The European Challenge

The European Initiative

Series Editor: PROFESSOR DAVID G. MAYES
National Institute of Economic and Social Research, London, and Co-ordinator
of the Economic and Social Research Council (ESRC) research project *The
European Initiative*.

The late 1980s and early 1990s have produced major events and changes in
Europe which are set to produce fundamental shifts in the economic, political and
social changes throughout the continent. The European Community's Single
Market Programme due for completion at the end of 1992 and the sweeping
political reforms and revolution in Eastern Europe have been the catalysts. This
new series of books has been established to publish the best research and
scholarship on European issues and to make an important contribution to the
advancement of knowledge on European issues.

Professor Mayes is Co-ordinator of a major research initiative on European issues
by the Economic and Social Research Council. The Series, in addition to
publishing the leading contributions made by that initiative, will also publish
other titles drawn from all disciplines in the Social Sciences, including Economics,
Political Science and Sociology.

Titles in the Series:

The European Challenge: Industry's Response to the 1992 programme
edited by David G. Mayes

The New Europe: Changing Economic Relations between East and West
by Susan Senior Nello

The European Challenge:

Industry's response to the 1992 programme

Harry P. Bowen
Elisabeth de Ghellinck
Gernot Klepper
Joëlle Laudy
David G. Mayes (editor)
Isabelle Pouplier
Didier Salvadori
Leo Sleuwaegen

HARVESTER
WHEATSHEAF

New York   London   Toronto   Sydney   Tokyo   Singapore

First published 1991 by
Harvester Wheatsheaf,
66 Wood Lane End, Hemel Hempstead,
Hertfordshire, HP2 4RG
A division of
Simon & Schuster International Group

Distributed in North and South America by
The University of Michigan Press
839 Greene Street, P.O. Box 1104
Ann Arbor, Michigan 48106, U.S.A.

Typeset in 10/12pt Times by
Keyset Composition, Colchester

Printed and bound in Great Britain by
BPCC Wheatons Ltd, Exeter

British Library Cataloguing in Publication Data

The European challenge: Industry's response to
the 1992 programme.
 I. Mayes, David G.
 382

   ISBN 0-7450-1034-2

---

1   2   3   4   5   95   94   93   92   91

Contents

Foreword

Michael Emerson

This book is a kind of mid-term review for the European Community's Single Market initiative. The early phases were those of the years 1985 and 1988. The first phase, 1985 and 1986, was when Jacques Delors and Lord Cockfield conceived the objective of finally suppressing all remaining administrative barriers to internal movements of goods, services, labour and capital. They set out the programme of legislative action required (the 300-item White Paper *Completing the Internal Market*), and secured political agreement to fulfil this by the end of 1992. The second phase, 1987–8, was marked by an important research effort to establish what the likely economic effects would be. This resulted in the so-called Cecchini Report, which estimated 200 billion ECU of potential gains.

The third phase, 1988–9, was that during which the business world – in the Community and outside – came to take the European single market as a new datum of strategic importance. Signs of the programme's credibility multiplied, be it in opinion polls of business leaders or in their activities to restructure their own enterprises or take over others.

A natural sequel was then to work out in more concrete detail what was actually beginning to happen at the level of individual industries. This is essentially the task of the present volume, edited by David Mayes, and based on contributors by leading industrial economists for a dozen major industrial sectors.

The study as a whole shows that there is no scope for easy generalisations on how 1992 affects each branch of industry. The intensity and type of impact is widely different. However, the industrialist, economist, journalist or banker will find in this volume a realistic and completely independent account of how Europe's industrial structure does now adjust to its new environment.

Having recently moved from the Brussels of 1992 to open the EC

Commission's new delegation to the USSR in Moscow, one is struck by a number of overwhelming contrasts which offer a further perspective on David Mayes' volume. For all of the importance of the single market and economic and monetary union projects of the EC, these are nevertheless carefully controlled and relatively predictable events. The framework of analysis, empirical and theoretical, is stable and well established. Information is rather transparent and the statistics quite good. In this other half of Europe little is either controllable or predictable or stable or transparent . . . The industrialist in the European Community and reader of this book should count their blessings. Even if not every chapter here is sensational in its content, its information value is of a high order and will be for many a necessary output into well-honed business strategies.

Moscow, 18th February 1991

Preface

Chapters 2 to 13 of this book were commissioned by the European Commission as part of its monitoring of the impact of the completion of the European Single Market. The views contained in them are the authors' own and have not been subject to any editorial control by the Commission. The authors are thus very grateful to the Commission and to Michael Emerson and Pierre Buigues and their colleagues in particular for supporting this research, for encouragement and comment, and for obtaining the agreement to publish.

We hope that these studies will go at least some of the way to providing an understanding of the complex responses to 1992 and to easing the path of integration in Europe. The studies by Elisabeth de Ghellinck, Isabelle Pouplier and Didier Salvadori have been translated from the French by Michael Cunningham to whom we are most grateful, particularly for the unequal struggle with technical expressions. The chapter by Joëlle Laudy was translated by David Mayes. Otherwise the studies are largely in their original form with the exception of omission of appendices, annexes and case studies for reasons of space. In general these missing sections are available from the individual authors. Unfortunately lack of space caused the omission of a further study on textiles and clothing by Christine Huttin.

David Mayes is grateful for the help and enthusiasm of Peter Johns and for the comments and advice of Alan Shipman.

1
Introduction
David G. Mayes

This book provides an assessment of how industry is responding to 'The European Challenge', which is how the Cecchini Report (1988) describes the European Community's programme to complete the 'internal market' by the end of 1992. It goes on to forecast how that response will continue into the future. The individual chapters were originally reports commissioned from independent consultants by the European Commission as part of the process of monitoring the impact of the programme.

Up to now quantitive assessments of '1992', as the programme has been dubbed, have tended to be both hypothetical and largely general. They have not attempted to estimate how markets will actually respond and hence to identify the actual as opposed to hypothetical gainers and losers. This book changes that. The eight experts drawn from six countries have examined over a dozen individual industries in detail, covering most of manufacturing industry.

This is not just an analysis of general trends at the industry level but a detailed examination of the principal strategies being followed by the main firms in these industries, not just within Europe, but worldwide, as all can and in most cases do participate already in the European market. The individual studies have a common format, although of course the particular authors employ their own individual style in following it. This format involves an exposition of the structure of the industry and the main forces affecting it, an examination of the way in which the Single Market measures could affect the industry and then an analysis of the strategies being followed by firms in the industry, distinguishing between external strategies – mergers, acquisitions, joint ventures, licensing arrangements, etc. – and internal strategies – relocation of production, new distribution patterns, changes in product market focus, scale, etc.

In this introduction we draw together some of the common threads from these individual studies. We begin by setting the estimation of the impact of the 1992 programme in its context.

The estimation of the impact of the 1992 programme

The European Community's programme for completing the 'internal market' is one of the most ambitious changes to the trading environment to be undertaken in peacetime. Indeed, were it not for the opening up of the Eastern and Central Europe in 1989/90 it would probably be the most ambitious change. The process of agreeing the changes is not yet complete and many of them, particularly those relating to technical harmonisation, will not be agreed for several years to come. Nevertheless, we have quite a good picture of what is intended.

Naturally, there is enormous clamour to estimate what the impact of these changes will be on European industry, the member states and, indeed, the rest of the world. The changes are so large and the European market and producers so important that the repercussions are global, not just internal to the Community. Early in the process the European Commission undertook a major study entitled 'The costs of non-Europe'. This was published in 'popular' form as the Cecchini Report (1988) in more detail in *European Economy*, No. 35 (reproduced as Emerson *et al.* (1988) *The Economics of 1992*), with a set of seventeen volumes of detailed reports from an army of consultants hired to undertake the work.[1]

However, this was very explicitly not an assessment of what would happen but an attempt to measure what the costs were to the Community of having the various barriers preventing a single market in goods, services, labour and capital. It did not attempt to estimate whether all the barriers would go or whether European industry would respond in such a manner so as to exploit the full potential gains. There have been a number of attempts to alter this by making assumptions about the extent to which the possible gains are actually realised (Bakhoven, 1989, and Dell and Mayes, 1989, for example) resulting in estimates which still suggest that growth in Europe may increase by about ½ a per cent a year to 3 per cent a year (see *National Institute Economic Review*, November 1990, for example) which is an improvement of around a quarter.

Not all objections to the Cecchini Report criticise it for being overoptimistic. Baldwin (1989) in particular has drawn attention to the poor representation of the dynamics of the process of change. Although the macroeconomic section does contain some model simulations, which are set out in more detail in Catinat *et al.* (1988) the Cecchini Report is essentially an examination of static costs. However, the process of competition is essentially dynamic, with each of the players trying to get an edge over the others by producing new and better goods and services or improving efficiency so that they can offer better prices or profit margins. The 1992 programme can affect this dynamic process in a number of ways: by enhancing the pressure of competition through lowering the ability to segment markets; by increasing the size of firms and hence increasing their world market power and ability to reap the benefits of dynamic economies of scale and scope; by lowering the price of capital and hence encouraging investment; by improving the efficiency of the labour market including the quality of skills through the social dimension and hence the knowledge base; and through the flanking policies enhancing the rate of growth of research and development.

However, there is considerable reluctance to quantify such possible gains because the empirical evidence on their extent is so weak. In the most recent edition of *European Economy*, No. 44, entitled 'One Market, One Money', these possibilities are explored but in fairly cautious terms in the wider context of Economic and Monetary Union. The largely theoretical calculations suggest that an outcome over a ten-year period of an additional 30–130 per cent of the static gains would be possible. (My own estimates of the dynamic gains from integration, made twenty years ago (Mayes, 1971), suggested a result towards the middle of that range, say, some 70 per cent additional benefit.) Thus, even if we do play down the initial static effects of the Single Market programme and suggest that only perhaps half of the costs of non-Europe are removed, adding a dynamic element to it could restore half the difference and, on the more optimistic assumptions, all of it.

Introducing dynamics, however, poses a new challenge to the arithmetic of gains and losses. In those regions and industries where the initial impact of the Single Market is unfavourable it could lead to dynamic disadvantages. It is therefore important to try to understand how this dynamic process of change takes place and, in particular, how it is taking place on this occasion. The main agents in this process of change are firms and it is therefore essential for the focus of attention to be on them.

Looking at aggregate figures obscures much greater changes at a detailed level, some positive and some negative. Some industries like chemicals are already very open – highly traded – with international standards and multinational companies, where European companies are very efficient world traders and, hence, are already close to a single market. Other industries like local services are not traded and subject to relatively little influence from the single market programme. It is the remaining industries, which are currently a relatively long way from a single market and which have considerable scope for response, where the effects are likely to be greatest. Buigues and Ilzkowitz (1988) made an attempt to identify the forty most sensitive sectors where 'sensitive' means 'most likely to be heavily affected by the Single Market programme' (see Table 1.1). This work has been built on in *European Economy*, Special Edition 1990, 'The impact of the internal market by industrial sector: the challenge for the member states', by examining which are the most sensitive sectors in each of the member states. (We return to this issue in more detail later in this chapter.) However, this is still an assessment of potential, not an analysis of what is changing nor a forecast of the sectoral composition of the impact of the Single Market programme.

Forecasts of the impact of completing the internal market, industry by industry, are scarce. Burridge and Mayes (1990) examine the prospects for a 91-sector breakdown in the UK using Oxford Economic Forecasting's Industry Model while *Europe in 1995* (BIPE *et al.*, 1990) tries to provide a more informal assessment of the prospects for various key sectors in the four largest states. However, the BIPE *et al.* study is not aimed at separating out the influences which stem from the Single Market programme. The Burridge and Mayes results are only partial, but they do show that for the UK the main favourable impact falls on the investment industries, not just plant and equipment but also construction.

An inevitable consequence of having change is that some existing capital will prove irrelevant to the new needs and hence the requirements for new capital rise. At the same time, there will be downward pressures on the average cost of capital with the opening up of capital markets in Europe and moves towards monetary union. Since Burridge and Mayes only look five years ahead it is too early to say how much the surge is due just to adjustment to the new conditions and how much to a continuing increase in the rate of investment. However, the lower cost of capital would normally ensure such an increase. The major losses occur in consumer industries, particularly in the field of textiles and clothing. In these industries increased foreign competition has a harsh impact on industries already under pressure. It is assumed, for example, that in so far as there is a renegotiated MFA the only restraints are on a Community-wide basis. As a result there would be little effective protection for the UK industries. Furthermore, the impact of the Single Market programme extends right through the economy into the services and non-tradable sectors as well. There is thus a striking contrast between the impact of the Single Market and that of previous moves towards integration in Europe which have, the Common Agricultural Policy excepted, been focused on the reduction of tariff barriers on manufactured goods. However, the study of output alone disguises much of the nature of the change, which involves ownership as well. This again points to the need to consider the subject in detail. Even the level of the industry is not enough.

The scope of the study

The chapters that follow were designed to cover a wide range of European industry and, in particular, the sensitive sectors set out in Table 1.1. All the major sectors of manufacturing are covered, although there are some considerable gaps in mechanical and electrical engineering and in manufactured foods. The former gaps are intentional, as it seemed more helpful to consider two of the sensitive industries in some detail rather than provide a fairly superficial coverage of much of engineering. What the studies do not cover, except marginally, is the three-quarters or so of the economy which is not manufacturing.

The major reason for the partiality of this coverage is that manufacturing dominates trade both within the Community and with Third World countries. This would have achieved its object for most earlier steps in the process of European integration but this is no longer true, and a complete understanding of the full impact must await the findings of the second set of studies of the services industries which is about to begin.

As a result of the wide coverage of manufacturing, between them the chapters cover the whole range of industrial structures. These structures are set out in the first part of each of the chapters and have a very considerable influence on the resultant patterns of reaction by the companies. They interact with the various combinations of influences from the Single Market programme.

The three most important features which emerge from this analysis of structure are the importance of openness to world competition, the degree of specialisation or differentiation in the products and the level of concentration of firms in the industry. This is very clearly illustrated by the motor car sector. The major European markets are all protected to a considerable extent against Japanese competition not just by a tariff but by quantitative restrictions. Exports to other countries outside Europe are by and large weak. The Single Market will result in a major decline in the effectiveness of external protection and hence a period of harsh competition within Europe which will lead to a loss of market share by existing European producers. In chemicals, on the other hand, or even trucks which is a much more similar industry, the main players are already competitive and successful on the world stage. The Single Market will mean far less to them in respect of new exposure to external competition.

Where the product cannot be readily differentiated, as in fertilisers, or close competitors can emerge, as in cars, the appropriate strategy has to involve a volume increase to gain a cost edge. It is very instructive to see the number of exits in fertilisers and other base chemicals by major firms in recognition of this problem. In the car market Salvadori distinguishes the 'generalists' and the 'specialists'. The latter, by picking specific segments, like Land Rover or Rolls-Royce or Ferrari, can dominate that

Table 1.1 The industrial sectors most affected by the Internal Market

NACE Codes	Sector	No. tariff barriers	Dispersion prices net of taxes	Share in value added	Share of intra-EC imports in demand	Share of extra-EC imports in demand	Extra-EC export/import ratio
	High-technology public-procurement sectors						
	Group I						
330	Office machines	high	7.44	2.45	30.91	36.30	57
344	Telecommunication equipment	high	8.89	4.29	22.44	28.76	117
372	Medico-surgical equipment	high	21.12	0.38	31.48	31.38	139
	Traditional public-procurement or regulated markets						
	Group 2						
257	Pharmaceutical products	high	32.65	2.48	10.61	6.40	248
315	Boilermaking, reservoirs, sheet-metal containers	high	22.12	1.00	2.54	1.10	1,108
362	Railway equipment	high	21.74	0.35	4.97	3.48	680
425	Wine and wine-based products	high	15.88	0.34			
427	Brewing and malting	high	20.94	1.21	3.27	0.20	2,047
428	Soft drinks and spa waters	high	24.87	0.53	4.56	0.33	721
	Group 3						
341	Electrical wires and cables	high	8.89	1.40	11.21	8.79	163
342	Electrical equipment	high		3.42	17.91	13.04	182
361	Shipbuilding	high		0.78	7.75	21.72	178
417	Spaghetti, macaroni, etc.	high	8.86	0.14	6.72	0.38	1,038
421	Cocoa, chocolate and sugar confectionary	high	10.12	0.72	12.98	2.83	214
	Sectors with moderate non-tariff barriers						

Group 4

Consumer goods

345	Electronic equipment	moderate	7.65	1.84	19.71	28.80	63
346	Domestic-type electrical appliances	moderate	7.67	0.88	22.68	11.37	130
351	Motor vehicles	moderate	10.61	7.21	22.82	10.44	201
438	Carpets, lino, floor covering	moderate	15.76	0.23	44.85	23.65	122
451	Footwear	moderate	14.28	0.81	44.65	36.84	106
453	Clothing	moderate	10.17	1.98	13.43	18.37	57
455	Household textiles	moderate	13.42	0.21	26.05	31.68	59
491	Jewellery, goldsmiths' and silversmiths' wares	moderate	22.06	0.27			157
493	Photographic and cinematographic labs	moderate	10.12	0.16	15.99	10.23	128
495	Games, toys and sports goods	moderate	12.07	0.26	23.95	43.41	48

Capital goods

321	Agricultural machinery and tractors	moderate	8.30	0.66	19.75	5.40	442
322	Machine tools for metals	moderate	10.73	1.22	17.91	16.25	191
323	Textile and sewing machines	moderate	10.97	0.53	34.96	23.26	369
324	Machines for foodstuffs ind.	moderate	12.26	1.28	31.45	14.63	400
325	Plant for mines, etc.	moderate	18.06	1.68	29.40	14.81	342
326	Transmission equipment	moderate		0.73	23.79	13.48	178
327	Other specific equipment	moderate	12.92	0.76	38.66	20.92	330
347	Lamps and lighting equipment	moderate	15.70	0.36	31.84	12.70	252
364	Aerospace equipment, manufacturing and repairing	moderate	17.10	2.20	18.05	24.25	121

Intermediary goods

247	Glassware	moderate	21.46	1.11	21.29	7.39	213
248	Ceramics	moderate	21.46	0.90	20.93	8.62	255
251	Basic industrial chemicals	moderate		4.81			
256	Other chemical products for industry	moderate		1.81	30.39	11.41	249
431	Wool industry	moderate	23.02	0.62			
432	Cotton industry	moderate	23.02	0.94			
481	Rubber industry	moderate	17.85	1.48	20.45	8.43	175

Sources: *Panorama of EC Industry*, and estimates from Commission services

product area and make it hard for other entrants. Their strategies therefore differ markedly from those exposed to the open competition.

In concentrated industries like motor car manufacturing or airlines the scope for increased economies of scale or other advantages of size are relatively limited as the companies are already on the limits of market share under the Merger directive. The major emphasis for change therefore lies with internal efficiency, tightening the supply chain and links with non-European companies.

Buigues and Jacquemin (1989) have set out a simple classification of these latter two points using the two axes of the scope for differentiation and the advantages of being a leading firm (see Figure 1.1). This gives four categories and the industries they quote include examples from the thirteen industries covered in this book in each of those categories. Craft industries like machine tools have a widely differentiated product which is best tackled by specialist firms. Cars, as we have already seen, can be distinguished between the mass and specialist markets. Lastly, areas like steel and fertilisers, as we have just mentioned, face harsh competition in a world market where it is difficult to establish a market lead.

This set of four categories gives a further cross-classification to the four different categories of potential exposure to competition set out in Table 1.1 and emphasises the complexity which drives us towards having this set of industry studies.

The impact of the Single Market

Most of the main analyses of the impact of the internal market concentrate on just a few areas of current change. Emerson *et al.* (1988) pick out frontier barriers, public procurement, technical differences and fiscal harmonisation. In the special 1990 edition of *European Economy* import quotas and industry-specific issues are added. In this book the authors have taken a rather broader view looking at the programme as a whole, as set out in Table 1.2 by Alan Shipman in Mayes (1990), because it is this wider framework which governs the longer run view, choices over location, investment in capital and human skills, etc.

The first section of Table 1.3 sets out an approximate chart of the main influences on each of the thirteen industries from the 1992 measures as discussed in the individual chapters. The first point which is noticeable is that there are important areas of measures which are not mentioned in the chart, such as the free movement of persons, the removal of barriers on capital and the removal of barriers at the frontier. In the main, this last finding may reflect the fact that many of the product areas covered are relatively high-valued and not subject to deterioration from delays as in

	Fragmented	Specialised
High	catering (conventional) building (conventional) craft industries	pharmaceuticals DP software luxury cars
Number of possible differentiations	Impasse	Volume
Low	steel shipbuilding paper	aerospace tyres medium-sized cars electronic components television sets and video recorders domestic appliances
	Weak	Strong

Advantages of being a leading firm

Figure 1.1 Competitive environment matrix examples (Source: BCG, 1985; Porter, 1985; Buigues, 1985)

Table 1.2 The main features of the Single Market programme

The 1992 Programme calls for action in six main areas

Unified market in goods and services Removal of barriers to trade in financial and other services, and of remaining non-tariff barriers to visible trade. Simplification of customs procedures and elimination of vehicle checks. Harmonisation of technical standards and health/safety regulations, with mutual recognition of certification. Closer alignment of VAT and excise duties.

Unified factor market Free movement of capital, with removal of exchange controls. Alignment of savings taxes. Free movement of labour, with mutual recognition of qualifications.

Promotion of competition Common rules on regulation, takeovers, state assistance to industry, patents and copy-rights, company accounting and disclosure of information. Opening of public procurement of competitive tender. Reduced intervention in agriculture.

Monetary integration Exchange rate alignment (via ERM). To be followed by adoption of a single currency and creation of a European central bank.

Social protection Adoption of a Social Charter incorporating freedom of movement, fair wages and conditions of employment, vocational training, collective bargaining, consultation over technological change and company restructuring, protection of children, elderly and disabled people.

United response to external challenges A common external tariff. Infrastructure projects, especially high-speed rail and road links and integrated telecommunications. Co-operative R & D, especially in microelectronics and information technology. A common energy policy.

Table 1.3   The 1992 programme and responses to it by industry

	Airlines	Aerospace	Machine tools	Railway equipment	Microelectronics – semiconductors	Microelectronics – consumer goods	Metal goods	Cars	Trucks	Basic chemicals	Pharmaceuticals	Fibres	Textile products
1992 measures and opportunities													
Scale/scope economies from SEM		X			X	X		X		X			
R & D co-operation (via EC programmes)		X			X								
'Open' public procurement		X		X	X						X		
Removal of subsidies				X				X	X				
Environmental standards	X			X					X	X	X		
Deregulation, competition policy	X												
Technical harmonisation		X		X			X	X	X				
Common external tariff and protection from NICs						X	X	X	X			X	X
Responses													
Merger/joint ventures (via rationalisation)		X	X	X	X	X	X	X	X	X	X		X
R & D co-operation		X	X	X	X					X			
Sales/service co-operation	X		X							X	X		
Scale/scope economies via joint ventures		X		X	X					X	X		
Greater product differentiation		X	X					X		X	X	X	X
Restriction to speciality 'niche' markets	X	X						X	X	X	X	X	X
Cost-cutting to compete on price			X					X				X	X
Diversification to 'service' industries						X		X	X				X

the case of foodstuffs. However, it is very clear that the perceived impact of the various measures from the analyses in these chapters is rather less than might have been expected from, say, the surveys in the 'Cost of Non-Europe' (Nerb, 1988), where almost all of the various areas of measures were judged important before the event (see Figure 1.2).

Take the information technology industry, for example. Increased standardisation, both in hardware and software, has an obvious benefit for a segmented European market but the same advantages accrue also to the major non-European manufacturers, particularly those in the United

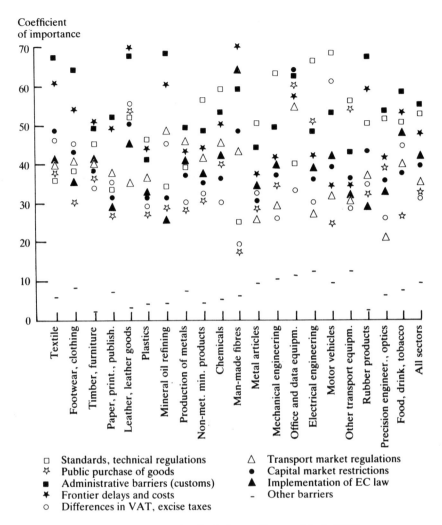

Coefficient
of importance

□	Standards, technical regulations	△ Transport market regulations
☆	Public purchase of goods	● Capital market restrictions
■	Administrative barriers (customs)	▲ Implementation of EC law
✶	Frontier delays and costs	– Other barriers
○	Differences in VAT, excise taxes	

Figure 1.2 Importance of barriers by industry (Source: Nerb, 1988)

States who are setting the standards anyway. These foreign suppliers
already have scale economies from their home markets, some also have
efficient production structures within Europe. Hence, removing barriers
within Europe helps them as well and they do not have to suffer the costs
of restructuring a production base which is distorted and somewhat
inefficient as a result of existing European divisions. In so far as these are
dynamic economies, these foreign firms will still have the opportunity to
remain ahead.

Several factors combine to suggest why the measures should not be perceived to be so important as the Nerb survey implies. The first is simply that although they may assist firms' strategies they do not in fact alter their direction. A second is that in some areas, such as fiscal harmonisation, agreement has been slow to come and hence, in the light of experience over the last two years since the survey, views of importance have been revised. Thirdly, the interpretation of the questions may be different.

Take two of the most obvious examples of greatest importance in Figure 1.2 – administrative barriers (customs) in the case of textiles and clothes (columns 1 and 2), and standards, technical regulations in the case of motor vehicles (two-thirds of the way across). The first of these is completely borne out in the sense that it is the threat of the removal of barriers under the Multi-Fibre Arrangement and competition from allowing goods in from Turkey and Eastern Europe which are the greatest threats to the industry. However, the question in the survey was actually aimed at the administrative costs of getting customs clearance within the Community, which is trivial by comparison. Similarly, in the case of motor vehicles, meeting all the standards and technical requirements is a really serious concern in the industry, although harmonisation of such standards across the Community has already gone a very long way. They are by no means the main explanation of the ability to segment the European market, as Salvadori sets out in Chapter 2. These prior views of importance and the revealed views of the importance of measures in the ensuing chapters are thus not really a comparison of like with like.

Added to these changes in perception is a general finding that in practice there are reasons why the measures should not be as significant as they appear in theory. Competition among airlines, for example, is restricted by limitations of landing/taking-off slots at the major hubs, while sunk costs limit the plausible degree of integration of the railway equipment market. In the truck industry major reorganisation to restructure the industry on a European basis has already taken place.

One theme comes through which was not well articulated in the earlier analyses, namely, the role of foreign competition. In most industries this threat comes from direct investment, particularly by the Japanese setting up production in Europe or, in some cases, buying European producers. This has already provided effective competition in areas such as consumer electronics, it is beginning in the motor car industry, and the potential exists in other industries such as railway equipment.

Not all competition is from direct investment. The basic chemicals industry, textiles and clothing face major competition from new producers in the Far East and in the case of chemicals from oil producers in the Gulf. The potency of this threat has two implications. In the first place, it suggests that from the point of view of the drive towards efficiency the EC has done well to avoid the pressures towards 'Fortress Europe' that seemed to be emerging in 1987 and 1988. Secondly, however, it appears that the distribution of gains between existing European producers and third country companies may be rather more towards the latter than was initially envisaged. Given the need for capital to provide the investment necessary for change, this inflow from overseas may actually be beneficial.

One final remark is also in order. Although these studies have been published quite quickly they are already being overtaken rapidly by events. The pace of change is so fast in Europe, especially in the East but also with progress towards economic and monetary union, that the concerns which dominated the firms in 1988–9 will have already been revised, particularly those in Germany. There are opportunities in the motor industry in the East, for example. The pressures on the clothing and textile industries are intensified. Decisions on relocation of production, particularly those which may have involved lower labour costs in peripheral regions of the Community, now have to take account of a possible new source of competition.

The response of firms to the Single Market

The studies in the chapters which follow are concerned with the impact of the Single Market down the whole of the value-added chain. And the framework in Figure 1.3 (*European Economy*, Special Edition 1990) was put forward to the authors by the European Commission. However, the analysis was cross-classified by the need to examine 'internal' and 'external' routes to change, i.e. the extent to which firms used organic structural change or mergers, acquisitions or other forms of linkage with other firms as their routes to restructuring in the face of the internal market measures.

The clearest response by firms to the Single Market comes from external growth shown in the second half of Table 1.3. We can see that all industries except airlines and fibres have made significant use of mergers and acquisitions in their strategies. The two exceptions are already highly concentrated which inhibits their ability to combine further as they attract the attention of the European competition authorities. There has been some activity for airlines with the purchase of Air Inter by Air France and the failed attempt by KLM and British Airways to take joint stakes in Sabena.

This experience fits with more general evidence (see Figure 1.4). There has been a merger boom in Europe. Mergers doubled between 1982/3 and 1985/6 and again by 1988/9. However, it is important to realise that this is

14   Introduction

Component of value added:	Possible nature of the impact:
1. Research and development	Growth in the number of joint projects
	More homogeneous environment at European level
2. Supplies	Wider range of suppliers
	Lower prices
3. Logistics	Lower transport costs
	Relocation of storage facilities
	(better adapted to an integrated market)
4. Production	Increased production at each plant
	Reduction in the number of production plants
5. Marketing and distribution	Centralisation of product management at European level
	Community-wide marketing campaigns
6. Consumers	Availability of a wider range of products
	Increased demand (growth effect) and lower product prices

Figure 1.3   Impact of the removal of non-tariff barriers on the value-added chain (Source: Commission services)

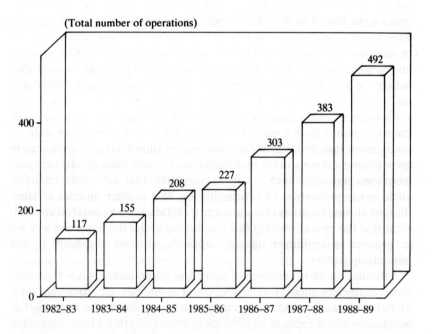

Figure 1.4   Number of mergers/takeovers undertaken by the 1,000 largest European industrial firms (Source: Reports on Competition Policy)

Table 1.4 Mergers and acquisitions by nationality of the firms involved

Year	National	EC	International
1983–84	101	29	25
	(65.2)	(18.7)	(16.1)
1984–85	146	44	18
	(70.2)	(21.2)	(8.7)
1985–86	145	52	30
	(63.7)	(23.0)	(13.3)
1986–87	211	75	17
	(69.6)	(24.8)	(5.6)
1987–88	214	111	58
	(55.9)	(29.0)	(17.8)
1988–89	233	197	62
	(47.4)	(40.0)	(12.6)

Note: Figures in brackets show the percentage of the total number of operations surveyed

Source: European Commission

part of a worldwide phenomenon, so quite a part of this phenomenon is unlikely to be due specifically to the Single Market.[2] More convincing is the shift in composition of the acquisitions (see Table 1.4). During the years from 1983/4 to 86/7, 65–70 per cent of activity was purely national while cross-border activity within the EC ran at 20–25 per cent. However, in just two years there was a major shift, with just under half of mergers and acquisitions in 1988/9 being national and 40 per cent cross-border within the EC. It obviously remains to be seen how long this trend will last.

Changes in ownership are an early step in the process of change. In themselves they alter nothing regarding efficiency, economies of scale, or innovation. It depends how they are used or followed up. The change in ownership gives control for making the subsequent changes. It is obvious from some industries such as railway equipment that subsequent changes, such as rationalisation of production on to a smaller number of sites, thereby closing facilities in some member states, is being delayed until it is clear that the operation of public purchasing under the new rules will not in practice discriminate against suppliers with no capability in the purchasing country.

Although there is evidence of more European linkages it is clear that some industries such as electronics and chemicals are operating on a global scale, and that the US and Japanese markets are so important as purchasers and sources of technological innovation that a large portion of non-domestic merger and acquisition activity is taking place there. In the same way that Japanese and US manufacturers feel they need a stake in production in the European market so European companies seek a stake in the US (the ICI takeover of Stauffer and the Bull acquisitions of Honeywell and Zenith, for example).

Current merger and acquisition activity is influenced by previous activity. It is clear, for example, that the truck industry has already rationalised on a European basis during the earlier part of the 1980s, moving away from the previous pattern of substantial American ownership to an industry with a smaller number of producers and some reverse ownership of US companies. Renault (RVI) for example owns 45 per cent of Mack.

The Single Market provides two short-run influences on merger and acquisition activity. On the one hand it makes linkages between companies more desirable, but on the other it is actually helping to make the formation of such alliances easier. Thus, acquisitions across borders which might previously have been frustrated by governments or other national interests may be rather easier to achieve. Hence, in the short run there will be a flow of changes reflecting previous disequilibrium between aspirations and constraints as well as the 'stock adjustments' to the structure of operations suitable for the Single Market.

Figure 1.5 shows that some other forms of linkage between companies seem to have risen relatively little since the beginning of the Single Market programme. The taking of minority holdings was running only 20 per cent above its 1985/86 level in 1988/9 while the formation of jointly owned subsidiaries was 60 per cent higher (compared with the 120 per cent increase in mergers and acquisitions over the same period).

The industries studied in this book suggest that agreements between firms provide an important facet of the response to 1992 in almost all industries. Three particular forms of linkage are revealed in Table 1.3: joint ventures to obtain economies of scale and scope, joint sales arrangements and R & D co-operation. These arrangements are most prevalent in the engineering industries. It is not yet clear whether there is any European competitive model to contrast with the strong Japanese domestic competition (Porter, 1990). Clearly, EC competition policy will want to take account of collaborative moves by European companies.

In many respects the 1992 programme is as much a response to the wishes of industry as it is a stimulus to industry, leading it to respond. In 1985, before the Single Market White Paper, the European Round Table of industrialists was advocating a single market introduced over a period of five years. Many of the Single Market measures are therefore swimming with the tide. In these cases we can expect industry to change rapidly, as it is being permitted to do what it wants to do anyway. There are other instances where the measures taken are not those wanted by the major firms. The simplest example is that industry had hoped for rather more effective external protection, wanting a situation more like that perceived to exist in Japan with strong domestic competition inside an

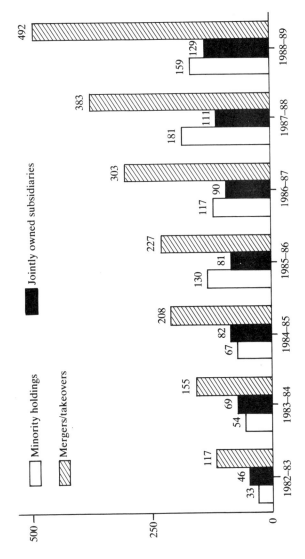

Figure 1.5 Number of takeovers, acquisitions of minority holdings and new jointly owned subsidiaries: situation for the 1,000 largest European industrial firms (Source: Commission services)

effective external barrier. A second is that competition policy has been strengthened, making the creation of new giant firms more difficult. The motor industry is a clear case in point. All the changes taking place are likely to lead to an intensification of competition and a fall in profit margins. At the same time, the industry is incurring heavy costs from technical and structural change. Demand, although rising, will not be sufficient to permit all the mass-market producers to operate at the minimum efficient scale. Losses and amalgamations seem inevitable. What the industry would like is an ordered process of change which would maximise the chance of European survivors, rather than a free-for-all which would favour companies with strong market shares in other countries like the United States and Japan.

Table 1.5 shows in the top part where some of the internal market changes complement existing trends, whereas the bottom half shows

Table 1.5   Complementarities and inconsistencies between the Internal Market measures and market trends

Trend	Complementary measure
New technology leads to reduction in minimum efficient scale through flexible manufacturing systems	Unified market enables greater access to new market areas but with substantial differences in buyers requirements likely to remain
Japanese surplus looking for reinvestment abroad	Incentive for Japanese to invest in Europe to get inside external tariffs and reap full advantage of Single Market
R & D scale economies and advantages of collusion at the 'pre-competitive' stage of R & D	Large co-operative R & D programmes in 'pre-competitive' areas (IT, telecoms innovation dissemination)
Scale economies, scope economies and competition incentives made available through cross-border ownership market	Capital-market deregulation and new legal framework making cross-border acquisitions easier
Growth of oligopolies within EC, prevent competition but unchallenged by domestic competition policy	European-level merger control to prevent anti-competitive concentration
Pressure for standardisation of technical/safety/environmental regulations, to reduce cost of modification before a product becomes exportable	Harmonisation, and removal of non-tariff barriers
Concern about the environment	Stronger environmental standards and regulations
Contracting-out and privatisation, as means to control public spending and increase revenue	Opening-up of public procurement, restriction of state subsidies to firms
Competition in concentrated markets requiring ease of entry/exit and reduced sunk costs (for contestability)	Single Market providing greater scope for potential entry and redeployment of fixed-cost resources to other uses
Fall in transport costs relative to production costs	Single Market allowing producers to locate in lowest-cost regions; infrastructure projects which further reduce costs

Table 1.5–*contd.*

Trend	Related measures
Shift to 'knowledge-intensive' production requiring higher skilled more autonomous workforce	Social Charter and structural funds providing for vocational training, participation
Increased external effects of national macro policies and interdependence of main macro instruments	Move towards common monetary and fiscal policies, economic union
Increased trade requiring exchange-rate stability to reduce costs of hedging/ exchange risk	Completion and 'hardening' of ERM

Trend	Inconsistent measure
Use of product differentiation to reduce competition and achieve market power	End to national standards as a basis for product differentiation
Restructing/re-allocation/building-up of new sectors requiring state intervention	Restriction of state aid to industry
Innovation for competitiveness with non-European firms requires collusion to protect monopoly rents, or subsidy to compensate for their loss	Competition promoted, collusion reduced, state subsidy restricted
Opening up of Eastern Europe as source of low production costs and direct investment opportunities	Attempts to attract inward investment and achieve higher investment within the EC
(In some member states) Return to 'free' labour market with weak trade unions, flexible wages	Social Charter conditions for union power, minimum wages, etc.

some that conflict. Although the coverage in the Table is by no means comprehensive, the general balance is clearly that the Single Market works with the trend rather than against it.

The complementarity emphasises why it is so difficult in the chapters which follow to sort out which of the steps that firms are taking are really consequent on measures in the Single Market programme and which would have been taken in any case. The Single Market is such an important event that it is often used as a reference point; it is cited as *the* cause when it is *a* cause. It is, so to speak, a convenient and widely acceptable hook on which to hang the reasoning for many commercial decisions.

The final part of Table 1.3 sets out the 'internal' strategies for change which characterise the various industries (only the stronger trends are shown as all changes tend to be present to some extent in all industries – the Table should be viewed in terms of substantial deviations from the average).

Whereas external strategies can be gleaned readily from newspapers and other published sources, information on internal strategies is much more difficult to come by and has involved detailed interviews with firms in the various sectors. However, as Salvadori notes, this itself is a biased process: firms say what they want people to hear, they do not necessarily reveal what is the case.

We can perhaps categorise the main strategies employed as being 'offensive' or 'defensive', depending upon whether they represent attempts to capture new markets or reinforce a position in existing ones. In the defensive group we see the following:

- Increased product differentiation, in part to preserve brand loyalty.
- A shift towards a smaller range of niche products where competition is less intense.
- Horizontal and vertical integration (or collusion) to increase market power and reduce competition.
- Diversification to spread risks and find less harshly competitive product-markets.

The offensive group includes the following strategies:

- Raising value added/quality in existing lines aided by training, process innovation and restructuring.
- Cost and price reduction.
- Product innovation (in contrast to the previous section this may involve taking risks rather than avoiding them).

The importance of all these moves is that they fit into the framework of business strategy. 1992 provides an excellent test-bed for strategic response – in particular because it changes the rules of behaviour for firms (Shipman and Mayes, 1991). The different rule systems of the various countries now come into direct competition, particularly where 'home country control' is the framework applied. It is by no means clear whether the outcome will be new European rules or the gradual domination of one or other national system (or, indeed, continued coexistence). What we can observe is strong tendencies to try to protect the existing rule systems rather than making positive commitments to change. This applies to governments as much as firms. The first choice in most cases is to retain existing legislation if possible.

We are reluctant to replace this heterogeneity of behaviour with a spuriously authentic generalisation of the internal strategies employed (the management literature is already too full of recipes and conclusions based on just a few case studies). This chapter therefore concludes by discussing each of the individual industry pictures.

The remainder of the book

The twelve chapters which follow contain eleven industry studies and an exposition by Joëlle Laudy of the European Commission, using their BACH database, of the extent to which the means and availability of financing in the different members states affects the strategic responses of firms in those countries to the Single Market programme. Added to the different pattern of company ownership and traditions of doing business this can result in strikingly different responses, as is revealed by the grant variations in merger and acquisition activity that we noted earlier.

Chapters 2–6 form a group, all related to transport and transport equipment. Transport forms a key ingredient of a geographical market and the removal of physical barriers in the Single Market should increase the demand for transport services directly. The impact of the rest of the 1992 programme will have negative as well as positive consequences on the demand for transport services as the incentive to relocate and the increased ability to set up in other markets can both alter the pattern of distribution and need to export.

The immediate facet of these chapters which is striking is the differences between them. The public sector is heavily involved in railways as the provider of services and the purchaser of most equipment other than goods wagons. It is heavily involved in airlines as an owner of airlines and indeed of airports, and a regulator of fares, routes, landing slots and air traffic. It is also the major purchaser of aerospace equipment, particularly for military applications. In the case of cars and trucks, the government provides the infrastructure of the road system, the regulations for the rules of the road, vehicle safety, environmental controls, etc., but it is not the major purchaser and the nature of the equipment is very much determined by private sector demand.

Didier Salvadori sees the European market being the focus of competition in the world by car makers in the 1990s, aided principally by competition from firms which are foreign-owned (predominantly Japanese). These producers will not only have greater access to the market through the reduction of external quotas hampering their exports to the EC but from production within the Community as well. As a result the relative price of cars will fall, and European producers will have to increase their efficiency markedly – not just at the stage of final assembly but all the way down the supply chain of subcontractors and component and equipment supplies. Indeed, it is the efficiency of the chain itself which will be a key element in maintaining the necessary competitiveness.

Thus in one respect this is a classic example of the intended impact of the Single Market. There will be major benefits to European consumers, particularly if fiscal and other harmonisation helps reduce pre-tax price differentials across the market of nearly 50 per cent. The outlook for the European producer must be more depressing. Total market growth over the 1990s is expected to be around 20 per cent but market share of existing producers will fall as their output rises by nearer 10 per cent and margins are heavily squeezed. There is no suggestion that as a result of this pressure European producers will enjoy a renascent surge in their exports to the major markets in the United States and Japan.

The truck industry might well have shown a similar pattern, given how much demand has been squeezed, were it not for two features which distinguish it from cars. As Leo Sleuwaegen explains with an illuminating set of diagrams, the European and indeed the world industry has been transformed in the 1980s. In Daimler-Benz Europe has the world leader and the pattern of US ownership of European companies has been replaced by European stakes in the United States, even in Mack, whose trucks symbolise the cinema image of the American truck. Also, the industry has effective protection against the Japanese, first, because the technical specification of vehicles is very different, and secondly, because to break into the market a supplier needs a distribution chain. Existing chains are controlled by current manufacturers and setting up new chains would be extremely expensive. In one sense, therefore, the truck industry has anticipated the Single Market. The progress in the 1990s is highly dependent upon whether the Japanese overcome the entry barriers.

It is also worth noting from Sleuwaegen's diagrams that the German, French and Italian markets are predominantly national, whereas the remainder are much more European. A real test of the reality of a single market would occur if those three national markets also became European.

Gernot Klepper has studied both airlines and aerospace. For airline behaviour there is the example of the United States where the market turned into a 'hub and spoke' system, with the main airlines having a base or, in some cases, bases out of which their main flights went and into which smaller regional airlines provided feeder services. Gernot sees the same pattern arising in Europe with London, Paris, Frankfurt and Amsterdam as obvious hubs, but the role of government is crucial here. Unless regulations change and regulatory support for 'flag-carriers' ends, a sub-optimal system is bound to result. These changes are in the main not part of the Single Market *per se* but are related policies. Initial steps show only limited promise and the withdrawal of the BA–KLM–Sabena partnership makes the difficulties of sustaining global competitiveness and competition within Europe simultaneously, very clear.

The military side of aerospace has fluctuated in recent years, first with the changes in Eastern Europe and arguments about the size of the peace dividend and now with the consequences of the Gulf war and the need to replace hardware. This and indeed the dispute in the Baltic states means that by the time of publication results could be very different from those anticipated when the chapter was written. As for civilian aerospace, there is already a highly concentrated market. Although Deutsche-Aerospace is emerging as a new force and Japanese participation in the market is increasing, entry costs are huge and existing suppliers, despite major support through defence spending, have found it difficult to compete in the main airframe and engine markets. Here the Single Market has little to offer. The industry is already global, and although, perhaps, the spirit of *juste retour* may change to enable a more efficient structure for Airbus Industrie, this is not a matter for 1992 legislation.

Finally, railways appear an archetypal case for the Single Market. Indeed, it is quoted as such in the Cecchini Report. In the mid-1980s it was characterised by small state-owned national equipment producers supplying domestic purchasers with little trade within Europe yet fairly considerable exports to developing countries. There are considerable economics of scale available, as evidenced by the major US producers, yet technical divisions between markets keep the countries segmented. In practice the scope for change is much more limited. There are already agreed technical requirements for international travel of rolling stock throughout the whole of Europe, not just the Community. There are enormous sunk costs involved in changing the main differences between the systems. In the UK every bridge and tunnel would have to be widened, in most countries every electric locomotive would have to be replaced as their power systems differ, etc.

Nevertheless, there has been a major programme of acquisition and merger, involving Swiss, Swedish and Canadian companies as well as those in the Community. However, production patterns have changed little as yet because outside the United Kingdom and countries without a significant domestic industry public purchasing behaviour has yet to change. This change in purchasing is a *sine qua non* for the success of the Single Market. Until purchasers treat all European suppliers as being 'domestic' major gains will not be realised. Behaviour thus far does not give any indication that there will be sweeping changes in purchasing patterns in most member states. The main 'European' hope for the industry lies in the development of a high-speed network, the Channel Tunnel and the increasing competitiveness of long-distance rail for goods, aided by environmental concerns about the alternative, road transport.

The second group of industries, Chapters 7–9, all relate to electronic products and their applications. The first two, on components and consumer electronics, were actually written as a single piece by Harry Bowen and the pressure of space has meant we have had to leave out his interesting analysis of each of the main companies at the world level, although fortunately they can be obtained directly from him. His chapters make rather gloomy reading for the European industry. We read how the US industries have been successfully attacked by the Japanese, especially in consumer electronics. Although a rearguard action is taking place in this area, which has strong tariff protection still, it is only through joint ventures and other forms of technical co-operation that it is possible to stem the tide. New chip manufacture is now so expensive that only a few of the very largest producers can contemplate it.

The saving grace comes through software which is now more important than hardware in the successful sale of electronic equipment. Isabelle Pouplier in her study of DP and IT equipment shows that there is a tendency of firms to move towards being universal service companies. European producers have a much larger share of their own markets than they do internationally. The major issue in the industry is standardisation, particularly in terms of connectability. However, this is not a European phenomenon and standards are being set on the world stage, heavily influenced by US interests. Those which cannot expand to export economies of scale and scope tend to move to specialised or niche products if they are to survive. In lowering internal barriers the Single Market forces firms to face up to more of the worldwide pressure. In so far as parallel policies are introduced through European programmes like ESPRIT II this may help contribute to the heavy R & D base required. However, as Harry Bowen points out, in the case of integrated circuits in the United States, it is by no means clear that Sematech, the government–industry partnership, is going to provide an effective counter to the Japanese.

The remaining three industrial sectors, chemicals, metals and machine tools, covered in Chapters 10–12 are very diverse – and, indeed, as is made clear in the case of chemicals, subject to considerable diversity within that single industry heading. Elisabeth de Ghellinck shows a very different pattern for fertilisers, in which economies of scale and low cost inputs are major factors in a fairly homogeneous products group where competition is based on price, from that in, say, pharmaceuticals where patent protection allows particular firms to dominate small sectors.

In general the chemical industry is highly international already and the major European players are competitive on the world scene. Here the Single Market has little to offer. It is in areas like pharmaceuticals where governments control purchasing and pricing that changes could occur. With high R & D costs, firms need a period of protection to be able to recoup their outlays before substitutes can be developed. If EC governments were to drive prices down, that would actually harm EC producers compared to overseas competitors. The major gain in terms of efficiency comes from the new rules for gaining acceptance for new drugs in member states, through which companies have the choice of getting acceptance at European level or in their own state, subject to European requirements. This will greatly speed up the ability to sell in a wide range of markets while patent protection is still effective. One of the main reasons for the rapid growth of the UK company Glaxo in the world league on the back of Zantac, an anti-ulcerant, was the much greater rapidity with which it introduced the product in the main markets round the world.

Within metals, considered by Gernot Klepper, the primary attention is on iron and steel. This is in a sense the very first sector to go into a single European market with the formation of the European Coal and Steel Community in 1952. The industry is dominated by a handful of giant firms, including three out of the top five in the world. The effect of the Single Market has to be seen in the light of the actions in the 1980s which involved the contraction of a industry subject to severe overcapacity and its progressive exposure to the forces of international competition. In the light of such major reorganisation Gernot feels that any major consequences are yet to be revealed.

The downstream industry of machine tools, right at the heart of mechanical engineering, is also a prime candidate for change as a result of the Single Market according to the Buigues and Ilzkowitz classification of the forty most sensitive sectors. However, a closer examination reveals that this is not really the case. Although the industry is characterised by a large number of small firms, particularly compared with Japan, many of these are world leaders, especially those concentrated in Germany. The reason is simply that machine tools are highly specialised products, which are often customised for the individual buyer. The Japanese have focused on the computer-controlled, highly flexible machines which can do many tasks, but these are not cost effective for many applications where specific tools are required. The gains which seemed possible from economies of scale in the industry are thus to a large extent imaginary. No doubt co-operation agreements for joint marketing and research can be improved, as positive attempts in the Italian and Spanish industries have indicated, but the disastrous experience of the consequences of going for large size on its own, as evidenced by the collapse in the United Kingdom of Alfred Herbert, the world's largest machine tool company, is a lesson well learned.

Concluding remarks

Taken together, therefore, we see a manufacturing sector in the midst of major change. Some of that is clearly due to the Single Market which in many respects is swimming with the tide of global change. However, it is that global change which itself tends to be the driving force for change in

Europe. It is Japanese competition in cars and consumer electronics, US and Japanese competition in electronic components and chemicals, US competition in aerospace and computers, developing country competition in textiles and clothing, and the threat of Japanese competition in trucks and railways which have the major influence. By removing internal barriers the chance of successful European response is increased, particularly where size is important. But the major gain comes from the stimulation to investment and the extension of competition to areas like services and industries dominated by public procurement.

The European consumer is going to be a clear gainer as efficiency rises and relative prices fall. The extent to which the existing European producer gains rather than the foreign investor or exporter is much more debatable. We are able to see several cases where the competition is too harsh and the Europeans are likely to lose market share – in cars, in electronics, in textiles and clothing. However, that is not the comment on the success of the 1992 programme. We have to ask how much worse European industry would have fared without it. The disadvantages of the fragmented system were obvious and industry was already trying to surmount them. Although the industry studies in this volume make it very clear that many theoretical and 'expected' gains from aggregate analysis are not going to happen in reality, it is also clear that all sectors have received a shot in the arm and are changing rapidly, responding and, in some cases, leading the forces of international competition. The mergers and acquisitions boom may be worldwide and it may have shown many examples of European purchases in the United States but it is, nevertheless, a surge in cross-border alliances in Europe and it will help restructure the industry.

This is a study of the main traded areas of manufacturing industry. Clearly other parts of the economy with greater natural protection and less existing exposure to trade are likely to show different patterns. We eagerly await the Commission's next set of studies on the service industries. What the studies do show is that the various Single Market measures are part of a longer period of change. The pace has increased recently and there will undoubtedly be major overshooting. Not everybody can gain, although they may hope to. In the 1990s we will see the shakeout of the losers. In common with past experience a large proportion of acquisitions will be shown not to generate the returns that purchasers hoped for.

Such losses will be exacerbated in areas like public purchasing. Other measures in the field of fiscal harmonisation are far off agreement and the extent of 'Single Market' will still fall far short of that which prevails in the United States or Japan. Nevertheless, it still represents a major process of structural adjustment in European industry whose consequences will be felt for an extended period.

References

Bakhoven, A. F. (1989), 'The completion of the Common Market in 1992: macroeconomic consequences for the European Community', Central Plan Bureau Research Memorandum No 56.

Baldwin, R. (1989), 'Completing the European Single Market in 1992: how Cecchini underestimates the benefits', *Economic Policy*.

BCG, (1985), *Strategic Study of the Machine Tool Industry*, European Commission, Brussels.

BIPE, Cambridge Econometrics, IFO and Prometeia (1990), *Europe in 1995*.

Buigues, P. (1985), *Prospective et Compétitivité*, Paris: McGraw Hill.

Buigues, P. and Ilzkowitz, F. (1988), 'The sectoral impact of the internal market', EC Brussels II/335/88-EN.

Buigues, P. and Jacquemin, A. (1989), 'Strategies of firms and structural environment in the large internal market', *Journal of Common Market Studies*, vol. 28, no. 1, pp. 53–67.

Burridge, M., Dhar, S., Mayes, D. G., Meen, G. and Tyrrell, N. (1991), 'Oxford Economic Forecasting's system of models', *Economic Modelling* (forthcoming).

Burridge, M. and Mayes, D. G. (1990), 'Industrial change for 1992', ch. 10 in P. Dunne and C. Driver (eds), *Structural Change and the UK Economy*, Cambridge: Cambridge University Press.

Catinat, M., Donni, E. and Italianer, A. (1988), 'Macroeconomic consequences of the completion of the internal market: the modelling evidence', ch. 10 in *Studies on the Economics of Integration*, vol. 2 of *Research on the 'Cost of Non-Europe'*, European Commission, Luxembourg/Brussels.

Cecchini, P. (1988), *The European Challenge 1992: the benefits of a single market*, Aldershot: Wildwood House.

Dell, E. and Mayes, D. G. (1989), '1992: the environment for European industry', Centre for European Policy Studies, Brussels, July.

Emerson, M., Aujean, M., Catinat, M., Goybet, P. and Jacquemin, A. (1988), *The Economics of 1992*, Oxford: Oxford University Press.

King, M. (1989), 'Takeover activities in the UK', in J. Fairburn and J. Kay (eds), *Mergers and Merger Policy*, Oxford: Oxford University Press.

Mayes, D. G. (1971), 'The effect of alternative trade groupings on the United Kingdom', PhD dissertation, University of Bristol.

Mayes, D. G. (1990), 'The external implications of closer European integration', *National Institute Economic Review*, no. 134, pp. 73–85.

Nerb, G. (1988), *The Completion of the Internal Market: a survey of European industry's perception of the likely effects*, vol. 3 of *Research on the 'Cost of Non-Europe'*, European Commission, Luxembourg/Brussels.

Porter, M. (1985), *Competitive Advantage*, New York: Free Press.

Porter, M. (1990), *The Competitive Advantage of Nations*, London: Macmillan.

Shipman, A. and Mayes, D. G. (1991), 'The evolution of rules for a Single European Market', National Institute Discussion Paper.

Notes

1. These are listed in both Cecchini and Emerson *et al.*
2. This and previous merger waves may have resulted from a phase of relatively rapid economic expansion at a time when rising stock markets, followed by increased costs of borrowing, raised the attractiveness of growth by acquisition (King, 1989).

Table 1.1 and Figures 1.2–5 are drawn from *European Economy* No. 40 with permission.

2

The automobile industry

Didier Salvadori

Introduction

The aim of this chapter is to analyse the strategies of firms in the automobile sector (i.e. vehicle manufacturers and component suppliers) and to identify the impact on these strategies of the setting up of the 1993 Single Market. Within this context, there are four objectives:

1. To describe the structural climate of the automobile sector (e.g. state of the market, relationships of competition) in which the setting up of the Single Market will take place.
2. To describe the strategies developed by firms in order to respond to the new market.
3. To analyse the impact of the setting up of the Single Market on these strategies.
4. To set out the perspectives of structural changes that can be expected in the coming years.

Our approach is based on the fact that a strategy developed by a firm in a given economic environment is unique. Companies elaborate their strategies on the basis of both their perception of the environment and their understanding of their own strengths and weaknesses within this environment. Therefore, in the three sections of this chapter we will present the following:

1. A description of the environment of the automobile sector and an analysis of the main changes which the sector has undergone in the last few years. This description will include a focus on the principal characteristics of the companies' responses during this period.
2. An examination of the Single Market's dynamic. We will look at the most important changes within the statutory environment and in the

field of competition brought about by the setting up of the Single Market, and we will also analyse the effects of the latter on the market itself and on the ways in which agents perform.
3. An analysis of the current strategies adopted by firms in Europe. We will consider company strategies in the recent past and try to identify the impact of preparations for 1992 on the strategies that have been developed.

From the outset, it is essential to emphasise the weakness of the theoretical and empirical tools available. Macroeconomic models make it possible to be very precise about the effects of certain cyclical or structural measures, thanks to modes of conduct that have been presumed to be stable over a period of time, backed up by the law of large numbers. If we study the impact of a structural measure on the behaviour of firms, and particularly on their strategies, the starting point is the *im*permanence of behaviour. Hence, the analysis has to be based on an examination of scenarios and simulations. Broadly speaking, it is rare for the link of cause and effect between the implementation of policies and modification of behaviour to be formally established. There is no evidence that behaviour would not have changed if the measures had not been taken; equally, there is no evidence that the measures adopted are solely responsible for these changes in behaviour.

This study will concern itself with the way in which firms perceive the changes introduced by the setting up of the Single Market. Interviews with senior company representatives therefore appear to be the method that is best adapted to the problem as set out. However, we need to be clear about the limitations of such a method particularly in the case of a sector that is oligopolistic and in the focus of the media. Detailed analysis of the market and competition and the strategic decisions taken are not matters of public discussion; they are items of debate for company boards alone.

Furthermore, the elements of analysis and strategy as articulated by firms go hand in hand with a policy of internal communications (employees) and external communications (shareholders, customers, suppliers and competitors – even the State).

Notwithstanding these difficulties, the method employed is based on a collation of data coming from a number of different sources (company reports, studies, examination of commercial documents, discussions and interviews with senior staff in the firms themselves and in client and supplier firms, press articles, financial documentation and so on); this information then needs to be selected and cross-checked. The way in which the information about a sector is organised makes it possible to produce a synthesis of each firm's strategy and also a synthesis of the strategies adopted within the sector.

This study has certain important limitations. It is not possible to examine every firm in detail, and with some companies the problems of non-response and strategies of disinformation are also encountered – obstacles which can only be overcome, and then only in part, by sending the firms a clear statement outlining the objectives of the study and by assuring the interviewees that they will receive plenty of feedback. Also, in some cases, desirable cross-checks and detailed questioning could not be carried out. Thus, as in all impact studies, there remains an underlying feeling of dissatisfaction with the final format of the study.

Basically, though, the chapter contains a large amount of information about the strategies being followed in the automobile industry and about the impact of 1993 in particular. The reader will be able to identify certain elements of methodology that will be applicable to other sectors.

Current structures in the automobile sector and main structural developments since the first oil crisis

The automobile sector has undergone many important changes in the last few years: demand has become increasingly complex, growth has been subjected to violent fluctuations and markets have become less and less national. Furthermore, supply has become very concentrated and has above all been decisively internationalised. As these developments are well known, we limit ourselves to a brief analysis of the prospects for demand and a schematic presentation of the companies in the sector.

It is worth noting that firms in the automobile sector in Europe are currently redefining their strategy, now that most of them have carried out significant internal reorganisations.

Characteristics of the markets

Quantitative aspects of the European market

Developments in recent years In the course of the last few years, the 12 countries of the European Community have become a market that is quantitatively more important than the North American market (see Table 2.1 (a) and (b)). Growth in demand has been sustained by the economic vitality of southern Europe and by a marked acceleration in demand for replacement in the principal markets of Western Europe.

Table 2.1(a)   Market characteristics: world market statistics

Geographical areas	Pop'n (m.)	car prod'n (m.)	cars/ 100 pop'n	Annual sales ('000s) 1985	1988	1995[1]
Western Europe	365	123	33.7	10,609	12,944	14,035
(EC only)	325	113	34.8	9,539	11,786	12,995
US, Canada	268	147	54.9	11,632	11,646	11,600
Japan	122	28	23.0	3,104	3,717	4,400
Rest of world	4,145	85	2.1	7,142	6,945	7,200
World total	4,900	385	7.9	32,487	35,252	37,235

Note: [1]forecast

Table 2.1(b)   Market characteristics: market development by country – number of private cars

Country	1985	1986	1987	1988	1989 (est.)	1990	1991 (forecasts)	1992
France	1,766	1,912	2,105	2,217	2,310	2,325	2,250	2,300
West Germany	2,379	2,829	2,916	2,808	2,750	2,862	2,860	2,900
UK	1,832	1,882	2,014	2,215	2,286	2,150	2,250	2,300
Italy	1,747	1,825	1,977	2,184	2,365	2,260	2,300	2,400
Spain	543	647	874	998	1,050	980	1,150	1,250
Netherlands	494	560	555	482	505	540	650	700
Belgium	360	395	406	425	430	440	470	490
Luxembourg	28	32	32	34	40	45	50	55
Denmark	157	169	124	89	90	95	150	170
Portugal	94	110	124	212	215	220	230	240
Greece	78	65	46	58	70	70	90	100
Ireland	61	60	49	64	75	70	80	90
EC	9,539	10,486	11,222	11,786	12,186	12,057	12,530	12,995
Switzerland	267	302	306	321	350	340	340	250
Sweden	263	270	316	343	320	340	345	250
Austria	243	262	243	252	270	250	255	260
Norway	159	167	115	68	60	85	90	95
Finland	138	143	151	174	185	170	180	185
Europe (17 countries)	10,609	11,630	12,363	12,944	13,371	13,242	13,740	14,035
US	10,974	11,398	10,225	10,591	9,800	9,600	10,100	10,200
Japan	3,104	3,146	3,275	3,717	4,203	4,280	4,300	4,400
World market	32,487	34,174	33,963	35,252	35,274	35,222	36,490	37,235

By virtue of the diversity of the countries and the existence of cyclical time lags in their economic performances, the European Community has had a buffer against cyclical fluctuations. Indeed, trade cycles in Europe are demonstrably less important than those obtaining in North America.

Developments on the horizon for 1995   The prospects of growth in the European market are favourable for the following reasons:

- Demand for equipment and accessories which is still clearly lower than that in North America (this is particularly true of countries in southern Europe, an area where it is expected that there will be sustained economic growth).
- The effects of replacement of cars flowing from the introduction of technical controls on vehicles or from a strengthening of existing controls (this mainly applies to Italy, Spain, France and Greece).
- The effects of replacement of cars brought about by a movement towards the top of the range, which is potentially important in several European countries; this trend will be stimulated by the effects of supply (e.g. the attraction of a new car and improved standards).

Qualitative aspects

The automobile sector occupies a market strongly characterised by technological development. Producers are constantly being faced with the need to come up with new ideas as consumers find these aspects very attractive. In this way, the market is stimulated by a 'quality effect' which needs to be analysed separately from 'volume' effects (the number of registrations) and 'price' effects. A distinction needs to be drawn between the following:

- The 'whole range' effect (i.e. the category of the vehicle as distinct from a presentation of segments of the market).
- The 'mix' effect (i.e. different versions of a single model of vehicle – engine performance, standard of equipment, special models, sports models).
- The 'equipment' effect (i.e. the development of standard features on the basic model).

The car market can be divided into 7 segments, shown in Table 2.2 (a) and (b). The 'whole range' effect is to be found amongst segments 2, 3, 4 and 5 but its development is limited to a short-term market. Furthermore, it is closely linked to phenomena of national supply in those countries where vehicles are manufactured locally. The 'mix' effect is important in segments 2, 3, 4 and 5 and is of minimal relevance in segments 1, 6 and 7. In segments 2, 3, 4 and 5 the 'equipment' effect creates circumstances in which the tendency to lower the relative price of vehicles can be counteracted. By constrast, the drop in relative price is observable in segment 1 despite the presence of an increasingly wide range of equipment; in segments 6 and 7, the characteristics of vehicle equipment

Table 2.2(a) Market characteristics: segmentation of the European automobile market

Segment	Characteristics	Principal models		
1 economy	<1,100cc price <45,000FF	Austin Mini Maruti 900 Yugo 45	Citroën 2cv Renault 4	Fiat Panda Seat Marbella
2 small	1,000–1,450cc price 45–65,000FF	Austin Metro Ford Fiesta Mazda 121 Peugeot 205 VW Polo	Citroën AX Honda Civic Nissan Micra Renault 5	Fiat Uno Lancia Y10 Opel Corsa Seat Ibiza
3 medium (lower)	1,100–1,600cc price 60–80,000FF	Alfa Romeo 33 Ford Escort Lada Samara Nissan Sunny Renault 19 VW Golf/Jetta	Austin Maestro Ford Orion Lancia Delta Opel Kadett Rover 213 Volvo 340	Fiat Tipo Honda Accord Mazda 323 Peugeot 309 Seat Malaga Yugo 65
4 medium (upper)	1,500–1,950cc price 76–100,000FF	Alfa Romeo 75 Citroën BX Honda Prelude Nissan Bluebird Renault 21 Volvo 440	Audi 80 Fiat Regata Lancia Dedra Opel Vectra Toyota Corolla	Austin Montego Ford Sierra Mazda 626 Peugeot 405 VW Passat
5 large	1,600–2,000cc price 95–160,000FF	Alfa Romeo 164 Citroën XM Honda Legend Mercedes 190 Renault 25 Volvo 240	Audi 90/100 Fiat Croma Lancia Thema Mitsubishi Galant Rover 820	BMW 3 series Ford Scorpio Mazda 929 Peugeot 605 Saab 900
6 de luxe	>2,000cc price >160,000FF	Audi 200 Saab 9000	BMW 5,7 series Volvo 740/760	Mercedes 200, 300, 500
7 prestige, sport, leisure	sport prestige de luxe sport offroad concept-van	Alpine, Ferrari, Porsche Bentley, Jaguar, Rolls-Royce BMW M3 M5, Audi 200 Lada Niva, Mitsubishi Pajero, Nissan Patrol, Land/Range Rover, Jeep, Toyota Land Cruiser Chrysler Voyager, Nissan Prairie/Vanette, Renault Espace		

do not correspond to a market dynamic but rather flow from a specific image of the vehicles.

Analysis of these qualitative market developments calls for explanations and specific forecasts for the various segments of the market shown in Table 2.2 (a) and (b) and even for certain sub-segments. They may be distinguished as follows:

1. *Segment 1* The cheap car market is characterised by extreme sensitivity to price under the constraint of a given standard of features and of minimum performance.

Table 2.2(b)   Estimated European market structure by segment, 1988

Segment	Registration ('000s)	Share (%)
1	550	4.25
2	3,689	28.50
3	4,077	31.50
4	2,556	19.75
5	1,197	9.25
6	647	5.00
7	227	1.75
of which		
sport	13	0.10
prestige	4	0.03
de luxe sport	20	0.15
off road	90	0.62
concept-van	110	0.85
Total	12,944	100.00

2. *Segments 2, 3, 4 and 5*   These four segments represent 90 per cent of the European market; demand is sensitive to supply effects, while sensitivity to price is mitigated by sensitivity to the vehicles' technical characteristics, by phenomena relating to image, and by behaviour concerning brand loyalty.

3. *Segment 6*   The 'de luxe' vehicle market is extremely sensitive to effects of image and there are powerful attachments to particular makes; it is also a market which is fairly consistent throughout the world.

4. *Segment 7*   This needs to be split up into five sub-segments, the first three of which have achieved a degree of worldwide consistency:

- sports cars – a fluctuating market in which the effects of image are highly important;
- prestige cars – this market is marginal in terms of volume, avoids cyclical fluctuations and effectively does not evolve in any particular direction;
- sports car versions of 'de luxe' four-door saloons – this market, too, is marginal in terms of volume and is sensitive to the vehicles' technical performance and how they are presented on the news media (e.g. the Audi Quattro phenomenon);
- 'off road' vehicles – a resilient market and very dependent on image phenomena;
- the 'van' concept – also very buoyant and particularly sensitive to innovations in concept.

For an analysis of company strategies of adaptation, it is therefore necessary to study segments 1–6 together with the 'off road' and 'van' concept sub-segments.

An improvement in the quality of vehicles is likely to result from the three 'effects' referred to above. There will be a certain standardising of features which are currently reserved for vehicles at the top end of the market or for special models. However, not all technical options will be available throughout the range.

Quantification of the markets

By contrast with previous years, a drop in the relative price of vehicles is anticipated. Car manufacturers have benefited from a rise in vehicle prices which was greater than the average for consumer goods, thanks to an 'over-valuing' of 'quality' goods. In this sense the automobile industry occupies a unique place in consumer durables and semi-durables. What is more, it can be seen that companies in other sectors (electric household equipment and clothing, for example) are not in a position to pass on the entire increase in those manufacturing costs which are linked to an improvement in the quality of their products: they concede part of their improvements in productivity to the customer and to dealers. This difference is brought about by a number of phenomena, of which the mode of distribution and the intensity of competition play vital roles. Notwithstanding the developments expected in these two areas, there is likely to be a moderate tendency for the relative prices of vehicles to fall, the relative price being defined by the following formula:

$$\text{index of relative price (year } n+1/ \text{ year } n) = \frac{\text{index of increases in catalogue prices, model by model}}{\text{index of improvement in quality} \ast \text{general index of prices}}$$

Manufacturers will therefore have to concede some of their productivity gains to consumers – or secure certain productivity gains from their suppliers.

Assuming a stable technical and economic situation, there is more likely to be a more sustained growth in the market of extras than in the motor car market itself. As a result of the development of demand for vehicles with improved equipment, an increased preparedness on the part of consumers to shop around together with the attraction of technology (even if it is not actually used), there will be a tendency for components to contribute more to the value of the vehicle; the equipment and accessories market will therefore be stimulated, independently of developments expected in manufacturers' integration strategies and in their technical organisation (see Table 2.3). Independent producers of components will be able to increase the cost of their know-how and

Table 2.3   Estimates and forecasts for the European market

	1985	1988	1992	1995	Average rate of growth p.a. 1985–8	1988–92	1982–5
Car market:							
'000 vehicles	10,500	12,944	13,740	14,035	7.2	1.5	0.7
bn ecu 1988	60.00	87.39	95.00	100.00	13.3	2.1	1.7
Potential market open to suppliers prod'n in Europe:							
'000 vehicles	11,500	13,850	14,500	15,000	6.3	1.1	1.1
bn ecu 1988	50.00	68.18	75.00	80.00	10.7	2.4	0.8
Market for primary equipment:							
at 1998 rate of integration ecu bn 88	24.00	30.50	36.00	39.00	8.3	4.2	2.7
with falling rate		30.50	39.00	43.00		6.3	3.3
Market for subcontrac'rs:	15.00	18.00	21.00	23.00	6.2	3.9	3.1
Market for parts/accessories:							
products bn ecu	14	15.6	18	20	3.6	3.6	3.5
services	15	18.7	23	27	7.6	5.3	5.4

technology, which will hence be only partly dominated by vehicle manufacturers; other suppliers (subcontractors and suppliers of inter-mediate products) will be in a less favourable market position.

Changes in the technical and economic organisation of the sector suggest a sustained enlargement in the equipment market. The market estimates and forecasts set out in Table 2.3 rely on calculations based on modest information relating to vehicle prices, purchases by European and non-European manufacturers who have set up in Europe, and important modifications to manufacturers' practices in the context of the integration rate. This rate corresponds closely to the production of components or to vehicle in-house subassembly. It is often closely linked to the relationship between added value and the manufacturers' turnover, although this system of measuring is highly unsatisfactory. There is likely to be a drop in the average integration rate in Europe resulting both from modifications in strategies expected from European manufacturers and from the opening up of new markets linked to the presence of non-European manufacturers.

All in all, the outlook for the European market is an attractive one. By comparison with the American market, it is more important, more dynamic and geographically more concentrated; it is also three times larger than the Japanese market. Developing countries and the countries of Eastern Europe undoubtedly have huge growth potential, but access is difficult and they can boast of little homogeneity.

There is no doubt that the European market will increasingly become the target market of manufacturers and suppliers the world over. This will intensify competition, which will be expressed in price, quality characteristics of the vehicles and in those services associated with the use and ownership of vehicles.

The principal players

The automobile industry occupies an important place in the economies of many countries – and not just those that are direct producers of vehicles – by virtue of the importance of the purchases made by automobile manufacturers: intermediary items account for over 50 per cent of the cost of a vehicle, and this is not counting the manufacturers' distribution networks. Alongside the major vehicle manufacturing companies which are seeking to structure the sector stand firms of all sizes and of widely differing characteristics.

As far as the suppliers to the vehicle manufacturers are concerned, this study will concentrate on those firms that supply the industry directly. We will identify and then give a schematic introduction to the main firms concerned, and this will be followed by a brief look at the relationships between the industrial (production capacity, setting up of new factories) and commercial (market share) strengths of the manufacturers. Finally, we will discuss the vertical and horizontal relationships between the manufacturers: their supply systems and their after-sales distribution and service structures.

The manufacturers

The list of manufacturers in Table 2.4 is far from being exhaustive; the main manufacturers appear on the list according to the nationality they nominally belong to, this being a fairly pertinent criterion if we are to construct a world map of manufacturers. The main limitation of this Table is that there are no references to 'joint venture' factories in developing countries and in East European countries.

European manufacturers can be grouped in two categories:

1. 'Generalist' manufacturers that produce over 500,000 vehicles a year with a range covering segments 1–5.
2. 'Specialist' manufacturers that produce fewer than 500,000 vehicles a year, including vehicles in segments 5–7.

In Japan, there are nine main manufacturers. Toyota and Nissan have an annual production level which is greater than that of the most important European manufacturer and comparable with that of the

Table 2.4   Car manufacturers: the main players

Car manufacturers	Production ('000s) 1985	1988	Turnover (bn ECU) Total	Cars	(bn ECU) % Cars/tot.	Profits (bn ECU)	% turnover
European							
Generalists							
Austin-Rover	480	520			95.0		
Fiat	1,320	1,840	29.21	23.71	81.2	1.86	6.4
Ford-Europe	1,450	1,660	19.57	17.61	90.0	1.36	6.9
GM-Europe/Opel	1,570	1,770	15.83	14.25	90.0	1.61	10.2
PSA	1,600	2,140	19.79	16.82	85.0	1.27	6.4
Renault	1,670	1,890	23.06	17.64	76.5	1.29	5.6
VAG	2,350	2,550	29.14	26.23	90.0	0.37	1.3
'Specialists'							
Daimler-Benz	520	550	35.71	26.57	74.4	0.83	2.3
BMW	440	470	9.66	7.73	80.0	0.19	1.9
Volvo	370	390	13.80	8.28	60.0	0.47	3.4
Saab	110	130	7.14	2.39	33.4	0.46	6.4
Porsche	25	25	1.25	1.06	85.0	0.01	1.0
Jaguar	40	50	1.53	1.45	95.0	0.07	4.4
Japanese							
Toyota	3,500	3,750	52.29	39.21	75.0	2.29	4.4
Nissan	3,100	2,850	30.29	24.23	80.0	0.64	2.1
Honda	1,260	1,700	21.43	13.93	65.0	0.69	3.2
Mazda-Datsun	1,190	1,350			90.0		
Mitsubishi	1,170	1,300	12.14	10.32	85.0	0.10	0.8
Suzuki	780	840			80.0		
Daihatsu	450	520			95.0		
Isuzu	430	510			95.0		
Subaru/Fuji	260	260			80.0		
American							
General Motors	6,800	4,900	98.57	73.93	75.0	4.34	4.4
Ford	3,500	3,900	82.71	62.04	75.0	4.74	5.7
Chrysler	1,900	2,100	31.71	28.54	90.0	0.94	3.0
Other							
Hyundai (Korea)	200	580					
Daeweo (Korea)	40	170					
Kia (Korea)	20	130					
Lada (USSR)	800	750					
Polski (Poland)	250	250					
Zastava (Yugoslavia)	170	220					

second most important American producer, while Honda, Mazda and Mitsubishi are approximately the same size as the European generalists. Japan also boasts small independent producers which rarely look to external markets.

American firms are undoubtedly large, but it is worth remembering that each of them is in fact a federation of makes, all of them old independent firms.

Looking at the final category we can see that South Korea is probably the fourth largest vehicle producer in the world.

The component suppliers

The list of firms in Table 2.5 confines itself to a small number of suppliers to the automobile industry.

As far as the European firms are concerned, it is important to remember that they need to be analysed according to both their size and their degree of market diversification. In the automobile industry, it is traditional to draw a distinction between those component manufacturers that devote the vast majority of their resources to designing and developing finished products specifically for the vehicle industry and those for whom the industry is only one outlet. The former are not just custodians of some industrial know-how or of the mastery of a technology which is used in the industry; they are 'function specialists' involved in the car market. However, we will see later on that this distinction loses some of its validity with the entry into the motor car market of large, medium-sized and small firms: they increasingly employ techniques and products that have been developed in other sectors.

For the moment, however, let us keep this distinction between specialised manufacturers and other suppliers. The first category contains two types of firm: four large multi-product firms dealing in a wide range of products and product-functions and the others which specialise in just one function or one kind of component.

In addition to these firms, there are now large European groups which have made the automobile industry into a major axis of their development. They boast high technological skills and know-how which are energetically sought by the industry all over the world.

Other smaller European companies (with a turnover of under 50 million ecus) draw clear lines between those parts of their activity that impinge on the automobile industry and those that do not. However, as these firms are not quoted on the Stock Exchange there is very little information on them, but it is nevertheless possible to state confidently that they, too, have a considerable level of technical expertise – enough to give them a certain independence from the manufacturers.

As for non-European firms, only some of the most important have been listed. American manufacturers characteristically have subsidiaries within the main group which produce components. By contrast, Japan has an independent components industry, but one needs to bear in mind that Japanese manufacturers own shares in the principal firms producing components; this might be termed the 'spheres of privileged supply'.

Table 2.5 Suppliers to the automobile industry: the main players

Companies and groups	Turnover			Activities	
	bn ecu total	cars	% car/tot	Car components	Other products
European firms					
Large multiproduct					
Bosch (Ger)	9,286	5,107	55	Electrical equipt, injection, brakes	elec. household appl. and electronics
Valeo (Fr)	2,286	2,263	99	Electrical equipt, lights, heating, clutch	none
Magenti-Marelli (I)	1,786	1,518	85	Elec. equipt, lights, heating, injection	ind'l elec. and electronic
Lucas (UK)	1,714	1,114	65	Brakes, injection, wiring	aeronautical
Specialists					
BBA auto products (UK)	917	779	85	Brakes, suspension, transmission	aeronautical
Epeda/Bertrand/Faure (Fr)	1,114	780	70	Seating, seating engineering	bedding, luggage
VDA (Ger)	533	427	80	Dashboard equipt	ind. measuring eqpt.
Teves (Ger)	1,048	995	95	Brakes	aeronautical
Lignotock (Ger)	227	227	100	Interior fittings, inside of doors, dashboards	nil
Reydel (Fr)	243	146	60	Interior fittings, rearview mirrors	kitchen eqpt., lighting
ECIA (PSA) (Fr)	829	580	70	Silencers, steering wheels/cols.	tooling, car repairs
Sommer-Alibert (Fr)	586	234	40	Interior fittings, fuel tanks	plastics
Labinal (Fr)	414	228	55	Dashboard equipt, wiring	aeronautical
Montupet (Fr)	157	141	90	Engine parts, aluminium wheel rims	aluminium foundry
Teksid (Fiat) (I)	331	215	65	Engine castings, brakes, suspension	foundry, heavy lorry, agric. machinery
ZF (Ger)	2,190	1,446	66	Gear boxes, transmission	heavy lorries, agric. machinery
Fichtel-Sachhs (Ger)	1,190	1,012	85	Suspension, clutches	heavy lorry, agric. machinery, cycles
Kolbenschmitt (Ger)	410	205	50	Engine parts, pistons, cylinders	heavy lorries, agric. machinery
Boge (Ger)	267	213	80	Shock absorbers	heavy lorries, bicycles
Delanair (UK)	63	51	80	Heating equipment	heavy lorries
Allevard Ind (Fr)	118	88	75	Spring suspension	spec. steels, springs, bicycles
Plactic-Omnium (Fr)	314	126	40	Interior fittings, bumpers	plastic products
Rejna (I)	225	146	65	Suspension, shock absorbers	heavy veh. suspension
CEAC (Fr)	214	171		Batteries	heavy lorry batteries
Manducher (Fr)	171	146	85	Interior fittings, bumpers, fuel tanks	plastic prods
L'Ectricfil (Fr)	21	17	80	Spark plugs	IT
Sogefi (de Benedetti (I)	400			Filters, suspension	filters, lorry and rail suspension
Foggini (I)				Interior fittings, rearview mirrors	injection plastics

				Automotive products	Other products
Leistritz (Ger)	57	49	85	Silencers	lorry silencers
Wimetal (Fr)	19	19	100	Silencers	none
Large diversified					
Siemens (Ger)	12,333	617	5	Electrical equipt, injection, brakes	dom. elec., elec., electronics
GKN (UK)	3,667	1,650	45	Transmission, suspension	mech. eng. machinery
TI (UK)	1,833	458	25	Susp'n tubing, exhausts, seating	tubes
Hutchinson (Total, F)	714	321	45	Rubber joints	rubber products
Turner & Newall (UK)	1,833	825	45	Spare parts, clutches, brakes	ind'l prods, filters, mech'l parts
BTR (UK)	7,500	750	10	Plastic parts, rubber products	plastics, rubber
Sat-Sagem (Fr)	1,371	41	3	Electronic equipt	aeronautical, arms
Small specialists					
Lebranchu (Fr)	100	90	90	Prototypes and diestamping	
Small diversified					
Forges Stephanoises (F)	90	41	45	Forgings	forgings, tools
Fonderies de Leman (F)	50	20	40	Aluminium engine castings	aluminium castings
Fonderies Waeles (F)	30	17	55	Alloy castings	industrial castings
Defontaines (F)	47	24	50	Clutches, starters	machined parts
Large non-European					
Japanese					
Nippondenso	7,333	6,600	90	Electrical equipt, injection, clutches	friction materials, electronics
Aisin Seiki	3,400	2,890	85	Transmission, engine parts	ind. mech. parts
Tokai Rika	867	823	95	Dashboard equipt	elec./electronic parts
Kayaba Inds	800	440	55	Shock absorbers	aeronautics marine
Diesel Kiki	1,400	1,260	90	Injection, air conditioning	
Atsugi	567	453	80	Engine and chassis parts	industrial parts
Akebono	533	480	90	Brakes	heavy lorry brakes
Yuasa				Batteries	instruments, compressors
Tokico	653	457	70	Shock absorbers	
American					
AC Products + other GM	16,429	15,607	95	Engine, chassis and bodywork	
Ford Components				Engine, chassis and bodywork	
Acustar (Chrysler)	3,111	2,956	95	Engine, chassis and bodywork	
Dana	5,000	3,000	60	Gear boxes, transmission, suspension	hydraulic equipt
Borg Warner	3,889	1,361	35	Gear boxes, transmission	chemical products
Eaton	3,556	711	20	Brakes, transmission	lorry equipment, industrial parts

The manufacturers' relative strengths

Table 2.4, which shows the main manufacturers, enables us to judge relative strength in terms of turnover and annual production. European manufacturers (including the subsidiaries of American groups) turn out between 12 and 13 million vehicles a year and export about 1 million (of which half are vehicles in segments 5, 6 and 7). American manufacturers produce approximately 9 million vehicles annually, but it is appropriate to add the production figures of Japanese firms that are established there; exports from North America are marginal. Japanese manufacturers, for their part, have a combined annual production of some 12 million vehicles of which more than 20 per cent are built abroad; more than half of all vehicles made in Japan itself are exported.

Although Japanese and American manufacturers produce their goods worldwide, European production is concentrated on Europe (see Table 2.6) and particularly in six EC countries with the addition of Sweden. However, European manufacturers are setting up production lines on a 'European level' by developing their penetration into Spain and Portugal: the overwhelming majority of vehicles produced in these countries are models from segments 1 and 2 and other models which are less important and involve little automatisation at the assembly stage (4-wheel-drive models and small industrial vehicles). Investment planned by European manufacturers is likely to take their combined annual production over 14 million units if projects involving East European countries are included. The figures of Japanese producers should be added to this.

The increase in capacity by Japanese firms bears some resemblance to the European-level division of labour carried out by the European manufacturers themselves. The major Japanese factories in Europe and their most important projects there are referred to in Table 2.7. For the most part they are in Britain and Spain, and there is some penetration in Portugal. In addition to the factories built by the Japanese, there are numerous co-operation projects between European and Japanese manufacturers to build utility vehicles or 4-wheel-drive cars. The development of Japanese vehicle manufacturing capacity in Europe is in line anyway with their global policy of accelerating investment plans and extending production capacity abroad.

Investment by Japanese vehicle manufacturers should have reached about a thousand million ecus for the year 1988–89, an increase of more than 19 per cent over 1987–88. Part of this investment is aimed at developing capacity in North America which is estimated to be already producing about 800,000 units a year. In 1991–92, the production capacity of Japanese manufacturers is likely to total 2,100,000 units. What is more, the Japanese have announced that they will be building

Table 2.6 Location of production in Europe

| Manufacturers | Number ('000s) 1988 | | | | | | | | | | | | |
| | Country of production | | | | | | | | | | | | |
	Germany	France	Italy	UK	Belgium	Spain	Portugal	Other EC	Tot. EC	Sweden	Austria	Total	Non-Europe
Austin-Rover	–	–	–	470	–	50	–	–	520	–	–	520	–
Fiat	–	–	1,840	–	–	–	–	–	1,840	–	–	1,840	–
Ford-Europe	610	–	–	390	280	280	–	–	1,560	–	–	1,560	–
GM-Europe/Opel	890	–	–	170	360	350	–	–	1,770	–	–	1,770	–
PSA	–	1,820	–	80	–	220	20	–	2,140	–	–	2,140	–
Renault	–	1,380	–	–	180	280	50	–	1,890	–	–	1,890	–
VAG	1,800	–	–	–	190	310	–	–	2,300	–	–	2,300	250
Daimler-Benz	550	–	–	–	–	–	–	–	550	–	–	550	–
BMW	470	–	–	–	100	–	–	–	470	–	–	470	–
Volvo	–	–	–	–	100	–	–	–	100	290	–	390	–
Saab	–	–	–	–	–	–	–	–	0	130	–	130	–
Porsche	25	–	–	–	–	–	–	–	25	–	–	25	–
Jaguar	–	–	–	50	–	–	–	–	50	–	–	50	–
Nissan	–	–	–	60	–	–	–	–	60	–	–	60	–
Other	–	5	40	20	20	30	10	23	148	–	7	155	–
Total	4,345	3,205	1,880	1,240	1,130	1,520	80	23	13,423	420	7	13,850	250

Table 2.7   Japanese plants in Europe

Manufacturers	Location	Type, production	Production 1988 units	Projected volume Date	Projected volume Units
Nissan	Sunderland (UK)	assembly cars	80,000	1992–93	200,000
Nissan	........(Spain)	assembly vans, 4 × 4	4 × 4		
Nissan (with Ford Eur.)	........(Spain)	assembly vans, 4 × 4	–		
Nissan	........(Greece)	assembly cars	100,000		
Nissan	........(Spain)	assembly cars	–	1992	150,000
Toyota	Burnaston (UK)	assembly cars	–	1997–98	200,000
Toyota	Shotton (Wales)	engines	–	1997–98	200,000
Toyota (with Volkswagen)	........(UK)	manufacture vans	–		
Toyota	........(Portugal)	assembly vans	–		
Honda	Longbridge (UK)	assembly cars	–	1990	40,000
Honda	Swindon (UK)	assembly cars	–	1994	100,000
Honda in co-op. with Rover	........(UK)	engines	–	1990	70,000
Suzuki	........(Spain)	assembly, 4 × 4	20,000 4 × 4		
Suzuki	........(Wales)	assembly, 4 × 4	15,000 4 × 4		
Suzuki (with Land Rover)	........(Spain)	manufacture 4 × 4, vans	–		
Isuzu (with GM Eur.)	........(UK)	assembly vans	–	1990	70,000
Mitsubishi (with Mercedes)	........(Spain)	manufacture 4 × 4, vans	–		
Hino	........(Ireland)	assembly lorries	3,000		
Hino	........(Portugal)	assembly lorries	–		
Hino	........(Norway)	assembly vans	–		

factories in the main East European countries in co-operation with existing firms. This investment programme goes hand in hand with a wish to control developments in the principal markets and to escape possible import restrictions. It is also in line with a strategy of an international division of labour which finds its most advanced form in the development of 'top end of the market' models of specific brands. These models are actually built in Japan in very modern factories and using highly sophisticated forms of organisation. The marketing of these vehicles demands the mobilisation of considerable sums of money in order to set up new distribution networks and promotional operations leading up to the launch. For example, the publicity costs of launching Nissan's new 'Infiniti' model in the United States came to $60 million in a single year.

Commercial penetration by vehicle manufacturers into the three principal markets is extremely unequal. In the European market, each of the six generalist manufacturers occupy between 10 per cent and 15 per cent. Of the remainder, about 20 per cent is shared out amongst the specialists (roughly 5 per cent each), and the rest is occupied by small and medium-sized European operators and non-European firms, mainly Japanese (see Table 2.8).

The American market is notable for a level of imports which is significantly higher than that of the European market – about 30 per cent as opposed to something under 10 per cent (see Table 2.9). What is more,

Table 2.8   The European market: number of registrations ('000s)

Manufacturer	1986 '000s	1986 %	1987 '000s	1987 %	1988 '000s	1988 %	1989[4] '000s	1989[4] %
Group: Rover[1]	408	3.5	420	3.4	376	2.9	406	3.0
Group: Fiat[2]	1,634	14.0	1,758	14.2	1,928	14.9	2,001	14.8
Ford Europe	1,360	11.7	1,476	12.0	1,460	11.2	1,555	11.5
GM Europe	1,268	10.9	1,301	10.5	1,339	10.5	1,460	10.8
PSA	1,326	11.4	1,501	12.1	1,671	12.9	1,717	12.7
Citroën	499	4.3	580	4.7	619	4.8	649	4.8
Other Peugeot	827	7.1	921	7.4	1,052	8.1	1,068	7.9
Renault	1,234	10.6	1,310	10.6	1,313	10.3	1,393	10.3
Group: VAG[3]	1,704	14.7	1,844	14.9	1,925	14.9	2,014	14.9
Mercedes-Benz	437	3.8	434	3.5	436	3.5	406	3.0
Volvo	221	1.9	247	2.0	272	2.1	270	2.0
Japanese	1,363	11.7	1,401	11.3	1,446	11.2	1,460	10.8
Other	896	7.7	918	7.5	997	7.7	838	6.2
Total	11,630	100.0	12,363	100.0	12,953	100.0	13,520	100.0

Notes: [1]Group Rover: Austin + Rover (incl. Land Rover & Range Rover) [2]Group Fiat: Fiat + Lancia + Alfa Romeo + Autobianchi + Ferrari [3]Group VAG: VW + Audi + Seat [4]estimated

Source: CSCA

Table 2.9 The American market: number of registrations ('000s)

Assembled in United States and Canada

	1987		1988	
	'000s	%	'000s	%
GM	3,555	34.8	3,641	34.4
Ford	2,019	19.7	2,205	20.8
Chrysler	962	9.4	1,062	10.0
Honda	316	3.1	375	3.5
Nissan	119	1.2	112	1.1
Toyota	44	0.4	72	0.7
Mazda	2	0.0	31	0.3
VW	61	0.6	24	0.2
Mitsubishi	–	0.0	1	0.0
Other	3	0.0	3	0.0
Total local prod.	7,081	69.3	7,526	71.1
of which US	6,539	64.0	6,911	65.3
Jap.	481	4.7	590	5.6
Eur.	61	0.6	24	0.2

Imported

	1987		1988	
	'000s	%	'000s	%
Toyota	583	5.7	616	5.8
Honda + Acura	421	4.1	393	3.7
Nissan	409	4.0	360	3.4
Mazda	206	2.0	224	2.1
Other Jap.	283	2.8	262	2.5
VW	130	1.3	143	1.4
Mercedes-Benz	89	0.9	83	0.8
BMW	87	0.9	73	0.7
Audi	41	0.4	22	0.2
Porsche	23	0.2	15	0.1
Hyundai	263	2.6	264	2.5
Volvo	106	1.0	98	0.9
Saab	45	0.4	38	0.4
Peugeot	8	0.1	7	0.1
Other	450	4.4	467	4.4
Total imported	3,144	30.7	3,065	28.9

	1987	1988
Total registrations ('000s)	10,225	10,591

the control of the American market as carried out by home producers is of even less importance since registrations of vehicles of non-American makes manufactured in North America account for no more than 5–6 per cent of the total market – most of them vehicles built in Japanese factories. Vehicle imports in the strict sense of the word are headed by Japanese manufacturers with over 20 per cent of the market.

European manufacturers have made little impact on the American market. Only Volkswagen experienced any sort of commercial success; this has been based substantially on the popularity of the 'Golf'. The other European manufacturers operating in North America are specialists in top-range vehicles; this particular penetration reached its high point when exchange rates made the prices particularly attractive, but the period 1987–89 saw a significant reduction in the sales of such vehicles.

More than 95 per cent of the Japanese market is dominated by home producers. The main imports are German and most of them are vehicles at the top of the range (see Table 2.10).

Supplies and distribution structures

Component supply The methods used by manufacturers to get their supplies go a very considerable way towards explaining the equipment and specific features of motor cars. Until recently, the sector was very national in character. However, producers of equipment have to follow the lead of the technical developments of vehicles, and these in turn evolve a global character as a result of the manufacturers' overall strategies. Furthermore, vehicle manufacturers have been indicating certain reservations about this in view of the component producers' own internationalist strategy; it is believed that this development could make more available certain technical innovations which have been developed following co-operation with the equipment producers.

The situation is changing, but with two constraints. The first is of a technical nature: the technical development of vehicles demands a very high degree of technological and technical skills which must become increasingly elaborate and specific; thus manufacturers have found themselves obliged to hand over an increasing share of design and production work on equipment to their suppliers. The second constraint is economic: the autonomy of the component producers and the increase in the number of their outlets are enabling them to lower their unit manufacturing costs and therefore their output prices as passed on to the vehicle manufacturers. Developments of this kind have found their inspiration in Japanese modes of organisation.

Japanese vehicle manufacturers are a long way from being integrated,

Table 2.10 The Japanese market: number of registrations ('000s)

Manufactured in Japan	1987 '000s	1987 %	1988 '000s	1988 %
Toyota	1,453	44.4	1,633	43.9
Honda + Acura	337	10.3	401	10.8
Nissan	764	23.3	860	23.1
Mazda	198	6.0	217	5.8
Mitsubishi	158	4.8	180	4.8
Suzuki	62	1.9	64	1.7
Daihatsu	75	2.3	90	2.4
Isuzu	58	1.8	55	1.5
Subaru/Fuji	68	2.1	79	2.1
Other	4	0.1	5	0.1
Total	3,177	97.0	3,584	96.4

Imported	1987 '000s	1987 %	1988 '000s	1988 %
Volkswagen	23	0.7	27	0.7
BMW	21	0.6	26	0.7
Mercedes-Benz	18	0.5	22	0.6
Audi	8	0.2	11	0.3
Rover	5	0.2	7	0.2
Honda (US)	–	0.0	5	0.1
GM (US)	3	0.1	5	0.1
Volvo	3	0.1	4	0.1
Ford (US)	1	0.0	4	0.1
Porsche	2	0.1	3	0.1
Other	13	0.4	19	0.5
Total import	97	3.0	133	3.6

	1987	1988
Total registrations ('000s)	3,274	3,717

making very few components themselves, although they enjoy extremely close relations with the producers. The big manufacturers are controlling shareholders in the firms of the 'first tier' component producers. These firms have two vital roles: first, to design, develop and produce highly standardised components of very good quality and largely for the top end of the market; secondly, to organise industrial links with the other tiers of suppliers. They have the job of selecting the second and third tier suppliers, fixing prices and carrying out quality control. It is these firms that were involved in the early conception of such important technical developments as narrow lights and four-wheel drive, and they also have huge financial power and wide commercial influence.

Vehicle manufacturers in the United States are very closely integrated, perhaps as much as 70 per cent of equipment being built by the manufacturers themselves. Each of the big three vehicle manufacturers has subsidiaries producing components in such a way as to give them significant autonomy and to wrest commercial advantages from other manufacturers. This policy is difficult to put into practice, however, and one consequence is that there are relatively few equipment producers in the United States, which may go some way towards explaining some of the inertia in technical development of vehicles there. By contrast, Japanese manufacturers operating in North America have tried to develop working relationships with local equipment producers. They have then moved on to introducing Japanese firms into the market, and some of these have taken over the management of some American firms.

The situation in Europe is somewhat complex. The rate of integration varies considerably from one manufacturer to another although, as a general rule, the generalists are less integrated than the specialists. There even appears to be an opposite tendency prevalent towards disintegration.

Industrial structures are closely linked to national data. In West Germany, for example, with the exception of the Bosch group which enjoys considerable independence, component producers are small or medium-sized firms and are very specialised; they are also involved in very few foreign transactions. They have developed within the orbit of German vehicle manufacturers which have limited them to a steady technical development of high quality. French and Italian manufacturers have long kept the price of components down. The technical development and the quality of goods have suffered accordingly, and the profit margins of their producers have largely depended on replacement work. Changes are happening, however, and both countries now have one company which turns out a wide range of products. Nevertheless, the rest of the industry is changing slowly, partly because its commercial penetration of foreign manufacturers is extremely limited.

Vehicle distribution The marketing of vehicles is currently carried out by networks of specialist dealers. This system brings with it a kind of protection for the manufacturers in the sense that the distribution is done by approved firms whose commercial policies the manufacturers largely determine and take some responsibility for.

Those manufacturers that are well established commercially have an exclusive distribution network, which, in turn, has an importing subsidiary in each country in which it operates. The latter is financially independent of the manufacturer. Manufacturers whose commercial penetration is more limited must go through an importing subsidiary and a 'multi-make' distribution network.

In the United States, there are numerous distribution networks because American manufacturers market a large number of makes, and the very great distances to be covered lead marginal manufacturers to make use of 'multi-make' networks. Dealerships are, generally speaking, of little importance as they are financially weak and tend to operate on a regional basis. Most attempts to develop business outside the manufacturers' networks have taken place on the West Coast.

The majority of vehicle distribution in Europe is carried out by manufacturer subsidiaries or by concessionaires who are independent distributors; they guarantee deliveries to branches by means of local agents. These local agents, which are often family firms, vary in size considerably from one country to the next, and there are even variations within a given country. There are, however, finance groups which control several 'multi-make' concessions like Lonrho in Britain and Scoa in France.

During 1987 and 1988, France saw attempts to set up large-scale distribution systems, but these have not been followed up. Instead, there are experiments involving large commercial centres concentrating on the distribution of several makes. So-called parallel networks, which involve an agent getting supplies from abroad and reducing prices, have also been tried out but they are no more than a marginal phenomenon so far.

Finally, in Japan, it is quite clear that vehicle distribution is the basis of home manufacturers' complete control over the internal market, particularly as land prices make it extremely expensive to set up commercial undertakings in town and city centres. Relations between distributors and manufacturers are very complex, with the distributors completing an important constructor's range by selling models produced by small and/or foreign manufacturers.

Servicing networks and spare part distribution One justification given for selective distribution is the need to maintain vehicles according to standards set down by the manufacturers. Indeed, servicing networks are an essential ingredient of the manufacturers' commercial policies since repairs are carried out by concessionaires and agents who make good profits out of the supply and distribution of 'original' spare parts. It is also significant that in the midst of the 'traditional networks' there are independent and 'multi-make' vehicle mechanics who get their supplies of parts from the manufacturers' own networks or from wholesalers. These independent or 'multi-make' agents and wholesalers enable 'marginal' manufacturers to offer appropriate repair services.

None the less, traditional networks have a tendency to face competition from new forms of financing. In France, for instance, and to a lesser extent in the United Kingdom, wholesalers have developed their own distribution networks selling direct to consumers who wish to service their cars themselves. In parallel, the big equipment producers have supported, or even participated in, the development of systems offering specialist repair work (e.g. carburettors and electrical work). For their part, large food chains have begun to market spare parts and accessories and have even set up small repair depots independent of the main shops. Finally, some specialist distributors are now opening many more shops, frequently under franchise.

Manufacturers are fighting back by strengthening their distribution and after-sales service structures, and by setting up 'free service areas' in certain districts.

To sum up, there are a great many people in the automobile industry. The relationships between them are often complex, and the relative industrial and commercial strengths of the manufacturers cannot be measured without taking into account the overall organisation of each of them.

Main structural developments

The description of the market and its main protagonists as set out in the preceding sections is aimed at giving a picture of the automobile sector in the late 1980s. We must move away from this static view, and to do this we need to focus on certain vital influences on the industry, beginning with the problems faced by the sector.

Analysis of household budgets shows a relative reprioritising of expenditure in favour of 'higher' functions (e.g. transport, health and leisure) and away from 'primary' functions (e.g. food, clothing and housing). Expenditure on motor cars has continued to grow even in developed countries. This situation is not going to last for ever, and this makes it a very important facet of the fundamental characteristics of demand.

We can think of the purchase of a motor car under the following three headings:

1. A means of satisfying the need to travel around in a given technical, societal and economic environment.
2. A relationship between the consumer and technology – the choice of vehicle is linked to the wish to control certain technologies (or simply to have the possibility of doing so).
3. The identification between the vehicle and the social image.

In time, as socio-economic conditions – and individuals – change, so the balance between these three areas shifts.

The need to travel and the degree to which the car meets these needs are subject to the following modifications:

*   Life style (living in a semi-urban setting, working in city centre, going shopping on the outskirts, types of leisure activity and their importance);
*   demographic and socio-professional developments;
*   earnings levels;
*   changes in running costs (fuel and tax);
*   views on traffic congestion and on environmental problems;
*   competing and complementary means of transport.

The attitudes of the consumer to the new technology are undergoing changes that are very difficult to predict: for example, there is currently a demand for further introduction of new technological means of increasing reliability, safety, comfort and performance. However, it may be that this increased technological complexity will only be properly used by a tiny minority of consumers, with certain developments not being used at all: for example, it is said that an average of only two of the many channels on a car radio are ever used, and that digital information panels are ignored.

The relationship between the vehicle and social status is no more secure: at the moment, the process of social identification is enlarging the market for cars at the top of the range, but the process could easily move in the opposite direction at some point in the future (the status accorded to the Citroën 2CV in West Germany is an example of this phenomenon).

We can see that the market in which the manufacturers are operating is fundamentally uncertain. Every new model, every innovation is a risk which relies on the ability of the firms to understand and predict the characteristics of the market, themselves closely linked to socio-economic considerations.

The design of a vehicle is a long process – it takes 2–3 years – and it is complex because it is difficult to separate out the various phases: for example, the amount of noise the vehicle makes depends on tyres, wheels, transmission, mechanical parts, suspension, passenger space and the exterior design of the car. However, innovation is essential – if risky (for example, the failure of new designs for dashboards). The prototype development phase is one that has been revolutionised by systems perfected by CAO, but there remains the old problem that design and development rely heavily on technology, know-how and various materials, and this obliges manufacturers to fall back on suppliers who themselves have a wide diversity of industrial cultures.

Vehicle production is fundamentally no different from a large-scale assembly of components but, as in activities of this type, the various tasks have to be divided up and some of them carried out manually. What is more, the average size of parts makes it imperative to have a technical and logistic organisation that is specific to the work in hand, and one that is to be observed to the letter: industrial management comes out of the search for a compromise between flexibility and mechanisation. Automation has made it possible to reconcile mass production and something very close to product uniqueness. At the present time, there are in practical terms no longer any constraints preventing a wide diversity of models of cars within a series. The amount of investment necessary to set up automated assembly is extremely large, and it is generally thought that an assembly line has to reach an annual production of 200,000 vehicles to be profitable.

In addition to the problems associated with production, the manufacturer needs to feel confident that later stages will be reliable: delivery, the ability of suppliers to operate at the appropriate rate (850–1,000 cars per day on average) and to keep their stocks to a minimum. When delivery systems are working well, it can be said that there exists a moderately advanced form of integration between equipment producers and manufacturers. As far as marketing is concerned, the very existence of an exclusive marketing system has its quid pro quo: obligations for guarantees and for stocks of spare parts.

In conclusion, the problems facing the automobile sector can be summarised as follows: how to predict market tendencies 3–4 years in advance; how to manage a gruelling design/development/production process; and how to put into practice a commercial policy of direct access to the final market which generates long-term relationships. The problem of managing the industrial and commercial operations over a period of time is fundamental to the industry: to illustrate the point, it is a matter of anything between twenty-five and thirty years from when the first line is made on the drawing-board to the moment the car is driven out of the showroom, and the various companies in the sector have to manage resources throughout that time.

Now that we can see the main areas of difficulty, we can move on to the development of the automobile sector over the last twenty years.

New directions 1975–1985

The early 1970s coincided with a period marked by great convulsions which arose out of various tensions caused by rises in the costs of raw materials and energy products. There was also a breaking away from certain established patterns of behaviour, and this profoundly destabilised the automobile industry.

The sector underwent an upheaval because the motor car was becoming a product of mass consumption at a rate which was severely stretching the market and at a time when disposable household income was shrinking. Socio-cultural influences were also having their effect on the nature of demand. There began to be an increasing awareness of the fact that Western economies suffered from energy dependence, and, at the same time, it could be seen that customers were beginning to have sharply individualised aspirations.

At the very time demand was changing its rhythm and its very nature, the modes of production were beginning to reveal their intrinsic weaknesses. The Taylorian model was finding its limitations with the first signs of a rejection of the old order of man management associated with this mode of production (compartmentalising of tasks, lack of autonomy), and this rejection of the system was sharpened by increasing absenteeism at the workplace and by falls in productivity. Another reason for the discovery of Taylorian shortcomings was the tendency for the market to diversify: the organisation of production under that system was not adapted to an increase in the range of models; nor did it enable the industry's supply side to diversify.

In the late 1970s and especially in the early 1980s, the motor car industry carried out a unique process of adaptation. It consisted of the following steps in chronological order:

1. Placing commercial activity in the very centre of those national markets, well controlled in terms of distribution networks, demand – and, above all, profit.
2. A shift in the design and development of new models: generalist manufacturers sought to extend their ranges, began to operate on a more generalist footing using the 'base platform' approach, and attempted to integrate automation into all stages, including design.
3. A change in modes of production: manufacturers looked for ways to automate welding, casting, painting and final assembly, and began to acquire technical and social skills necessary for a major reduction in the workforce and in the size of production units.
4. Manufacturers tried to establish new relationships with their suppliers, both first tier producers and subcontractors: they entrusted these suppliers with more of the design and development processes of their products and promised them longer orders, but demanded in

return higher performance in terms of improved quality, reduced supply delays and cost.

A new problem, domination by competition: 1985–1990

During the period 1985–90, the process of adapting industrial structures continued: the pursuit of investment, an increase in research, a speeding up of the importance of electronics and the development of partnership relations with other companies. What was at stake with this adaptation policy was the need to get established in a sector which had become strikingly more competitive, for the following reasons:

- Competition between manufacturers intensified because the costs of research, design, development and production had to be met from increased volume of sales; the manufacturers adopted very aggressive marketing policies in external markets while temporarily maintaining the profit levels in their home markets.
- It followed that systems of marketing had to be modified because of the need to cover markets more efficiently (an increase in the number of sales outlets, reorganisation of import subsidiaries, development of new marketing services); at the same time, the manufacturers wished to take precautions against the entry into the sector of new firms specialising in distribution.
- Commercial advantage now began to favour suppliers, with component producers achieving a very high degree of technical and commercial autonomy; it followed that commercial relationships were acquiring a much better balance. This situation seems likely to be a lasting one in view of technical and technological developments in vehicle manufacture, although specialist firms (notably in electronics) are now making major interventions as suppliers. Manufacturers are thus confronted by firms doing business worldwide. They have to negotiate with them over improvements in productivity and they have to learn to live in their industrial culture.

To sum up, the setting up of the Single Market is taking place at a time of a major restructuring of the automobile sector. At first sight, this means that the Single Market is amplifying certain problems and making the search for solutions more urgent, although basically the nature of the constraints does not seem to have been overturned. On the other hand, the Single Market might bring about a modification of the solutions used in the control of these industrial and commercial restraints.

The information set out in the foregoing Tables aims to clarify the basic data underlying the technological, industrial, commercial and financial strategies of companies in the automobile sector. It is important to bear in mind the diversity and complexity of the range of firms linked to the manufacturers and the colossal amount of production and commercial activity throughout the sector. Modifications to statutory obligations, particularly with regard to competition, will ask serious questions about the ability of the whole sector to function effectively. In this context, reactions to 1993 can be seen to be highly complex but also enormously interesting, since the Single Market is being set up at exactly the same time as new strategic directions are being developed in Europe.

The setting up of the Single Market

The setting up of the Single Market is founded on the adoption of directives relating to all areas of economic, industrial and tertiary activity. In a great number of sectors, the negotiations are dealing with problems of a technical nature, and it is a question of defining common standards. These undoubtedly form very important stakes for industrialists from the various countries and are therefore also the concern of the member states themselves, but fundamentally the nature of the debates is technical. This is not so in the case of the automobile sector: the debate here is less technical (there are only three minor directives still to be adopted) than political. How strong is the wish to move into markets outside Europe? Which industrial risks can be taken?

Firstly, we will try to focus on the effects which the Single Market is expected to have on the automobile sector, and we will then develop the key issues of harmonisation; finally, we will try to formulate perspectives for the sector within the framework of the Single Market.

The line of argument applicable to the automobile sector

The White Paper and the Cecchini Report have set down the gains to be expected from the removal of barriers hindering the circulation of products and the provision of services within the European Community. In this section, we will try to apply the line of argument adopted by the Cecchini Report in respect of the automobile industry.

The general framework: the barriers to be removed

The work of the Cecchini Report has led to the identification of three kinds of barrier (fiscal, physical and technical) which are found throughout the automobile industry:

1. *Fiscal barriers* The fiscal barriers are VAT, fiscal problems specific to particular countries and the fiscal implications of certain laws:

● VAT rates vary considerably from one country to the next (see Table 2.11). Bringing these rates closer together by lowering the very highest rates will lead to a reduction of the disparities without getting rid of them completely.

● Member countries have introduced their own fiscal measures: Denmark and Greece, for instance, impose a tax on the purchase of vehicles. All EC countries have taxes covering fuel and car ownership, laws dealing with vehicle registration and, in some cases, taxes relating to car insurance.

● Disparities arising out of certain laws (e.g. taxes on company profits, income tax, ways of amortising investment in vehicles) can result in an additional cost being passed on to the consumer because they distort the competition.

2. *Physical barriers* The physical barriers impeding the circulation of new vehicles are customs controls, import limits and the authorised acceptance of specified vehicles into the country in question:

● Customs controls hold up the movement of new vehicles in so far as the function of getting through customs takes time and ties up resources. It is a factor in increasing cost.

● Import restrictions (the quota system) limit supply and may even encourage distributors to raise their prices.

● The authorised acceptance of specified vehicles into a given national market is based on conformity with the regulations in force at the time. As these regulations can vary somewhat between different countries, non-European manufacturers are constrained from importing certain models into certain countries. Potentially, this practice can reduce competition and limit consumer choice.

Table 2.11   The range of rates of VAT in the EC

Country	Rate %	Comments
Belgium	25	33% for larger than 3 lt
Denmark	22	+ 105% purchase tax
Spain	33	
France	28	
Greece	6	
Ireland	23	
Italy	18	38% for larger than 2 lt (2.5 lt diesel)
Luxembourg	12	
Netherlands	19	
Portugal	16	
Germany	14	
UK[1]	15	+ car tax 10%

Note: [1]Changed to 17.5% in 1991 Budget

3. *Technical barriers* The technical barriers take the form of homologation regulations referred to above. As far as producers are concerned, these national specifications stand in the way of potential economies of scale at the different stages of the design, production and marketing of features as well as the design, assembly and marketing of the finished vehicles.

To conclude, the line of argumentation proposed in the Cecchini Report can be applied a priori in the automobile sector. Some of the barriers can be lifted in such a way as to increase the level of competition and encourage companies to perform better and give better value to consumers. The impact of the lifting of these barriers in the market is what now needs to be studied.

The likely impact of lifting the barriers

The likely consequences for the consumer of lifting the barriers come under four headings: a reduction in the price of vehicles; a reduction in the costs of running a car; an increase in the range of vehicles on the market; and a worldwide improvement in value for money and supplementary services; as follows:

1. A reduction in the price of vehicles in absolute terms may first proceed from a substantial and abrupt decrease in fiscal influences on consumption (VAT). There may also be a reduction in relative prices as a result of some lightening of fiscal charges sustained by companies.

    There could also be a major reduction in vehicle prices due to a modification of the manufacturers' own pricing policies, itself a consequence of intensified competition. There is considerable disparity in prices for certain models exclusive of tax in different EC countries (see Table 2.12): in the main, this is caused by the manufacturers' pricing policies and, to a lesser extent, by distributors' remittance practices.

    Finally, a reduction in production costs might flow from greater efficiency at the production stage and from more intensive use of economies of scale (see pp. 60–2); equipment producers and vehicle manufacturers will both be affected, and the latter will be able to acquire supplies more cheaply. Competitive pressure will encourage manufacturers to pass on the lower unit costs to the networks of distributors, possibly by conceding certain advantages to them (e.g. stock financing); these advantages will come to light in the negotiations between distributor and customer.

2. There is likely to be reduction in the costs of running a car and of car ownership. The nature, basis and rates of particular taxes vary

Table 2.12   Disparities in prices of cars in the EC

Country	Average prices[1] (cheapest country = 100)	
	1987	1988
Denmark	100	100
Greece	–	107
Belgium	121	123
Luxembourg	122	127
Netherlands	122	130
France	128	132
Germany	128	137
Portugal	127	140
Ireland	130	145
Italy	129	148
Spain	142	149
UK	144	161

Note: [1]before tax

substantially within EC countries: taxes relating to ownership (e.g. registration documents, insurance tax and road tax) can be harmonised downwards, while there is likely to be pressure to lower other taxes connected with car purchase and ownership (e.g. purchase price and insurance) as a result of intensified competition in the affected sectors. However, any diminution in the costs of running a car will become significant if there were to be a reduction in the taxes levied on fuel. Any overall lowering of the costs of owning and running a car could have a favourable impact on the market: examples of this are an increase in the number of people considering buying a car, more access to mid-range and top-of-the-range vehicles, and more interest in renewing one's present car.

3. An increase in supply linked to the disappearance of import restrictions and procedures is likely to stimulate the market by means of both sharpened competition and 'supply effects': it has been noted in the past that periods of dynamism on the market have been explained by the models on sale being more attractive.

4. A worldwide improvement in value for money should affect both the vehicles themselves and supplementary services such as guarantees, financing and after-sales service. This improvement will be a consequence of intensified competition amongst equipment producers and car manufacturers and in the areas of distribution and after-sales service; distribution networks will in all probability play a major role in this process. The arrival on the vehicle distribution and

after-sales service markets of firms operating throughout the continent should force manufacturers to intensify their efforts to produce goods of high quality and should also introduce a more standardised after-sales service.

Altogether, the consumer is likely to get more satisfaction and the market is likely to enlarge, other things being equal. It has been implicitly understood in the above arguments that vehicle consumption will continue to expand at a favourable rate.

The likely impact on company practice

The likely impact on company practice and strategies will take two forms: 'normal' reactions of adaptation (e.g. re-organisation faced with a reduction in costs) and 'anticipative' reactions.

The lifting of barriers is likely to have the effect of turning company strategies and practice on their head. Firms will react in order to seek three objectives: high standards of quality and efficiency, the right size of operation and appropriate marketing networks.

Quality and efficiency standards at both design and production levels (i.e. equipment and finished vehicles) have risen markedly in recent years under pressure from Japanese manufacturers. Achieving these standards involves cutting the delay between the earliest design stage and the beginning of the marketing stage by the use of 'modular' systems: the vehicle is conceived as a sum of modules which is overseen by sections (belonging to the manufacturer or to the equipment producer) which are both independent of and interdependent on one another. It is not possible to entertain this approach without calling into question the previous work systems which were based on the primacy of certain areas of work over others. Furthermore, production problems will have to be increasingly tackled at an earlier stage of vehicle development. These new methods are acquiring widespread currency throughout European industry; the opening up of the market is making them indispensable and is forcing companies to introduce them urgently.

Theoretically, the achievement of the right size of operation enables component producers and vehicle manufacturers to benefit from economies of scale at all stages of production. The problem of finding the 'critical size' varies considerably from one sector to the next: the 'optimum size' is claimed to exist on the basis of technical production data (e.g. what sort of production it is, whether the financial rate of return is rising or falling). In practice, the 'critical size' argued by industrialists is not linked to any technical characteristics of the function of production: it is determined by data relating to competition. Industrialists explain it thus: in this sector, the top x companies dominating the market devote y

per cent of annual turnover to research and development and z per cent to investment in order to stay in the market; it is essential to continue with research and development and investment, by spreading the costs over an entire production process which represents at least w per cent of the market.

The logical consequence of this reasoning is that companies have to agree amongst themselves in order to achieve the critical size of operation. Such a policy takes a number of different forms: alignment with partners who are not competitors and who supply the financial resources to make the R & D available – in return they benefit themselves from the R & D or from other know-how; a reduction in the range of R & D activity by closing branches and by specialising in small, narrow fields; and working together with a competitor. The latter option itself takes a number of forms, including an agreement on technical co-operation, a common subsidiary, amalgamation and absorption. The opening up of the European market is tending to make the 'critical size' larger since the motor car market already has a European dimension, if not a global one, as far as certain components are concerned, and competition will unquestionably intensify the demands of R & D and investment.

The adaptation of the marketing structure will facilitate the entry of a much larger clientele. For manufacturers, that involves a significant strengthening of their sales networks abroad, with many more sales outlets and the provision of increased assistance (e.g. spare parts and financial services); for the equipment producers, it means becoming one of the suppliers of the new European and non-European manufacturers. At all events, the conditions are both technical (quality, reliability, the cost of products) and commercial (an adapted market strategy, in many cases the setting up of a marketing subsidiary and possibly a production centre as well). Obviously, these demands tend to enlarge the 'critical size', but they also make it virtually essential to have a policy of co-operation with other firms if only to avoid takeovers.

This rational approach to the practice of firms demonstrates that the 'objective' area of company activity is scarcely modified by the creation of the Single Market, except for an increase in demands on these developments and a reduction in manufacturing delays. It is clear that constraints such as the need to introduce new products, quality control and automation have already been noted by companies in the sector. Equally, differences in technical specifications are limited and are efficiently handled by firms involving themselves in diversification of ranges. Meanwhile, the big companies retain control of the market and are already establishing marketing and production outlets in external markets.

Throughout this analysis of company reactions, it must be borne in mind that the industry is an oligopoly and this leads industrialists to 'over-react': they anticipate an increase in competition and 'anticipate the anticipations' of their competitors and partners. A firm's reactions can accurately be explained by its perception of the sector and expected developments, but also by its interpretation of operations carried out (or supposedly carried out) by other companies within the sector. An analysis of the implications of the Single Market for company strategies could really be based on theories of chance.

In effect, access to the final market (i.e. the motor car market) is such that it basically consists of a game between a limited number of actors; the same goes for the intermediary markets (component producers and suppliers of other products). Access to these markets is conditioned by an understanding, an anticipation and an acceptance of manufacturers' strategies. The most important analytical tools are to be found in the area of inter-company relations, hence the importance of reactive strategy.

In conclusion, the 'objective' structure of the automobile industry has not been fundamentally modified by the setting up of the Single Market, in so far as the industry is in the midst of restructuring and reorganising itself in response to both the market's restraints and those technological restraints which have nothing to do with the Single Market. However, the Market is decidedly changing the way in which these constraints are being perceived. There is a kind of 'over-reaction' of companies 'anticipating the anticipations' of competitors and partners.

The new environment: a debate centring on sensitive issues

The automobile industry is one of the most delicate areas in the programme of European harmonisation. It is largely a political matter, and since this chapter cannot deal with the problem under that heading: we will limit ourselves to a presentation of the relevant 'sensitive issues'.

The opening up of the European market

The main problem facing the automobile sector is the opening up of the European market to other countries. It means departing from a system of import quotas on Japanese vehicles entering certain home markets. It will be helpful to recall the origin of these quotas, which concern three main countries (France, Italy and Spain) and certain other countries at a much less important level.

In France, the quota was placed on Japanese manufacturers (or, to be more precise, on the importers) in the course of negotiations that took place in 1976, partly at the insistence of French manufacturers. It was set at 3 per cent of annual registrations and only affects private cars (small utility vehicles and 4-wheel-drive vehicles are excluded). The procedure followed is as follows: at the beginning of each year, Japanese importers fix the number of vehicles to be imported by reference to forecasts of the number of registrations on the French market; then, each importer is allotted a portion of the overall quota. However, in recent years, registrations of Japanese cars has not reached 3 per cent, as market forecasts have been systematically overtaken. This system also allows the large Japanese manufacturers who are present on the French market to make it difficult for their compatriots to enter, since they divide the quotas amongst themselves very strictly.

The establishment in Italy of a bilateral quota of 5,000 vehicles a year was negotiated in the 1950s at the insistence of the Japanese government. A study carried out by MITI had shown that the Italian motor car industry had the greatest capability in Europe of competing with the Japanese industry at the very time that vehicle manufacture was beginning to play a critical role in Japan's industrial development. It was a device for protecting the Japanese market in order to allow Japanese manufacturers to develop while being sheltered from competition. The 3 per cent quota exists to this day in the same form, although it has been distorted by registrations of 4-wheel-drive and utility vehicles and by the importing of 'second-hand' cars from other European countries.

The introduction of a quota system in Spain originally set very high import charges, although these have been slowly removed in consequence of Spain's entry into the European Community. Japanese vehicles registrations account for no more than 0.9 per cent of the total market. The market is undoubtedly protected because of the existence of a national manufacturer, but it is difficult to believe there was no pressure from the French, the main manufacturers in the country.

As far as other countries are concerned, the United Kingdom has a voluntary agreement according to which Japanese manufacturers undertake to market prudently, which has remained below 11 per cent of the market; in West Germany, there is no formal limit but the Japanese manufacturers' share of the market has stabilised at 15 per cent, a surprising state of affairs in view of the phenomenal penetration of the market between 1979 and 1985.

The arguments in favour of keeping the quotas are as follows: on the one hand, Japanese manufacturers benefit from a protection of their home market which enables them to carry out an aggressive price war overseas, and they benefit from a more favourable economic environment (e.g. social climate, tax and sub-contracting); on the other hand, generalist European manufacturers have had to put up with a general slowing down of the market and have also had to deal with important technical developments. These European manufacturers are, further-more, in the middle of a major reorganisation of their industry and it suits them not to be disturbed by a price war.

Another argument surrounds the 'Europeanness' of vehicles produced by Japanese firms in Europe. The debate has focused on the 'local content' to be achieved: some believe it ought to be 70 per cent, some believe 80 per cent, but in fact there are many ways of calculating it (see Table 2.13). Over a longer period of time, a rate of 70 per cent seems easy to achieve, whereas a rate of 80 per cent implies a higher level of

Table 2.13   The local content of a car and a breakdown of the costs of a mid-range model

The calculation of the local content of a vehicle is based on the relationship of the value of the components that have been purchased, the operations carried out locally and the vehicle's overall value. The 'numerator' and the 'denominator' of this relationship can be varied.

1. *The numerator*   the value of the components purchased or the operations carried out later can be valued in different ways according to the 'price' of local labour; also, the components themselves can be valued within the context of the factory where they are being worked upon.
2. *The denominator*   there are three ways of looking at the value of a vehicle:
    *   production costs;
    *   the selling price to the dealer;
    *   the selling price exclusive of tax.

The principle used in discussions on local content in Europe was a reference to the selling price to the dealer (i.e. approximately 55–65 per cent of the selling price exclusive of tax). A local content of 50 per cent is thus easily achieved if only through engine fitting, assembly and painting, to which need to be added the costs associated with marketing and preparation for sale.

Breakdown of the selling price to the dealer:

	%		%
Raw materials	7.5	supplies	7.5
Exterior equipment	3.4		
Electrical equipment	7.7		
Interior equipment	9.8	total equipment	47.7
Chassis equipment	13.0		
Engine and transmission	13.8		
Body assembly	7.9		
Painting and assembly	6.8	total manufacture	19.5
Tooling for fitting	4.8		
Studies/projects/prototypes	3.6	design	3.6
Miscellaneous (marketing logistics)	10.1		
Manufacturers' profit	9.3	marketing (incl. profit)	21.7
Guarantee	2.3		
Total	100.0		100.0

investment whose profit return would be very difficult to achieve in production centres turning out fewer than 100,000 units a year.

In any case it would be extremely difficult to account for all these vehicles in any specific way in commercial operations outside the EC. It is understood that the solution reached in June 1990 does not propose the inclusion of vehicles built in Europe in the quota but the reduction of the quota on the proportion of new Japanese cars. This appears to be the only technically applicable solution. Problems surrounding the import control system (or 'autolimitation') also seem to have been resolved: a period of five years has been agreed starting in 1993, and all that remains is agreement on ways of getting rid of national quotas and the overall quota covering the entire European market. Predictions in this area are difficult, but it is hard to see anything other than a gradual opening of protected markets up to a threshold of 10–15 per cent.

Technical and fiscal harmonisation

The second matter that negotiations need to make progress on is technical and fiscal harmonisation. The problem consists of a number of separate issues.

Technical harmonisation of new vehicles is not a problem in itself; in fact, there are really no technical problems at all. The adoption of the most recent directive concerning vehicle characteristics will be the same *ipso facto* as the setting up of an EC acceptance system: any vehicle authorised to be registered in any one EC country will automatically be entitled to registration in any other country in the Community. This system outlaws all import controls and, for example, gives the right to a Japanese manufacturer who is 'not recognised' in France to invoke European law with a very strong chance of succeeding. EC acceptance is therefore closely connected to the problems of quotas.

Technical control of vehicles once they are on the road, however, poses a double problem. Currently, each country has its own system of checking vehicles, and early plans to harmonise these appear to have been abandoned. National variations create problems of inequality for European consumers and safety problems for the vehicles themselves. There is also the problem of the buying and selling of second-hand cars. Countries where control is least strict run the risk of being a dustbin for vehicles which do not have the authorisation to be driven in other countries. This will have an impact on the second-hand market, influencing the practice of distributors picking up vehicles when a new one is bought, and ultimately leading to a distortion of the way the European markets function.

Harmonisation of VAT is also an important ingredient in the unification of the European market. It is inconceivable that a given vehicle should have two different prices a few miles either side of a frontier: distribution networks (and therefore after-sales services) in areas close to borders would not be able to survive, and operators would probably derive commercial advantage from differences in VAT. The problem is to define the difference in acceptable rates: given normal pricing practices, a margin of 3 per cent over the final selling price might be the maximum acceptable.

Although it might be thought that 'specific' VAT rates are on the way out, there is still substantial disparity in the taxing of fuel and of car ownership. These variations are irritating from the point of view of consumers wishing to be treated equally, but they do not look as if they will create distortions of competition or upset the motor car market. So, bearing in mind how important these taxes are for the financing of national budgets, it is extremely unlikely that any attempts will be made to seek harmonisation in the short or medium term.

Tax harmonisation is, however, taking place in the second-hand car business. At the moment, there are two major principles covering VAT: either the basis of the taxation corresponds to the total value of the transaction or the taxation is based on the profit margin fixed officially at the time of the transaction. Harmonisation is being imposed to head off the possibility of disparities arising inside commercial competition: such disparities will become less and less acceptable because second-hand trade will experience considerable growth amongst distributors as profit margins on new cars drop.

All in all, technical and fiscal harmonisation should be resolved in tandem with other negotiations on such issues as import controls and VAT. Likely changes will be limited, but they will be by no means negligible.

Exclusive dealing

The problems associated with exclusive dealing derive from both negotiations and interpretations dealing with various European texts. The problems are slightly different for the sale of vehicles and for the sale of spare parts.

The sale of motor cars is the exception to the Community principles of the free circulation of goods and freedom to sell. Clauses dealing with exclusive rights of sale have been included because of the complexity of activities connected with vehicle servicing.

European Community texts relating to the concession contracts controlling car distribution were adopted in 1985 and are known as Rule 123/85. This Rule is still the subject of widely diverging interpretations concerning the exclusive territorial rights accorded to an agent by a concessionaire who in turn may have been mandated by the manufacturer; certain clauses can even bind the manufacturer and even an agent if the concessionaire disappears.

The issue most fiercely debated, however, is the 'parallel importation' problem. In practice, Rule 123/85 gives 'exclusive' rights to sales networks, but it also gives the consumer the chance to go and buy a vehicle in the country of his or her choice: a consumer can also 'mandate' an intermediary to acquire a vehicle in another country and have it registered in the consumer's country of residence.

This is the legal basis for 'mandatory' and 'parallel' importation networks: 'mandatory' business is carried on by a number of smallish firms (40,000 vehicles in France) and is based on differences between prices exclusive of tax. It is worth noting that, at the time when negotiations were taking place over Rule 123/85, the margin between prices charged in different EC countries was limited to 12 per cent. Parallel importation relies on significantly bigger margins.

The PSA company attempted to limit goods reaching a 'mandatory' firm called Ecosysteme by forbidding its concessionaires in Belgium and Luxembourg to supplying it: the European Commission became involved and issued a statement ordering PSA to withdraw its interdiction and limiting the number of vehicles re-imported into France to 1,211 units. This was described as a 'conservatory' decision and was issued without prejudice to a further decision which is pending.

The legal and economic aspects of the sale of spare parts is slightly different from that relating to the sale of finished vehicles. Manufacturers market 'original' spare parts on the basis that they bear the maker's brand 'label', but also assume responsibility for the parts even if they have been made by an equipment producer or a subcontractor. Original parts are sold by the concessionaire's intermediary to agents and independent motor mechanics, with a tiny proportion going to private individuals; however, parts can also be got hold of – and more cheaply – through wholesalers who sell spare parts that have been made by component producers and marketed under their name.

Body parts avoid this double marketing in so far as they are made by the manufacturer and are protected by a law relating to intellectual and artistic property. There are nevertheless 'parallel imports' of body parts and of other parts whose origin is unclear: they are known as 'adaptable' parts.

Manufacturers and their trade associations try to hang on to their exclusive right to sell 'original' parts, mainly by refusing to sell to wholesalers and by 'advising' their equipment producers against reaching agreements with them. This practice is based on Rule 123/85.

There has, however, been an initial breakthrough as a result of an agreement between Ford (UK) and the European Commission: Ford (UK) will only exercise its rights to intellectual and artistic property of body parts for a period of five years after the launch of a new model; thereafter, the manufacturer will renounce his rights or will grant licences 'on reasonable conditions'.

To sum up, the statutory and economic fields are still prey to several uncertainties which will only be removed slowly and through negotiations. It cannot be emphasised too strongly that, in an industry so markedly characterised by enormous investment and by resources being tied up for many years, the time factor is of paramount importance. Manufacturers would like to have the maximum amount of time to prepare themselves for certain changes (for example, the changes in anti-pollution laws did not allow industrialists enough time to adapt), but they also want their competitors to have the minimum amount of time (for example, as a result of negotiations on the opening of the European market being protracted, Japanese manufacturers were obliged to give simultaneous consideration to several lines of access). The most important changes unquestionably concern two areas: the ways of opening up the market to Japanese manufacturers and the development of the conditions in which distribution networks will function.

Foreseeable effects

We have attempted so far to draw a picture of the new European order. We now need to try to anticipate the changes which could occur in supply and demand and within the context of supply and demand as adapted to the needs of the automobile industry. The ideas that follow constitute no more than the basis for a more detailed examination to be undertaken in the future.

Analysis of the possible impact of measures taken to deal with demand

Demand is likely to have been deeply affected by the changes discussed above. It is not possible here to construct a model of the development of demand, but we can set out the fundamental issues to be taken into account: income elasticity, price elasticity and supply effects.

The elasticity of income calculated over a long term for the automobile industry is clearly more than 1, and is even quite close to 2 – econometric studies demonstrate that the short-run elasticity could reach 8. This encourages speculation that, in a favourable economic climate in Europe, the automobile industry is well on course not only in the short term but over a considerably longer period of time. It is likely to be sustained by demand emanating from parts of the world experiencing a boom and where the demand elasticity is probably very strong.

It is important to point out that the calculation of elasticities – and more generally the lengthening of tendencies observed in the past – is an inefficient system of forecasting: statistical work on rates of replacing equipment and of renewing parts and engines at a European level is inadequate precisely because the basic data are in short supply.

Price elasticities measure how consumption of a product varies after its relative price has been changed. An elasticity of -1 indicates that an increase of 1 per cent in the relative price of the motor cars will turn into a consumption reduction of 1 per cent. In a climate characterised by a tendency for relative prices to drop following intensification of competition, demand can be expected to rise.

Statistical work in this area is difficult to use. Experience shows that some influences related to sales have a time lag, which falsifies measurements of this type: for example, at the time when VAT on car sales was being reduced in France, there were enormous variations in the numbers of registrations from one month to the next – consumers changed their minds (frequently on the advice of dealers) about when to buy in order to take advantage of the lower VAT rate. There is no evidence to suggest that vehicle sales went up as a result of reductions in price.

However, it is possible to visualise a phenomenon which is globally favourable to the motor car market and particularly to the producers of equipment and accessories. In general, in order to buy a car, households have a budget which is connected to a means of financing the purchase (credit): if the price drops below what was expected, this will generally mean that a car with better fittings and accessories will be bought.

Although it is very clear that this is how consumers behave in respect of motor cars, there is very little comparable information relating to other items of household consumption.

Supply effects have a tendency to operate in favour of an increase in demand. Improved quantity and quality of supply can stimulate a movement to replace old vehicles with new ones; they can also partly bring into question those sales cycles which have allegedly characterised replacement phenomena appropriate to a more constant climate. Clearly, there is nothing quantified about this phenomenon.

To conclude, it is reasonable to expect demand to increase, although this will have to fit in with a slow change in the structure of household budgets in favour of goods and services connected with leisure and health. The share of household expenditure occupied by the motor car is unlikely to increase by much. In this context, it is important to bear in mind that countries with a large potential growth in the market will be introducing roadworthiness checks, and the knock-on effect of this on the 'maintenance and use of car' segment of the household budget will be considerable. Where car budgets do not change, the sums of money likely to be affected by the purchase of new vehicles will be even more limited.

The total number of registrations in the seventeen European countries will probably level out at something over 13 million vehicles in 1990, an increase of 0.5 per cent over 1989. These are levels which analysts consider to be characteristic of the top of a cycle; a more 'normal' European market would be based on approximately 12 million vehicles rising by 1–2 per cent a year to a level of 13 million in 1993 and 14.5 million in 1998, the likely date of the complete opening up of the market.

An evaluation of potential supply in Europe

Potential supply in Europe during the period 1990–2000 can be calculated according to investment plans announced by European manufacturers and announcements by non-European manufacturers that they will be opening plants.

All the major manufacturers, whether generalist or specialist, are involved in projects to modernise and extend their production capacity. They are also introducing new systems of work organisation which will enable them to make better use of the production capacity. The plans that have been announced and the companies' investment data suggest that European manufacturers (including those in Eastern Europe) will be producing about 14 million private cars in 1995 and 14.5 million in 1998 (see Table 2.14).

According to the information currently available, plans by non-European manufacturers to open new plants only relate to Japanese firms. It is estimated that these plants will altogether produce approximately 500,000 units in 1995 and a million in 1998. The numbers of vehicles produced in Eastern Europe have not been taken into account.

We have divided the origins of imports into the European market into four categories: Japan, North America, Eastern Europe and the rest of the world. Imports from Japan are currently estimated at 1 million units and, in the long term, this is likely to increase as the European market is completely opened up, although not until after 1998. In the meantime, import controls will favour models at the top of the range. In practice, those Japanese manufacturers who are currently established in the European market benefit from importing medium-range and top-of-the-range vehicles since the constraint takes the form of a maximum number of vehicles; in a market characterised by quotas, they have the opportunity to set up distribution networks which suit the sales of such vehicles. The large Japanese manufacturers will now cease to oppose the entry into the European market of 'small manufacturers': these firms will be restricted to building vehicles at the bottom of the range, and will be hamstrung by low profitability; they may even be absorbed by the large manufacturers.

Imports from North America could reach 500,000 vehicles a year

Table 2.14   Potential supply in the European market

	('000 cars)		
	1990	1995	1998
European manufacturers			
Generalists	11,500	12,500	13,000
Specialists	1,500	1,500	1,500
US	25	35	60
Japanese			
Imports from Japan	1,000	800	800
Local production	250	500	1,000
Imports from elsewhere	–	30	500
Other imports			
Developing countries	15	25	60
Other Eastern countries	25	150	500
Total potential supply in Europe	14,315	15,540	17,420

during 1995–98, but this takes into account the extensions carried out to the productive capacity of Japanese manufacturers in the United States and Canada: they appear to have resulted in overcapacity and some of this extra production could be aimed at the markets of Western Europe. Exports to Europe by American manufacturers should stabilise at about 100,000 units; only Chrysler will attempt to increase its share.

Countries in Eastern Europe will probably be exporting something in the order of 500,000 private cars in 1998. Plans currently being announced take current production of 1.7 million private cars (the USSR included) to more than 3 million in 1995: internal markets will not be able to absorb this number of vehicles easily and from now on the target market for them will be Western Europe.

Surplus imports will come from developing countries. Many of them (e.g. Korea, India and Malaysia) would like to make the motor car industry one of the pillars of their industrial programme but, in view of the size of accessible markets in these countries and the production constraints on assembly work, part of their production will be sent to the markets of developed countries. Given the standards of reliability that obtain in these markets, it is likely that the position of these manufacturers will remain marginal. At all events, imports will not rise above 100,000 a year.

In conclusion, the potentially available supply on the European market will probably comprise some 17–18 million vehicles in 1998.

Scenarios of supply-and-demand adaptation

On the subject of the production and marketing of vehicles, the adaptation between a potential supply of 17–18 million vehicles and a demand of 14–15 million can take the form of increased exports or an adjustment to production (i.e. underutilisation or decreased use of capacity). The determining factors of supply and demand are difficult to follow in the case of producers of components and accessories.

European exports will not be able to find substantial outlets in developing countries: demand is out of kilter with European production. The only target markets can be marginal ones involving considerable expenditure, and the majority of these are in developed countries: North America and Japan – countries where there is potential overcapacity, where competition is fierce, and where not a single European manufacturer has achieved commercial penetration of any significance.

The most likely scenario is an adjustment of capacity; in fact, manufacturers have already reduced their break-even point considerably and it is thought that generalist European manufacturers now cease to make profits after producing an equivalent of 1.2 million vehicles. This suggests that there could well be underutilisation of capacity, but it is important to analyse things dynamically – the break-even point is a theoretical threshold.

If we bear in mind that manufacturing costs are no more than 55–60 per cent of the total cost, the risks of commercial war are that it is very difficult to retain control of marketing and that costs could rise very steeply; it is also an area where productivity gains are very limited. A climate in which capacity is being underutilised is generally speaking well suited to a price war, which in turn leads to the disappearance of the weakest participants. However, in those sectors which are strong oligopolies and where distribution is effectively controlled, there can often be a rise in prices accompanied by some cartelisation of the market – air transport is an instance of this. At all events, the problems of distribution have not disappeared.

The equipment and accessories market – and, more generally, the manufacturers' component supply market – is strongly influenced by the overall situation in the automobile market. Even in the unlikely event of the international component equipment and accessories business becoming considerably stronger, the producers would lose out badly if vehicle manufacture in Europe were cut.

On the other hand, the strengthened presence of Japanese manufacturers in Europe presents them with an opportunity. The Japanese have much to gain from equipment and accessories producers responding to their expectations. Indeed, although it may be true that assembly techniques in different parts of the world are very similar, vehicle characteristics have remained different. Japanese manufacturers have reserved for themselves the know-how and market knowledge of the equipment producers, who in turn (unlike their American counterparts) have brought their methods and factories up to date over the last few years; they seem to be in a favourable position.

It is on the European market that the future of the world's main manufacturers will be fought out. The opening of the European market makes it even more attractive, and competition will increase significantly.

An analysis of the new European market shows that the European motor car industry will undergo a severe test in the coming years. It will have to face up to a degree of competition it has never known, and not one segment of the market will be spared. The setting up of the Single Market will accelerate changes which were set in motion in the late 1970s and early 1980s.

The strategies at work

Our examination of company strategies takes account of long-term developments in the automobile industry, and the setting up of the Single Market in particular. We will now try to demonstrate how firms have integrated the observations and analyses we have set out above. Firstly, two preliminary comments:

1. We have judged it necessary to present a critical analysis of strategies in the automobile sector so as to give a concrete meaning to the various policies mentioned (e.g. research and development, products, marketing and finance).
2. The elements of the strategies explained below cannot be all traced back to the setting up of the Single Market. As we have shown elsewhere, the Single Market does not change the nature of the problems that companies have to face up to.

General thoughts on company strategies in the automobile industry: drawing up an analytical framework for analysing the strategies

Companies draw up strategies on the basis of an analysis of the market and of the state of the competition in which they operate. The principles of the strategy that can be identified outside the firm and the main issues to be concentrated on (as communicated by senior managers) make it possible for outside observers to reconstruct (in part) the view of the market underpinning the strategies that have been put into practice.

The strategy fundamentally consists of a defined balance between the analysis of the business environment and ways of appropriating financial and human resources, bearing in mind the company's strong and weak points at the various stages of producing and marketing its products. We will therefore examine the following areas:

- the management of research and innovation potential;
- the management of product definition potential;
- the management of technical potential (e.g. materials and accessories);
- the management of human potential;
- the management of financial resources;
- the management of logistics potential (e.g. stocks and delivery);
- the management of relations with suppliers;
- the management of relations with other firms involved at later commercial stages (e.g. clients and distribution networks);
- marketing policies (e.g. targeting customers, publicity, image policies and pricing policies);
- policies of external communication (e.g. relationships with the news media).

Company strategy will be applied to each of the above areas, and there will be key questions particularly relating to the automobile industry. What emerges, together with ideas about the company's view of the market and of the competition, will be the foundation of the strategy that has been adopted.

Analytical framework looking at the company strategies in the automobile industry

The analytical framework that has been drawn up will look at each of the policies enumerated above.

The management of research and innovation potential

Companies possess a potential in terms of research and innovation which is based initially on research workers, then on patents and finally on project management. The fields of application to be looked at are the following:

- Industrial research (i.e. physics, chemistry and thermodynamics). There are also areas of specific importance: combustion (for the manufacturers) and the structure of plastics (for suppliers);
- Product innovation (i.e. the ability to translate technical research and market analysis into a product). Up-to-date examples include an innovation from a manufacturer (hydractive suspension) and two innovations from equipment/accessories producers (antilock brakes and air conditioning requiring low energy consumption).

● New work processes appropriate to the new modes of production. The main innovations in this arena are automated systems (for manufacturers) and stocking systems of the 'just-in-time' variety (for suppliers).

Research and development is unique as far as management methods are concerned. Companies need information from outside and they are prepared to exchange information with other organisations, but there is a limit to how far this can go (the exact nature of the work being carried out and the problem of competitors learning about innovations).

Firms in the automobile sector have made use of several formulas. One criterion concerns the type of firm involved, based on the following characteristics:

● association with a public research body;
● association with a private research body;
● participation in national or European research programmes;
● association with industrial firms outside the sector;
● association with firms inside the sector but not competitors;
● association with competitors.

Another criterion of these policies is the kind of legal arrangement chosen by the company, for example:

● a research contract;
● a research contract followed by production;
● a joint venture;
● an economic interest group.

The management of product definition potential

Industrialists in the automobile sector have enormous experience in product policy. For the vehicle manufacturers, it is a question of clarifying the way they want to focus their marketing within the various segments of the market; for the producer of equipment and accessories, the task is to propose solutions in relation to that marketing focus.

The manufacturer's marketing focus is based on a choice between placing the vehicle in one of the following categories:

● in each segment;
● in some segments or only one;
● in one segment but only marginally (e.g. sports, luxury, safety).

There is also the question of choosing the means of moving forward, for example:

● using the company's own resources;
● co-operating with another company;

- picking up a vehicle that has already been developed by another manufacturer.

This marketing focus policy is completed by a 'mix policy':

- several versions of a given model;
- few but distinctive versions;

and also, by a policy covering equipment and accessories:

- standard;
- options.

Finally, throughout the life of a model, decisions frequently need to be taken relating to updating it and restyling.

The producers of components and accessories work with the manufacturers and share their philosophy in terms of the product; they also have a growing role in the development of small, specific features (e.g. the development of narrow lights). Their policy is to attempt to develop new products for two reasons: because the manufacturers wish to put it on the market; and because they have come up with it first.

To achieve this, they adopt a number of tactics, for example:

- development by self-financing;
- development by co-operation with the manufacturer;
- co-operation with potential competitors;
- co-operation with firms that are not competitors.

The management of technical potential

The automobile industry has classic difficulties as far as the management of technical potential is concerned – the increase in investment needed is extremely fast (approximately 10 per cent of annual turnover for one manufacturer). In general terms, the nature of investment can be defined as follows:

- extension of a unit;
- introduction of a new unit;
- modernisation of a unit.

The methods used to acquire the money include the following:

- buying back of plant;
- renting/lease-back;
- from the company's own funds;
- by associating with another firm.

The most important aspect of investment policies in recent years has undoubtedly been the development trends of technical potential; there have been three main trends:

1. the policy of developing automation:
2. changes in the organisation of production (just-in-time and 'modular' production);
3. the policy of internal and external integration/disintegration (making production units autonomous and the growing importance to suppliers of sub-contracting).

The management of human potential

There have always been problems relating to the management of human potential in the automobile sector, although the industry has now moved from the problems associated with massive reductions in the workforce to a much sharper form of management.

Policies of recruitment and/or of staff reductions have currently three aims:

1. preventing cyclical over-employment;
2. ensuring proper distribution of age;
3. ensuring the passing-on of know-how.

The methods used to achieve these aims have multiplied as follows:

- use of part-time work and fixed-term contracts;
- adjustment of social contracts;
- use of outside agencies;
- agreements with competitor and non-competitor firms;
- a policy of encouraging entrepreneurship and hiving off activities into separate small companies.

In addition to the quantitative management of human resources, a policy has been developed for training personnel with a view to improving product quality.

To sum up, internal communication policies have made great strides, but initiatives connected with income and motivation policies have made slower progress.

The management of financial resources

The management of financial resources has occupied an important place in the strategies of firms in the automobile industry by virtue of the huge sums invested and because of comparisons made with Japanese industry – Japanese manufacturers and producers of equipment and accessories tend to have few debts, if any, and some of them even show substantial profits.

The first canon of financial strategy in the case of firms quoted on the Stock Exchange has been a modification of the shareholder structure, enabling large amounts of investment to be realised without significantly increasing the ratio between debt and equity.

Next, the problem of how to reduce debts was tackled. First, the amount of working capital was cut thanks to improved management of stocks throughout the industry, and then there was an increase in cash flow which generated financial resources exceeding investment needs. The underlying problem of surplus self-financing was solved by a reduction in debts by means of accounting operations which were sometimes highly innovatory (e.g. Defeasance PSA). The introduction of better balance sheet structures has been an important factor in the reduction of debt costs, and expenses have been cut back to a level out of proportion to the overall debt. Finally, a return to satisfactory cash flow levels has encouraged companies to re-examine their policies of distributing dividends.

Generally speaking, industrialists are aiming for a policy of self-financing for their current investment, and are only prepared to revert to being in debt in order to achieve external growth or to assist the company to undergo an important restructuring.

The management of logistics potential

Logistics have assumed great importance in the automobile industry as a result of the policy of stocks reduction. In several cases, certain logistical activities which have even been integrated at an earlier stage have been placed in autonomous firms (sometimes subsidiaries), and have been set up in competition with other group concerns.

The management of relations with suppliers

Manufacturers' policies of devolving work to outside firms has not resulted in an increase in the number of suppliers; on the contrary, it is estimated that the number of direct suppliers has halved in ten years.

Relations have changed enormously. Manufacturers' main suppliers now operate on the basis of 'internal quality control' (i.e. the parts are no longer checked at the manufacturer's factory gate), and component and accessories producers are attempting to replicate this practice with their own suppliers. The practice has developed as a result of overall standardisation.

Relations have also changed in respect of what the contracts say: the idea of 'partnership' needs to be more sharply defined by experience, and agreements involving small quantities are becoming rarer and rarer. Producers of components and accessories are becoming increasingly involved in commercial risks side by side with manufacturers as they now participate at an early stage of product definition and also in the development of the products themselves.

The management of relations with other firms involved at later commercial stages

Manufacturers appear to have decided against major changes to the structure of distribution networks, and the consequence has been a slight change in the number of firms concerned:

- import subsidiaries;
- local branches;
- a network of concessionaires;
- agents.

Generalist manufacturers have made great efforts to take advantage of a healthy market to re-establish the networks' profitability although, in a less buoyant market, manufacturers will have to take responsibility for a growing number of commercial operations (e.g. promotion, recovery of second-hand cars and financing); they will also have to oversee the ways in which concessionaires hold their stocks.

Manufacturers have therefore started adapting their networks back to the size they originally were. They have done this by seeing sales through to their conclusion (lists of clients, financing, guarantees, repairs).

Marketing policies

Firms in the motor car industry place their marketing policies at earlier stages of development than distribution networks. Their objective is to determine ways of entering the market and staying there. For the manufacturers, the main decisions concern activities associated with launching new models, publicity policies and supply priorities (this is essentially a choice between the home market and foreign markets). The producers of parts, components and accessories need to decide on sales policies outside the manufacturers' networks – distribution circuits and promotion policies.

Policies of external communication

Policies of external communication are separate from marketing policies in that they aim to promote the image of the company rather than the image of the products; decisions centre on the degree and form of participation in sports events that attract a strong media presence (e.g. rallies and Formula 1 races). In this context, it is important not to forget economic and financial communications between firms. Also, when senior managers in a firm take part in public debates and the firm is involved in sponsorship deals, this further boosts the company's image.

Our analytical framework has made it possible to understand the strategies of firms in the automobile industry. The strategy basically takes the form of supplying a satisfactory analysis of the market, the strengths and weaknesses of the competition and the firm's own strengths and weaknesses. To discover the definition of the strategy, it is necessary to answer these two questions:

- Which part of the market should the firm occupy?
- What should be done to achieve this?

The analytical framework makes it possible to answer the second question; with the help of certain extra information concerning the market, it becomes possible to answer much of the first question as well.

The manufacturers' strategies

This examination of the manufacturers' strategies will be in three parts: a presentation of industrialists' analysis of the market and of competition; a study of the options available in respect of market position; and a discussion about ways of carrying the strategy through.

An analysis of the environment of the automobile sector

Manufacturers generally agree on an analysis of what the main tendencies of demand will be over the next few years, as follows:

- Demand will tend to be less buoyant as a result of economic growth (the share of household expenditure devoted to the motor car is likely to decrease and the amount of money spent on cars will probably decrease in proportion to the Gross Domestic Product).
- Demand will become more segmented, with the emphasis on vehicles that are more distinctive, in response to an underlying psychological tendency in the direction of differentiation.
- Demand will become more difficult to predict: powerful fluctuations in the quantitative and qualitative characteristics of demand can be partly expected for reasons of cyclical phenomena (e.g. changes in household expenditure patterns, the cost of running a car); but also

for psychological and sociological reactions that cannot be foreseen (e.g. a rejection of modern design, a new importance for ecological issues, a lessening popularity of the motor car because of traffic congestion).

By and large, manufacturers are expecting demand to behave favourably in the short and medium term because of the favourable economic climate anticipated over the next few years. However, their view of the sector's future is marked by uncertainties concerning consumer behaviour.

Manufacturers also have reached a general agreement over how the competitive situation will develop. They will be obliged to go for an increase in their share of market volume in order to write off the ever-increasing expenses associated with research, development, production and marketing. The overall programme of design, production and distribution will have to remain flexible, and this makes it imperative to invest heavily in information technology, materials and, above all, in work systems.

As far as design and production of vehicles are concerned, the manufacturers' maximum production levels will be significantly lowered as a result of co-operation agreements and the increased use made of the producers of equipment and accessories and of other suppliers. One consequence will be intensified competition amongst distributors: there will be more discounting and trading-in of vehicles in the style of the American market, and marketing costs (publicity in particular) will increase very sharply.

The overall intensifying of competition will affect all segments of the market, with the exception of relatively marginal segments such as prestige cars. The reason is that the dynamic of the market and the constraints relating to the incorporation of new technologies into new vehicles are pushing manufacturers towards the top of the market.

It will be completely out of the question for manufacturers to pass rising prices back up the production line. They will be faced more and more with big suppliers who control very complex areas and they will refuse to see their prices reflect commercial tensions at the end of the line.

As far as demand is concerned, the likely impact of the Single Market is an increase in registrations, particularly in the countries of southern Europe and in those countries which will have to introduce periodic vehicle checks. However, despite the fact that this effect can be foreseen, it plays a very marginal role in the analysis of demand. Managers nevertheless see a substantial threat coming from environmental issues and possible problems relating to a rejection of motor cars; they are also afraid that rapid changes in public opinion will be translated into EC statutory measures (e.g. on diesel) which will have a constraining influence on them and which will be very difficult to abide by at the levels of production and marketing.

Competition will be affected by the harmonisation of European markets in the sense that the importance of 'national sanctuaries' in producer countries will be reduced and even removed more quickly than predicted. This will come about all the more quickly as we get closer to the opening of the markets currently protected from Japanese manufacturers.

The strategies

There are probably five kinds of strategy, which are not all contradictory:

1. *The volume strategy* This strategy consists of increasing market share until achieving the position of leader, while the volume effect enables research, development, design and (above all) production costs to be paid off; it also aims at controlling distribution and marketing. It involves a period of price war, but this can be won if the firm is in complete command of automated production processes.
2. *The challenger strategy* The aim here is to remain in the market with a policy of offering a product and service of outstanding quality. In this way, there is always favourable comparison with competitor products.
3. *The strategy of engaging in external markets* This strategy involves developing both production and sales in markets outside Western Europe. Its objective is to take advantage of lower production costs and privileged access to 'new markets', thereby defraying certain costs associated with research, development and plant construction.
4. *The strategy of development on the edges of the market* This strategy is all about developing on the edges of certain segments like sports cars, off-road vehicles, safety, or a car used exclusively in town. It is a strategy that is most effective as a complement to other approaches.
5. *The strategy of technological diversification* Here, the firm reorganises its activities in the direction of operations that are less competitive and therefore less demanding in terms of research and development.

Ways of applying these strategies in the context of the Single Market

The question is one of deciding exactly what companies do to succeed in establishing themselves in the appropriate market position, and there are two approaches to answering the question: a 'vertical' analysis and a 'horizontal' analysis.

First, *the vertical analysis*, based on the analytical framework used earlier, and using specified areas of application.

Activities associated with research and innovation are the result of the biggest constraints as perceived by the manufacturers: the environment and traffic congestion. Research work is shaping the future of the whole automobile industry, and manufacturers therefore view favourably the idea of co-operating amongst themselves under the aegis of national or Community agencies: examples of this are the European research programme on radio location and the French 'clean engine' study.

Work on product definition varies according to which strategies have been followed. Manufacturers wishing to establish themselves as market leaders try to impose a fairly low standard of vehicle specifications; manufacturers controlling luxury or sports cars, and even those playing the 'challenger' role, seek to make the equipment and exterior appearance of their vehicles distinctive.

Investment practice is difficult to follow, although it is noticeable that the biggest investment is carried out by manufacturers who are looking for commanding market positions. Automation is a particularly important reason for investment.

The implementation of personnel policies can also be interpreted in the light of market position. It is worth noting that a qualitative policy of staff management has been introduced more quickly by manufacturers seeking a challenger position or one on the fringes of the market than by those aiming at market leadership.

The workings of financial policy appear to be quite independent of industrial strategies. The tendencies described above (appeals of shareholders, a reduction in the need for working capital, self-financing of investment, getting out of debt) vary little from one firm to the next; the elements that explain the financial strategy are to be found in the data specific to the firm in question (e.g. the shareholders and the relationships with suppliers) and in its financial environment.

Relationships with suppliers furnish an example of how firms approach the problem differently. Manufacturers seeking to be market leaders have a more marked policy of reducing the number of suppliers and seem to exert more pressure in order to lower the price of what is supplied to them; manufacturers who do not have advantages of volume appear to develop the concept of 'partnership' further.

Distribution and marketing are performed very differently in different firms. Large-scale manufacturers have invested less qualitatively in these two areas than those who have opted for a more specific market position. Indeed, some of the latter have begun to regain control of networks (e.g. by repurchasing from importers), to choose new operators, and to give higher priority to the 'service' side of distribution.

Communication practice seems to have little to do with the strategies selected. A global image policy is, however, being evolved, while the resources being put into it are closely linked to the overall financial situation and to expediency.

Second, *the horizontal analysis*, which interprets growth activities and policies of agreement between firms.

Horizontal analysis of strategies considers the numerous co-operative ventures that have seen the light of day in recent years. The automobile industry has traditionally had many such ventures and intercompany agreements; there are four 'traditional' types, as follows:

1. *Technical agreements*, which aim to develop components and technical solutions; examples include the Peugeot–Renault–Volvo engine, the Fire engine studied by Fiat and Peugeot together but developed solely by Fiat, and the production of interchangeable components. These examples of companies working together are based on them having identical interests in a limited area of work.
2. *Distribution agreements*, whereby some manufacturers undertake the marketing of another manufacturer's model in order to enlarge their own range without incurring the development costs – the reciprocal distribution agreement between Renault and Chrysler is a good example. It is also a way of testing market reaction to a new product or brand.
3. *Financial share in a firm*, with the aim of developing it without controlling it. In 1970, American manufacturers acquired a share of the capital of Japanese manufacturers in exchange for technical co-operation; more recently, they have acquired majority shares in the manufacturers of luxury cars like Jaguar and Saab.
4. *Taking over a firm*, with a view to carrying out an industrial restructuring; examples include Citroën (by Peugeot), Alfa Romeo and Lancia (by Fiat) and the minority takeover of Rover by Honda.

The Renault–Volvo and Daimler-Benz–Mitsubishi agreements are examples of new ways in which companies can work together. They aim to research into areas of multiple co-operation, and what is new about them is that they are less concerned with projects than with a market-wide perception of a whole range of sectors outside the automobile industry:

- The two companies in the Renault–Volvo agreement have similar interests in that they have chosen complementary market positions (for one, top of the range; for the other, a generalist challenger position based on quality products and services), and have opportunities to collaborate in the area of industrial vehicles.
- In the case of Daimler-Benz–Mitsubishi, we have two firms that have chosen a multiproduct strategy and want to prioritise technological skills. Thus, these agreements make good sense because their

respective areas of technological competence complement one another and because they share the industrial leadership of the projects by virtue of technological and industrial skills and commercial opportunities.

There is no way in which the setting up of the Single Market can be linked to the increase in the number of 'traditional' operations and new-style operations; however, the competitive climate and the worldwide dimension of the markets cannot be an insignificant factor in these strategies.

The strategies of suppliers in the automobile industry

Component suppliers see the automobile industry developing in a similar way to vehicle manufacturers; they always have to include manufacturers' strategies in their own.

Analysis of the sector

There is considerable agreement amongst vehicle manufacturers about how they think demand will go. The main factor in their favour is the general tendency of manufacturers to reduce the share of components and accessories produced in their factories because of both cost and the highly skilled nature of production. In time, demand will be stimulated by the technical development of the 'car product' and by the tendency of manufacturers to entrust a growing share of design work to suppliers. This realignment of dependence between manufacturers and suppliers will probably resolve itself in favour of the latter, with costs benefiting them particularly.

The global market for spare parts will fluctuate gently between growth and decline, but certain segments may be stimulated by the introduction of periodic vehicle checks and by new forms of marketing.

The current process of selecting suppliers in the automobile industry is likely to continue. Producers of components and accessories are suffering at the moment from constraints of investment and from changes in work systems and training: the elimination of marginal competitors will have a favourable effect on commercial relationships with manufacturers.

The main producers of components and accessories to the automobile industry have identified the need to look for outlets away from their traditional area of activity. The Single Market creates a stimulating climate in which to give this strategic issue high priority. For the major producers of these items, the debate on the penetration of Japanese manufacturers into Europe has created a climate that is quite favourable to the development of commercial or technical agreements with Japanese vehicle manufacturers or producers of accessories.

The strategies of producers of components and accessories

There are four types of strategy in this sector of the industry, as follows:

1. *The strategy of the 'size' effect*   This consists of being the right size to enable the firm to be a leader or challenger in important markets; by controlling the technical development of a 'vehicle function', it will almost oblige manufacturers to do business with it.
2. *The strategy of flexibility*   This involves a systematic search for partnerships with manufacturers covering a limited number of products, and taking part in – even anticipating – developments in terms of products and organisation.
3. *The strategy of technical know-how*   A firm following this strategy becomes the leading producer in the field, and certain techniques can only be developed through it; the strategy of the 'size' effect is not specially important in this case.
4. *The strategy of diversification*   According to this approach, the firm looks to other sectors for new outlets or opportunities to apply its control of certain techniques.

Ways of applying these strategies within the context of the Single Market

Any analysis of the strategies of producers of accessories poses certain problems because of the compartmentalised nature of the information available. We can none the less attempt a 'vertical' analysis and a 'horizontal' analysis.

First, *the vertical analysis*. Policies relating to research and development and innovations have considerable influence over the strategies in force. Indeed, the production and size of the firm are also very relevant.

As a general rule, the workforces of vehicle manufacturers and component producers are integrating increasingly, but it is also true that the manufacturers' design departments are only opened up to large producers of accessories – that is to say those that can offer an innovation potential, or those that strongly side with the manufacturers.

As far as the multiproduct operators are concerned, vehicle manufacturers are beginning to look upon them as everyday partners in the field of R & D and innovation. They now dominate a wide range of 'generic' technologies, and this gives them very great power in areas that were once the domain of the manufacturers. On the other hand, specialist firms (of all sizes) bring 'solutions' to the manufacturers by displaying their technological and technical skills in the areas where they are dominant.

Investment practice is closely linked to the market positions they have sought. Large multiproduct groups or firms developing a strategy of market leadership invest heavily in accessories and materials; they also attempt to expand their operations on a European level, if not world-wide, as a means of gaining access to new manufacturers in these new markets. Firms following a strategy of flexibility are more likely to opt for a policy of setting up production units close to the manufacturers' assembly lines. Those preferring the strategies of know-how or diversification invest in a more concentrated way on techniques where they have established competence and in those parts of the country where they have traditionally operated.

The ways in which personnel policies are implemented are difficult to identify but firms which are heavily involved in partnership projects with manufacturers and which are in the business of producing quality goods have developed personnel policies whose aim is to increase the staff's involvement and level of responsibility.

Financial policies are significantly linked to the overall size of the firm in question. Large companies wishing to occupy positions of power in the market have been able to develop, thanks to relatively independent financing. Firms working more closely with vehicle manufacturers have received advice from the latter about ways of expanding their external operations: carefully planned financial packages have enabled these firms to play the role of 'pole federateur' in certain segments. There are significant limitations to this policy.

Relationships with lower tier suppliers have suffered the backlash of the demands that the vehicle manufacturers have made of the first tier producers of components and accessories. The major producers in this sector have been 'integrateurs de fonction' and therefore indispensable in the production chain; their own suppliers no longer have any direct contact with the vehicle manufacturer and participate in the development of a component under the control of one of the major producers. This kind of joint policy has encouraged some firms to diversify, or even to leave the automobile industry. At all events, leading businessmen believe that the loss of direct contact with the manufacturer is a loss of market control, and they refuse to base their future in the market on such conditions.

As to the marketing of spare parts, the large producers of equipment and accessories have a policy of reducing their dependence on the vehicle manufacturers' networks and of distributing through wholesale outlets or specialist networks that have direct access to the consumer. This involves setting up sales networks, but it is a policy that could work very successfully in the medium term.

Second, *the horizontal analysis*. In the mid-1980s, companies de-veloped policies towards setting up agreements with other firms, extending their areas of operations and redrawing their business bound-aries. We will now distinguish between 'traditional' operational agree-ments and new ones.

'Traditional' operations are related to a policy of defining privileged areas of industrial activity: Lucas, the Italian group Magneti-Marelli and the French firms Valeo and Matra have all withdrawn from certain operations recently (lighting, heating and carburettors respectively).

A second type of 'traditional' operation involves a large number of firms: those firms which have succeeded in 'emerging' as the most skilled in a particular sphere try to establish themselves as 'key producers' in their sector and extend their market control by expanding outside it; they also apply their know-how in firms which they take over. A third type has large non-specialist groups creating specialist subsidiaries and developing new activities with a view to ultimately buying existing firms: an example of this was the decision of Siemens to buy back Bendix. Finally, there has been a dramatic increase in the number of technical and marketing agreements (e.g. Bosch–Nippodenso, Valeo–Akebono and Magneti-Marelli–Lucas).

However, new types of agreement have also been making their mark. These can take the form of medium-performance firms attaching themselves to a large company which has interests in the automobile industry but which allows the supplier to develop its own strategy (examples include the participation of Cockerill-Sambre in Ymos and of Usinor-Sacilor in Allevard). Companies approach this in very similar ways and it is worth noting that co-operation is mostly in the field of marketing (helping to gain access to foreign manufacturers and to manufacturing plant abroad). The second 'new' type of agreement was made between a big Japanese components producer (Kasai, a subsidiary of Nissan) and a medium-sized European producer (the Reydel group): there is little industrial content in such an agreement, with the Japanese firm seeking access to the European market and the European company wanting access to Japanese manufacturers in Europe and worldwide. The real interest for the European firm in this kind of agreement is less important than the fact that both companies complement one another's production; recent events make it impossible to give a fuller picture of this development.

It is hard to establish a formal link between the increase in the number of 'traditional' operations, the appearance of new types of agreement and the setting up of the Single Market. The explanation given by leading industrialists is that these operations go hand in hand with the enlarge-ment of their 'natural' markets as they grow from national entities to continental, or even worldwide, activities.

Analysis of this broadening of the market – a 'natural' broadening in the case of equipment producers – is uncertain: it is difficult to know how much weight to give to the effects of the 'normal' growth of a firm, to the return of the financial situation to normal, and to the industry's view of a more open Europe. The overall climate for this broadening can be said to be favourable.

We have tried to give as complete a presentation as possible of the strategic trends of firms in the automobile sector. It is a sector that is unusually rich in operations of very different types, and it would appear that the more recent operations follow a logic which scarcely differs from the agreements and attitudes that obtained before. The trend is less industrial and more commercial and technological, and this would suggest that the enlarging of the markets demands huge developments to be made in tertiary functions – research and development, design and marketing.

Conclusion

The setting up of the Single Market does not fundamentally call into question the strategic trends in the automobile industry that date back to the early 1980s, but they need to undergo three main modifications before we move on to recommendations concerning Community policy.

The transparency of competitive conditions in Europe

The debate about the Single Market in the automobile sector has largely focused on the nature of competition (loyalty/disloyalty) between Japanese and European vehicle manufacturers on the one hand and amongst European vehicle manufacturers on the other. Two important issues emerge: pricing, and government aid to home manufacturers.

Earlier developments have shown that the problem of government aid (punctual intervention but at a difficult time for companies in the midst of restructuring) is of less importance than the mechanisms involved in setting prices in an industry where prices are more durable than the aid.

We need to examine what goes to make up costs and selling prices. The ability of a manufacturer to maintain his position in the market, or even to move upwards, depends basically on the following factors:

- *The cost structure* Unlike the discussion on competition, the question here is whether the cost structure is 'abnormal', but it is also necessary to be absolutely clear about the criteria of 'normality' from the point of view of working conditions, relationships with suppliers, technological advances and so on. It would appear that this cost structure is acceptable in a competitive framework as long as all producers can potentially gain access to it.

- *Pricing practices in different markets* The question here is whether some manufacturers take 'unfair' advantage of their dominant position in their domestic market or in other markets (even of a cartel) in order to carry out aggressive commercial policies in new markets.

In respect of the points raised above, the main modification introduced by the Single Market is as follows: the Single Market will not irrevocably bring complete harmonisation of conditions of competition as far as the structure of costs and prices is concerned; it will, however, be possible to know what the conditions of competition in Europe are, thanks to the harmonisation of economic information and regulations. This is not the first time that we have drawn attention here to the decisive role played by information in company strategies.

An examination of the conditions of competition between manufacturers begs the question whether it would be as easy to study the production and sales conditions of non-European producers.

Changes introduced within the domain of the manufacturers themselves

The setting up of the Single Market has brought about little change as far as the markets and production of vehicles are concerned. By contrast, in the commercial arena problems will be somewhat different, particularly the technical and strategic aspects.

On the technical side, the ways in which import subsidiaries in exporting EC countries operate may well be called into question; not even their existence is guaranteed. As far as strategy is concerned, manufacturers will need to reconsider their pricing and distribution policies and maybe set up their own EC marketing policy involving promotion, publicity, management of distribution networks and various other services.

Changes introduced within the domain of the producers of equipment and accessories and of suppliers

The setting up of the Single Market has played a dynamic role in this sector of the industry. Access to new European and non-European manufacturers seems to be both necessary and easier within the framework of a more homogenous Europe; the effect is largely psychological but it is all the more important in that the firms involved are relatively small. The changing size of the firms is forcing them to reconsider their industrial and commercial presence, and this could result in entry to the American and Japanese markets.

It is precisely because of this last criterion that it is important to appreciate the real range of the agreements; these may be fairly formal for the time being, but they bind European and Japanese producers together during a period when respective strengths are quite unbalanced.

What form of intervention should the Community be recommended to carry out?

This chapter describes itself as a 'clinical analysis' of the automobile industry, and no major dysfunction has come to light. It follows that any recommendation relating to 'industrial policy' should be concerned with the setting of standards and should take due note of certain political and social objectives (even strategic objectives like the winning of foreign markets) that have not been examined closely here.

Put in another way, it seems to be difficult to arbitrate between the interests of the consumer (a rapid opening up of the markets, a speedy harmonisation of taxes, an early removal of technical constraints) and those of the businessman wishing to be in control of market developments. We cannot ignore the possibility that the consumer who is eager for competition may also be either a direct or indirect employee of the automobile industry, whose job could disappear; he or she could also be the user of a public service which would be withdrawn in the absence of fiscal resources.

It must be made clear that there is no such thing as a rigid standard in industrial policy, simply a number of methods used in the pursuit of economic, social or other objectives. An industrial policy which encompasses policies of research, training and various support services is no more than a tool that services what is more or less explicitly a political project. Thought needs to be given now to the project and to the industrial objectives of the Community.

3

The truck industry

Leo Sleuwaegen
(with the assistance of H. A. J. van Wijk)

Introduction

In the early 1980s the European truck industry was confronted with a sharp decline in demand. This was mainly caused by the collapse of the export markets in the Middle East and Africa and a severe recession in Western Europe. Between 1980 and 1984 production decreased by almost 33 per cent which, however, was not enough to avoid huge excess capacity in the industry. After 1984 a strong recovery reversed the trend. Some manufacturers reached full capacity in October 1989. This is quite remarkable for an industry that suffered from excess capacity of almost 50 per cent in the preceding years (see Table 3.1).

The most important manufacturers (Daimler-Benz, Iveco, Renault Vehicles Industries (RVI), Volvo, DAF, Scania and M.A.N.) reacted differently to the crisis period. Iveco, for example, postponed its plans to become a pan-European manufacturer and started a strong reorganisation within Europe. Daimler-Benz, Volvo and RVI sought expansion of their activities with US companies in order to penetrate the US market. M.A.N., a strongly national-based firm, was reluctant to react in an active way.

Since the changed market situation in the early 1980s the European market has become completely dominated by European producers. In 1987 the seven large European firms captured about 90 per cent of the EC market over 3.5t. gross vehicle weight (GVW). The US manufacturers – General Motors, International Harvester and Dodge – withdrew from their European bases in the United Kingdom, and when the Italian company Iveco formed a joint venture with Ford in the UK in 1986 the market came completely under the control of European manufacturers.

Table 3.1   Production of trucks in Western Europe ('000s)

1980	1984	1987
500	336	360

The manufacturers have since been preparing themselves for a further concentration within a smaller number of groups. The first large merger was the one between Leyland and DAF in 1987. Recently, in September 1989, the Austrian company Steyr was taken over by M.A.N. In October 1989 the Spanish public enterprise INI announced that the truck division ENASA was for sale (ENASA produces Pegaso trucks); Volvo, Daimler-Benz and DAF all showed interest, but ultimately ENASA was taken over by M.A.N. Also in October 1989 it became known that RVI and Volvo were having talks about a possible merger in which the truck division would play an essential role, while RVI and DAF agreed in the same month to co-operate in the development of a new light-weight commercial vehicle. At the same time, the major European truck makers are increasing the geographical scope of their operations beyond European borders.

H. Dietz of DAF gives the following characterisation of the development of the truck industry:

1. Before the Second World War: penetration in Europe by the US manufacturers.
2. 1970s: transformation of the conventional industry into a more technology-intensive industry.
3. After 1985: penetration of the US market and world markets by European companies.

Industry environment and structural analysis

The truck market in Europe

The product

In commercial vehicles a distinction is usually made between trucks, buses and vans. The rather vague distinction between trucks and vans poses an analytical problem. Some manufacturers, like Renault (RVI) and Fiat (Iveco), register their van production in the car division instead of the truck division. Other manufacturers like DAF no longer have a car division which implies that their commercial vehicle production figures include vans. Trucks and vans are often considered as two different industry segments characterised by different competitive environments. For instance, Japanese producers have a strong position in the van segment of the European commercial vehicle industry, but, as yet, they do not have such a position in the truck market.

In this study on the truck industry, the definition used is the same as the one used by the European Commission in dealing with the Iveco/Ford UK co-operative agreement: a truck must have a weight over 3.5t. GVW. The following subdivision will be used in the analysis:

- light GVW: >3.5t.–4.9t.
- medium GVW: 5t.–16t.
- heavy GVW: >16t.

On January 1st 1993 new uniform regulations concerning measures and weights will be applied for trucks and buses in the EC market (with a temporary exception for the United Kingdom and Ireland). Eight classes will be distinguished, based on the number of axles, number of wheels per axle, distance between axles and whether the vehicle is articulated or rigid. Such a technical division is not necessary for the purpose of this study.

The geographic market

There are clear differences in the geographical strategies adopted by the truck manufacturers in the EC. While some have recently adopted a European strategy in anticipation of the fact that Europe will be their relevant market in the near future, other larger manufacturers have already developed a true global strategy. Figure 3.1 shows total production volumes of the major truck makers for medium- and heavy-weight trucks.

The analysis is primarily performed on a European level, i.e. the European Community plus Sweden (since two of the most important suppliers are located there). Attention will be paid, however, to every manufacturing nation, including the United States and Japan as important competitors in certain segments of the world market.

Demand conditions

As mentioned in the introduction, the demand for trucks dropped markedly in the beginning of the 1980s. Two explanations were put

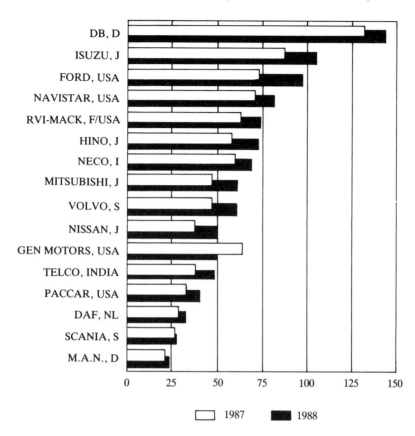

Figure 3.1 World production of trucks above 6t. GVW (× 1,000)

forward: the collapse of the export market, in particular the Middle East and Africa; and a recession in Western Europe. The demand for trucks is, indeed, a derived demand (as a part of the demand for road transport) and thus very dependent on economic growth conditions. The demand for trucks is also very dependent on a more structural element: the substitution from other transportation means.

When looking more carefully into the structural element, substitution from air and shipping transport can, in many cases, be ruled out for reasons of costs and/or speed. However, this does not completely hold for rail transport. It is broadly recognised that road transport cannot expand forever and in some parts of Western Europe clear signs of congestion are a well-known feature. Environment protection, which has become a hot political issue, could in the same sense increase the importance of rail transport. Rail transport has important advantages over road transport: it is less polluting than road transport; it helps decrease traffic jams; and, because of diminished road transport, maintenance costs of road infrastructure could be reduced. Reliable time schedules for rail transport also help develop efficient logistic planning systems for geographically dispersed companies in Europe.

There are, however, several reasons why these advantages may not be sufficient to erode the demand for road transport quickly. The major reasons are as follows:

- There is a tendency for the centre of the economic activities to shift south inside Europe, in particular to south Germany and northern Italy. If Spain and Italy continue their infrastructure adjustments this tendency could be enforced. This might decrease traffic problems in north-west Europe.

- Along with the ongoing deregulation of transportation in Europe and the introduction of new advanced technology, refined logistical systems are being developed which will have a significant influence on the improvement of the efficiency of road transport. However, this might decrease the growth in the number of trucks. H. Werner of Daimler-Benz even expects that these efficiency gains will be so high that in the year 2000 road transport demand will still be covered by the current fleet.

- It is expected that the demand for medium-range trucks will be squeezed between the demand for light/medium- and heavy-range trucks (see Figure 3.2). This is based on the idea of local distribution centres evolving throughout Europe between which long-distance transport will occur. This development should be viewed in relation to improvements in logistical efficiency.

- In EC Member States such as the Netherlands where congestion is a serious feature, the policy of the government is primarily aimed at the

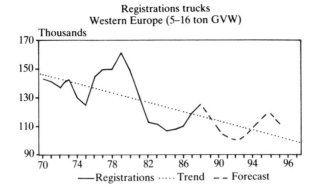

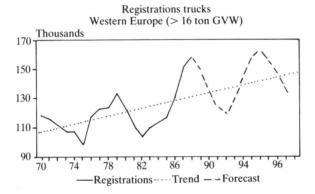

Figure 3.2   Trends in registration of trucks (Source: NoB-wegtransport)

reduction of car traffic rather than on reducing road transport. This has to be seen in connection with the fact that both rail and road transport each still seem to have their specific market segments. Rail transport is traditionally used for bulk transport (coal, iron/steel, construction materials) whereas road transport is more directed to the transportation of goods with a higher added value. Table 3.2 shows that national rail transport in the five major transport markets of the European Community dropped, in favour of road transport, from 27.1 per cent to 22.4 per cent in 1987. A similar tendency can be identified for international transport (see Figure 3.3).

More generally, road transport has the important advantage in comparison with railways of being more flexible, having better penetration possibilities and in many cases being less expensive.

Table 3.2   National rail/road transport in five European Community markets

	1979	1982	1987	1993
France				
road transport	94.6	77.1	89.9	102.9
rail	70.0	53.9	51.3	50.4
total	164.6	131.0	141.1	153.3
West Germany				
road transport	123.9	119.8	142.7	164.7
rail	66.3	57.4	59.1	60.0
total	190.2	177.2	201.8	224.7
Italy				
road transport	81.6	94.9	108.9	125.6
rail	18.4	17.7	19.3	21.5
total	100.0	112.6	128.2	147.1
Spain				
road transport	92.2	91.5	95.7	114.0
rail	10.3	10.5	11.5	12.2
total	102.5	102.0	107.2	126.2
United Kingdom				
road transport	104.6	96.8	107.0	118.5
rail	19.9	16.5	15.6	15.3
total	124.5	113.3	122.6	133.8
EC Total				
(12 Member States)				
total	797.4	739.7	814.0	907.0

Sources: Commission of the EC, undated documents

Rail transportation in the separate Member States has been indirectly favoured by restricting measures on road transport in the past years. Apart from the fact that many of these measures were primarily introduced in order to control road transport itself (cabotage, price regulations, safety demands, etc.) it cannot be denied that they also made the nearest substitute more attractive.

Combined rail/road transport could 'merge' the advantages of both road and rail transport. The investments in infrastructure that are required, however, are very high, which implies that in spite of its attractive features such an option is not easily realisable in the short run. The Channel Tunnel will undoubtedly contribute to the attractiveness of the train–truck combination. For the Alp nations like Austria and Switzerland, which are suffering from the increasing volume of transit traffic, combined rail/road transport may also prove to be an attractive direct solution.

From all these considerations it follows that unless substantial measures are taken to reduce road transport on a European level, the industry will continue to grow into the next decade. This is reflected in Figure 3.4 which shows the expected registration of trucks in Western European countries.

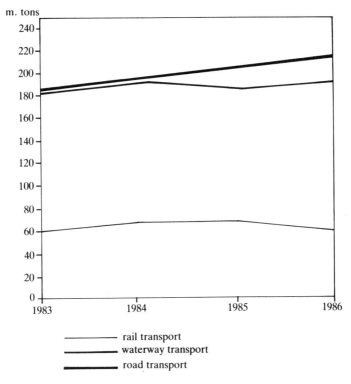

m. tons

rail transport
waterway transport
road transport

Figure 3.3   Cross-border transport (Source: DG-Transport EC)

Supply conditions

Production and employment

Table 3.1 shows total truck production in Western Europe for the years 1980, 1984 and 1987. Forecasts for the period after 1990 do not indicate a major change in the total volume in the coming years. However, the composition of production may change substantially by putting more emphasis on the light and heavy categories.

Table 3.3 shows employment figures for the major European truck makers over the period 1984–9. The figures for the year 1989 are estimates. For RVI no reliable figures for the years 1984–6 were available, but it is known that the workforce diminished substantially in these years, as the estimates show. The growth in total employment suggests that there have been no drastic rationalisations coupled with a loss in employment. On the contrary, there appears to be an increase in the number of specialised employees, which may largely be explained by

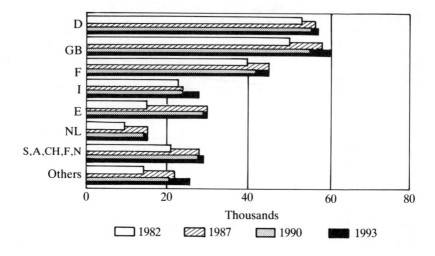

Figure 3.4   Expected registration of trucks in Western Europe (>3.5 ton)
(Source: *Financial Times*, 8 November 1988)

Table 3.3   Employment

	1984	1985	1986	1987	1988	1989
DB	70,372	77,352	81,182	82,039	82,000	81,000
Iveco	36,263	34,585	36,053	35,962	38,110	37,800
RVI	40,000 E	40,000 E	36,000 E	34,792	34,151	34,000
Volvo	15,700	16,150	16,500	17,600	17,700	17,850
Scania	19,758	20,129	21,334	22,755	23,000	23,250
DAF	8,710	8,678	9,304	16,631	16,491	17,250
M.A.N.	16,353	16,438	17,144	17,142	18,487	17,500
Total	207,156 E	213,332 E	217,517 E	226,921	229,939	228,650

the fact that trucks become technologically more complicated with
increasing customisation of the product.

It is tempting to make a comparison of labour productivity across the
different truck makers. However, this is not feasible in view of the
important differences in vertical integration and product mix of the
different truck makers. Table 3.4 shows the ratio of number of trucks

Table 3.4 Trucks produced per employee[1]

	1984	1985	1986	1987	1988	1989
DB	2.9	2.8	2.8	2.9	2.9	2.9
Iveco	2.3	2.9	2.6	3.0	3.3	3.7
Volvo	2.6	2.6	2.7	2.6	2.6	2.7
Scania	1.1	1.1	1.2	1.2	1.2	1.2
DAF	1.5	1.5	1.6	2.5	3.2	3.1
M.A.N.	1.1	1.1	1.1	1.2	1.2	1.4

Note: [1]Number of trucks produced divided by total number of employees

divided by total employees. The production figures that are used, are derived from annual company reports and from specialized industry sources. For RVI no reliable production figures were obtainable. The figures in Table 3.4 show the lowest figure for the heavily vertically integrated Scania and a very high figure for Iveco, which company depends considerably on outsourcing for its components. This is also true for DAF, which, in addition, has broadened its product line through the merger with Leyland. For the more stable truck makers, such as Daimler-Benz and Volvo, no significant changes in the ratio have emerged over the period 1984–9.

Technological progress

The truck industry has been characterised by fast technological advances in product development in the most recent years. These advances should be seen in connection with the following factors:

* Enhanced environmental and safety demands that are coming up from the national and the European level.
* Increased competition among hauliers which has resulted in a competitive demand for technologically advanced trucks in order to obtain/maintain a good position in the transport market.

A deregulated market for free transport after 1992 could increase this competition. According to W. Lochte of M.A.N., the creation of an internal market will induce more competitive demand which, in turn, will require more co-operation with external suppliers of components if manufacturers are to be able to meet this demand. Increased competition among hauliers could shorten the life of a truck and put pressure on manufacturers to put new models on the market sooner.

The suppliers and their national markets

West Germany

Daimler-Benz   Daimler-Benz (DB) is the world's largest truck manufacturer with production facilities in all major continents of the world. In the United States DB has its subsidiary Freightliner which it acquired in the early 1980s. DB holds a strong position in the medium range (5–15.9t. GVW). In the heavy segment there is strong competition from other suppliers, especially from imports and from the other German truck maker, M.A.N. In West Germany DB is dominant market leader, but DB also reached a market share of 25.8 per cent in the European market in 1987.

Daimler-Benz is a strongly diversified concern, with – in addition to the car industry – interests in aerospace (Dornier and MBB), electronics (AEG) and related activities. This gives DB a broad basis for its R & D activities without the immediate need for co-operation with other firms.

M.A.N.   The second German supplier of importance is M.A.N., a mainly national-oriented concern. M.A.N, which holds a good position in the heavy-range segment, has interests in related activities such as diesel engines for ships. The company has developed a strategy to become a full-range truck manufacturer. In connection with these plans M.A.N. has become involved in a co-operation agreement with Volkswagen (VW) to develop a middle-range truck. In addition, M.A.N. reached similar co-operation agreements with DB and Eaton (transmissions and axles), mainly in order to keep R & D costs down.

Another element of M.A.N.'s strategy is directed towards developing a European dealer network. M.A.N. expects that after 1992, when the inner frontiers will have disappeared, the now relatively protected position of German hauliers will be affected. Foreign companies might prefer another truck manufacturer if M.A.N. had no broad service and dealing network outside Germany. Expansion of this network is therefore of vital importance. Some years ago M.A.N. made an agreement with the Spanish company ENASA to set up a marketing network in Spain, and in 1989 ENASA was taken over by M.A.N. In the same year, M.A.N. also took over the Austrian truck maker STEYR. M.A.N. also had a joint interest with Daimler-Benz in DTV, a manufacturer of diesel engines, until DTV was completely taken over by Daimler-Benz in 1989. However, in spite of the formal dissolution of this joint venture there are still many ties in components development and sourcing between DB and M.A.N.

Through the acquisition of Freightliner in the US by DB and the co-operation agreements with Japanese manufacturers, the German truck industry has evolved into a global network structure. The intercompany relationships of the German truck industry are shown in Figure 3.5:

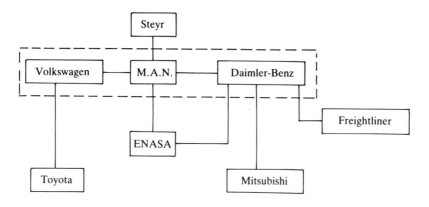

Notes: Volkswagen co-operates in the car division with Toyota in the development process on a new pick-up truck; DB and Mitsubishi are both involved in the Spanish Iberica plant in the development of new commercial vans

Figure 3.5   The West German truck industry

Italy

Iveco   Since the early 1980s Iveco has been part of the Fiat group. Iveco is the second largest supplier in Europe after DB. Like DB, it is a full-range manufacturer.

In 1982 Iveco integrated the German firm Magirus-Deutz. Mainly because of the production plant of this company in Ulm (Germany), Iveco has been capable of achieving a substantial market share in Germany. Then, in 1986, Iveco formed a joint venture with Ford (UK). Iveco is known as a less vertically integrated manufacturer. The Italian company has many co-operation agreements with sub-suppliers such as Rockwell (axles) and Eaton (gear-boxes).

The Italian truck market is the fourth largest in Europe. An expanding transport market in 1987 and 1988 made it possible for many Italian hauliers to renew their fleet and hence to reinforce their competitive position in the Common Market. This fleet renewal was an important boost for Iveco's production.

France

Renault Vehicles Industries Renault Vehicles Industries (RVI) is part of Regie Renault, the French state-owned concern. In 1984–6 RVI suffered accumulated losses of up to FF5.32bn but in 1987, after a large reorganisation, these losses were turned into a profit of FF195m. RVI is the sole French truck manufacturer since Iveco closed down the UNIC plant in Trappes in 1984. The French truck market – which was, like the UK market, cutthroat – has become more profitable in the past few years as a result of expanding demand. It should be noted, however, that import penetration in France is much larger than in Germany and Italy (see Figures 3.6, 3.7, 3.8).

Besides the French production facilities RVI has plants in the United Kingdom where RVI established Renault Truck Industries (RTI) in the Dodge plant which it acquired. Furthermore, RVI has its own plant in Spain, owns 45 per cent of the shares of the US manufacturer MACK, and also has a strong presence in the African market.

Sweden

Apart from West Germany, Sweden is the only nation with two suppliers among the 'big seven': Volvo and Scania.

Volvo Volvo produces an extensive range of medium trucks as well as heavy-range trucks. In 1986 Volvo and the US company White–GM created a joint venture, making Volvo the third European manufacturer

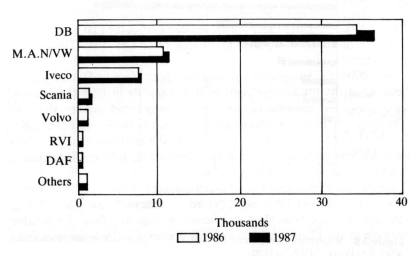

Figure 3.6 Registrations in West Germany (> 3.5t. GVW) (Sources: industry sources, AID)

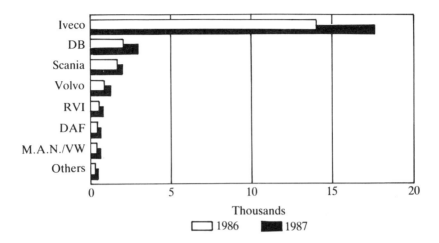

Figure 3.7 Registrations in Italy (> 3.5t. GVW) (Sources: industry sources)

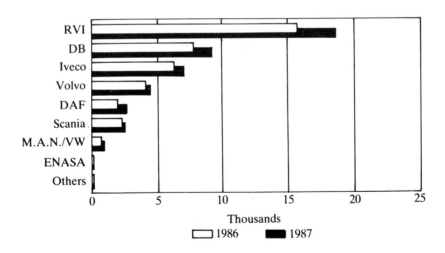

Figure 3.8 Registrations in France (> 3.5t. GVW) (Sources: industry sources, AID, *L'Argus*)

to penetrate the North American market in this way. Manufacturing in the United States is best described as 'assembling', but Volvo is trying to introduce its own vertically integrated production system in its US subsidiary.

Volvo is one of the most diversified firms among the European rivals. Apart from the facilities in Sweden and the United States, Volvo has plants in Belgium, Scotland, South America and Australia. According to Volvo it would be a logical step to expand its production to southern Europe.

Scania   Scania has a reputation as a very successful and profitable manufacturer. Unfortunately, the profits of Scania are very much needed in the Saab/Scania concern in order to support the car division of Saab which is suffering heavy financial losses.

Scania is specialised in the heavy range (16t.plus GVW). Its production system is best described as strongly vertically integrated. In doing so, Scania emphasises its independent structure of operation, which also explains why Scania chose to penetrate the US market through greenfield entry, unlike DB, RVI and Volvo.

The Swedish market accounted for 7,042 trucks in 1987 (1986: 5,994), with Volvo registrations equal to 3,170 (2,750) and Scania 2,348 (2,191). This means a penetration by EC truck makers of about 22 per cent (17.6 per cent) in the Swedish market.

Netherlands

DAF   Of all the important manufacturers, DAF is the only company which is completely dependent on the truck business. Apart from a special product division for army vehicles, the core activity of DAF is formed by its truck division (see Figure 3.9). DAF has always been a strong competitor in the heavy range of the market. The merger with Leyland in 1987 gave DAF the necessary expansion to the lower segments and provided extra production facilities in a relatively inexpensive way. DAF needed extra capacity because the plants in Eindhoven (Nether-lands) and in Weverlo (Belgium) had almost reached full capacity. The third advantage of the merger was the creation of a third home market, besides the Netherlands and Belgium.

As a smaller company DAF does not have the financial assets of the bigger (diversified) companies and needs to make clear choices about R & D activities. One of those choices by DAF was to stay out of the horse-power race in engine building. Another example of such a strategic choice is the co-operation agreement with ENASA. In the joint venture 'Cabtec' (1984) these two firms developed a new series of truck cabins.

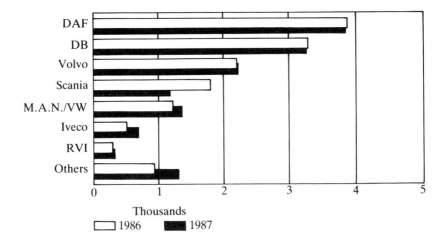

Figure 3.9 Registrations in the Netherlands (>3.5 t. GVW) (Source: RAI)

Just as in other national markets, DAF is market leader in the Netherlands.

Apart from DAF there are some small Dutch truck makers which are best considered as very specialised 'niche' competitors: Terburg, F.T.F. and GINAF. Import penetration in the Netherlands is high.

United Kingdom

The UK industry has undergone drastic changes in the 1980s. When DAF and Leyland merged in1987 the last important UK manufacturer lost its independence, in spite of the fact that the UK market is still the second largest sub-market, after West Germany in the EC. US manufacturers, who were dominant in the United Kingdom before 1980, saw their role diminishing, mainly after RVI took over control in the Dodge plant, Iveco started a joint venture with Ford (UK) and General Motors (GM) closed down Bedford. GM tried to merge with Leyland, ENASA or M.A.N., but none of these attempts proved to be successful. Figures 3.10 and 3.11 illustrate the following changes:

* Dodge was transferred into Renault Truck Industries (RTI).
* AWD is what remained of Bedford after the withdrawal of GM.
* Seddon-Atkinson broke up with International Harvester (US) and was taken over by ENASA in 1986.

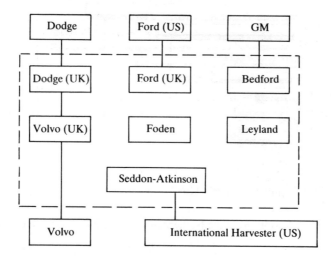

Figure 3.10   United Kingdom market, 1980

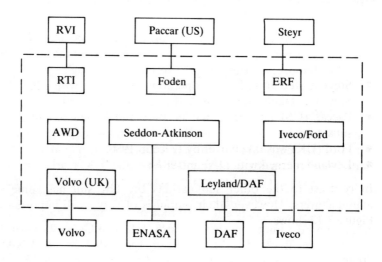

Figure 3.11   United Kingdom market, 1989

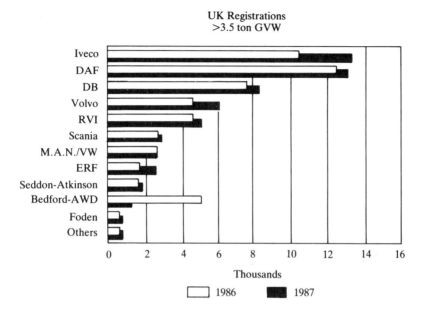

Figure 3.12   Registrations in the United Kingdom (Source: SMMT)

- Steyr started an R & D co-operation agreement with ERF in 1987. Steyr was taken over by M.A.N. in September 1989.
- Paccar (US) bought Foden in 1981 and Foden is still a Paccar subsidiary.
- Ford (UK) was taken over by Iveco in 1986.
- Leyland merged with DAF in 1987.

In contrast to the other sub-markets the UK still has some small manufacturers. However, their output is of very small importance, as Figure 3.12 shows.

Spain

Spain no longer has an independent national-based truck maker. ENASA became part of M.A.N., and Motor Iberica, with activities mainly in the 3.5–9t. GVW, is owned by Nissan. Major truck makers, such as RVI, operate assembly plants in Spain.

Linkages between the European truck makers

In Figure 3.13 all the existing (known) intercompany relationships of the European truck industry are put together.

The excess capacity that existed shortly after the market breakdown in the beginning of the decade has fallen considerably, but has not fully disappeared. Some manufacturers (Volvo, DAF, M.A.N., Scania) have reached full capacity while others such as DB, RVI and Iveco are still believed to suffer from some excess capacity.

The following factors are pertinent to the present overall situation:

- Although EC truck makers continue to spread their activities worldwide, the European market is still their core market.
- The United Kingdom has suffered most from the recession, and has undergone strong structural changes as a result of which the leading manufacturers came under foreign control. Looked at from the output side, however, this sub-market is still the second largest in the EC Market.
- West Germany, France and Italy together make up about 45 per cent of the Western European market. As yet, these markets are marked by a low degree of import penetration. One cannot speak, therefore, of one European truck market. Transport deregulation, such as abandoning of the cabotage system, is very likely to change this situation.

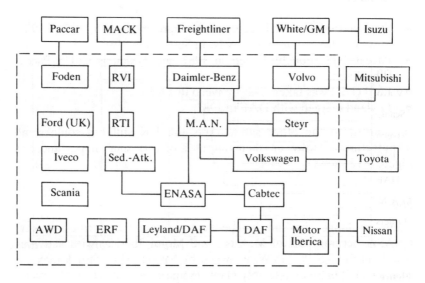

Figure 3.13 European truck industry

- Daimler-Benz is also the market leader in Western Europe. This position is particularly significant in the medium range. Within the heavy-range market, shares are divided somewhat more equally as Figure 3.14 shows.

The competitive process

Pricing behaviour and dealer networks

The truck market largely corresponds to a textbook description of a heterogeneous oligopoly with a fair degree of product differentiation. There is not only the distinction of the product according to weight classes, but also inside a separate weight class itself there is considerable room to differentiate the product.

Additionally, the European truck industry is still fairly fragmented, following national markets. This offers room for price discrimination and this, indeed, appears to be the case. Markets with a low degree of import penetration in which the national manufacturer holds a strong and well-protected position seem to be highly vulnerable to price discrimination. This is illustrated by the contrast between the situation in Germany and Italy, which is characterised by low import penetration and dominant producers, and that in open economies such as Belgium and the Netherlands.

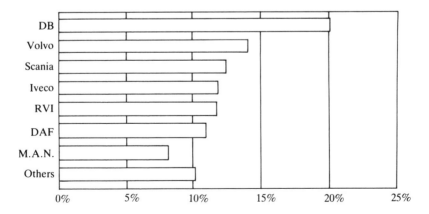

Figure 3.14 Market shares (> 16t. GVW) (Source: Own estimates for the year 1987)

It is essential for a manufacturer to keep access to European markets by maintaining an extensive dealer network. In view of the diverse needs of a typical transporter a dealer can hardly restrict his business to selling only heavy-range trucks but is often forced to sell a broader range, including other types of trucks and vans, and to establish a good service and maintenance reputation. A good-quality product coupled to a dealer network with a well-developed service and maintenance system appears a major advantage in gaining market share. Several observers note, for instance, that one of the major reasons why the UK manufacturers suffered so much from the market breakdown in the early 1980s is that they had failed to create an extensive dealer network on the European continent.

These considerations do not completely remove the importance of price competition. Excess capacity in a capital-intensive industry makes the truck industry very vulnerable to price competition. The huge excess capacity in the early 1980s induced a strong pressure on prices. The United Kingdom in particular became a cutthroat market after the US manufacturers left the country.

R & D strategic alliances

Research and development (R & D) has become of increasing import-ance in the truck industry. In trying to enhance the quality of their products by the introduction of electronics in the development of a new truck, financial needs of truck makers have increased substantially. This has created serious problems for manufacturers lacking a broad financial basis. These companies have to make choices about the areas (often major components of a truck) in which they want to become leaders and those where they might adopt a follower's position.

Exact figures on R & D are not available but the estimate of 3–4 per cent R & D to sales ratio for DAF seems to be a reliable estimate. Volvo and Scania achieve a higher rate, with 5 per cent and 7 per cent respectively. In R & D expenditures, it is useful to make a distinction between kinds of research and development. Basic research is very restricted in the truck industry. Applied research programmes exist, but mainly in large and diversified companies. Development programmes are of major importance, and assume greater importance the smaller the manufacturer.

Economies of scale in manufacturing tended to become subordinate to scale economies in R & D in the past decade. Economies of scale in manufacturing are still very important, but have lost some of their importance as a result of the introduction of flexible manufacturing. Scale economies also differ considerably among components, as illustrated in Table 3.5.

To illustrate the importance of development costs, Table 3.6 presents estimates of capital expenditures for developing a new truck and the installation of a new production plant.

Smaller manufacturers try to overcome the disadvantages in the R & D area by relying on outsourcing for some components and by establishing co-operation agreements or partnerships with other manufacturers or sub-suppliers. Examples of these types of co-operation are, for instance, the relationships between Steyr and ERF and between ENASA and DAF (Cabtec, 1984), and the co-operation between DB and M.A.N. Daimler-Benz, as a larger company, advertises openly that its broad diversification provides substantial advantages for its R & D efforts.

Entry and substitutes

In view of the current overcapacity and the continuing rationalisation, there are no indications of rapid new entry into the European truck industry. American manufacturers penetrated the European market long ago, but withdrew from their activities in the early 1980s. However, in line with the ongoing globalisation of the industry, American truck

Table 3.5   Minimum annual volumes for optimal production

Cabins	200,000+
Frame	40,000+
Axles	40,000+
Engines	200,000+
Final assembly	100,000+

Source: Estimates from Muller and Owen, 1981

Table 3.6   Financial requirements for the construction of a commercial vehicle, 1982 (£m.)

Design and development costs:	
• complete new truck	120–200
• truck with existing components	50
• new cabin	60
• new axles	80
• new engine	150–200
• new gearbox	50–100
Assembly unit costs	150–300
Sub-assembly unit costs	150
Research and design department	40
Company investments for a new series of commercial vehicles (using existing components)	350

Source: Estimates from Muller and Owen, 1981

makers have engaged in many agreements with European truck makers which could easily develop into a renewed participation in the European industry.

A competitive entry threat comes from Japanese manufacturers. Nissan, Toyota and Mitsubishi already capture a considerable market share in the European van market, in spite of the fact that Italy, France and West Germany impose some restrictions to protect the national industry. It seems likely that Japanese entry will indeed happen from 'below', i.e. by penetration of the light range instead of the medium or heavy ranges. The demand for transport (and thus the infrastructure) in Japan has developed in a different direction from that in Europe. As a result, Japanese trucks in the medium and heavy ranges are completely different in product specification from the European trucks. Because of the lack of technological synergy the Japanese find themselves confronted with a serious adaptation problem in the heavy-weight range.

These are also indications that Japanese manufacturers will try to enter through establishing more extensive co-operation agreements with European firms; Toyota with Volkswagen, Mitsubishi with Daimler-Benz and the (unsuccessful) negotiations between Hino and ERF in 1983 point in this direction. Nissan started with a co-operation agreement but later on acquired the Motor Iberica plant in Spain. In developing co-operation agreements it is easier to exchange essential complementary technological knowledge and it also becomes possible to gain access to a dealer network. As emphasised before, such a network is essential for a truck manufacturer since no potential buyer will buy without the insurance of an extensive service network.

If globalisation (in the long run) in the truck industry progresses as in the car industry, further co-operation is likely to take place.

As to competitive threat from substitute products, rail transportation may, to some extent, constitute a threat for the future development of the truck industry. Technological developments will have to be directed towards this threat. Particularly, the development of combined rail–road transportation systems appears as a probable development, which will, very likely, be stimulated by the EC authorities.

Government intervention

In previous paragraphs it was concluded that the European truck industry was still fairly fragmented and, hence, nationally oriented. This gives room for national governments to intervene and influence the market process substantially by supporting their *own* manufacturer. For example, the EC could hardly agree with the intervention by the

Spanish government to help ENASA. The company received a large amount of money in the early 1980s to help its further restructuring. Apart from ENASA several other cases of government support are known, as follows:

- The French government subsidised Renault industries. The European Commission approved this under the condition that RVI would restructure its organisation thoroughly.
- The German government provided substantial support for the DB–MBB merger.
- As non-EC-based truck makers, Saab–Scania and Volvo operate under the Swedish tax system that enables the creation of tax-free provisions. These funds can exist permanently and have the character of risk-bearing capital. Both Saab–Scania and Volvo have made use of this facility. In several Member States such as France and Spain, the government also provided substantial financial incentives to truck owners to renew their fleet.

European co-ordination will undoubtedly help to eliminate these distortions in the competitive process. In addition to improving co-ordination, the European Commission will also have to monitor closely the developments in the truck market. In several cases it has already reached a verdict concerning co-operation agreements, as follows:

- In 1982 the Commission approved a co-operation agreement between Volkswagen and M.A.N. for the development and production of a series of medium-weight trucks (6–9t. GVW). The Commission pointed out that competition in the medium range was not seriously affected. Joint distribution was, however, not allowed.
- A joint venture between Rockwell, a US sub-supplier, and Iveco was allowed in 1983 with a time horizon of eleven years. The motivation was that considerable technological spill-over advantages would emerge from this co-operation. Rockwell and Iveco co-operated in the development of a new axle and arranged joint distribution. The other truck manufacturers would be able to acquire their axles from alternative sub-suppliers.
- The joint venture between Iveco and Ford (UK) was given due attention. In 1988 the Commission approved this integration. On the basis of an analysis of market shares the Commission judged 'that effective competition exists in the part of the Common Market in which the co-operation has its main impact'. In establishing the relevant market the Commission primarily directed itself to the sub-market in the United Kingdom and, only secondly, to the European market.

Corporate strategies

Industry and company performance

Based on fragmentary information, industry experts estimate the rate of return on sales in the truck industry to be rather low, between 3 per cent and 6 per cent. However, as indicated before, there are important variations across the different truck makers, following their presence in different (fragmented) national markets. Truck makers also differ very much in their scope of operations, including a different degree of integrating the manufacture of components. In this respect, it is interesting to see how important the different components are in the final product.

Muller and Owen (1981) have made a rough estimate of the costs (ex-labour) involved in producing a truck, as shown in Figure 3.15. According to several experts interviewed these figures still seem to be valid. None of them wanted to make adjustments for their own situation. These figures only refer to the costs of producing components. Major excluded costs, of course, are the R & D expenditures in creating new components. These costs have increased substantially over the past decade. Only rough percentages are available: in percentage of total sales these expenditures would go from 3–4 per cent (DAF) up to 5 per cent (Volvo) and 7 per cent (Scania). The percentages for Volvo and Scania are higher because these firms are also more vertically integrated and diversified into other activities. For less integrated firms strategic co-operation alliances with other manufacturers become crucially important to maintain overall competitiveness of the product.

DAF, M.A.N. and RVI are clear examples of companies that have

Cab:	14%
Engine:	20%
Gearbox:	10%
Axles:	7%
Chassis:	4%
Line assembled components:	35%
Final assembly:	10%
Total	100%

Figure 3.15   Costs structure, excluding labour costs
(Source: Muller and Owen, 1981)

increasingly adopted this strategy. Daimler-Benz and Volvo are also involved in narrow relationships with other manufacturers (Mitsubishi and White–GM), while Iveco created a joint venture with Rockwell. Scania, emphasising its independence, has no R & D relationships with any other manufacturer or sub-supplier.

The entry of high-tech electronics in 'the truck of 1992' raised new R & D problems for manufacturers. Enhanced transport efficiency will be made possible through the introduction of computer technology. Although most observers expect no full vertical integration in that direction in the next few years, companies that are also involved in car manufacturing are likely to be able to benefit increasingly from the many spill-overs that exist in the development of car electronics and truck electronics.

Figure 3.16 shows the difference in performance among the European truck makers for the period 1984–7. Industry experts explains Scania's good performance by pointing out that Scania manufactures all components in-house and in doing so Scania has full hold on the lucrative spare parts and service market. This comment clearly indicates that not all truck manufacturers follow a common strategy. It seems useful, therefore, to examine in more detail some of the crucial strategic dimensions in which European truck makers differ from each other.

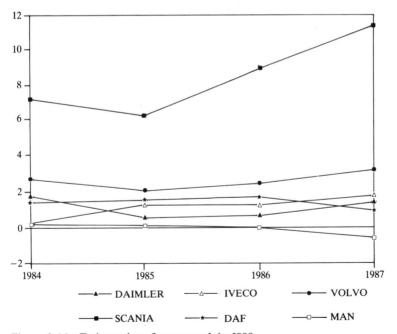

Figure 3.16 Estimated profits per truck in £000s

Corporate strategy and competitive scope

In analysing corporate strategy it is useful to look more closely at the decisions truck makers have made with respect to the following aspects of competitive scope:

- *Segment scope*: in which product segments is the company specialised?
- *Industry scope*: in which industries is the company active?
- *Vertical scope*: what is the attitude towards vertical integration, backward as well as forward?
- *Geographical scope*: which geographic strategy is followed; what is the relevant geographical market?

Industry and segment scope

A basic feature of the industry is that firms tend to diversify into similar activities, for example:

- Cars (DB, Fiat–Iveco, RVI, Volvo and Saab–Scania)
- Aerospace (DB, Fiat–Iveco, Volvo, Saab–Scania, M.A.N.)
- Buses (DB, RVI, Volvo, Scania, M.A.N., DAF)

Volvo has interests in almost every field of transportation: road, water, and air transport. Several manufacturers, among which Scania is a typical example, undertake activities in the engineering and machinery industries. DAF is the least diversified company, while Daimler-Benz is clearly at the other end of the spectrum. DB has spread its activities into many areas: electronics, aerospace, space industry, pharmaceuticals and engineering, in addition to the car industry. According to DB this diversification provides a broad basis for extensive research and development with many synergetic effects for all activities. It should be noted that five of the seven manufacturers (if M.A.N. is considered as being independent from Volkswagen) are not only competitors in the truck industry but also in the car industry.

There are also considerable differences in the range of products offered by truck makers in Europe. Some manufacturers, like Daimler-Benz, RVI and Iveco, offer a wide range of products in all size and weight classes and applications. Other manufacturers like M.A.N., DAF and Scania concentrate their efforts on the segment of heavy-weight trucks. This difference is very marked and should therefore best be combined with other strategic dimensions to understand the differences in overall strategy and performance of the major European truck makers.

Vertical scope

Volvo and Scania are known as heavily vertically integrated firms while, on the other hand, Iveco is often described as an assembler. Both Volvo and certainly Scania are successful manufacturers and their policy of vertical integration is often presented as one of the explanatory elements behind this success. Daimler-Benz seems more recently to have decided to bring some activities in-house (such as gearboxes).

Volvo's in-house added value on a truck amounts to 60 per cent of total value. According to H. Dubbelman this percentage declines to about 30 per cent for a manufacturer who performs only assembly operations. Again, it should be stressed that these figures are only tentative estimates.

Quality control is often mentioned as an explanation for extensive vertical integration. If a manufacturer decides to keep production of components in-house this creates the possibility of a solid integration of these parts into the total truck. Already, at an early stage of research and development, full synergies between components can be controlled which provides the basis for a reliable and high-quality truck. Sub-contracting is often less expensive, but when economies of scale in component production can be achieved, this cost disadvantage may quickly disappear.

In view of the different scale economies in component development and manufacturing (see p. 113), a large production volume therefore appears as a prerequisite for the successful integration of the different sub-activities. Alternatively, integrated truck manufacturers could try to sell part of their components to independent smaller manufacturers. To some extent, this seems to be the strategy followed by M.A.N. in coupling the supply of components to the development of co-operation agreements with smaller specialised commercial vehicle manufacturers.

In Figure 3.17 the degree of vertical integration is plotted against the range of products offered by the major European truck makers. A full-range producer who has adopted a strategy of vertical integration is, on the one hand, forced into higher investment but, on the other, may benefit from scope economies across the different products because of the introduction of standardised components.

Substantial changes are also taking place on the forward side of the business system. The dealer and service networks are of vital importance for a truck manufacturer. With 1992 coming, the presence of a dealer and service network throughout Europe is essential. The structure of such networks will be different from the current networks. Multifunctional dealer stations are likely to emerge in which not only regular service and maintenance are available but also those activities that in the past decade

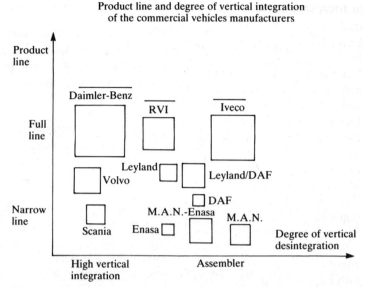

Product line and degree of vertical integration
of the commercial vehicles manufacturers

Note: The size of the squares represents the European market share

Figure 3.17 Vertical integration and product line (Source: adapted from Simaey, 1987, and Reekmans, 1989)

were provided in stations outside the network. Examples of such activities are tyre services. It is expected that activities that were left to these 'niche-stations' will again be integrated in the regular dealer networks. The emergence of large multifunctional dealer and service stations throughout the European market is likely to be accompanied by a substantial decrease in the number of dealers. These larger dealers will be supplied directly from the manufacturer without importers' intermediation. Further standardisation in truck components will increase the efficiency of such a system.

Geographical scope

In the first section of this chapter it was argued that several European truck makers are very dependent on their national market. This situation, in anticipation of further European integration, seems to be changing markedly (see Figure 3.18). For instance, M.A.N. restructured its internal organisation to be able to meet the challenge of a single market. After the recession of the early 1980s M.A.N. became extremely dependent on its national market, but qualifies now – after the takeover of ENASA and Steyr – as a pan-European manufacturer. DAF which traditionally has acted more as a European firm, has broadened its European scope through merging with Leyland in the United Kingdom. In doing so, it now considers its home to be in three markets: the Netherlands, Belgium and the United Kingdom. Iveco, being Europe's number two, has a solid basis, both in Italy and the United Kingdom. DB and Volvo are companies that developed a global strategy in which Europe is considered as the main sub-market. Volvo has restructured itself into European, American and rest-of-the-world divisions, thus creating the infrastructure that is necessary to challenge Daimler-Benz as the world's largest truck manufacturer; co-operation with General Motors might enhance this position. RVI has interests in North America (MACK) and a relatively strong presence in Africa (the former colonial regions), but Europe firmly continues to be the core market. Finally, Scania appears as a European firm, specialised in the heavy range.

Some manufacturers are making prudent attempts to acquire further interests in Eastern Europe. Daimler-Benz is engaged in a joint venture with Fap Famos in Yugoslavia. M.A.N. has reached an agreement with

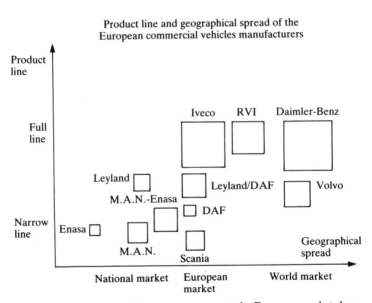

Note: The size of the squares represents the European market share

Figure 3.18 Product line and geographical spread (Source: adapted from Simaey, 1987, and Reekmans, 1989)

the Soviet firm Belavtomaz concerning the supply of M.A.N. engines and DAF started a service network in Eastern Europe.

Future developments

This section attempts to combine the findings of the preceding sections with the views of experts/managers of the major European truck makers about the future development of the European truck industry. Clearly, in the previous section it appeared that there is a tendency towards more concentration in the industry. It seems logical therefore to concentrate primarily on this feature. Scale economies in production and distribution, and the fact that R & D is becoming more and more important in the truck industry, are often cited as the major reasons behind this concentration. To create sufficient financial assets for extensive R & D programmes, size (diversification) and market share seem to be major factors. For relatively small manufacturers, such as DAF and M.A.N., this poses serious problems. Co-operation agreements with ENASA (Cabtec), the merger with Leyland and more recently the joint venture with RVI indicate that DAF is indeed seeking external help. M.A.N. has adopted a similar strategy (see p. 102), although it should be noted that M.A.N. has potential access to the technological knowledge of DB through its narrow relationship with Daimler-Benz. More generally, the different views expressed by the industry experts led to the formulation of three scenarios which, as will become clear, may be interpreted as consecutive stages in the development of the industry.

Three scenarios

Scenario One

In the first scenario experts expect that six to seven manufacturers will survive. In fact, there will be no shake out, neither will there be any mergers among the big seven. *Ad hoc* co-operation agreements over R & D activities may arise to make it possible for each manufacturer to conduct the necessary research. When, for instance, DAF and RVI get involved in a joint R & D programme for the development of a new van, they may continue to compete at the same time in the heavy-weight truck segment. In this scenario there is no room left for non-EC manufacturers. The Japanese–European co-operation in the car industry does not extend to the truck industry. Japanese firms are not able to overcome the major entry barriers: the different specifications of a European truck and the lack of a comprehensive dealer network. There is no real competition from imports from outside the Common Market, but the threat remains. The time horizon of this scenario extends from the next five to seven years.

Scenario Two

A true Europeanisation will occur in the second scenario. Manufacturers who would survive in the first scenario because of a profound national basis are integrated into three to four large pan-European companies. In this scenario these three to four large manufacturers compete in an integrated Common Market in which there may be competition from imports, basically in the lower segment of light commercial vehicles. These European firms would increasingly invest abroad, especially in the American market. A real globalisation of the industry would not occur, however.

Scenario Three

This scenario is the most globalised scenario. Truck manufacturers in the United States and Japan will co-operate on R & D and eventually on production with the remaining three to four European firms. As such, this scenario is strongly based on the global truck concept. Each major region in the world will continue to have its own specific needs for road transport. These needs will be dealt with through customisation, without having to sacrifice the benefits from scale economies in the development and manufacture of key components. The European firms in this scenario operate on a global basis.

In the three scenarios there was no explicit mention of the role of Eastern European firms, such as Tatra (Cz), RABA (Yu), ROMAN (Ro., licensed by M.A.N.) and Zil (USSR) as the better known manufacturers in that region. Most experts excluded them because of their poor technological basis and financial potential, and the absence of a comprehensive dealer and service network.

Most experts agreed, however, that Eastern Europe could provide a new market for the European truck industry. Co-operation with the truck industry in Eastern Europe could include the transfer of knowledge and enhance the industrial development of this area. For the European truck industry this could mean new truck demand and, in the short run, attractive location conditions to open new plants. Again, co-ordination at Community level is required. If national governments adopt their own 'Ost-politik' this could induce inequality in the competitiveness of the European truck industry.

Concentration in the truck industry and its impact on performance

In a recent contribution Jacquemin, Buigues and Ilzkowitz (*European Economy*, No. 40, May 1989) have developed a method of establishing whether concentration through merger or takeover in a particular industry is likely to enhance efficiency and/or reduce competition. In analysing the impact of increased concentration they use four indicators, as follows:

1. *Demand growth* In a market with low growth of demand concentration is more likely to reduce competition.
2. *Import penetration* With strong competition from imports concentration is less 'dangerous' than in a protected, closed market. In this respect it is important to consider whether globalisation takes place or not. This could mean that a different geographical market than the EC market should be considered.
3. *Economies of scale* If substantial economies of scale exist, concentration may enhance efficiency.
4. *Technological content* In R & D-intensive industries concentration could provide efficiency gains in the R & D area: economies of scale, financing, etc.

Indicators (1) and (2) show whether there is a substantial change in the competitiveness in the relevant market, and (3) and (4) point out possible efficiency gains.

Within this Figure 3.19 four different categories emerge:

1. Industries in which mergers could induce a reduction of competition without any prospect of efficiency gains (I, III).
2. Industries in which mergers are not likely to have an effect on competition nor enhance efficiency (II, III).
3. Industries in which mergers could increase efficiency without reducing competition (II, IV).
4. Industries in which mergers could enhance efficiency as well as bring forward a reduction in competition (I, IV).

By characterising the truck industry with the help of the four indicators – demand, import penetration, economies of scale and technological content – some tentative conclusions as to the effect of increasing concentration emerge.

Demand

As Figure 3.15 showed, Western European truck registrations are forecast to increase slowly until at least 1993, with a temporary decline in 1989/90. According to H. Dubbelman this decline could induce substan-

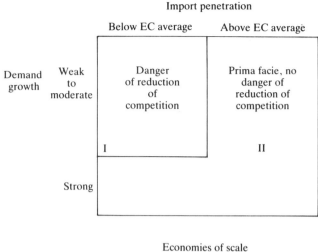

Figure 3.19   Indicators of the likely impact of increased concentration
Source: Buigues, Jacquemin and Ilzkovitz (1988)

tial problems for those manufacturers who have only recently recovered from large financial losses in the 1980s. Deregulation of road transport is likely to enhance efficiency (i.e. fewer trucks required) but increased competition among hauliers could, as was concluded earlier, create a competitive demand.

The US industry can serve as an example of what the effects of deregulation are on the transport and truck industry. According to several observers, deregulation in the United States increased efficiency and pushed inefficient hauliers out of the market, irrespective of their size. Structurally, there has been a polarisation towards large (interstate) firms and small local distribution companies. Entry was relatively high: instead of the usual 3,000 entrants per year, 18,000 new firms entered the market between 1980 and 1985.

Also increasing environmental demands, in order to reduce pollution, are likely to diminish the technological life cycle of a truck.

It remains to be seen, however, if this growth of demand will come in time for the financially vulnerable smaller firms, which face increasing competition from manufacturers who have developed a global network. With further deregulation of the transport market in the EC, some segments, like part-load shipments, may become dominated by large international hauliers who are developing pan-European networks to provide full service to their customers. These larger groups would gain bargaining power in their dealings with truck manufacturers and thus force prices down to lower levels.

Import penetration

In view of the characteristics of the products, it is not surprising to find that import penetration from truck makers outside the EC is very low. But also *within* Europe, as shown in the introduction to this chapter, import penetration is also rather low, with nationally based companies dominating the national market. A threat may come from the entrance of new foreign suppliers in the EC market. But, as emphasised before, the cost of developing a dealer and service network is considered as a major obstacle for foreign firms to penetrate the market. However, along with changes in distribution, when multifunctional dealer/service centres arise, some dealers might be left without a manufacturer to serve. E. Enschedé considers this as a real possibility for Japanese manufacturers to acquire their own dealer network if further co-operation with European manufacturers should fail. Important in this context is the observation that in spite of the fact that the number of truck manufacturers has decreased significantly over the past decade (from about fourteen in the late 1970s to seven at this moment) the number of dealers has stayed almost the same.

The possible entry or exports of trucks from Eastern Europe seem to be a less serious threat in the short run. Eastern European trucks may be attractive in terms of initial costs to acquire them. But again, a dealer and service network is missing, and from a technological point of view there is an estimated gap of about fifteen years. The introduction of just-in-time systems has shifted storage from company warehouses to trucks, thus also shifting the storage risk to hauliers. Reliability and efficiency in transport are of vital importance for the competitive position of a haulier. With respect to these considerations, Western European trucks are much more competitive than their Eastern European counterparts.

Finally, it should be observed that the major Western European truck makers already compete in world markets, which has many direct and indirect consequences for their strategic behaviour in the Western

European market. These interactions will undoubtedly grow in importance along with further globalisation in the strategies of Western European truck makers.

Economies of scale

In a capital-intensive industry economies of scale often play an important role. In the preceding sections it was shown how these scale economies differ substantially according to the different components (axles, engines, cabin, etc.). There are indications that the truck industry has not fully exploited scale economies in production. Standardisation in component specifications will undoubtedly make it easier for manufacturers to exploit these scale economies. It follows that scale economies will play an increasing role in the competitive process. In the long run (10–15 years) globalisation is likely to take place and volume in production will be more than ever a major competitive tool. If European firms want to compete successfully with Japanese and American manufacturers, the development of efficient large-scale production techniques will be of major importance.

Technological content

Co-operation agreements among truck makers have increased significantly in recent years. This was largely due to a substantial rise in R & D costs and the need to invest in large R & D programmes. There is no sign that these costs are likely to fall in the future. Two aspects are of crucial importance in these R & D programmes: environmental demands, and the demand for more efficient trucks from hauliers. Safety, noise limitations and emission standards will become more stringent and require new technological developments in all the major components of a truck. Efficiency and reliability are the most important competitive tools for a competitive haulier in a deregulated transport market. Manufacturers are expected to deliver trucks that meet these demands.

With regard to these efficiency considerations, integration of trucks in integrated logistics systems will be very important. It is obvious that only trucks with 'on-board' computer systems are able to fit in such concepts. The importance of electronics in this area is likely to increase and manufacturers who do not develop activities in this area will have to look for reliable and qualified sub-suppliers. Co-operation among manufacturers could provide a better basis for undertaking risky R & D activities in the application of electronics in the creation of a new generation of trucks.

Quality considerations are often mentioned as the major reason why many of the truck manufacturers are seeking further vertical integration.

But again, large volume is a prerequisite in order to adopt such a policy of vertical integration successfully, which forces the company into making higher R & D expenditures to develop the different components.

Conclusion

On the basis of the foregoing elements, while the truck industry offers considerable opportunities for potential efficiency gains through mergers and acquisitions, further concentration implies a considerable potential threat to competition. There is an arguable case for increased concentration when we look at the aspects of economies of scale in combination with the increasing technological content of truck manufacturing. The relevant market is changing fast from nation-led to Europe-wide and increased concentration could help European manufacturers to compete successfully in world markets. However, the necessity of developing or acquiring a dealer and service network in order to penetrate the market, seems to act as a serious barrier to enter the European single market. Further consolidation of the industry into fewer manufacturers and the less optimistic forecasts about demand do cause concern about possible anti-competitive procedures in the near future.

References

Buigues, P., Jacquemin, A. and Ilzkovitz, F. (1988), Horizontal Mergers and Competition Policy in the European Community, European Economy, 73 pp.
County NatWest Truck Overview (1989), 13 October, pp. 13–23.
FEBIAC/Bulletin d'information (1984), 'Immatriculations de vehicules à moteur', No. 6, 20 February, pp. 727–30.
Financial Times (1985), 'Commercial Vehicles', section III, 29 November, pp. I–VIII.
Hinterhuber, H. H. and Kirchebner, M. (1986), 'The analysis of strategic groups of firms', *European Management Journal*, vol. 4, no. 2, pp. 95–103.
Instituut voor wegtransport (1986), 'Ondernemingen van geroepsgoederenvervoer over de weg in België sinds 1965', Brussels (April), 25 pp.
International Automotive Review (1985), 'Europe's truck industry: manufacturers changing performance and corporate activity', 2nd quarter, pp. 94–108.
Jaarverslagen DAF Trucks, Nissan, Volvo, Saab–Scania, M.A.N., Iveco, Mercedes-Benz.
Ministry of Industry (1988), *Swedish industry and industrial policy*, p. 88.
Muller, J. and Owen, N. (1981), 'Determinants of structural change in the European commercial vehicles industry: scale, coordination and vertical integration effects', mimeo.
Ohmae, K. (1985), 'Becoming a triad power: the new global corporation', *McKinsey Quarterly Review*, spring, pp. 2–25.

Pearce, C. (1985), *The West European Truck Industry, Automotive Special Report, No 3*, London: *The Economist* Publications Ltd, 107 pp.
Porter, M. E. (1980), *Competitive Strategy: Techniques for analyzing industries and competitors*, New York: The Free Press, 396 pp.
Reekmans, M. (1989), Industriele analyse van de Europese bedrijfswagenindustrie en toekomstperspectieven, Katholieke Universiteit Leuven, Department Economie, Leuven, 121 pp.
Rhys, G. (1984), 'Heavy commercial vehicles: a decade of change', *National Westminster Bank Quarterly Review*, August, pp. 25–35.
Scherer, F. M. (1980), *Industrial market structure and economic performance*, Boston, 2nd edn.
Sharman, G. (1989), 'What 1992 means for logistics', *McKinsey Quarterly Review*, spring, pp. 104–20.
Simaey, J. (1987), Studie van de Europese sector der bedrijfsvoertuigen, Katholieke Universiteit Leuven, Department Toegepaste Economische Wetenschappen, Leuven, 172 pp.
Truck en Transport Management (1987), 9 September.

Notes

This report benefited from discussions with the following experts:

- H. H. Dietz, Board of Directors DAF Trucks N.V., Eindhoven
- A. S. P. S. Van Hoogstraten, Marketing service department Mercedes-Benz Nederland B.V., Utrecht
- H. R. Dubbelman, Manager Volvo Bedrijfswagens B.V., 's Gravenhage
- E. L. Enschede, Marketing manager Renault Bedrijfswagens Nederland B.V., Vianen
- D. Van Tol, Vice-President M.A.N.–VW Truck & Bus B.V., Vianen
- L. Glaumann, President Scania Nederland B.V., Zwolle
- H. C. Van Leuven, Marketing manager and sales operation services Iveco Nederland B.V., Apeldoorn.

Furthermore, the author would like to thank Rita Sepelie and Peter Van Dijcke for their competent assistance in the final preparation of this paper. This report was written before the decision of the German anti-trust authorities not to approve the M.A.N.-ENASA merger. ENASA now belongs to the IVECO group.

4

The railway industry

David G. Mayes

Introduction

At first blush it would appear that if any industry is going to reap major efficiency gains from the completion of the European Single Market it will be the railway equipment industry. In the past almost all the purchasers have been nationalised industries or local public authorities which have tended to buy locally in relatively small quantities. There are substantial economies of scale available in some parts of the industry, so efficiency gains can be reaped from increased competition among producers and increases in size of production runs as markets become European rather than national.

However, despite enormous activity in forming linkages between companies in the supplying industries, major fragmentation of the market is likely to continue because of the structure of demand. In the first place, the purchasers are largely unchanged and, with the exception of special projects like the Channel Tunnel, are likely to remain so. That said, the trend is clearly towards closer international co-operation, with the proposals for developing a European high-speed passenger network and a better international freight system all leaning in that direction. Specialised equipment apart, there are as yet no clear indications that many major railway authorities will be purchasing their main equipment from suppliers outside their own countries. A glimpse of the possible way forward is offered by the experience of British Rail and London Transport, which have been operating an open policy for several years. Even in these cases the acceptance of major foreign tenders has only occurred slowly.

Secondly, although track may link one country with another this disguises very considerable incompatibilities between the various systems. The gauge is different in the Iberian peninsula, although ambitious plans are in progress to change major parts of this. The United Kingdom and Ireland have a different structural gauge; not all track is electrified; France, West Germany, the Netherlands and Belgium each have different electric power units and so on. The pattern of travel is primarily national and will remain so, although cross-border freight, commuting and travel will be encouraged by the single market.

There is an enormous sunk cost in existing systems, which in most cases will mean that the costs of changing far outweigh the gains for purchasers from lower prices resulting from larger-scale production of common 'European' equipment. There is thus little incentive for rapid change. However, economies in the production of many components are not only possible but realised already. There are specialist suppliers of brakes, bogies and other smaller components and fittings, whose products are incorporated by several final suppliers. Indeed, some final suppliers really only run a complex assembly operation and do little original manufacture as such. It is only with new measures like extensions to the high-speed network that a more 'European' railway may be developed, as is clearly illustrated by the major investments in the Spanish railway system.

The foregoing remarks all relate primarily to the national rail networks but the railway systems in the member states have a second component, the mass transit systems of urban areas. Light railways within cities have even less reason to have regard for compatibility with other countries, as they do not usually connect with them. However, there is a rise in the popularity of these systems and, by the same token, new, physically distinct, light railways do not have to show the same regard to compatibility with existing equipment, track and established patterns of operation. Hence, local authorities are more inclined to purchase systems which already operate elsewhere, thus increasing the opportunity for reductions in cost and cross-border purchases.

The picture of the railway supply industry painted only a few years ago has become rapidly outdated because the European railways are going through a period of renaissance. After undergoing decline in the 1960s and 1970s investment in railways is increasing rapidly for a variety of reasons, only one of which is 1992. As a result, the 20–50 per cent underutilisation of capacity estimated in the Cecchini Report has now been substantially reduced. The short-run pressures to reduce capacity to enable remaining firms to make a reasonable profit have consequently fallen. Hence, despite the major changes in the pattern of ownership of the railway equipment industry, there has as yet been rather less change in the location of production or rationalisation of its structure. However, it is early days yet and mergers and acquisitions made with restructuring in mind will go a number of years before the changes are fully implemented. In any case, part of the current upsurge in demand is cyclical, so the problem of overcapacity will again rear its head and companies which are doing less well will be forced to restructure. The change in the industry is not likely to occur all at once before the end of 1992 but gradually, as the behaviour of purchasers changes and suppliers have time to react to their changed circumstances.

The typical evolutionary pattern of the past has been to keep firms going during downturns in the domestic market by aggressive bidding for overseas contracts in the developing world, which could be offset by government assistance and high margins on domestic contracts. Now, with increasing competition within Europe, export contracts will have to be more viable in their own right as there will be less opportunity to offset losses. The immediate losers in this process would be the developing countries if contract prices rise. There will also be some loss of business for European producers in so far as contracts are now won by third countries, Japan, Korea and the Eastern bloc for example. Since spare capacity will still have to be held to meet peak demand in Europe, the costs of that idle capacity will have to be borne by someone and will hence tend to fall on the contracts which are let. It is only by spreading the work better among a smaller number of European companies that costs can clearly be reduced. The current surge in demand will postpone that adjustment.

Currently we are a long way from any 'single market'. There are few overseas parallels to look at to see how such a single market might evolve. The US system, with its great distances and domination by freight, is not comparable. The existence of only two major producers in General Electric and General Motors, with a limited product range, is not in itself a good indicator. Japan, with its predominantly passenger railway and a number of separate railway companies, might provide a better comparison. Australia with three major differences in gauge may suggest how compatibility can be slowly approached. The clear message from Australia is that heavy investment is required. Give the lack of profitability of most European railway companies this implies that the major impetus for more rapid progress towards European integration will have to come from government funds unless demand continues to rise strongly.

In the sections which follow, the first sets out the structure of the railway equipment industry and the railway equipment market and examines how it has changed in recent years. The second examines the forces for change in the industry imparted by the 1992 programme. The next two sections explore the implications for the internal and external strategies of firms in the industry, tracing them out for the whole of the value-added chain, from technological change and component supply to distribution and finance. Some case studies are then explored in detail and the final section concludes.

The structure and recent history of the rail and railway equipment industries

Rail transport

The state of the European railway equipment industry is intimately bound up with the state of European railways. Following explosive growth in the nineteenth century the importance of the railway in the transport system has peaked in the face of competition from roads and, more recently, air. The share of railways in total transport has continued to fall in recent years (see Table 4.1). Both passengers and freight can be transported more quickly from origin to the destination of the journey by road when the distances are relatively short, because the track of the railway system is fixed and runs between a series of fixed stopping points. In many cases goods require transhipment by road at both ends of the trip, from the factory to the rail head and from the rail head to the customer. Only where the two are conveniently sited, or the goods heavy or the distances long will rail transport show a clear advantage. This helps

Table 4.1 Percentage of transport using railways[1]

	Passengers		Freight	
Country	1979	1987	1979	1987
Belgium	9.5	7.2	26.2	20.0
GB	8.3	7.2	14.8	9.8
Denmark	4.3	7.9	6.7	6.7
France	10.5	9.4	33.9	23.9
W Germany	6.7	6.6	27.8	22.8
Italy	8.6	7.2	13.5	8.7
Netherlands	6.3	5.6	5.7	4.8
Portugal	10.6	8.1	–	–
Spain	10.0	8.5	8.0	7.2
Total	8.9	7.6	19.4	14.7

Source: *Europe in 1994*

Note: [1]excluding metro

explain the importance of rail travel in France and West Germany (see Table 4.1). Passenger travel is further assailed when it comes to long distances because, despite the high cost of air travel, time becomes more important; return journeys can be completed in a day which would otherwise have to be accomplished over several days incurring not just the cost of people's time but overnight accommodation as well.

There is, however, one exception to this picture, which is travel within urban areas, whose roads have become increasingly congested. Here the trend is towards expanding the rail system, particularly with the use of light rail and underground systems. With frequent stops and faster rates of travel the disadvantages of the rail system can be offset, aided in many cases by having an integrated passenger transport system which brings together buses, light rail, underground and conventional railways. On the whole, however, railways have been uneconomic and have had to be subsidised to continue in operation. In general, this has meant that they have also become publicly owned and operated. The railway equipment industry thus faces a set of national and municipal purchasers who face clear financial constraints.

Although orders are placed by the railway companies, demand for railway equipment is clearly a function of the usage of the system by customers, and it is also affected by the pace of technical change. Higher-speed travel, which has been facilitated by advances in a wide range of technology from traction and bogies to signalling, has arrested the decline and promises growth for the future aided by improvements in quality relating to comfort, timeliness and the other services available, such as catering. The outlook for the railway industry and hence its suppliers has changed during the 1980s. While goods traffic has remained stagnant (see Table 4.2), passenger traffic has risen slowly in all the member states, except Belgium, Luxembourg and Portugal, since 1980. It now looks as if there will be much healthier growth over the next few years both in longer-distance travel and within urban areas. All this requires investment which implies increased sales by the railway equipment industry as the new services are provided – in many cases, sales involving considerable technical advance.

There are two additional forces for change which are affecting the industry. The first is major new projects, the foremost of which is the Channel Tunnel, whose construction cost is now estimated to be 10bn ECU, making it one of the largest projects in the world, dwarfing most of the other rail projects in Europe. Added to this will be the new high-speed links on both sides of the Channel, which are also major projects, sufficiently major in the case of the United Kingdom that it is not at present clear how much of the line can be built in the face of the high cost and environmental constraints. Elsewhere Spain has made the major decision to convert its main network to the same gauge as the rest

Table 4.2 Rail transport, 1980–86

Country	Passenger km (bn)		Freight (bn t km)	
	1980	1986	1983	1986
Belgium	7.0	6.1	2.4	2.3
Denmark	3.8	4.5	0.6	0.6
France	54.5	59.9	39.2	34.8
W Germany	38.4	41.4	34.5	36.4
Greece	1.5	2.0	0.3	0.3
Ireland	1.0	1.1	0.6	0.6
Italy	40.0	40.5	6.9	7.0
Luxembourg	0.2	0.2	0.1	0.1
Netherlands	8.9	8.9	1.0	1.0
Portugal	6.1	5.8	1.0	1.1
Spain	13.5	15.6	10.6	8.8
UK	30.3	30.8	17.9	17.7
EC(12)	204.7	216.8	115.0	110.8

Source: Eurostat, *Transport and Communications Statistical Yearbook* 1970–86

of the continental EC. The second force for change is the economic integration of Europe itself, which by reducing barriers at the border will enable the smoother flow of freight as well as passengers. In so far as this encourages trade, a portion of this increase will fall on railways – a share which may be increased by governmental encouragement of rail rather than road travel through regulation.

The railway equipment industry

The railway equipment industry is complex. As is shown in Table 4.3 the supply can be broken down into locomotives, other rolling stock – passenger coaches, trucks, etc. – and track and trackside equipment, particularly signalling. Although railways themselves tend to buy completed vehicles, the final suppliers may do little more than assemble a set of major components, such as traction unit, control system and bogies from elsewhere. Hence, to form a proper view of the industry these component suppliers, which are often small and highly specialised, also need to be considered. They may not fall under the specific NACE heading 362 which covers the industry.

In the world as a whole, track improvements and new lines provide about a quarter to a third of total expenditure, but within Europe in the past, rolling stock, both locomotives and drawn vehicles, tend to form an important component of expenditure. The Channel Tunnel, high-speed network and gauge change in Spain are changing that. Trackwork is generally undertaken by large, usually national, construction and civil

Table 4.3 The pattern of railway investment at the end of 1986 ($m.)

Country	Locomotives	Passenger coaches	Freight wagons	New lines	Track improvements	Electrification	Signalling	Other	Total
Belgium	–	22	8	–³	87	39	38	53	247
Denmark	3	19	2	–	10	21	10	47	112
France	–	–	–	509	–	–	–	1,122	1,632
West Germany	6	–	–	1,115	405	26	92	1,414	3,052
Greece	–	11	11	–	29	–	6	18	81
Ireland	–	23	–	–	–	–	3	1	27
Italy	–	–	–	–	–³	–	–	–	–
Luxembourg	4	2	2	–	–	4	5	6	19
Netherlands	7	59	7	51	75	10	31	89	326
Portugal	8	17	7	–	22	2	5	55	115
Spain	–	102	11	–	156	35	38	276	626
UK	19	170	19	–	–	111	121	236	676
(EC Twelve	47	425	67	1,675	784	248	344	3,317	6,913)
World¹ total	645	894	858	2,288	2,497	683	689	6,293	14,848
Total (1988)²	705	1,992	576	1,664	2,066	350	536	8,164	16,053

Notes: ¹44 main countries excluding USSR, China, Canada and US   ²October 1988 ($m.)   ³less than $0.5m., otherwise no figures are available where none are given

Source: International Railway Journal. January 1987/9

engineering companies. These may have interests in other trackside equipment. Balfour-Beatty in the United Kingdom, for example, have acquired Henry Boot Railway Engineering. Links with the provision of electrification and signalling equipment are common, through companies such as Hawker-Siddeley in the United Kingdom.

Most of the industrialised countries have a capability for producing locomotives, other rolling stock, and trackside equipment and constructing the track itself. On the whole they supply their own domestic markets, trade between them, except in specialist items, being uncommon. They also supply the developing world where most of the new lines are being built. This export market plays an important role for most producers, especially those in the smaller countries, because domestic demand for new equipment tends to be intermittent, with orders for several units on each occasion. Producers therefore had to have the capacity to meet these peaks in demand. While there is a steady requirement for repair and maintenance this was rarely sufficient to fill the gaps between peaks. It was therefore worthwhile to bid aggressively for export contracts provided they covered the marginal costs. Indeed, given that domestic markets were protected it was possible to recoup losses on overseas contracts from the domestic markets, and some suppliers have averred that their competitors have had covert agreements with their public sector purchasers to enable them to obtain subsidised export contracts.

In 1986 there were approximately 100 companies in the world involved in substantial production of railway equipment with actual or potential sales in Europe at the time of the inception of the Single Market programme, as set out in Table 4.4 (the three Chinese companies are shown because of their size not because of their current plausibility as suppliers). UNIFE in *Panorama of EC Industry 1989* suggest there are 85 manufacturers in total in the Community: 17 locomotives, 44 rolling stock, 24 both. We have identified 60 and a further 20 elsewhere in Europe outside the Soviet Union. The countries with strong industries within the EC were France, West Germany, and the United Kingdom and to a lesser extent Italy and Belgium. However, Sweden and Switzerland are also significant players and with the merger of ASEA and Brown-Boveri created the largest supplier in Europe.

Adding up the sheer number of firms is misleading as this gives no indication of size. The structure of the industry and its market is outlined in Table 4.5. Output statistics in the Community are only partial. Table 4.5 (e) suggests that the French industry is the largest, although there is substantial production in Italy, West Germany and, to a lesser extent, Spain. Using more comprehensive employment figures, shown in Table 4.5 (f) it appears that the French, German, Italian and UK industries are of equal size. However, this takes no account of productivity and if we

Table 4.4 Railway equipment suppliers: vehicles and parts, 1987

Country	Company	Details (where known)
European Community		
Belgium	1 ACEC	locos and rolling stock, electrical
	2 BN	locos and rolling stock, mechanical
	3 BREC	wagons and bogies
	4 CMI	locos
France	5 Alsthom	all main areas
	6 AFR	
	7 ANF Industrie	diesel, elec. locos, coaches
	8 CFD	diesel locos and units
	9 Francorail	group includes firms 10–13
	10 Carel et Fouche	wide capability among group
	11 Creusot Ivoire	
	12 De Dietrich	coaches, bogies, etc.
	13 Jeumont Schneider	
	14 Matra	unmanned rapid transit
	15 Remafer	special wagons
	16 SFL	shunting locos
	17 Soulé	railcars and passenger coaches
West Germany	18 AEG	electrical
	19 Diema	shunters
	20 Duewag	passenger cars/light rail
	21 Kaelbe-Gemeinder	diesel locos
	22 Knorr-Bremse	
	23 Krauss-Maffei	locos Maglev (TRI)
	24 Krupp-MAK	locos, some coaches
	25 Linke-Hoffman-Busch	coaches
	26 M.A.N.	
	27 MBB	light vehicles
	28 Siemens	electric and diesel electric
	29 Talbot	railcars, passenger, freight
	30 Thyssen–Henschel	locos
	31 Waggon-Union	freight cars
Italy	32 Ansaldo	locos (signals)
	33 Badoni	shunting locos
	34 Breda	sets
	35 CFC	coaches, wagons
	36 Ferrosud	locos, coaches, wagons
	37 Fiat	wide range
	38 Firema	locos, underground
	39 OMS	locos, units, coaches, wagons
	40 Reggiane	
	41 Soccini	
	42 SOFER	locos, units passenger coaches
	43 TIBB (part of ABB)	locos
Spain	44 Ateinsa	locos, sets, wagons
	45 Babcock & Wilcox	several
	46 CAF	locos, wagons, coaches
	47 Macosa	locos, coaches
	48 Maquinista	elec./diesel locos, sets
	49 Tafesa	rolling stock
UK	50 Barclay	shunting locos
	51 Balfour-Beatty	
	52 BREL	rolling stock
	53 Brush (Hawker-Siddeley)	elec. traction
	54 GEC	locos
	55 Hunslet	light locos
	56 Metro-Cammell	rapid transit, underground, etc.

Country	Company	Details (where known)
	57 MLE	
	58 Powell-Duffryn	wagons
	59 Procor	special wagons
	60 Standard	wagons
Netherlands	61 Holec	elec. equipment
Portugal	62 Sorefame	locos, units, coaches
Other Europe		
Austria	63 Plasscher-Teurer	tracklaying and maintenance
	64 SGP	rolling stock
East Germany	65 Ammendorf	passenger, restaurant cars
	66 Bautzen	coaches
	67 Dessau	wagons
Finland	68 Rautaruukki	special wagons
	69 Valmet	locos
Hungary	70 Ganz Electric	
	71 Ganz Navag	diesel locos
Norway	72 Strommens	elec., diesel, passenger, freight
Poland	73 Kolmex	
Romania	74 Electroimport Export	
Sweden	75 AGV	rolling stock
	76 Alusuisse	aluminium components
	77 ASEA	electric traction
	78 Kalmar	locos, wagons, coaches
Switzerland	79 Brown-Boveri	electric traction
	80 Schindler	rolling stock, light rail
	81 SIG	rolling stock
	82 SLM	locos, railcars
Other		
Australia	83 Clyde	locos
	84 Comeng	locos, coaches, light rail
	85 Goinan	locos, wagons, coaches
Canada	86 Bombardier	locos, bogies
	87 Hawker-Siddeley	
	88 MLW	
China	89 Beijing	locos
	90 Changchun	passenger cars
	91 China National Railway Loco and Rolling Stock Co.	
Japan	92 Alna-Koki	coaches, wagons
	93 Fuji	sets, coaches, wagons
	94 Hitachi	locos
	95 Kawasaki	locos, coaches
	96 Kinki-Sharyo	light rail cars
	97 Mitsubishi Electric	electric locos and units
	98 Tokyu	rail cars
	99 Toshiba	locos, railcars
Korea	100 Daewoo	
	101 Hyundai	elec. motors
US	102 GE	locos
	103 GM	locos
	104 Thrail	freight cars
	105 Westinghouse	elec. equipment

Note: this list is not comprehensive but covers most of the main players

Source: W. S. Atkins, *Jane's World Railways*

Table 4.5   The structure of production and trade

(a) Main indicators for railway rolling stock in EC[1] (bn ECU ('000s))

	1980	1983	1987	(other countries excluded)
Apparent consumption	1.4	2.5	2.1	UK, Spain, Portugal
Net export earnings	0.3	0.5	0.4	Spain, Portugal
Production (excl. parts)	1.7	3.0	2.5	UK
Employment	(68.2)	(66.7)	(51.6)	UK, Netherlands

(b) Trends in EC[2] production by product (bn ECU)

	1980	1983	1987
Locomotives	0.26	0.68	0.66
Passenger coaches	0.91	1.70	1.31
Goods wagons	0.52	0.60	0.49

(c) Production and foreign trade (bn ECU (Index))

	1980	1983	1987
Production (current val)	1.68	2.98	2.46
	(100)	(177)	(146)
(constant val)	1.68	2.17·	1.43
	(100)	(129)	(85)
Imports extra EC	0.03	0.05	0.04
	(100)	(152)	(119)
Exports extra EC	0.35	0.52	0.43
	(100)	(148)	(124)
Exports/imports	10.90	10.70	11.40

(d) Market trend by product in EC[3] (bn ECU)

	1980	1983	1987
Locomotives	0.20	0.56	0.57
Passenger coaches	0.80	1.44	1.06
Goods wagons	0.41	0.73	0.43

(e) 1987 national production by product (m. ECU)

	B–L	Dk	Fr	WG	Gr	Irl	It	Ne	P	Sp	UK	Total
Locomotives	41	0	268	67	0	0	268	0	6	11	–[5]	659
Passenger coaches	70	26	538	217	0	0	247	0	8	203	–	1,310
Goods wagons	18	6	97	191	0	0	140	0	19	21	–	492

(f) 1989 employment ('000s)

	B–L	Dk	Fr	WG	Gr	Irl	It	Ne	P	Sp	UK	Total
	1.1	0.8	12[4]	11[4]	–	–	11.7[4]	2.5	0.7	8	11.5[4]	59

Notes: [1]excluding Luxembourg, Ireland and Greece   [2]excluding UK, Luxembourg, Ireland and Greece   [3]excluding UK, Spain, Portugal, Ireland, Luxembourg and Greece   [4]may be slightly underestimated   [5]figures are not available where none are given

Source: (a)–(e) Panorama of EC Industry, (f) CEGOS-IDET (1989)

assume that differences in manufacturing industry as a whole are replicated in the railway equipment industry this would imply that the German and French industries are the largest in terms of value added followed by the United Kingdom and Italy.

Although General Electric and General Motors in the United States are among the world's largest companies and indeed have significant sales of railway equipment in the United States and third countries, they have little involvement in Europe, except with the sale of private freight locomotives to private purchasers in the United Kingdom (privately owned locomotives and rolling stock can operate on British Rail track) and technical agreements with German producers so that the latter could use American expertise to build diesel-electric locomotives (GM with Thyssen-Henschel and GE with Krupp). GM in particular is the world leader in diesel locomotives with 60 per cent of the market (EC, 1988)[1]. More significant competition comes from the Japanese who have had considerable success in selling to third markets against European competitors. Indeed, one might also look at Daewoo/Hyundai in Korea as a competitive threat in view of their rapid growth and success in developing countries.

The pattern of production and trade within Europe summarised in Tables 4.5 and 4.6 is straightforward and an excellent brief description of the industry is given by UNIFE in *Panorama of EC Industry 1989*. National purchasers have usually bought from national suppliers except when there is no domestic capacity in a particular niche. Thus, for example, the United Kingdom has little experience in light-rail vehicle manufacture so it has tended to order vehicles from foreign suppliers.

Table 4.6 Trade in railway vehicles by OECD countries, 1987 ($bn. percentage)

	World	Exports to EC(12)	non-OECD		Imports[1] from OECD	EC
OECD	2.94	0.45(15)	1.39(47)	France	0.06	0.03(52)
EC	1.40	0.33(24)	0.69(49)	Germany	0.07	0.04(63)
France	0.79	0.06(8)	0.19(24)	Italy	0.07	0.05(66)
W. Germany	0.45	0.19(42)	0.33(73)	UK	0.05	0.04(80)
Italy	0.09	0.01(11)	0.06(67)	Neth	0.10	0.08(80)
UK	0.16	0.03(19)	0.07(63)	Belg–L	0.03	0.03(93)
US	0.35	0.04(11)	0.17(49)	Denmark	0.03	0.03(90)
Japan	0.52	0.00(1)	0.12(23)	Ireland	0.01	0.01(98)
Canada	0.37	0.02(5)	0.30(81)	Portugal	0.01	0.01(91)
				Spain	0.01	0.01(71)

Note: [1]All trade measured by exports, thus all imports from non-OECD sources are omitted

Source: OECD Trade Statistics (NEDO–DOTS databank)

However, there is considerable variety in urban mass transit systems. Thus, despite the lack of light rail, the United Kingdom has strong capability in standard gauge urban transit systems, Metro-Cammell supplying the Hong Kong system.

There are considerable differences between the specialisms of the various European producers, reflecting in large part the differences in the way in which their railways have developed. Thus, the United Kingdom has developed high-speed diesel units and, more recently, electric units to run on conventional track. Indeed, this was complemented by the attempt to build even higher-speed 'tilting' trains, a technique also pursued in Italy, Spain and Sweden. Problems with planning permission, reflected currently in the controversy over the route for the high-speed link through the south of England to the Channel Tunnel, have discouraged the approach followed in France with higher-speed electric units on a special, dedicated, track, as pioneered in Japan twenty years earlier.

In locomotives German companies have specialised in three-phase alternating current technology which helps keep weights low and gives considerable flexibility in enabling both heavy-duty and high-speed operation.

This separation of purchasing by national authorities has helped create a European railway system which is fragmented. Although there is a developed schedule of long-distance trains which run across international frontiers – France to Greece, Denmark to Spain, Netherlands to Russia, etc. – it is the carriages and wagons which make the through trip not the locomotives. This is largely because the countries use different electric systems: e.g. 15 kv 16⅔ Hz West Germany, 25 kv 50 Hz France, 3kv DC Belgium, 1/2 kv DC Netherlands. Indeed, the UK operates more than one system with catenary pick-up AC north of London, a third rail with 750V DC south of London, and a fourth rail for the London Underground.

The fragmentation extends into another dimension. If we ignore the various other services, the rail business can crudely be divided into three: freight, inter-city passengers and commuters (within travel-to-work or catchment areas). Normally, the first two will be operated by the same company, while commuter travel will be operated by municipal undertakings which frequently combine bus with light-rail or subway systems. Added to this will probably be commuter trains on the main rail network. The United Kingdom is somewhat unusual because of the importance of the main rail system in commuter traffic.

Comparable statistics are difficult to find. In the Community as a whole gross tonne kilometres worked are divided fairly evenly between passengers and goods at around 480bn tonne km in 1985, but while goods traffic has been static or falling, particularly in France and the United

Kingdom, passenger traffic has actually risen in recent years, again principally in France (prior to the TGV). Most traffic is internal. Only 1–2 per cent of passenger traffic was international in 1986. Figures on traffic outside the main rail system as a measure of the importance of commuters to long-distance travel are not available. UK figures suggest that urban transit systems other than British Rail carry as many passengers but take them on average only a fifth of the distance. The decline in rail travel until the mid-1980s has been reflected in the supplying firms, which also contracted and found themselves with spare capacity. During 1983–6 employment fell by 15 per cent (on the basis shown in Table 4.5 (f)) aided by technological advance which improved productivity.

Thus, in general, we see the following factors in Europe at the outset of the Single Market programme:

1. Demand dominated by national and local public sector purchasers which tended to favour their own markets.
2. A large number of producers often on a small scale.
3. Substantial overcapacity because of fluctuations in demand.
4. A strongly fragmented market in technical terms along national lines.
5. A growth in demand for railway travel which is likely to ease overcapacity problems.
6. Innovation with the high-speed network and the Channel Tunnel.

The forces for change from the 1992 programme

The importance of the Single Market programme has to be judged in terms of the state of the railway industry at the time. The major impact of the Single Market programme on the railway industry comes through the public purchasing directives, as it is the behaviour of these purchasers which has been the major reason for a departure from Single Market conditions. All the major purchasers in the past were public entities, either publicly owned national railway companies or municipal transit authorities. The major exception to this in recent years is the Channel Tunnel operation which is financed and owned by an Anglo-French private company Eurotunnel and is being built and will be operated by a second Anglo-French company Transmanche-Link. With the exception of countries like Denmark, Ireland and the Netherlands with little productive capability of their own, contracts have usually been awarded to domestic suppliers.

It is not fair to blame this purely on protectionist attitudes, because it reflects the conditions under which the railways were built up in the first place and the extremely high costs of change. When railways were constructed, largely in the middle and second half of the nineteenth century, labour costs were low and the effective competition was from the horse or walking. The payoff to investment was thus high. Each railway tended to be constructed on a fairly local basis and international connection was a secondary rather than primary consideration. Delays at frontiers and the need to change trains or locomotives was a minor consideration compared with alternative transport. With steam locomotion this was less of a problem but the gradual introduction of electrification also proceeded on a national and piecemeal basis.

When it came to considering the requirements of longer-distance travel much of the investment was already in place. By then, much more effective substitutes existed in the form of road and air transport. Major investments to achieve compatibility between countries were therefore out of the question and existing national systems were improved incrementally. International linkage, through the Union Internationale des Chemins de Fer therefore concentrated on what was necessary to allow rolling stock to pass across borders rather than on wider harmonisation. Nevertheless, even allowing for this 'natural' differentiation between countries there was substantial scope for permitting more open tendering for contracts. Although a local supplier has natural advantages of knowledge and experience these are not necessarily overwhelming. Technical innovation may be able to offset the value of the local knowledge and, indeed, the possibility that this could be the case will be a pressure to increase competitiveness – the phenomenon usually referred to as 'contestability'.

There is some experience of what can happen if public purchasing is opened up. The United Kingdom has opened its market during the last five years as British Rail has been required to undertake competitive tendering. Prior to that it not only provided detailed specifications developed by its own engineering department but also had its own heavy-engineering division which undertook most of the repair work and the assembly and production of much of the new stock. This division, renamed BREL, has now been privatised and has to compete with other suppliers. The basis of seeking supplies has also changed, and performance criteria are now set which transfer the onus for how to meet the requirement from British Rail's engineers to the supplying companies.

The full effect of this opening up is yet to be seen but already BR has been faced by a greatly improved choice (as indeed has the London Underground, which is also undertaking a substantial investment programme and looking more widely for contractors). However, the first contracts are only now coming to fruition. The full extent of the gains (or losses) will only be shown once the experience and costs of operation are taken into account. (Similar opening of the market for buses has had mixed results.) However, at least this is an example of the Single Market type of purchasing requirements actually being applied in public.

In other member states, although the link between purchaser and supplier may have a clear distinction of ownership, the technical ties between the two may be strong (and likely to continue). In Germany, for example, a 44bn DM development project has been set up to produce a high-speed train that can run on other voltage systems (ICE-M), principally French, for the proposed Paris–Frankfurt/Stuttgart links and Italian for a link through the Alps (the current German high-speed train, ICE, is only compatible with the Austrian and Swiss systems). This is being financed jointly by the Federal Ministry for Research and Development, the Deutsche Bundesbank and the companies themselves. Having spent that sort of money there will be an enormous temptation to continue into production, whatever tendering process is ultimately used.

It is instructive to see the arguments reported (*International Railway Journal*, September 1989) for wishing to pursue a German option rather than adopting existing French designs. These relate first to technical differences and second to different German consumer requirements, comfort, for example. It is difficult in these rather thin markets to assess whether increased competition improves the product and reduces the cost to the purchaser or whether it merely increases the overall costs which then have to be borne by consumers in the ultimate prices. Experience thus far suggests that, for a Franco-German link, where both parties expect to have the technology, the expectation must be that the result will be a shared contract between Alsthom and a German consortium.

The initial assessments of other barriers to the Single Market in the background papers to the Cecchini Report did not stress any other facets as having a major impact on railways. One might have expected technical differences to be important, but these lie rather outside the Single Market programme. International travel has already been made thoroughly compatible through UIC. National differences are not particularly hampered by problems of standards or certification. It is simply that behaviour is different and there is an extremely high sunk cost in existing systems. The widening of the UK loading gauge to French standards is prohibitively expensive because it would involve altering bridges and tunnels all round the country. Similarly, increasing the axle loadings on French railways to those which apply in Germany would involve enormous expenditure. It is far cheaper to have a separate set of locomotives with lighter axle loadings – especially since the trend with high-speed trains is for lighter vehicles anyway.

Nevertheless, there are already extensive opportunities for the use of common components. Indeed, most railways vehicle manufacturers are assemblers of components, many of which come from specialist manufacturers who are themselves supplying many different companies. Clearly, there is considerable scope for further standardisation. The research organisation of UIC, ORE (Office for Research and Experiments) is involved with many programmes of co-operation. One of the main ones at present, for example, is on bogies involving Swiss, Austrian and Italian producers. This emphasises, incidentally, a further facet. UIC is not an EC organisation but a European one. Since trains between parts of the Community have to pass through Switzerland, Austria and Yugoslavia it would be mistaken to exclude them from any technical harmonisation. Similarly, trains need some measure of eastward and northward compatibility. Although trains to Moscow and Istanbul, for example, are a commonplace it would clearly be ridiculous if West German trains could not run to Berlin because of incompatibility with the East German railway system. Thus, the railway 'community' is a much wider affair.

In one respect the foregoing analysis exaggerates the position because one category of rail vehicles, namely, goods wagons, are often not owned by the railways but by private companies, particularly leasing companies. Although these also have a strong national flavour, in other industries lessors have had an important influence on the development of products. One of their advantages is the ability to buy in large quantities and hence provide some sort of competition for the other large purchasers, the railways themselves. However, entry to the freight system is through privately owned railheads in some countries. The enhancement of the Community's competition policy will not extend to breaking these monopolies which were alleged by some of those interviewed to inhibit exploitation of the full potential of rail transport.

The removal of frontiers themselves will clearly be a help. Costs can fall as the need for frontier officials to check goods and passengers is removed. The Cecchini Report estimated that costs might fall by as much as 1.8 per cent of the value of the goods traded. Incompatibility of traction systems may still require a stop at the border, although even this may be removed as current research on multisystem engines comes fully into operation. This will be of particular advantage to goods traffic which customers sometimes feel gets lost in the marshalling yards at the border.

In many respects, however, the major implications for railways, other than public purchasing, lie in other more indirect effects. In particular, it relates to the degree to which travel itself may be encouraged and rail travel encouraged compared to other modes of transport. If the removal of frontier controls increases the tendency of firms to ship their products from just a few locations rather than having distribution centres in each country, each operating at below minimum efficient scale, then traffic will increase. Current indications suggest this. Firms like Seiko-Epson are concentrating their European distribution systems – in Amsterdam in that particular case. Thus, this is a change not just for Community producers but for third country suppliers as well. The exact form of the impact on rail rather than other forms of transport will depend upon the way in which individual industries restructure. Rail is more attractive for bulk goods, for large consignments and for distances in excess of 250–400 kilometres. An exact limit is not appropriate as it varies with the relative quality of the road system, the regulatory restraints, such as those on lorry drivers, and the costs and preferences of potential users.

However, while railway travel is restricted, the road goods-vehicle market and the civil aviation markets are even more restricted. The cabotage restrictions mean that at least 30 per cent of lorries are travelling empty on their return trips. The comparison between US airfares and European fares reveals even greater distortions. It is cheaper to fly to a large number of destinations in the United States and Canada, for example, from the United Kingdom than it is to fly to Athens. The shortest routes, like London–Brussels, are the most notorious. Currently, progress on getting changes in these competing industries is slow. As the high-speed network develops and the Channel Tunnel is completed, city centre to city centre journey times will extend the range of trips for which rail is more convenient than air. Lower price will extend the range. At some point, of course, airlines will respond and force their regulators into change rather than inhibiting it as at present. Indeed, initial agreement was reached at the end of 1989. In the longer run, ecological considerations may also increase the attractiveness of rail travel.

The pressure for a European rail network, through CER (the Community of European Railways) is not a part of the Single Market programme as such, although it is in part a response to it. The major influence remains the removal of national public purchasing restrictions, however, and the response to that is greatly assisted by the measures to increase the freedom of capital and labour. This assists the formation and operation of transnational corporations and operations. It particularly assists the operation of the various shorter-run international agreements that are necessary to fulfil many recent contracts which require new specialisms or different combinations of existing capabilities.

Thus, the Single Market is both a stimulus for change and a means of increasing the ability to change. The economic rationale for such change is clear, namely, the exercise of market power. There are economies of scale to be reaped, hence there is an incentive for companies to expand through amalgamation. Given the small size of markets outside the United Kingdom, France, West Germany and Italy, this inevitably implies cross-border linkages. The stimulus for these linkages is increased by the feeling that genuine relaxation of national purchasing patterns will be slow – as the British Rail example illustrates. Hence, to participate in a foreign market requires participation in a company producing in that market, whether partially or by full takeover.

The implications for strategic change in the industry

In this and the following section we explore the factors influencing the strategic response of firms in the industry. As it is still early days in what is likely to be quite a long period of adjustment, only some of these responses have actually been revealed. Some were discussed in interviews with the companies, but in such a tight market firms were not surprisingly reticent where the strategy is not already known or obvious. In the current section we begin by looking at the forces affecting the market as Single Market develops and then assess the options. The firm has two basic forms of action it can take. It can reorganise internally, altering its product market focus, restructuring its organisation, marketing, finance, etc. It can also pursue an 'external' strategy, forming linkages with other companies for production, marketing, consortium bids, etc., or develop even closer relationships through cross-shareholdings or even takeover and acquisition. In this section we concentrate on the external route, leaving internal moves largely to the next section.

The process of market development

The immediate impact of the Single Market has not been on production but on ownership of railway equipment companies. During the last three years the picture shown in Table 4.4 has changed and there has been a consolidation of the major groups (see Table 4.7). This is a reduction by a third in the effective numbers of companies – the necessary proportion suggested by W. S. Atkins in the papers for the Cecchini Report for reduction in capacity in the industry. There are many other more limited agreements for joint marketing, etc., which are listed in an Appendix available from the author. The most important move has been the merger of ASEA and Brown-Boveri in January 1988, followed by the merger of GEC and Alsthom's power systems division later in the year and a consolidation of the German industry.

These arrangements have not yet broken the mould of European production and purchasing as rationalisation of plants across the EC countries has been limited. Similarly there has been little 'foreign' buying by the national authorities. A link-up like that between GEC and Alsthom enables the two companies to benefit from activities in each other's markets rather than for Alsthom to supply the UK market or

Table 4.7   Consolidation of major groups

(a)   Three main groups have been formed:

International
1. ASEA (77), Brown-Boveri (78), includes 40% of BREL (52), EB (Norway) ML (57), LM Ericsson (signalling) Ansaldo (32)
2. GEC (54)–Alsthom (5)
    includes ACEC (1), Jeumont Schneider (13), Carel et Fouche (10), Metro-Cammell (56), Ateinsa (44), Macosa (47), Maquinista (48)

National
3. German alliances
    Siemens (28), Krupp (24), Krauss-Maffei (23), Thyssen (30)
    (Eurotraco)

(b)   Smaller groupings:

4. Ansaldo (32), CSEE (France), EMT (Italy), Union Switch and Signal, Wabco Westinghouse
5. Hunslet (55), Navag (71)
6. Remafer (15), ANF (7)
7. Arbel (France), Fauval (France)
8. Bombadier (86), BN (2), ANF (7)

Note: numbers in brackets are those used in the list of firms in Table 4.4

GEC the French. On the Channel Tunnel, initial work seems to have been divided, with equal shares going to the United Kingdom and France and a smaller share to Belgium, commensurate with their involvement in the project. With the contracts for locomotives and rolling stock the net has been cast wider and the mould may be breaking. ABB (Switzerland) and Brush (UK) have received the contract for the locomotives while the wagons are divided half to a Bombardier–ANF (France)–BN (Belgium) grouping and the other to Breda–Fiat (Italy).

We are thus seeing a process which has a number of stages. The market at the outset was segmented, with public purchasers facing national producers, and with only limited competition between producers in countries such as the United Kingdom and Germany where there was more than one supplier. Such markets tend to be inefficient. While profitability is likely to be maintained within reasonable levels (because, on the upper margin, the purchasers can strike a harsher bargain in the future if excess profits are earned on any particular contract and, on the lower, the supplier can insist on adequate profits to remain in business) the checks on efficiency have to be largely administrative. The purchasers require adequate engineering knowledge to assess what technologies and products can be developed to meet their requirements. They also require knowledge to check the validity of the suppliers' costings and schedules. Given incomplete knowledge and a lack of effective sanction, this permits the supplier to operate at less than the maximum efficiency possible and to absorb inefficiencies in higher costs, which can be passed on. It is for this reason that the newly privatised industries in the United Kingdom – gas, telecommunications, etc. – have a watchdog authority to try to ensure efficient operation. In those industries there are multiple small purchasers, each with no market power or access to information. But even a monopoly purchaser cannot be fully informed, especially when it is in the interests of suppliers for him not to be. The supplier thus has considerable power if he knows that the purchaser has no choice.

In the first stage of the opening up of the market there is in theory a choice of strategies for suppliers to maintain market power. The first is merely to bid across borders and hence gain market share using the domestic market as a base. However, this is a high-risk strategy as it relies upon purchasers suddenly becoming completely open-minded and upon the absence of important local knowledge or specific requirements possessed by the local firms to meet the specific characteristics of the railways in that country. Neither of these assumptions is realistic. The new public purchasing rules are not yet in effect and even when they are it will take some time for both purchasers and suppliers to get used to operating them.

It is very expensive to mount proper bids for major contracts. Firms which do not expect that they have much chance of winning – whether or not that perception is correct – will either not bid or will put in a less thorough bid with a relatively high price to cover the unexpected costs which they may discover if they win the contract and have to develop the product. This occurs in part because, except in some specific cases relating to vehicles for new light railways or repeat contracts, it is not a matter of buying an existing product 'off the shelf' so to speak. A substantial degree of 'customisation' is required – far more than that involved in aeroplanes, for example, where customer requirements may relate to choice of engines and aspects of internal layout.

A major change has occurred in the case of British Rail which previously used to provide an extremely detailed specification of its requirements that it was then up to their own engineering subsidiary to produce – mainly through purchasing and assembling components from other domestic suppliers. Now it specifies 'performance criteria'. These set out what the products are to be able to achieve, including compatibility with existing equipment. This gives the supplier much more scope and reduces the predetermined uniqueness of British Rail's equipment. This particular change may do more to open up the market than merely compelling purchasers to make their tendering process open, as it permits the incorporation of more components and design elements which can be used elsewhere, hence both increasing the scale of production and reducing the learning costs of each individual project. It also enables a wider basis for competition, because the tighter the specification by the purchasers the smaller the opportunity for the producer to compete on the basis of technological innovation, design, quality and other non-price factors.

The first stage in the market evolution is, therefore, not to attempt to cross borders directly but to increase market power in two respects: first, by reducing the number of competitors, and second, by forming agreements with companies in other countries so that joint bids can be made. These may be one-off arrangements so that a consortium bid can be put together as, for example, with Euroshuttle (Brush, ABB, ANF-Industrie, BN and Bombardier) or they may go the whole way to a merger such as those between GEC and Alsthom and ASEA and Brown-Boveri or a takeover as with Alsthom and MTM and Ateinsa in Spain. There is a whole range of intermediate arrangements, such as the joint holdings in BREL where ABB has 40 per cent, Trafalgar House 40 per cent and a management buy-out team the remainder.

All these have the initial characteristics that they are changes in ownership rather than changes in the location of plant and methods of operation. They are devices for enabling producers to get over the national barriers in the sense of being able to earn a return from operations in the other countries. Thus, in the immediate instance ABB can earn profits from participating financially in BREL rather than by ABB supplanting BREL by winning a contract itself to supply British Rail. No doubt the proportion of ABB components in BREL's products will rise and the proportion of the total value added emerging from BREL's workshops rather than those of suppliers may change. Nevertheless, the market remains much more fragmented than is apparent from the computation of the sheer number of companies.

Does this mean the market becomes more competitive? The answer to this must be 'yes', quite simply because foreign competition becomes a realistic threat. However, the effectiveness of this threat will begin to lose its validity if, in fact, no substantial contracts are awarded to foreign contractors in Italy, West Germany, France or the United Kingdom. The demands from the other countries are relatively small. Spain and, to a lesser extent, Portugal have taken the decision to link themselves into the European high-speed network, which entails a major investment in track and rolling stock. As they do not have the necessary technology this has resulted in a deal with Alsthom which involves a takeover of the major Spanish producers. This enables Spanish production to continue at the same time as making the technological step forward. It is not clear how such a co-operative deal like this advances efficiency. Given that this network has to link with the French system, competition will have been limited. However, part of the contract for the locomotives has gone to a German consortium, so here again there are signs of a widening of the market, although much of the assembly work will take place in Spain.

We can therefore now set out the steps in the adjustment process or stages of market development, as follows:

1. Announcement of Single Market programme.
2. Formation of alliances, takeovers, mergers.
3. Success of co-operative/competitive bids.
4. Reorganisation of production.

Internal strategies for the firm in the face of competitive pressure

Sources of competition

Thus far, our discussion of the development of the market has been very much in the narrow terms of the relationships between the immediate suppliers and the purchasers. The key to increased competition lies with the purchasers who actually let the contracts. The behaviour of suppliers within Europe has been to reduce competition in the sense of reducing the number of suppliers markedly by merger and takeover and by putting in consortium bids for major contracts, thereby reducing the effective number of bids to a handful. However, this is not in practice actually a reduction in competition, as what it replaces in some cases represented no competition at all and in others only competition between a small number of suppliers.

Competition will be limited in practice if having a small number of suppliers results in explicit or implicit collusion or if the technological requirements mean that one supplier has an obvious advantage over the others. While collusion may be an illegal restrictive practice it is, nevertheless, very difficult to overcome 'rationing' behaviour whereby one supplier tends to corner a particular part of the market. Others, believing they have only a limited chance of success, place much higher bids. They participate in the 'game' because unless the game is played on each occasion they will not be able to obtain the contracts in their own markets.

This approach would be invalidated if the market is contestable by a reasonable number of third parties who do not have a market segment they can claim as their own. To determine this it is necessary to show that competitive bids are possible from third country suppliers and that European companies believe that there is a real chance that such bids might succeed.

Railways are one of the few areas where European companies are world leaders despite the inefficiencies and fragmentation of the domestic market. In a sense the one forces the other because overcapacity within Europe and restrictions on trade with each other mean that exports to third countries are the only means of retaining viability. Without detailed knowledge of internal company accounts we cannot know the extent to which tied domestic sales have been subsidising 'competitive' exports. All we can observe is the extent of those exports (Tables 4.5c and 4.6).

By comparison we can get an indication of the competitiveness of other non-EC suppliers by observation of their success in these third markets. Given the degree to which these are Eastern bloc or Japanese suppliers, one might be concerned by the extent that success is dependent upon the ability to raise finance on attractive terms rather than simply the comparative costs of production. Nevertheless, what emerges is that the Japanese are strong competitors in many areas, aided by the degree of co-ordination they exhibit in mounting bids. In view of the concentration of the European market it could be argued that full efficiency will only be achieved when the market is fully contestable by these outside producers. Currently, with one or two exceptions the market has not been contested and no major contracts have been secured. Since there are tariff barriers on these imports and no requirement to lift non-tariff barriers there is no reason to expect that this competition will be admitted anywhere except the United Kingdom.

It is readily possible therefore to envisage a Europe where there are two major EC producer groups. GEC–Alsthom and a German grouping in which Siemens has a strong role, with the perpetuation of Fiat and a small number of other players. The only serious contestability comes from ABB, which already has production facilities within the Community. Because of its technological strengths, the lack of tariff barriers through EFTA agreements and existing links, there is a real possibility that effective competitive pressures will come from this source. In any case, ABB has production facilities within the EC.

In assessing the demand for railway equipment it is important to bear in mind that not only is the market fragmented but demand is uneven. In general European railways have declined in size during the 1960s and 1970s. There has, however, been technical change, in part in response to changes in relative energy prices, replacing steam locomotives and electrifying the track. In addition, speeds have increased, with the HST (125 mph) system of diesel-powered trains in the United Kingdom running on existing track and the TGV electric system in France running on new specially constructed track. These high-speed systems are now extending into Belgium, West Germany, Italy, Spain and Portugal. Plans are well advanced to increase speeds further, with 140 mph electric trains appearing in the United Kingdom and a faster TGV Atlantique in France. In addition there is the unique stimulus of the Channel Tunnel through which there will be two groups of trains – the shuttle service ferrying passengers and vehicles just through the tunnel itself and the longer-distance trains conveying passengers and freight between locations in the United Kingdom and the continent. The specially constructed shuttle trains will have the largest loading gauge in Europe to accommodate lorries and double-decker passenger/vehicle wagons, and long-distance stock the smallest, in order to run in the United Kingdom, thus increasing rather than reducing diversity.

There is thus a series of four stimuli which are affecting demand for rail travel at the same time as the single market is being formed: an abnormally high cyclical peak in replacement of stock which has become obsolete; the rise in popularity of high-speed travel; the special Channel Tunnel project; and a rise in the popularity of rail compared with road transport, particularly within cities. Thus, for example, while the United Kingdom phased out trams and went without metropolitan light rail, a light-rail system has been introduced into Docklands in London and further systems are in progress in a number of cities, linked in cases such as Tyne and Wear and Glasgow with the existing main railway system. This trend seems set to continue as congestion increases.

The Single Market itself has undoubtedly contributed to this growth in demand, aiding the spread of the high-speed network and contributing to the final success of the Channel Tunnel project after a century of proposals and initial attempts. Further linkages are likely to follow, with discussions of a European rail network, for example.

The process of reorganisation is thus eased because it is not merely one of seeking to find a means of achieving an orderly rundown of a declining industry, characterised by overcapacity. Although there is overcapacity it is in part because of the inherent wide fluctuations in orders in national markets, met by national suppliers. The buoyancy of demand means that it will be possible for national authorities to see the reorganisation of supply without the prospect of immediate closure of the production facilities in their country. This reduction in capacity is likely to occur later when demand falls and when suppliers feel that they will remain competitive in the bidding procedure even if they can offer little local value added. That point is some distance off.

Forces for increased competition come not just from within the railway market but also from industries which could substitute for it. There are, of course, several effective competitors for rail travel which have contributed to the relative decline of railways in the period after the war. These are road, air and sea. The extent to which these sectors are affecting the restructuring of the railway equipment sector is also influenced by the Single Market programme. One of the reasons that high-speed trains are proving popular over distances where air travel might have been expected to compete more strongly is because of the failure to deregulate the airline system within the Community and the failure to reorganise air traffic control on a European rather than a national basis. Were this situation to change, then the growth of long-distance rail travel might be more restrained, with a consequent impact on the strategy of suppliers. Similarly, the failure to get agreement as yet on the removal of frontier barriers on the roads and the limits on cabotage – that is, back-loading – mean that road costs are still much higher than they need to be in a genuine single market.

Companies' strategies are clearly different in the face of uncertainty from what they would be if the doubts are dispelled. Since capacity already exists, it may not be sensible to close it where it can be competitive at higher levels of demand, until it is clear that such demand is unlikely to materialise. Clearly, companies must make a judgement about the relative costs of retaining capacity and opening new capacity.

This decision is most pertinent in so far as it applies to labour rather than to buildings, plant and equipment. The larger companies such as ABB, GEC–Alsthom and the German group – Siemens, Krauss-Maffei – do not manufacture solely railway equipment. They are much larger companies of which railway equipment is only a part. (Indeed, their strategies for railways may be far more determined by their strategies in other larger volume parts of their businesses.) They are hence able to switch resources between various parts of the company in response to the relative fluctuations in demand. This emphasises the advantages not so much of being a large company but of being one with a portfolio of activities which are readily interchangeable.

Thus, one of the advantages being exploited is economies of scope rather than economies of scale. The latter will also be obtained if either the pattern of orders becomes concentrated on a smaller number of producers or if producers in turn reduced the number of plants. There is much less reason why the orders themselves should, in the short run, become more homogeneous unless the railway companies also decide to co-operate further. Compatible systems tend to imply higher capital costs, as, for example, with the Thames Link services connecting the north and south sides of London which have to be able to use both the third rail and the overhead catenary system. While this may improve the service for the customer it will only cut costs if it reduces the amount of rolling stock and time required for travel. Here, the economies apply not to producers where costs rise (and quantities purchased fall) but to the consumer and to the economy at large.

In the component industries the position is different. Smaller companies which supply specialised parts to a number of final equipment producers can be relatively insulated from the fluctuations in demand in particular European markets. The importance of these component suppliers must not be underestimated, as typically two-thirds of the value of a train is bought in by the final manufacturer. It is noticeable that all the main players, GEC–Alsthom, ABB and the German grouping are parts of other groups including heavy electrical engineering. They thus provide common components and skills themselves, although the sectors setting the form of those common components may very well not be railway engineering.

Other influences on the market

The remaining influences on the development of the market and the various parts of the value-added chain are a rather mixed bag. First of all there are regulatory influences on the industry, as member states encourage traffic to move from road to rail. In Germany, for example, it is proposed to confine the transport of hazardous goods to rail as far as possible (ostensibly for reasons of safety, although the chemical industry in the United Kingdom feels this is partly a new non-tariff barrier to increase the competitive advantages of German suppliers, which tend to have access to railways).

Although the railway equipment industry is bedevilled by differences in technical specifications between countries, the general run of technical harmonisation measures in the Single Market programme will have little impact on the industry. The problem is not that suppliers are inhibited by technical barriers from selling their products in other countries but that the specifications made by purchasers differ, largely as a result of different traditions rather than any wish to discriminate. Of course, since it is up to the purchaser to decide what specification he wants it is, indeed, possible for him to continue to demand special characteristic with which domestic suppliers are more familiar even if more 'European' standards exist. There is thus a continuing opportunity for purchasers to favour domestic producers, in so far as they exist, if they wish, completely legally, within the terms of the Single Market.

There is a set of European standards, developed by the UIC, already in operation which relates to equipment which moves between countries and needs to be 'connectable'. This also will not be affected by the Single Market proposals on European standards. The only relevant issues are whether the readier ability to cross borders will increase the proportion of vehicles which cross borders. The rules are not straightforward. For example, the Channel Tunnel shuttle sets do not have to conform to UIC because they do not need to connect with rolling stock in the rest of the European system.

The Single Market has had only a limited effect on research and development, at the beginning of the value-added chain. The European railway equipment industry already has a joint research association which is largely concerned with issues related to the UIC although it covers other areas of general importance, such as the friction between steel wheels and steel rails. Nevertheless, the main innovations have come

from companies, particularly the larger ones, developing bogie technology, high-speed traction units, tilting trains, etc. Although control over
these innovations can convey considerable market power, where it lies
with a component supplier, such as the Pendolino tilting train, the
technology can be licensed to others. Ironically, the Single Market
increases the innovators' market power, in cases where there was
previously a single purchaser. If more than one company can supply the
final equipment for a particular railway the innovator can negotiate
among them to get a better price for his product.

The picture is completed by considering the influence of the freeing of
labour and capital markets as part of the Single Market programme.
Here, in the case of capital, we need to distinguish between purchasers
and suppliers. Given that purchases are largely from public funds, the
Single Market has little impact. But the reorganisation of supply may
have benefited particularly from the lifting of barriers to cross-border
acquisition, which might in previous years have been imposed by
governments.

The labour market liberalisation may have some effect on these
multinational companies, allowing them to move people round more
freely at the technical and professional level, but this is unlikely to be a
major influence on the market. Skill shortages on the shopfloor are more
important, particularly if the amount of slack capacity is cut, but these
problems apply much more widely to the engineering industry.

The prime forces, therefore, remain the change in the behaviour of
purchasers in the public sector and the actions of suppliers in acquisitions,
mergers, joint ventures and other alliances.

Illustrations from particular firms

The argument in EC(1988) was that the European market was similar in
many ways to the United States. The number of locomotives in service in
1986 was of a similar order of magnitude, 20,000 compared with 25,000 in
the United States, but that there were ten major producers in the EC
compared with two in the United States. The inference was that with the
inception of the Single Market this number would be reduced to
American proportions. In practice, this is roughly what has happened in
that the number of major producers in Europe has fallen, leaving three
main suppliers and some smaller companies. The major suppliers are now
as follows:

- ABB – the product of the ASEA and Brown-Boveri merger.
- GEC–Alsthom – the product of GEC and Alsthom plus a number of
  other smaller companies which have been taken over, e.g. ACEC
  (Belgium), MTM, Ateinsa and Macosa (Spain).

- Siemens – Thyssen – Krauss-Maffei – Krupp – these linkages are more variable. K, K-M and Thyssen have links for mechanical parts. S and K-M have formed Eurotraco for high-speed trains. S and ABB and AEG for electrical equipment.

And the smaller groupings:

- Ansaldo Transporti – links with CSEE (France) and Enole Marelli Transporti, through Elettra. A joint company with Fiat Ferroviaria Savigliano was stopped by the Italian government, so there is significant Italian capacity in Fiat and Breda which is yet to be integrated.
- BN (Bombardier).

Thus, the expectation was that the industry would concentrate and would thereby be able to make economies of scale. The first aspect has been fulfilled but the second is much less likely to be realised. Gerhard Scholtis of Siemens puts it as follows:

> With the creation of a single EC market in 1993, it may be thought that longer production runs and economies of scale will become available. Frankly, I don't think this will happen. History has left Europe with a legacy of different electric traction systems, clearances and even track gauges. Railways will continue to invite bids for tailor-made rolling stock and equipment. Standardisation is only possible at the level of components – which is already the case. (*Railway Gazette International*, May 1989)

The increase in concentration might be taken to imply that the companies were all following a similar strategy, but, in fact, there was considerable variety. Klaus Milz of AEG–Westinghouse suggests that 'the ability to offer complete transport systems – including planning, erection, servicing and in some cases, operation – will substantially improve the position of a railway manufacturer' (*RGI*, May 1989) implying that a company has to have the full range of competences. However, this can be achieved by developing all the facilities oneself – probably by acquisition – or by forming flexible alliances. This latter is clearly the strategy of Siemens – Gerhard Scholtis again: 'Siemens wants to remain in a position where we can select local partners for production and installation' (*RGI*, May 1989). It is thus worth tracing out the strategies of some of the major players in a little more detail.

The prime mover was ASEA which merged with Brown-Boveri in January 1988. This was followed not long after by Alsthom-GEC. Previously Alsthom was following a strategy of taking over smaller companies, ACEC in Belgium and Ateinsa, Macosa and NTM in Spain. Alsthom had hoped to become the world's largest producer on its own but required a strong partner, especially one in the United Kingdom after

ABB took a 40 per cent stake in BREL when it was sold by British Rail. (GEC has also picked up Metro-Cammell, one of the smaller UK producers, from the Laird Group.)

Thus, the ABB and GEC–Alsthom strategies appear to be twofold, first to increase in size and second to have international holdings, both by full and partial participation, to get a foothold inside other member states. Richard Hope summarises this strategy clearly:

> There is a marked trend for the big groups to buy up companies in order to gain a foothold in national markets. Obviously they have little faith in the 'single market' concept when it comes to securing orders from railway and metro operators who are beholden to politicians with an unemployment problem.
> (*Railway Gazette International*, May 1989)

The response by the German companies – there are twelve members of the German Locomotive Industry Association:

- AEG–Telefunken Anlagentechnik AG
- Brown, Boveri & Cie AG
- Carl Kaelble u. Gmeinder GmbH & Co
- Knorr-Bremse GmbH
- Krauss-Maffei AG
- Fried. Krupp GmbH
- Krupp Mak
- MTV Motoren und Turbinen-Union
- Motoren Werke Mannheim AG
- Siemens AG
- Thyssen Industrie AG Henschel
- J. M. Voith GmbH

– has been far more national as has that within Italy. There are two main groupings within the German industry: Kraus-Maffei, Krupp Mak and Thyssen Henschel which supply the mechanical parts of locomotives (the latter two are important diesel engine manufacturers) and Siemens, AEG and ABB which supply the electrical parts. They have tended to put together consortium bids for major European contracts and, indeed, succeeded in the case of the German high-speed trains, ICE, and the Spanish, TAV – although in the latter case there is a substantial domestic content in the locomotives, much of which will be supplied by the recently acquired Alsthom subsidiaries.

This 'marriage' between electrical and mechanical suppliers is common. BN and ACEC in Belgium, for example, supply the mechanical and electrical parts respectively. Although now controlled by non-Belgian companies – Bombardier (Canada) in the case of BN and Alsthom in the case of ACEC – they have recently secured a joint contract for the

Brussels Metro and a contract (with ANF of France) to supply the wagons for the passengers and their vehicles for the Channel Tunnel shuttle. The locomotives for these trains are being supplied by an ABB/Brush Electrical Machines consortium, with ABB providing the electrical component and Brush the mechanical.

The 'national' approach in Germany applies to coaches and trucks as well as locomotives. Duewag and Waggon Union are supplying a third of the coaches for the ICE and Linke-Hofmann-Busch, M.A.N. and MBB most of the remainder. Similarly Siemens and Krauss-Maffei have formed Eurotraco to improve their ability to bid for high-speed trains (their Italian subsidiaries are included with an eye on that market). It is also interesting to see that M.A.N., in winning a contract in China, was, in part, able to keep its costs down by subcontracting to East German firms. The same strategy seems to apply in Italy. Breda and Fiat combined to win the contract for the heavy road-vehicle carriers for the Channel Tunnel. The Japanese manufacturers, Hitachi, Mitsubishi and Toshiba, have also joined forces in their approach to the European markets although they have yet to achieve a serious breakthrough.

This does not imply that there is no room left for the smaller suppliers. Wagonfabrik Talbot (Germany) are supplying double-decker trains to the Netherlands. Transtech (part of Rauturuukki, Finland) are supplying container wagons to Denmark. Also in a specialised area, EB Signal (Norway) has won a contract for ATC equipment from Portugal. Plasser-Theurer of Austria, of course, continues to have a virtual monopoly of track-laying and maintenance equipment. Small companies have two routes to maintaining a position in the market. One is specialisation, what is often referred to as 'niche marketing'. The other is to team up with larger suppliers for particular contracts where they have a special advantage, say, by being a local supplier, or the supplier of existing equipment with which continuity is required.

These smaller firms thus will offer specialisation or an entry point to the market. Although Brian McCann from GEC sees a continuation of the process of concentration:

> I believe that mergers between large groups will continue until there are perhaps only two in Europe. Prices will come down, and world standard designs will emerge. Capacity and employment in the railway manufacturing industry, as in the railways themselves, will gradually reduce and the EC may end up with a centrally controlled rail network. (*RGI*, May 1989)

Others think that there will be clear limits to the process. Siemens wants to remain 'in a position where we can select local partners for production and installation' (Gerhard Scholtis, *RGI*, May 1989).

Conclusion

Much of the onus for further growth in efficiency in the railway equipment industry therefore lies with the purchasers. If there really is good cross-national success in securing contracts, then small plants in various countries, maintained largely to get contracts, can be closed. But this closure in many cases would only make sense if there were more standardisation in the railway system, which implies greater international co-operation between European railway authorities. This is at best a slow process – and an expensive one. Thus we see in the railway equipment industry a dramatic change in the structure of the ownership of industry, which may continue further. But with fragmented demand we will continue to see a lot of small-scale production. This may retain competitiveness within Europe, in part because there are few independent partners left for foreign producers to buy to get a good foothold in the market, but it will not necessarily help export competitiveness so much, where there are important economies of scale currently in the United States, Japan (and Canada). Europe's strengths relate especially to technology and quality. Given that the major overseas markets are in the developing world, this may not necessarily provide the most appropriate characteristics.

Of the nine major countries in the EC, five – Denmark, Netherlands, Portugal, Spain and the United Kingdom – could already be described as fairly open before the Single Market measures; three – France, west Germany and Italy – are largely closed; with Belgium in an intermediate position. Principally, the closed markets were closed because they had important domestic suppliers and Belgium was open only to the extent that it did not have some capabilities. The United Kingdom had already chosen, for reasons other than compliance with the Single Market, to open up its market although it had a full range of production capability. The remainder had relatively little choice but to be open. The success of the Single Market measures will thus depend in a large part on the actions of the three 'closed' markets. So far, the traditional suppliers of these markets have each consolidated, thereby increasing their domestic market strength. Technological differences could be used to keep the markets distinct. The strategy of the suppliers implies that this is their expectation. Only time will provide the answer.

Notes

1. *The 'Cost of Non-Europe' in Public-Sector Procurement*, Vol. 5 of *Basic findings, Research on the Cost of Non-Europe*, EC 1988.

5

Airlines

Gernot Klepper

Since World War II trade in manufactured goods has been subject to international rules set out in the GATT. In several rounds of negotiations tariff barriers have been reduced significantly; quantitative restrictions and discriminatory practices have been brought under control to some extent. In contrast, trade in services has so far been left out of international agreements. Similarly, with the creation of the European Community, policy initiatives have first focused on liberalising trade in manufactures. Only with the advent of the 1980s has a common policy towards the air transport sector been developed in the EC. Finally, the Single European Act in 1987 explicitly provides for the establishment of an internal market for air transport.

Although first steps have been taken already, this process is not finished yet and further adjustments within the industry will be necessary. The need for adjustment is particularly important in the air transport sector, since under the past system national airlines not only had a virtual monopoly in their home market, but also they were – and many still are – nationalised companies with all the advantages of having direct political support in their activities. Markets for other transport services undergo significant changes in the internal market programme. Adapting to new competition, and possibly to new ownership structures at the same time, will constitute a major challenge to the industry.

Structure

Demand trends

Demand for transport services can be met by different means of transport, one of which is air transport. Demand for air transport therefore depends on several factors: geographical conditions of the desired route, population density, speed relative to other modes of transportation, prices – absolute and relative to those of other means of transportation – and, most important, income.

World demand for air transport has been rising by 7.3 per cent a year on average between 1970 and 1987. From now to the year 2000 a slight decline in growth rates to 5.9 per cent is expected which will probably further decline to 4.2 per cent in the period 2000 to 2005 (Boeing, 1989). Figure 5.1 shows the development of regional travel markets and a forecast for the year 2000 by Boeing.

Such forecasts depend crucially on the expected growth in GNP and consequently per capita incomes, since they dominate demand trends. Several attempts to estimate the relation of income development, price, and air travel demand can be found in the literature (Doganis, 1985; Gillen *et al.*, 1985; Meyer and Oster, 1985; Mutti and Murai, 1977; Straszheim, 1978). Estimated income elasticities range around 1.5, i.e. a 10 per cent increase in income leads to a 15 per cent increase in demand for air travel. Business travel seems to have a slightly lower elasticity than vacation travel.

Price elasticities vary according to different fare categories as well as different routes. For international flights where alternative modes of transportation are practically non-existent, price elasticities must by construction be equal and opposite to the value of the income elasticities, i.e. around −1.5. For domestic flights, especially in short-range categories, substitutes for flying such as trains and cars are readily available, hence price elasticities are lower (i.e. more negative). For domestic US passenger service Baldwin and Krugman (1987) found a value of −2.85. For some European routes where substitutes are available elasticities might be even higher, although the Baldwin/Krugman estimate is already high compared to other studies.

The impact of this demand structure is obvious and can be readily seen from Figure 5.1. Demand will grow much faster in regions with high income growth. The fastest growing markets are routes to and from Asia and the intra-Asian traffic which have been growing between 9.2 per cent (intra-Asia) and 13.1 per cent a year (Europe to Asia) in the period 1970 to 1987. These routes will also experience the largest expansion between 1987 and 2000 with growth rates of 7.1 per cent and 9.4 per cent respectively. In absolute numbers the American market will still have the

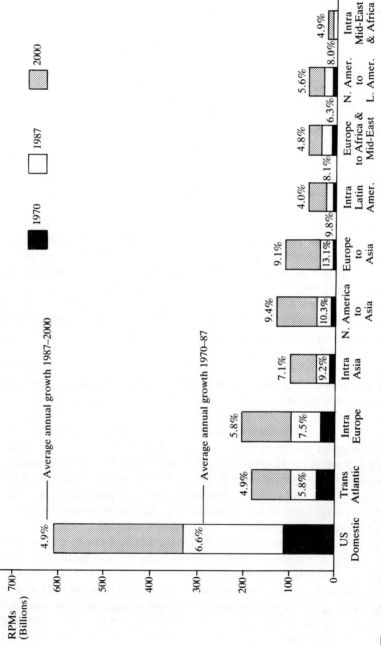

Figure 5.1 Major world air travel markets (Source: Boeing, 1989)

biggest increase, but only because of its large size. In percentage terms it will grow by less than 5 per cent.

In light of the estimated elasticities of income, demand in intra-European traffic will grow moderately. The proposed deregulation of European air-transport markets will lead to lower fares and, through relatively high price elasticities, to a further increase in demand. The extent of this price effect depends on the exact impact on fares. These two effects together account for the above-average growth perspectives for intra-European traffic. Intercontinental traffic originating from or coming to Europe participates mainly from the demand push in the Asian countries.

Supply

Technology of providing air transport services

Air transport is a service with very specific product characteristics. Each city pair on which the service at a particular time is offered is essentially a different product which can hardly be substituted by other city pairs, but it can be substituted to some extent by different times. In this sense, a large number of differentiated products define the market for air transport. Of course, further differentiation comes into play through different classes offered on a specific route and potentially different services by different airlines.

On the other hand, air transport services are not offered by a different company on each city pair. It obviously is advantageous to supply several city pairs concurrently. Economies of scale and economies of scope are important in explaining market structure in the air transport market.

Economies of scale would typically refer to increasing the number of airports served. Economies of density describe an increase of output inside a given network, i.e. either by adding new departures to routes which are already served or by increasing the size of the aircraft on these routes, keeping other factors unchanged. Finally, economies of scope describe the addition of new products, e.g. the establishment of charter services or air cargo transport in addition to scheduled services.

A number of studies have estimated these different effects (e.g. Gillen *et al.*, 1985; Kirby, 1986; White, 1979). Table 5.1 summarises Kirby's results which do not contradict those of other studies. Strong economies are only present in load factors and aircraft size. Increasing the number of destinations served and increasing the number of departures reveal even slight *dis*economies of scale. Since on a particular route load factor and aircraft size work in opposite directions *ceteris paribus*, economies of density are most likely to have a cost elasticity of approximately unity.

Table 5.1 Cost elasticities with respect to selected output dimensions

Factor	Elasticity
Average number of ports	1.041
Average stage length	0.911
Average load factor	0.314
Average aircraft size	0.495
Number of departures	1.084

Note: all elasticities are significantly different from unity

Source: Kirby (1986), Table 2

One can therefore conclude that the production of airline services overall does not exhibit strong economies of scale. With regard to economies of scope, Gillen *et al.* (1985) found that scheduled services and charter services are complementary only for low proportions of charter services (below 5 per cent).

Cost structure and contestability

These estimates need an important qualification. All numbers are estimated from markets which were more or less in equilibrium. Consequently, one cannot say that airline services are at all scales produced with constant returns to scale. Rather, competition has led to an industry structure in which there are just enough firms such that economies of scale are exhausted. Such an industry structure has been described by the same contestability (Baumol et al., 1982). A market is contestable – i.e. even with few firms an allocation equivalent to perfect competition arises – when there are no sunk costs of operating the firm.

The cost structure of airlines differs across airlines in different countries mainly because several inputs are differently priced across countries. Wages and salaries especially vary considerably. On average operating costs are composed as follows (Doganis, 1985):

- Direct variable operating cast   50 per cent
- Direct fixed operating cost   24 per cent
- Indirect operating cost   26 per cent

Hence, fixed costs are about half the size of operating costs. But not all of them must be treated as sunk costs. Doganis (1985) estimates that in the medium term as much as 90 per cent of operating costs can be varied easily. However, this depends on regulation of factor markets. Labour laws which raise the cost of firing may increase sunk cost. Aircraft themselves can easily be sold, since a well-functioning second-hand market exists, so that part of capital is not sunk. One area which might exhibit sunk costs is distribution of airlines services, such as reservation systems, marketing channels, etc.

Also several studies (see Baumol and Willig, 1986) have shown that routes from and to crowded airports have higher prices than those using less congested airports, indicating that landing slots may be an important entry barrier for new airlines. This result should, however, depend on the way landing slots are allocated. If slots are sold on a first come, first served basis established airlines will block important landing times, thus creating entry barriers. In contrast, under a regular auctioning framework such entry-preventing behaviour would not be rational. In general, one can conclude that airline markets are not perfectly contestable.

Industry structure

The European airline industry has historically been characterised by dominant national carriers which were usually state-owned and a number of small airlines serving regional, domestic, low-density traffic. The large carriers had a virtual monopoly on the dense routes in their domestic market. International routes were shared through bilateral agreements of the respective national carriers.

This structure has started to change in the light of the emergence of an internal market in the EC and proposed deregulation of the (so far) regulated air transport market. The current major European carriers are shown in Table 5.2. Compared to the American 'mega-carriers', European airlines are small. Since the acquisition of Eastern and Continental by Texas Air the American airline industry has become even more concentrated.

This concentration process has started only recently with the deregulation of the American market in 1978. After a period of intense competition and market entry of several new firms, a process of consolidation started. It resulted in an industry structure having a few 'mega-carriers' with roughly a 70 per cent share in the American market and a large number of regional airlines. The big carriers control the major hub into which the regional airlines provide feeder services. The market has become segmented into these two groups of airlines. The dominating companies are, of course, the mega-carriers which through their control of the big hubs and through co-operative agreements control about 95 per cent of the transport capacity in the US.

In Europe the competitive situation is slightly different. Past regulation

Table 5.2   Major European airlines in terms of total capacity offered

	Airline	ATKs (m.)
1.	British Airways	10,669
2.	Lufthansa	7,828
3.	Air France	6,443
4.	KLM	5,427
5.	Iberia	3,437
6.	Swissair	3,312
7.	Alitalia	3,090
8.	SAS	2,418
9.	Olympic Airways	1,513
10.	Sabena	1,496
	International Comparisons	
1.	United	19,682
2.	AMR (American Airlines)	17,103
3.	Delta	12,801
4.	Continental	12,652
5.	JAL	10,645

Source: IATA, ICAO, AEA

and the beginnings of deregulation have resulted in three groups of airlines with different competitive positions in the market, as follows:

1. *The flag carriers* They can still rely on a number of privileges, on their historically developed market position, and on their access to landing slots and airport facilities.
2. *The 'independent' carriers* They are essentially new entrants in the market for scheduled service. Some of them were charter carriers before and have expanded their activities into scheduled services.
3. *The regional airlines* They serve only less dense shorter routes either domestically or inside Europe. Their competitive position is quite different, since they usually use smaller aircraft so that they do not compete directly with the flag and independent carriers.

Development comparable to the US market is unlikely to happen. Most major European carriers are still state-owned or under some state control and they have dominating market shares in their domestic market. There are no signs that these companies are attempting to challenge this structure.

In terms of market dominance in international traffic, the European industry structure is still similar to the American industry to some degree. Each European country has its flag carrier which provides most of scheduled international flights. International routes have been shared under a 50/50 rule between the flag carriers of the two participating countries, i.e. each flag carrier supplies 50 per cent of the traffic on a specific international city pair. Domestic traffic was either supplied by the flag carrier or by an independent regional airline. Often regional airlines were only allowed to serve routes which could not be profitably served by the large aircraft of the flag carriers.

This structure has been somewhat softened through the competition of charter airlines. They were founded to undercut the cartel prices of the flag carriers in the vacation market segment, but have become competitors to scheduled services to some extent as well. Flag carriers have responded to this challenge with special discounts and by supplying charter services themselves. For example, Lufthansa owns its own charter airline, namely, Condor. Also a number of domestic regional carriers have begun competing on dense domestic routes.

Regulation of markets

Today's regulation of air transport markets is in transition. Historically, there were two different types of market regulations: the markets for domestic flights which were controlled by national authorities, and the markets for international flights which were and are to some extent controlled by IATA. IATA is a cartel of airlines providing international services and was founded in 1945. The cartel set prices for each route which were usually granted by the respective governments. Traffic on a specific route was shared between the two flag carriers on a 50/50 basis at the agreed price.

Since carriers were not allowed to supply domestic flights in a foreign country, domestic traffic was and still is completely controlled by the national authorities and supplied by domestic airlines. Whereas in the past airlines usually had a monopoly on a domestic route, with prices approved by the regulating authority, authorities have begun to grant several domestic airlines permission to compete on dense routes. These more liberal policies seem to expand as governments see deregulation in all transport markets becoming inevitable.

A part of the industry is essentially deregulated anyway. Charter carriers can freely choose routes and prices. They are not allowed, however, to offer scheduled services. Several loopholes have resulted in a situation where they can compete with scheduled traffic to some extent. This is one of the reasons why discount fares have been introduced by carriers offering scheduled flights.

In summary, the European air transport market is not very different from other transport markets in that it is highly regulated. Regulation of air transport in particular was and, to some extent, still is concentrated on restricting the right to supply air transport services, i.e. market entry, and to set prices for transport services freely. These are the areas where the Commission of the EC has started to relax regulations step by step.

1992 impact: deregulation

The logic of deregulation which the Commission has adopted is based on two premises. The American example of deregulation is not appropriate for the EC. Reforms should therefore be introduced step by step and through a development of the existing bilateral agreements between countries towards more liberal regulations. The second is that deregulation of the European air transport market should first be directed towards traffic between member countries and later towards traffic with third countries.

In 1987, a first package of air transport measures was introduced which addressed three aspects of regulation:

1. *Rules governing fares were relaxed.* Previously, fares for a specific route had to be identical for all carriers. Now no government can prevent the introduction of economy fares, as long as no dumping is involved.
2. *Capacity sharing rules were relaxed.* The strict rule in bilateral agreements for a strictly equal division of seat capacity between carriers which are authorised to operate a route was dropped. Now a carrier who wishes to expand capacity could do so, provided the capacity remained inside a specific ratio. This ratio was 55:45 per cent in 1988 and 60:40 per cent after October 1989.
3. *Community competition rules were defined.* Powers of investigation and sanction were conferred on the European Commission to ensure that competition rules are respected in the air transport industry. At the same time, a series of exemptions from competition rules were adopted. They allow companies to keep certain agreements which are clearly advantageous for passengers, such as co-ordination of air services, interlining agreements, ticket sales systems, etc.

Right now a second phase of deregulation is in the process of being introduced. The following items of the proposal are supposed to liberalise air transport markets and increase competition:

- *Limiting governments' power to block fares.* Any new fare introduced on a particular route can only be blocked by the authorising governments, if both governments oppose the fare. Otherwise fares are automatically approved. This system is called 'double dis-approval'.
- *Relaxation of traffic sharing rules.* Since 1988 an airline may not acquire more than 60 per cent of traffic on a city pair which is served by the two carriers. This percentage will be increased in steps to 75 per cent in 1992, and it is planned to eliminate it completely after 1992.

- *Cabotage*. First steps towards cabotage, i.e. the right to supply services between third countries, will be taken. One consists in raising the size of aircraft which are excluded from bilateral capacity controls from 70 to 100 seats. The new right of 'multiple designation' permits a government to authorise several carriers to serve the same route. Finally 'fifth freedom' rights are given to carriers for intra-community traffic, i.e. an airline can pick up and set down passengers on intermediate points of a route in third countries.

These measures will not free competition from government intervention completely, but, overall, they amount to a significant reduction of the monopoly power of flag carriers and offer easier market access for new suppliers.

Company strategies in a deregulated market

Describing the impact of a single market in air transport on company strategies is difficult. For one thing, by 1992 there will be no truly 'single' market. Secondly, even the process towards a single market is in rather an early stage. Company strategies are therefore changing in order to adapt to a constantly changing competitive environment. Thirdly, air transport has been growing at a rate much faster than expected, such that airlines are confronted with all types of capacity limitations, in the air as well as in airports. Company strategies, therefore, need to be adjusted to this process which occurs parallel to, but independently from, the creation of a single market. Therefore, only general trends in company strategies can be illustrated. They describe the current adjustments to the changes in the competitive environment.

It has already been mentioned that the European market is served by carriers which can be categorised into three groups: the flag carriers, independent carriers, and regional airlines. Each group has a different competitive position in the same environment in terms of market segmentation or market position. Regional airlines operate in a market niche which depends to a large degree on the activities of the large carriers. The strategies of regional airlines will therefore be discussed parallel to those of the flag and independent carriers.

Strategies of airlines in the face of an internal market can conveniently be grouped into internal and external strategies. The matrix in Figure 5.2 describes the different aspects of company strategies. In the following sections some facts will be presented, but most judgements about these strategies will be little more than speculations, since the industry is just starting to respond to the expected new environment.

	Internal	External
Flag Carriers	Capacity choice Pricing policy Marketing	Hub concept Intra-EC mergers Global mergers
New Carriers	Booking systems In-flight service Route selection	European co-operation Global co-operation

Figure 5.2   Company strategies

Internal strategies

In the proposed Internal Market framework flag carriers will be losing their monopoly position in large segments of the market. They will therefore need to react to the new competition with a reallocation of resources.

One of the most important areas, of course, is prices. Strictly administered prices for all traffic between city pairs disappeared years ago. Yet, flag carriers have started to segment the market by offering discounts to specific groups of consumers, e.g. APEX tariffs for travellers who book return flights and stay for more than a week, or weekend specials like the 'Spar-tariff' of Lufthansa. The idea behind segmentation is to levy full monopoly prices on those who need maximum flexibility and to lower prices step by step with increasing restrictiveness of service.

This process has started with the competition of charter airlines who often offered flights inclusive of hotel accommodation at the destination at lower prices than the flag carriers charged for the flight alone. As the restrictiveness of the IATA cartel eroded, discount pricing by flag carriers flourished. With the starting of liberalisation in the EC and the United States, not only discount fares but overall tariffs started to fall. On heavily contested routes in Europe fares fell by as much as 15 per cent. The percentage of fares sold at a discount to the administered official IATA tariff has increased significantly over the last few years (see Table 5.3).

Capacity choice for routes also depends on the degree of competition. A bilateral cartel with monopoly power will offer flights well dispersed over the day. The total capacity offered will be smaller than if there were competition from another airline. Load factors and profits are therefore high. With additional competition airlines have an incentive to increase the frequency of flights and use smaller aircraft. Consumers gain through shorter waiting times.

In Europe, strategies of increased frequency and smaller aircraft will conflict with airport congestion on many routes. How increased competi-

Table 5.3   Number of fares in Europe below economy fare

Percentage of economy fare	April 1988	January 1989	Change
65–45%	17,072	17,526	+2.7%
45–40%	2,898	3,449	+19.0%
40–35%	1,661	1,963	+18.2%
below 35%	742	1,151	+55.1%

Source: IATA

tion will work under such a constraint and whether competition will increase at all is still an open question. There are claims by new entrants that dense routes and congested airports are effectively closed to newcomers. For example, London's Heathrow airport has an explicit ban on new airlines, while Lufthansa is said to control the most profitable slots at the heavily congested Frankfurt airport.

If such claims are true, the liberalisation effects of air transport regulation will be limited by the congestion of airports and the inefficiency of the distribution system of landing slots. Allocation rules for landing slots are a topic which would need further investigation, especially in the context of competition in the air transport market.

In the case of London's Heathrow airport, newcomers are left with the option of flying to other London airports such as Gatwick, Luton, or Stansted. In other cases, airlines may fly similar routes to the flag carriers by using smaller less-congested airports in the neighbourhood of the big hubs. This option has been extensively used by charter carriers. The disadvantage of this strategy in the case of scheduled traffic is that passengers lose the option of convenient connecting flights which often go through the hubs.

Air transport services not only differ with respect to time, location, and price. On-board services, check-in and other services offer possibilities for differentiating the overall service of an airline. Parallel to the differentiation of prices, flag carriers are reversing the trend towards single-class seating. Whereas on intercontinental flights three classes are standard, international intra-European traffic has been operated with two classes in the aircraft. Most carriers are now going back to a separation of business and economy class.

Different on-board service has also become a strategy for product differentiation among airlines. German Wings, for example, is a new airline which competes directly with Lufthansa. It charges the same price on its routes as Lufthansa does, so that it has won the right to interlining before German courts. It claims, however, to offer superior on-board service. The opposite strategy is followed by the other German competitor to Lufthansa. AeroLloyd offers 'Lufthansa quality' at 10–15 per cent lower prices.

Under the IATA regulations, marketing, booking, and ticket sales have been of minor importance to airlines. Fares were fixed and in each country the national flag carrier had listed both carriers in its schedule. Since several airlines can now offer identical routes at different prices, the whole booking system has become a major item on the list of new company strategies. Most airline tickets have been sold so far through travel agencies; Lufthansa sells 85 per cent of its tickets through travel agencies. Together with the elimination of ticket price fixing, commissions, which up to now have been fixed, will also be free.

The freedom to set prices will offer airlines the opportunity to sell more tickets directly. This enables them to pass part of the commission to consumers. In the United States so-called 'consolidators' have begun to buy large amounts of tickets directly from the airline at a considerable discount. Such a system is also expected in Europe. It is especially attractive for customers with a large demand, such as large companies.

This tendency is alleviated by the emerging electronic booking systems. Previously, each flag carrier had its own computer reservation system. New airlines claim that these systems have been used in discriminatory ways.

Ryanair, an independent, Irish airline, is an example. When Ryanair started low-priced flights to England, Aer Lingus, the Irish flag carrier, refused to list Ryanair's schedule in its computer reservation system. It did get its flights into the British Airways computer for a fee. The twist, however, is this: Luton Airport, which Ryanair uses, is not listed as a London destination on British Airways computers. Hence, it does not appear with competing London–Dublin destinations on the computer.

American booking systems have put pressure on European firms to create larger networks. Two international booking systems are now emerging in Europe, called Galileo and Amadeus. All major European carriers participate in one of the systems (Table 5.4). Both systems are linked to American reservation systems. Some Galileo owners have shares in the Apollo system of United Airlines. The Amadeus software is bought from Texas Air Corporation's SystemOne reservation system and Amadeus has agreed to market SystemOne outside the United States. It also has signed a co-operation agreement with the Asian Abacus reservation system.

Overall these systems offer more transparency for travel agents and consumers, but they are susceptible to discrimination. Seemingly minor features can have major anti-competitive effects. The case of assignment of airports to cities – Luton to London – is just one example. Another one

Table 5.4 Ownership and participation in Europe's air reservation systems

Galileo		Amadeus	
Airline	Number of passengers (m.) (1987)	Airline	Number of passengers (m.) (1987)
British Airways	21.8	Lufthansa	16.9
KLM Royal Dutch		Air France	13.4
Airlines	5.9	Iberia	14.1
Swissair	6.8	SAS	12.6
Alitalia	14.3		
Covia Corporation[1]	55.2		
Associated companies:		*Associated companies:*	
Olympic Airways	6.6	Air Inter	12.8
Sabena	2.4	JAT Yugoslav Airlines	4.0
TAP Air Portugal	2.6	Linjeflyg (Sweden)	4.0
Aer Lingus	2.3	Finnair	3.4
Austrian Airlines	1.7	Braathens SAFE	
		(Norway)	2.9
		Icelandair	0.9
		Adria Airways	
		(Yugosl.)	0.6
Total	119.6	Total	85.6

Note: [1]51% owned by United Airlines, 49% by USAir, British Airways, KLM, Swissair and Alitalia

is the order in which flights on a particular route are listed when a travel agent uses the system for booking. Airlines which always appear on the screen first naturally have a chance of getting more orders than an airline which is listed later.

Both systems address this problem in the same fashion. A travel agent can call two different screens. One which is organised by criteria like route and time of day, and another one which shows the flights of a particular carrier. The advantage of this system is that the owners of the booking system do not seem to be able to discriminate against airlines which belong to the consortium. Compared to the previous situation competition inside the consortium will probably increase.

The problem of the booking systems in terms of competition is not so much that there are only two in Europe and probably five worldwide. Booking systems have increasing returns to scale by their very nature which requires an integrated system – ideally, one system which offers all flights. The number of systems will therefore be small. The problem is that they are owned by some airlines. These airlines have incentives to discriminate against non-owners. As long as the ownership structure does not change there is need for regulation of booking systems.

External strategies of established carriers

The prospect of 1992 for established carriers is clear: they will lose monopoly power. Whereas internal strategies were focused on product and price differentiation which are followed by the necessary internal adjustment, external strategies can be summed up under the following headings:

- Getting prepared for global competition.
- Using bottlenecks efficiently.

Prior to deregulation, flag carriers had at least a home market monopoly. This contested situation will disappear, but competition from foreign established carriers and from domestic and foreign newcomers will encounter several bottlenecks.

Besides the potentially anti-competitive effects of booking systems, airport congestion will be the other primary obstacle for new competitors. Airports have only a limited capacity of landing slots and passenger terminal facilities. The best landing times and the best locations of facilities have been used or possessed by the flag carriers who will continue to control this position. These are the direct and obvious effects. They would indicate that flag carriers will invest a lot of effort into securing this position.

A more subtle effect comes in through a number of changes in the competitive environment:

- Air traffic is growing at a rate which surpasses the increase in airport facilities. A reorganisation of air traffic is necessary to streamline traffic flows.
- Short-range domestic flights which become contested by new entrants will not be all that profitable for flag carriers. They will therefore focus more on international air transport.
- Intercontinental traffic from any country was controlled by the flag carrier. Under price competition foreign carriers can take away this traffic through feeder services to their home airports. Because of the short distances inside Europe this can be done without cost disadvantages. For example, Copenhagen and Frankfurt are at approximately the same distance from Hamburg, and so are Zurich and Frankfurt from Munich.
- Easy and flexible flight connections are important attributes for travellers, especially for business travellers who pay full fares and form an important part of net revenue of airlines.

All these factors seem to indicate that Europe is in the process of developing some form of a 'hub-and-spoke' system as in the United States. A small number of airports – a guess would be five to seven – in

Europe will become 'hubs' through which intercontinental traffic is routed. These hubs are served by short-range domestic and intraEuropean feeder services.

Those airports which will become international hubs will, of course, give the airline which is located in the hub a competitive advantage. Control of airport facilities, landing slots, or flexibility in the use of aircraft are such advantages. But most important is the ability to supply a worldwide network of flights which more or less rests on the existence of a 'home base'.

It seems – and this speculation is supported by the American experience – that in the future only airlines situated in a hub will become so-called 'mega-carriers'. It is expected that future intercontinental traffic will be supplied by a relatively small number of mega-carriers which serve practically every major airport worldwide.

The planned deregulation of air transport in the EC obviously has accelerated this process of concentration and competition. In this light, strategies of flag carriers have to be seen; in other words company strategies may not be a direct reaction to deregulation, but deregulation has forced upon airlines activities which they, sooner or later, would have to do anyway.

Right now, it is not clear exactly which airports will become major hubs, except for those which are apparent, like London, Paris, or Frankfurt. Other contestants are Brussels, Amsterdam, Copenhagen, Rome, etc. The strategies of European firms, however, seem to indicate some movement towards the hub system and the corresponding mega-carriers.

In the past few months and years several mergers and co-operation agreements have been signed among European carriers. The most recent ones are shown in Figure 5.3. Numbers in parentheses indicate the share which the airline owns; arrows without numbers indicate co-operation agreements or undisclosed shares.

Company strategies reveal the following pattern:

- Mergers of flag carriers with smaller airlines are often confined to domestic firms.
- There are no mergers of large carriers. They rely on co-operation agreements and/or the holding of small shares.

Three arguments could explain the first observation: the flag carriers concentrate on improving their domestic base by investing in regional airlines which serve their hub; or flag carriers do not expect a truly internal market, hence they do not expect the takeover of foreign regional airlines to be profitable; or, finally, even in an internal European market they do not expect to gain from controlling foreign airlines. There

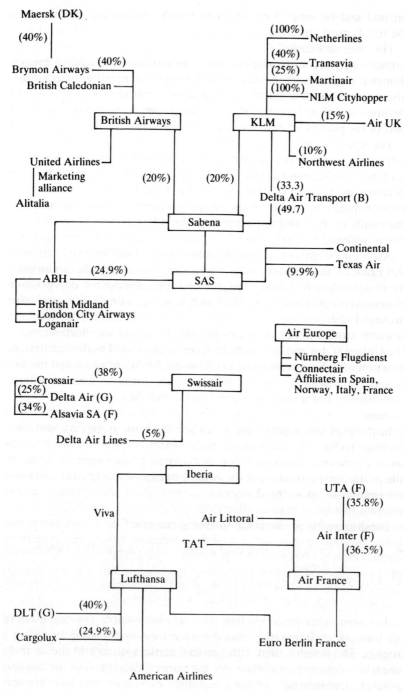

Figure 5.3   Recent company mergers and co-operation agreements

are no facts revealing which argument is valid, but one can speculate that the first is most important.

The 'hub-and-spoke' philosophy would mean that a potential mega-carrier wants to control as much of the spoke system as possible. Hence, domestic regionals are the most important in this context. This logic could also explain the big exception, namely the partnership of SAS with Airlines of Britain Heathrow (ABH); it is claimed that this investment is part of the plan of SAS to develop London to an SAS hub.

The situation involving British Airways, KLM, SAS and Sabena is interesting, but it is not possible to determine what these partnerships will lead to. Some sources say that Sabena, KLM, and British Airways plan to develop Brussels as a charter and regional hub, Amsterdam as either the European hub or a second long-haul airport, and London's Heathrow as the major intercontinental departure point. How SAS's plans will fit into this is unclear.

According to this logic the second co-operation will involve Lufthansa, Air France and Iberia, together with some regional and charter airlines. More speculation would then forecast the emergence of two con-glomerates: one around British Airways, KLM, Sabena, etc.; the other around Lufthansa and Air France. This would fit into the tendency towards around ten to twelve mega-carriers worldwide which started in the United States and the Far East. It is also supported by the fact that the two potential European groups (except for SAS) are owners of the two respective booking systems Amadeus and Galileo. This may be a coincidence, but it is an interesting fact in any case.

Another aspect which is apparent from Figure 5.3 is the fact that practically all flag carriers have started ties with American airlines – Swissair/Delta, SAS/Texas Air, British Airways/United, KLM/Northwest, Lufthansa/American. The reasons for such activities seem to rest on the protectionist structure of the American air transport market, but also on pessimistic views of American carriers about the openness of the internal European market after 1992.

Landing rights at American airports are given on a very restrictive basis, foreign airlines are denied fifth freedom rights, and American airlines must not be controlled by foreign capital. This makes the transfer of passengers at American destinations rather difficult for foreign airlines. Since mergers are forbidden, European airlines try to arrange co-operative ties with only small share holdings just below the legal limit.

In summary, strategies of flag carriers point towards a globalisation of air transport markets which are not necessarily confined to the EC as a region. The development of a hub-and-spoke system and the mergers seem to follow more a global trend than the establishment of the Internal Market. The Internal Market programme may, however, have acceler-ated this process.

New entrants

There is almost general agreement that new entrants will not be able to compete with those flag carriers which will eventually become mega-carriers. It takes a long time to develop a worldwide network of flights because of the immense start-up investments and also because of the know-how required to operate such a system. Consequently, new airlines have not attempted to challenge the position of the flag carriers head-on. They choose to compete in specific niches mostly on short routes.

Internal strategies are concentrated on product and price differentia-tion *vis-à-vis* the established carriers. For example, in Germany Aero-Lloyd and German Wings now offer flights on some of the densest routes to and from Frankfurt and Munich. AeroLloyd does this by offering 10–15 per cent lower fares than Lufthansa, whereas German Wings offers more service at the same fare as Lufthansa. Both companies are still focused on the German market, but at the same time they claim that they are waiting for the Internal Market to expand to European-wide network.

A different approach is followed by Air Europe. This British company has begun to develop a pan-European network of airlines before the deregulation has been completed. A series of European airlines was formed which would be owned and registered in their country of origin – as it is required by national law – but would share a common fleet, common standards, joint computer reservations, common staff and pilot training, etc. In doing this, a European airline has been founded inside the regulated institutional framework. The different Air Europe airlines offer fares 10–15 per cent below those of the national carriers.

This type of strategy essentially rests on a pessimistic expectation about the Internal Market programme in air transport. Air Europe's structure gives it a competitive advantage in a regulated institutional framework, but these advantages may disappear with deregulation, since such a complex structure of ownership in different companies will not be needed any more. But the philosophy of the chairman of International Leisure Group, the umbrella organisation of Air Europe, Harry Goodman, is: 'I don't believe in 1992' (*Wall Street Journal*, 13 April 1989). Ironically, the Air Europe airlines are so far the only 'European airlines'.

Structure and performance after 1992

What will the industry look like if the Internal Market programme for air transport is completed? This question can hardly be answered with much certainty. The deregulation of air transport markets has only started and it is open how far additional measures – which go beyond those already planned by the European Commission – will go. Even more so, it is open whether they will be accepted by the political process in the member countries. Nevertheless, a speculative list which represents the author's expectations about the future industry structure will be given.

The factor which will be crucial for all speculations about the future of the European air transport markets is how much the current national orientation of the industry will change. Flag carriers are often state-owned with all the consequences of political influence in the national regulatory authorities. Registration of foreign firms is still almost impossible. Fifth freedom rights are slow to be given to foreign carriers.

If this national orientation prevails, the European industry structure will not change very much. Global competition and the overall process towards an internal market will, however, eventually reduce this orientation. The resulting industry structure will then change in terms of the following factors:

- The geographical allocation of airports.
- The emergence of mega-carriers based on these hubs.
- The replacement of activities of companies which have been using regulatory niches, e.g. charter airlines.
- The new role of regional airlines.
- The role of booking systems for competition.

The geographical structure of airports has been influenced in the past by national boundaries. Domestic monopolies and international cartels have resulted in a distorted airport network. In the way in which national boundaries for regulatory activities lose importance and flag carriers lose their power, a more efficient network of airports will emerge. It is expected to be a hub-and-spoke system with a small number of intercontinental hubs, possibly 5 to 7.

This development of hubs will go hand in hand with the growth of a few airlines into so-called mega-carriers which provide a worldwide network of flights. Each mega-carrier will use a hub as its base. A hub may be shared by two or more carriers, although it is hard to imagine how these carriers will compete against each other.

Under the IATA cartel a number of airlines have used loopholes in the system to offer cheaper air transport services; charter companies and non-IATA airlines are examples. In a deregulated market this artificial division of activities is not necessary any more. Scheduled and charter services will be offered by the same companies, their distinction may disappear completely.

The hub-and-spoke system will reinforce the division of the industry into international and intercontinental carriers on the one side and airlines providing feeder services on the other side. Of course, the structure will not materialise in such an extreme form. Some dense international routes will always attract airlines which function as a competitive fringe.

It is hard to predict how regional airlines will be organised. They may still be formally independent companies – especially when their stock of aircraft is different from the stock of the large carriers, such that no economies of scale in maintenance or aircraft use are present. However, they will have to depend on the mega-carriers for marketing and selling in their role as feeder services for intercontinental traffic.

A crucial factor in determining the future industry structure and competition will be the marketing and selling of flights. In the future, not only an airline ticket will be sold, but a complete package of transport services will be offered covering everything surrounding the travel, hotel, flight, rental car, etc. The two European booking systems and the other systems in the United States and East Asia will be used by practically all airlines. The way in which these systems operate and how they are controlled will have a major impact on competition among airlines.

Such booking systems have clearly increasing economies of scale; without capacity constraints on computers a computer reservation system may even be a natural monopoly. How such a situation could be regulated in order to keep competition alive is an open question. Company strategies as well as the worldwide industry structure will depend on the way in which these computer reservation systems will work.

References

Baldwin, Richard and Krugman, Paul R. (1987), 'Industrial policy and international competition in wide-bodied Jet aircraft', manuscript.

Baumol, W. J., Panzar, J. C. and Willig, R. D. (1982), *Contestable Markets and the Theory of Industry Structure*, London: Harcourt Brace Jovanovich.

Baumol, William J. and Willig, Robert D. (1986), 'Contestability: developments since the book', C. V. Starr Center for Applied Economics, New York University, research report 186–01.

Boeing Commercial Airplanes (1989), 'Current market outlook – world travel market demand and airplane supply requirements', Seattle, February.

Doganis, Rigas (1985), 'Flying of course: the economics of international airlines', London.

Eaton, Curtis B. and Lipsey, Richard G. (1978), 'The principle of minimum differentiation reconsidered: some new developments in the theory of spatial competition', *Review of Economic Studies*, pp. 27–49.

Gillen, David W., Oum and Tretheway (1985), 'Canadian airline deregulation and privatization', Centre for Transportation Studies, University of British Columbia.

Gillen, David W. *et al.* (1988), 'Entry barriers and anti-competitive behaviour in a deregulated airline market: the case of Canada', *International Journal of Transport Economics*, pp. 29–41.

Kirby, M. G. (1986), 'Airline economics of "scale" in Australia and Australian domestic air transport policy', *Journal of Transport Economics and Policy*, pp. 339–53.

Lin, Leesha (1986), 'The demand analysis of the scheduled Level I domestic air travel market'. Proceedings of the 21st annual meeting of the Canadian Transportation Research Forum.

Meyer, John R. and Oster, Clinton V. jr (1985), 'Deregulation and the new airline entrepreneurs'. Cambridge, Mass.

Mutti, John and Murai, Yoshitak (1977), 'Airline travel on the North Atlantic', *Journal of Transport Economics and Policy*, pp. 45–53.

Strandenes, Siri Pettersen (1987), 'Scandinavian airline industry – market structure and competition', Centre for Applied Research, Norwegian School of Economics and Business Administration, Bergen, report no. 21/1987.

Straszheim, Mahlon R. (1978), 'Airline demand functions in the North Atlantic and their pricing implications', *Journal of Transport Economics and Policy*, pp. 179–95.

White, Lawrence J. (1979), 'Economies of scale and the questions of "natural monopoly" in the airline industry', *Journal of Law and Economics*, pp. 545–73.

6

The aerospace industry

Gernot Klepper

The aircraft industry has historically been a well-defined sector producing airframes and aircraft engines. As the technology of flying has improved the industry expanded to what is now called the aerospace industry. Although today there is no clear definition or encompassing statistical nomenclature for the industry, the product structure is relatively easy to define but numbers are hard to obtain. The heart of the industry is still the production of aircraft, of their engines and of aircraft parts; the last is important since, due to high safety standards and the long lifetime of an aircraft, replacement of parts is a substantial activity. Since World War II space products as well as electronic equipment in the air and on the ground have been added to the product structure. Space products are guided missiles, space vehicles, space propulsion units and space equipment and parts. Electronic components have become an increasingly important part of aerospace activities. Avionics is increasing with the number of aircraft produced, but its share in value is increasing as well: Arthur D. Little International estimated in 1987 that the 8 per cent value-added share of civil aircraft in the late 1980s will increase to over 10 per cent in the mid-1990s. Military aircraft and space products have much higher avionic shares, more than 30 per cent in some cases.

This product structure must be divided into a civil and a military component. Not only do markets for civil and military aerospace products follow different rules and have different structures, products themselves differ increasingly in their technological characteristics. In civil aircraft developments fuel efficiency, noise reduction, safety, and cost effectiveness are guiding factors, whereas military developments are primarily determined by military demands which are in many cases contradictory to civil needs. This is clearly evident in the engine technologies. Of course, in some areas civil and military activities are very similar; some identical products can be put to both civil and military use, of which the space shuttle is just one example. In general, therefore, it is difficult to separate space activities into their civil and military components.

Industry structure

Demand trends

There are three very different types of demand for products of the aerospace industry: demand for military aircraft and military space products; demand for civil space products (mostly research and communication satellites); and demand for civil aircraft. Only in the last segment can demand be readily observed on a market where consumers are agents with a well-defined objective. Demand for military and space products comes mostly from government agencies where budget constraints and preferences are difficult to assess.

Civil aircraft range from large transport aircraft through commuter aircraft and business jets to helicopters and leisure aircraft. Since the large transport aircraft segment dominates the market – about 70–80 per cent in the United States (US Department of Commerce, 1986) – the assessment will focus on this segment. Demand for large transport aircraft is derived from the demand for air transport services which have been growing at an average 7.3 per cent per year between 1970 and 1987 and are expected to grow in different regions by between 5 per cent and 9 per cent into the next century (see Figure 6.1). Airbus Industrie and Boeing used base estimates of 5.3 per cent and 5.5 per cent growth rates respectively in 1986/7 (Airbus Industrie, 1987; Boeing, 1986), but the current demand development has led to forecasts of 5.9 per cent on average (Boeing, 1989). Air travel demand growth is closely correlated with income growth, so that all forecasts crucially depend on assumptions about world income growth rates.

From these demand forecasts for air transport, civil transport aircraft producers have derived demand forecasts for different types of aircraft over the next twenty years. The expected demand for transport aircraft according to aircraft size and regional distribution from 1987 to 2006 is summarised in Figure 6.2. North America will still be the largest market, not the least because it has an old aircraft fleet so that replacement demand accounts for a large share of total demand. The fastest growing market is in the Asian and Pacific region. This also explains the large

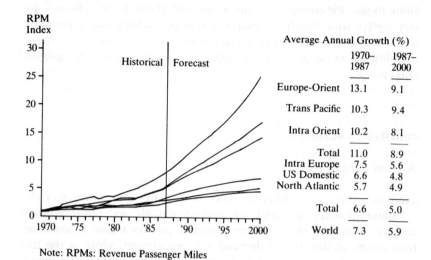

Figure 6.1   World air travel demand (Source: Boeing, 1989, p. 37)

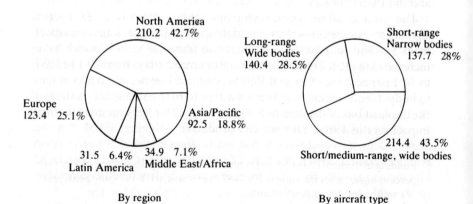

Note: forecast for 1987–2006 in 1986 $bn

Figure 6.2   Demand for large transport aircraft (Source: Airbus Industrie, 1987; own calculations)

share of the demand for long-range wide-body aircraft, of which 27 per cent comes from the Asian and Pacific region compared to a demand share of only 19 per cent of the total market.

Military demand is politically determined and depends on national perception about defensive needs as well as on the international relations. Military procurement is almost always heavily biased in favour of national companies such that – apart from exports to countries without a comparable industrial base – markets are confined to national boundaries. Budgetary constraints limit political demands for military products. Statistical information on weapons procurement in general and especially in the aerospace sector is scarce in most countries. Only in the United States is some information on the weapon acquisition process available which can be treated as an example for other countries.

Military procurement in the aerospace industry is an R & D-intensive activity. Normally, weapon procurement starts with R & D contracts, followed by advanced development, and ending with the actual procurement contracts. This whole process can extend over a long time horizon; a product cycle of twenty years for a military aircraft is not uncommon. Therefore, today's R & D budgets create a 'bow wave' of procurement contracts (Cain, 1987), i.e. every R & D contract is followed by much larger procurement contracts. An appendix, available from the author, illustrates typical 'bow waves' for the V–22 Osprey military helicopter and the Patriot missile.

The United States government has increased its R & D budgets significantly in the 1980s. National defence R & D outlays have increased from $14.5bn in 1980 to requested $46.9bn in FY 1989 which is an increase in the R & D share of national defence outlays from 10.1 per cent to 14.1 per cent (see Figure 6.3). This increase is expected to accumulate to budget requirements for which it will be hard to get funding. A study of the implications of the recent increase in R & D budgets summarises their impact on the demand for military products:

Funding in the final style of development – engineering development – was 40 percent higher after inflation in FY 1987 than it was in FY 1977, the peak year of engineering development funding prior to the 1980s buildup. The Administration's FY 1988 engineering development request represents 25 percent growth after inflation above the FY 1987 appropriation. (Cain, 1987, p. 2)

If all programs now in development are permitted to move into production as planned, the resulting procurement bow wave would require significant increases in the defense budget over the next five to ten years. However, such increases are unlikely, given the federal deficit and the rapid growth that the defense budget has already received. (*ibid*., p. 4)

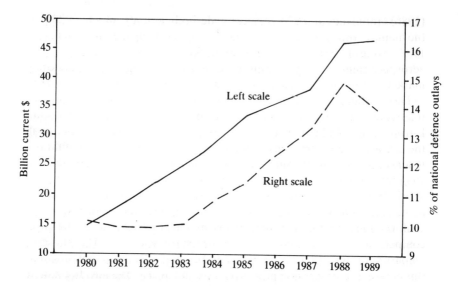

Figure 6.3   Research and development in the US defence budget (Source: Cain, 1987)

Similar results can be found for defence procurement plans in Germany (Wilke and Wulf, 1986). If the planned 3 per cent real increase in defence outlays is realised, simulations show that planned procurement would amount to between 27.6 per cent and 35 per cent of the federal budget, compared to 19.1 per cent in 1983 (Rodejohann, 1985). Another simulation study concludes that the defence outlays as a share of GNP in Germany will rise from 2.7 per cent in 1984 to at least 3.9 per cent in the year 2000; under unfavourable economic conditions it might rise to 5.3 per cent (Huffschmid, 1986).

Both the German simulations and the American 'bow wave' make clear that military demand is not likely to be realised as planned in the future. Budget restrictions will probably be more decisive in determining demand than military needs based on defence strategies. In that sense, military demand is difficult to predict even in the short run.

Supply

Regional industry structure

In market economies aerospace is a worldwide activity with international competition. By far the largest producer is the United States with 1.272m.

(1986) employees and $105bn sales amounting to 4.6 per cent of sales of the manufacturing sector (Aerospace Industries Association of America, 1987). American sales are estimated to cover about two thirds of world aerospace sales (Todd and Simpson, 1986, p. 7) so that one can expect a market of roughly $150bn in the Western world today.

The dominance of American companies in the aerospace sector is a relatively recent phenomenon. Aircraft design and production started in Europe after World War I. It was dominated by military production. In the 1920s demand for aircraft in the United States was boosted by the federal government through its heavily subsidised airmail activities. In 1935 the United States became the largest producer of aircraft. During World War II the production capacity was expanded massively, such that at the end of the war a large industrial base could be converted to produce civil versions of military aircraft. With its large distances and little competition by railroads the American market grew rapidly (US Department of Commerce, 1986). Parallel to the increase in demand in this period, major technological advances took place. The introduction of the jet engine both in Great Britain with the de Havilland Comet and in the United States with the Boeing 707 opened new opportunities in terms of speed and range.

The increase in demand and market size for civil aircraft was accompanied by increasing concentration of aircraft manufacturers. In Europe, French and British companies introduced new aircraft such as the Comet, the Caravelle, and the Concorde. None was successful commercially. In the United States the number of producers of large transport aircraft fell from about thirty in the 1920s to two after Lockheed opted out of the civil market in 1981. Today, there are three producers of large transport aircraft – Boeing, McDonnell Douglas, and Airbus Industrie, a joint venture of British Aerospace (20 per cent), Deutsche Airbus (a subsidiary of MBB) (37.9 per cent), (French) Aérospatiale (37.9 per cent), and (Spanish) CASA (4.2 per cent) (Airbus Industrie, 1987).

Industry structure by product categories

In value terms the civil side of the aerospace industry is dominated by large transport aircraft produced by these three producers. An estimated total market for civil aircraft of $35bn in the late 1980s is divided up as follows: 73 per cent large transport aircraft (>100 passengers), 19 per cent small commercial aircraft (<100 passengers), 5 per cent business aircraft, and 4 per cent for helicopters and leisure aircraft. Aircraft other than large transport are produced by smaller producers throughout the world, but even this market is still dominated by American and European producers.

The military side of the aerospace industry has a larger number of producers of which the largest firms are concentrated in the United States and Europe as well. European system firms developing new military aircraft are the same as those collaborating in the Airbus project. In addition there are some specialised companies focusing on military aircraft only.

Although American and European companies dominate the markets for aircraft and space products many countries have their own aerospace industry. These activities are, however, mostly confined to joint ventures with the leading firms where either components are produced or a whole aircraft is produced or assembled under a licensing arrangement. Licensing agreements are common for military aircraft whereas component supplies often occur in the production of civil aircraft. Aerospace industries in the Far East in particular use these activities in the hope of gaining technological know-how so that they can eventually develop their own products.

The aerospace industry is relatively small in most countries. The American aerospace industry is not only the largest in absolute terms but also in relation to country size. The share of aerospace turnover in GNP in countries with a large aerospace sector in 1986 was as follows (*Nachrichten für Außenhandel*, 4 April 1989):

- United States   2.50 per cent
- Great Britain   1.80 per cent
- France   1.53 per cent
- Canada   1.16 per cent
- West Germany   0.92 per cent

Figure 6.4 gives the development of the composition of aerospace turnover for the two largest production regions, the United States and the EC. The American increase in turnover came to a large extent from the expansion of military activities; their share rose from 55.3 per cent to 64.2 per cent. The American aerospace industry grew faster and was in 1984 two-and-a-half times larger than the European. The Japanese and Canadian aerospace industries are less than 10 per cent of the size of the European industry and are still small even compared to single companies like McDonnell Douglas or Boeing, but this might change in the future in the case of Japan.

Production by the EC aerospace industry in 1986 amounted to 39.2 billion ECU of which 36 per cent came from civil sales. The civilian share has been increasing from 30 per cent in 1980 because of the success of large transport aircraft (Airbus) and stagnating military markets. This tendency will probably continue in the 1990s. A breakdown by market segments shows a 49.2 per cent share of airframes (i.e. airplanes, helicopters, and missiles), 17.7 per cent of engines, 27.8 per cent of

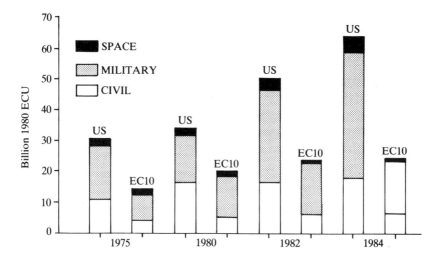

Figure 6.4 Composition of aerospace turnover (Source: Commission of the European Communities, 1986)

equipment, and 5.4 per cent of space products (See the Commission's *Panorama of EC Industry – 1989*).

International trade is dominated by the two large producing regions, the EC and the United States. The largest exporter and importer is the United States. It dominates the world market for aircraft with 46.8 per cent of exports of major industrial countries in 1986 and the market for missiles and spacecraft with a world export share of 62.1 per cent. The EC has roughly the same share in aircraft, but only 27.5 per cent in missiles and spacecraft. The aerospace industry is an important export industry in the United States with an export share of almost 10 per cent of manufacturing industry's exports and with the largest trade surplus of all industries. For the United Kingdom and France aerospace exports also contribute strongly to total exports. The EC overall has only a small trade surplus (see Table 6.1).

The commodity composition of trade in aerospace products is summarised in Table 6.2 for the United States and the EC. Whereas production in the industry was dominated by military activities, trade covers predominantly civil products. This clearly results from the bias of military procurement towards national suppliers. The EC has a trade deficit in civil aerospace products and a surplus in military products which leads to an overall trade surplus (Table 6.1). The Japanese trade figures show that Japan's aerospace industry is not yet an important competitor on world markets.

Table 6.1 Trade in aerospace products

	Imports (m. $)	Exports (m. $)	RCA*
US (1986)			
Total	7,902	19,727	1.67
Civil:	6,398	14,833	1.59
Aircraft	2,050	7,365	2.03
• Transports	742	6,276	2.89
• General aviation	1,053	243	−0.71
• Others	255	846	1.95
Aircraft engines and parts	2,198	3,074	1.09
Parts	2,150	4,394	1.47
Military:	1,504	4,894	1.93
Aircraft	35	1,502	4.51
Aircraft engines and parts	603	587	0.73
Parts	866	2,148	1.66
Missiles, rockets and parts	–	657	–
EC 12[1] (1987)			
Total	7,695	8,540	−0.37
Civil:	5,930	6,109	−0.44
Aircraft	2,142	2,657	−0.26
• Large Transports	1,635	1,465	−0.58
• Others	507	1,192	0.38
Aircraft engines and parts[2]	2,936	2,608	−0.52
Aircraft parts	852	385	−1.27
Military:	1,765	2,431	−0.15
Aircraft	325	449	−0.15
Aircraft engines and parts[2]	1,028	1,490	−0.03
Aircraft parts	412	492	−0.29
Japan (1988)			
Aircraft industry	2,024	300	−2.84

Notes: *Revealed Comparative Advantage RCA $= \ln (X_i/M_i) - \ln (X/M)$; X_i, M_i: Exports, imports of product group i; X, M: Manufacturing industry exports, imports   [1]EC without UK (1987)   [2]including UK

Source: *Nachrichten für Außenhandel* (04.04.1989); Statistical Office of the European Communities: External Trade, Analytical Tables, 1987; External Trade, Statistical Year Book, 1987; Aerospace Industries Association of America, 1987

The Revealed Comparative Advantage (RCA) of the United States aerospace industry is most pronounced in the area of complete aircraft, civil as well as military, whereas in the engine and parts group it is below the industry average but still above average when compared to the manufacturing sector. In contrast, the EC 12 only has a positive RCA in the group 'other aircraft'. The European aerospace industry overall has a trade performance slightly below the manufacturing industry average. Military products have higher RCA values than civil products, but are still slightly negative.

Table 6.2 Trade in (a) aircraft, aircraft engines and parts, and (b) missiles and spacecraft, 1984

(a)	Exports m. US$	Imports m. US$	Export share %[1]	World market share %[2]	RCA[3]
US	13,540	3,684	9.45	46.84	1.78
Germany	4,095	3,213	2.76	14.16	−0.27
UK	3,943	2,254	6.30	13.64	0.69
France	3,182	1,186	4.52	11.01	3.15
Canada	1,444	1,356	2.77	4.99	0.19
Italy	1,239	935	1.96	4.28	−0.20
Netherlands	682	680	2.02	2.36	0.02
Belg/Luxem	266	402	0.72	0.92	−0.53
Switzerland	183	295	0.75	0.63	−0.54
Japan	143	1,099	0.09	0.50	−3.55
Sweden	114	163	0.49	0.39	−0.61
Denmark	41	52	0.45	0.14	−0.06
Austria	27	34	0.68	0.09	1.29
Norway	11	293	0.17	0.04	−2.81

(b)	Exports m. US$	Imports m. US$	Export share %[1]	World market share %[2]	RCA[3]
US	962	227	0.67	62.09	1.93
Germany	21	N.A.	0.01	1.33	–
UK	188	N.A.	0.30	12.14	–
France	42	N.A.	0.06	2.72	–
Canada	75	N.A.	0.14	4.82	–
Italy	168	N.A.	0.27	10.82	–
Netherlands	2	N.A.	0.01	0.12	–
Belg/Luxem	4	N.A.	0.01	0.26	–
Switzerland	12	N.A.	0.05	0.79	–
Japan	8	N.A.	0.00	0.51	–
Sweden	56	N.A.	0.24	3.63	–
Denmark	2	N.A.	0.02	0.15	–
Austria	1	N.A.	0.02	0.04	–
Norway	9	N.A.	0.13	0.58	–

Notes: [1]Exports in % of manufacturing industry exports [2]Exports in % of major industrialised countries' aircraft exports [3]Revealed Comparative Advantage

Source: US Department of Commerce, unpublished data, own calculations

Major competitive factors

Competition in the civil aircraft industry is not confined to national boundaries. The market for commercial aircraft is truly international. Technological characteristics such as strong economies of scale and scope together with a world market which is small in terms of the number of units sold lead to a highly concentrated industry structure.

An aircraft is a complex product composed of thousands of components, each of which must be developed, produced and assembled.

Whereas radios and televisions require about 1,000 components and motor vehicles do not exceed 10,000, a turbojet has about 100,000 and a rocket up to one million components (Todd and Humble, 1987). Such numbers illustrate the difficulty in mastering the process of manufacturing aerospace products.

Consequently producers face high development costs.

> The investment prior to first deliveries of a new medium-size, medium-range commercial large transport can range from $1.5 to $2 billion over a four-year period. An additional $1 billion investment may be required in the two or so years following initial deliveries to compensate for the high production costs in the early phase of the learning curve and for the build-up of in-process inventory in the sub-assembly and final assembly stages of production. The result is that a new major aircraft project may accumulate a negative cash-flow of some $3 billion six years after the project is initiated. (US Department of Commerce, 1984)

These numbers may be even higher today; an estimate of $4 billion is given in *The Economist* (1988). Figure 6.5 presents the cumulative cash flow for a hypothetical aircraft project based on a simulation study by the US Department of Commerce in 1984.

It also shows that under favourable circumstances the breakeven point can be reached after twelve years. If demand over this period is slack and a smaller production rate has to be adopted the breakeven point is reached later or may be impossible to reach at all, as technical change or altered relative prices over such a long time may make other aircraft types more competitive.

This intertemporal structure comes essentially from the fixed cost of R & D and capacity development, but also from the learning effects that occur in the production of the aircraft. The learning effect turns out to dominate the economies of scale. There is worldwide consensus that aircraft production exhibits a learning elasticity of 0.2, i.e. production costs decrease by 20 per cent with a doubling of output (Berg and Tielke-Hosemann, 1987; US Department of Commerce, 1986). In Figure 6.6 examples for such learning curves are given. They also reveal that major modifications of an aircraft, so-called derivatives, move the learning curve upward, but by far less than would be the case if a completely new aircraft were designed. Of the overall economies of scale about 90 per cent are attributable to learning and the remainder to fixed costs.

These very special technological characteristics have resulted in a market structure with few large companies. In the market for large transport aircraft there are essentially three firms left: Boeing, McDonnell Douglas, and Airbus Industrie. The number of companies producing military products is somewhat larger due to a larger market and because of government policies favouring national producers.

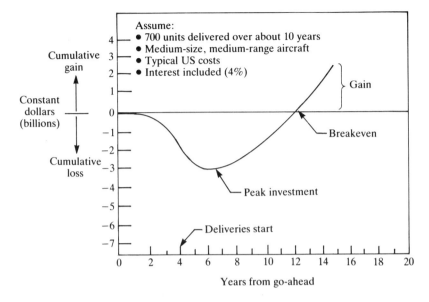

Figure 6.5 Cumulative cash flow for a hypothetical aircraft project (Source: *International Competition in the Production and Marketing of Commercial Aircraft*, Boeing Commercial Aircraft Company, March 1982, p. 11. Basic curve adapted from Report on Aviation Advisory Commission, 1973)

Institutions and industrial policy

Aerospace industries in all countries have had close ties to governments for a long time. The industries' first activities involved mostly military aircraft for which the respective government generally was the only customer. World War II and the following cold war made the strategic role of the aerospace industry even more important. Later, with beginning of space-related activities and with the increasing introduction of electronic components, the aerospace industry started to be viewed as a strategic industry with respect to most technology fields. Communication technology, electronics, advanced materials, aerodynamics, management and design techniques (CAD–CAM) are some examples (Aerospace Industries Association of America, 1985). All countries having an aerospace industry and those in the process of evolving their own industry are engaged in industrial and trade policy activities. The types of measures may vary but the basic goals such as national security and international competitiveness are common.

Industrial and trade policies appear in many different forms in European countries. Governments can directly influence the industry

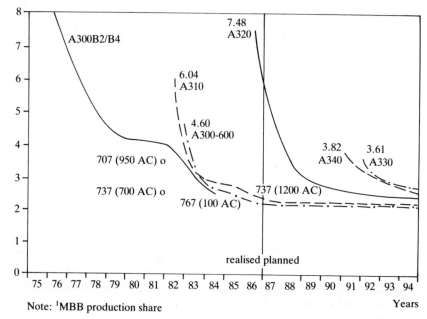

Note: ¹MBB production share

Figure 6.6   Learning curves for Airbus (Source: MBB, 1987)

through subsidies which are of particular importance to aerospace. Public procurement – especially in military and space products – also has immediate impact. More indirect and long-term measures include the general form of the procurement system, antitrust policies, and public vs. private ownership.

The countries with major aerospace industries – France, Germany, and the United Kingdom – have all reacted to unsuccessful launches of civil aircraft in the 1960s by actively supporting a centralisation of their aerospace industry. France has partially nationalised, the United Kingdom has been nationalising and then reprivatising, and in Germany the government owns large shares in the major aerospace firms. German firms such as Dornier, MBB, AEG, etc., are now in the process of being merged under Daimler-Benz AG into one large aerospace firm, Deutsche Aerospace.

In the military field co-production programmes among European firms and with American firms are supported by governments, often through NATO co-operation. Civil co-production is most visible in the Airbus project where – with government help – a competitor to the American large transport aircraft producers has been created.

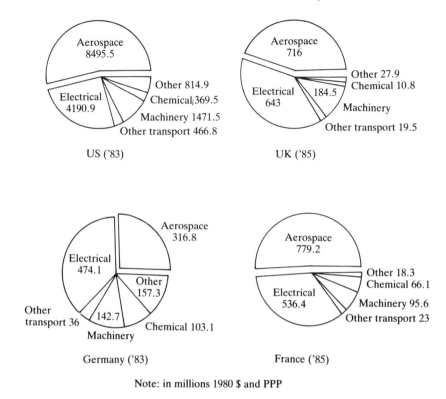

US ('83)

UK ('85)

Germany ('83)

France ('85)

Note: in millions 1980 $ and PPP

Figure 6.7 Government R & D funding of private enterprises for selected companies (Source: OECD Science and Technology Indicators)

Aerospace industries all over the world receive a large share of government R & D budgets. Figure 6.7 shows that the United States and France spend more than half of their government R & D funds in the aerospace industry. Only Germany has a relatively low share. Overall R & D spending of European firms is small relative to American expenditures. Figure 6.8 compares R & D expenditures according to source. Combined expenditures by German, French, and British companies amount to only 26 per cent of American expenditures. In terms of government subsidies they amount to only 21 per cent of American subsidies. Whereas practically all American subsidies come from military and space R & D contracts, European subsidies are also spent on civil aircraft projects, most notably those for Airbus Industrie.

The precise amount of aid that Airbus Industrie has received is unknown, but the accountants Coopers & Lybrand (1988) have estimated that Airbus has, up to 1988, received $13.9 billion of financial assistance.

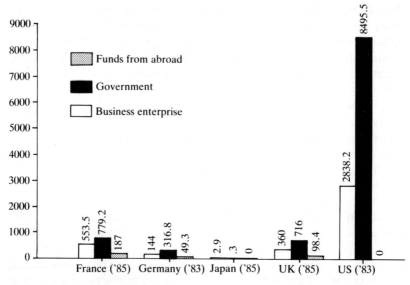

Note: in 1980 $ and PPP

Figure 6.8 Aerospace industry R & D expenditure by source for selected companies (Source: OECD Science and Technology Indicators)

If these grants had to be repaid on commercial terms it 'would amount to a charge of $10.2 million on each of the 1,650 aircraft which Airbus hopes to deliver up to the end of the century' (De Jonquieres, 1988). The information available about Airbus Industrie is 'insufficient to allow us to construct a reliable picture of the financial performance of the Airbus enterprise today' (Coopers & Lybrand, 1988).

Apart from the financial transactions, government commitment to support this entry into the market for large transport aircraft was essential for Airbus Industrie, because it gave a signal to incumbent firms that entry-deterring pricing strategies could not force Airbus out of the market (see Brander and Spencer, 1985 for the theoretical argument and Klepper, 1989 for the empirical analysis).

Trade policy on the import side has been confined to tariff exemption for all inputs in the production of large transport aircraft (Weiss *et al.*, 1988) and – as American firms claim – pressure on national airlines to buy European aircraft instead of foreign products.

Export-related trade policy measures concentrate on credit guarantees which function like interest subsidies. These measures are comparable to the conditions of the American Exim Bank. In the trade negotiations under the auspices of GATT in Tokyo the Agreement on Trade in Civil

Aircraft was signed in 1980 as an attempt to remove trade barriers and other impediments to free trade and competition in this market. In addition, the American and European governments have negotiated the 'commonline agreement' relating to large transport aircraft in which equal conditions of export financing through government agencies are laid out.

A particular problem for European producers of large transport aircraft is the fact that aircraft are sold in dollars worldwide. The uncertainty about exchange rate fluctuations as well as thin markets in long-term futures made pricing risky. The German government has recently given exchange rate guarantees to the German Airbus under which losses are covered if the exchange rate falls below 1.80 DM/$; but if the DM falls below 1.60 further losses will not be covered.

Other trade policy measures increasingly used are the so-called offset arrangements. An offset arrangement consists of an import order, mostly for military aircraft but increasingly in large civil transport aircraft, which is tied to a subcontract for maintenance or parts of the respective aircraft. The intention of importing countries is clear: technology transfer, foreign exchange savings and national employment objectives can all be met simultaneously. Exporting companies seem to be forced into such arrangement by the competition. Company representatives, however, claim that in civil aircraft contracts competitiveness of the offset arrangement *vis-à-vis* other suppliers must be assured. Whether this is the case in military contracts, is unknown. Practically all countries pursuing an industrial policy of promoting the development of a national aerospace industry use such arrangements.

Other aircraft-related offset arrangements are reported as well. 'Certain Airbus aircraft sales were obtained through such political horse-trading as trade agreements, route rewards, landing rights, and frequency rule adjustments, military weapons support and economic or regional assistance' (Harvard Business School, 1986). In these cases aircraft sales are not 'offset' by other aircraft contracts, but by more or less unrelated agreements (see, for example, the collection of press reports about government marketing support to Airbus collected by Boeing (Harvard Business School, 1986)).

Changing environment of 1992 for the aerospace industry

The European Community already has free movement of goods internally. In the case of the aerospace industry national quantitative restrictions do not exist either, in so far as the industry currently is not subject to internal or national direct trade impediments. Hence, 1992 will probably not have any effects in this respect.

Removal of technical and other barriers

There are several indirect barriers which are of importance for the industry. Governments are actively engaged in the aerospace industry in a number of ways. In most member countries large aerospace firms are partially or completely owned by the government. This relation gives firms enhanced opportunities to benefit from industrial policy measures.

At the same time, governments buy a large proportion of the industry's output. Roughly 30 per cent of overall turnover of the aerospace industry in the EC consists of sales to governments inside the EC. Another 30 per cent are extra-EC exports of which an unknown proportion is sales to extra-EC governments as well.

The dominant contractors for sales of military and space products are state agencies of the country of the producing firm. Whereas in the 1960s up to 80 per cent of the industry's sales were military sales, this proportion has declined due to the success of civil transport aircraft and due to the emerging space activities. Today military sales have increased in absolute terms, but their share has come down to roughly 70 per cent in the mid-1980s.

The aerospace industry is considered to be a key industry in terms of technological developments. It is believed that aerospace R & D and know-how spreads through the whole economy, thus creating positive externalities. Industries in all Western economies therefore get government support, either through military R & D contracts or through subsidies for R & D in civil activities.

Therefore, any changes regarding procurement policies and industrial policies will have a major impact on the industry. These policy areas are, however, subject to considerable controversy when it comes to the completion of an internal market. Although it is difficult to predict the dynamics of the Internal Market programme, military procurement will surely be rather late on the agenda. A European-wide military procurement agency will probably not materialise. National procurement systems will therefore remain, but it might be possible that non-discriminatory calls for tender will create a unified market with equal access available to all European firms at least.

Non-discriminatory military procurement

Although the Internal Market programme does not specifically address military procurement, the possibility of a non-discriminatory procurement system is taken as the basis of the following analysis. Prima facie, non-discriminatory procurement will lead to more competition among firms. Previously segmented markets with very few – sometimes only a single – suppliers will now still be segmented, but with free entry for foreign firms. Increased competition will reveal which firms have a comparative advantage on this market and a more concentrated industry structure might emerge.

But there are already other forces at work which reduce the expected pro-competitive effects. Three reasons for international collaboration seem to be important. First, complementary resources are shared efficiently as each partner contributes his comparative advantage to the project. Second, since access to foreign markets is often influenced by government policy, bilateral or multilateral joint ventures have a better chance of appearing acceptable to national regulating authorities. And third, projects in the aerospace industry have a long time horizon and involve – at the same time – large budgets, such that a company takes high risks in every project it starts.

The aerospace industry is therefore already engaged in intensive co-operation on specific projects in the military and civil area. The most prominent civil example is the co-operation on Airbus. On the military side several projects have been completed; new projects such as the 'Eurofighter', and 'Euroflag' (European Future Large Aircraft Group) are planned. These projects seem to exist quite independently from developments towards an internal market.

As far as military procurement is concerned, there is little chance that national procurement agencies will alter their bias towards domestic suppliers. The experience with international co-operation in several weapon projects is not encouraging. Perhaps the most difficult task in managing co-operative projects is the allocation of work among the different participants. In military as well as civil programmes, inefficiencies have been accepted because equity considerations among the partners constrained competitive bidding and efficient allocation of work. The F-16 and the MRCA programmes are reported to have suffered from such problems (Rich *et al.*, 1981).

Weapons procurement as well as civil aircraft production is a complex task in which a hierarchy of subcontractors is normally involved. These subcontracts also seem to go to domestic firms for reasons which are not clear, but national preferences or implicit quotas may account for this phenomenon. There are chances that an internal market will lead to subcontracting on a European-wide basis, not least because psychological barriers will eventually disappear. This might lead to increased opportunities for companies from countries with small aerospace industries. Since France and the United Kingdom with about 35 per cent of final turnover and Germany with below 20 per cent currently dominate Europe's aerospace industry, companies from countries like Italy, Spain and the Netherlands may benefit most as subcontractors from an internal market.

It has already been mentioned that the aerospace industry is composed of large so-called system firms, which own the know-how of producing the final product but depend on component technologies from other suppliers. Entry into the market of system firms seems to be difficult, if not impossible. Since World War II only Airbus has entered the market, and even in this case the companies in the Airbus consortium were all established producers. It is therefore highly unlikely that – even far-reaching – institutional changes in the EC will open up opportunities for entry of new firms. This might only take place in niches for specific components and subsystems.

Civil markets

In civil markets for aerospace products aircraft sales and space products follow different rules. As in the case of military procurement, space products are not commodities traded primarily on open, competitive markets. They are highly sophisticated items which must be co-ordinated within a large and complex systems-engineering framework. Co-ordination is typically achieved through a mixture of governance modes involving public administration, large integrated firms and co-operative alliances, as well as competitive markets. Up to now the main focus of the space sector has been determined by the interests of governments in defence-related issues, for scientific and extraterrestrial exploration, and in achieving national prestige. There is a tendency towards greater commercialisation of space activities which might change the structure of demand, but to what extent and when this will happen is as yet unclear.

European space activities are already quite centralised. Sixty per cent of the overall European space funds are appropriated for the ESA (European Space Agency); only the remaining 40 per cent fall under national control. But even in centralised activities such as the ESA programmes the 'principle of fair returns' is the rule. This rule requires that each country that finances x per cent of a project will get rewarded more or less x per cent of the later contract value for its national suppliers. This leads to inefficiencies and greater programme cost, but developments in the context of the 1992 programme are unlikely to lead to improved efficiency.

The civil aircraft market is dominated by sales of large transport aircraft, i.e. in the case of the EC by Airbus. This market is truly international from the demand side as well as from the supply side. Three producers – the American McDonnell Douglas and Boeing and the European Airbus – compete in a world market composed of a large number of international airlines. Airbus production efficiency suffers from national interests which have resulted in an inflexible production structure. For example, the Airbus programme is known for its Guppy airplanes which carry parts of the aircraft all over Europe for final assembly in order to assure work-sharing among partners. German producers of Airbus estimate that by changing final assembly of the A320 from two locations to one location would save about $30 million per year (*Der Spiegel*, 30 January 1989). Such political constraints, however, will have little chance of being alleviated by the internal market programme.

In conclusion, the impact of institutional changes affecting the aerospace industry are quite small and uncertain. There are very few explicit internal barriers. The industry is internationally oriented already. There is a chance for more co-ordinated government activities in procurement as well as R & D policies, but it remains doubtful whether compartmentalisation due to national interests will be overcome.

Company strategies in the completed Internal Market

Civil aircraft

International co-operation is the main feature of the civil aircraft industry all over the world. The Airbus co-operation has been cited as an example of European integration from proponents as well as opponents, and it exemplifies the difficulties which pan-European co-operation faces. The complexity and costliness of civil aircraft programmes is so large that only a few firms can profitably survive worldwide as principal builders of aircraft. At the same time subcontracting is becoming increasingly important. The major factors to which civil aircraft firms are responding are the booming demand for large transport aircraft, the strategic position of firms in the industry network as it has emerged in the past and the impact of industrial policy.

With full order books all producers of large transport aircraft are currently producing at their capacity limits and are still plagued by delays in deliveries. Consequently, they are looking for subcontractors which can ease some of the pressures. This opens up opportunities for aerospace firms of smaller countries which have not been strongly involved in co-operative ventures previously. Italy especially, but also many Asian companies, get an increasing share of subcontracts from the two American civil transport aircraft producers. Established co-operative groups like Airbus are trying to increase production capacities on their own. Overall the Internal Market programme does not seem to influence these decisions.

With Lockheed leaving civil aircraft markets and the Airbus consortium becoming a contender on international markets, three companies – Boeing, McDonnell Douglas, and Airbus – now dominate the market, with Fokker specialising at the lower end. Firms currently not engaged as primary suppliers will have to rely on subcontracts or co-production agreements. Practically all large transport aircraft are produced today with such international co-operation: Airbus has up to 30 per cent foreign, i.e. non-European, content; some Boeing and McDonnell Douglas aircraft have similar non-American content. National boundaries inside Europe do not seem to have any impact on this worldwide network of aircraft production.

Airbus is still a heavily subsidised aircraft; therefore, the firms participating in the Airbus consortium depend on support from their national governments. Although one has to speculate about tendencies favouring domestic firms, there are indications that national priorities play a role. As already mentioned, transport aircraft are composed of components produced worldwide. Nevertheless, subcontracting by members of the Airbus consortium seems to have a national bias. MBB's latest subcontracts of about $1 billion, for example, went increasingly to German companies. More than 50 per cent of MBB's share for components of the A320 comes from Germany; at 60–70 per cent, the shares of domestic production of Aerospatiale and British Aerospace requirements are even higher. (These numbers refer to 1987 plans.)

These shares may however fall as competitive pressure forces Airbus partners to look for more cost-efficient subcontractors and, at the same time, to respond to pressures in foreign markets. In many markets it is easier to sell aircraft to airlines which are frequently state-owned when domestic firms are involved in the programme. Aircraft producers therefore become increasingly interested in a widespread net of contractors. If there are tendencies in the Internal Market programme to centralise the allocation of government support, the internationalisation of component supplies might proceed with increasing speed.

Military aircraft and space products

The situation in military aircraft and space products is different since demand does not come from private profit-oriented companies, but from governments with varied interests. These interests range from buying a product best designed to meet the needs of the military to technology and industrial policy objectives. These interests favour domestic producers and has led to a segmented industry structure in Europe. But concurrently with these forces, new military aircraft or space products have become increasingly expensive to develop so that a single national firm in many cases is unable to accumulate the financial resources or the technological know-how by itself. Co-operation is therefore inevitable.

So far, this co-operation has resulted in the setting-up of consortia for specific projects. PANAVIA is a consortium composed of British, German, and Italian firms building the Tornado aircraft. Similarly the

Eurofighter consortium (BAe, MBB, Aeritalia, CASA) has been established to build the EFA (European Fighter Aircraft) and the Eurojet consortium (Rolls-Royce, MTU, Fiat, Sener) to build the engine of the EFA. This aircraft competes with the French Rafale aircraft and the American Hornet 2000. EUROFLAG (European Future Large Aircraft Group) is another joint venture (BAe, MBB, CASA, Aeritalia, Aerospatiale and, previously, Lockheed) founded to build a military transport aircraft for the late 1990s. These consortia seem to be a compromise between the interest of national government in relying on their domestic defence industry and the inefficient scale of domestic firms.

A trend towards a pan-European military procurement system might alleviate some of the constraint set by national interests. More flexible joint ventures without the 'principle of fair returns' could potentially lead to more efficient co-operation. Experiences with space programmes which are to a large extent already under the control of European agencies such as the ESA (European Space Agency) are not encouraging, however. Even in these programmes inefficiencies of compartmentalisation are hard to overcome.

These difficulties cannot be solved for military aircraft and weapons since demand comes from political institutions with special political interests. In the space sector chances are better, but a vicious circle has to be broken. Space activities are predominantly government financed with the consequences on efficiency and cost effectiveness just described. High costs, on the other hand, prevent the emergence of a commercial market which would impose fewer political constraints on aerospace firms. If the commercial market for space products grows, then there are chances that specialisation in Europe and the world according to firms' comparative advantage will take place. An internal market with free capital movements will surely support the development of such an industry structure.

Industry structure

Since most European aerospace firms do not specialise in military or civil products, overall strategies in the light of an emerging internal market must be considered. Until recently the European aerospace industry has been characterised by a process of national concentration. AEG, Dornier, MTU, and MBB have been merged under the control of Daimler-Benz in Germany; British Aerospace has also grown into a conglomerate and ranks fourth among aerospace firms worldwide. The French industry is still in a transitional phase, with declining military sales and increasing sales of commercial aircraft and space products; with

Aerospatiale and Dassault there are still two large aerospace system firms.

This development of concentration along national lines seems to be changing. Closer ties across borders may become more frequent. Just recently Daimler-Benz, Matra, and GEC have announced plans for joint ventures at the level of their subsidiaries with cross-ownership of stocks. Although this is only a first sign, it could indicate a trend towards a European industry structure. Whether the Internal Market programme was or is responsible for this potential development cannot be answered.

Conclusion

The European aerospace industry is characterised by a mixture of internationalisation of activities and compartmentalisation of production and ownership within national boundaries. This mixture is possibly influenced by the demand structure which the industry is confronted with. Civil aircraft markets are truly international, military markets and space product markets still have a heavy bias towards domestic suppliers.

Firm strategies on civil and military markets consequently differ. But since most aerospace firms are active in both markets, ownership structures seem still to be dominated by concerns for military procurement. Co-operation therefore takes place in the form of joint ventures on specific products but well-defined quotas for national producers.

The Internal Market programme seems to have little direct influence. Even in space programmes, which to a large extent are under European control, problems of compartmentalisation have not been overcome. Essentially, workloads in space programmes are still distributed according to the financial contribution of the member country governments.

Whether the Internal Market will have some indirect impact on firms' behaviour is rather speculative. It may be that some of the national orientation of merger activities and co-operation will make way for a more European orientation.

References

Aerospace Industries Association of America, 'Aerospace – facts and figures', Washington, current issues.

Aerospace Industries Association of America (1985), 'Technology diffusion – the movement of technology between aerospace and other industries', Washington, October.

Airbus Industrie (1987), 'Global market forecast: 1987–2006', Blagnac Cedex.

Ball, Nicole and Leitenberg, Milton (eds) (1983), *The Structure of the Defense Industry*, London.

Berg, Hartmut and Tielke-Hosemann, Notburga (1987), 'Branchenstudie Luft-fahrtindustrie: Der Markt für Großraumflugzeuge des zivilen Luftverkehrs', *Dortmunder Diskussionsbeiträge zur Wirtschaftspolitik*, no. 24, July.

Berg, Hartmut and Tielke-Hosemann, Notburga (1988), 'Vom Glanz und Elend staatlicher Technologieförderung: Das Projekt "Airbus"'', *Dortmunder Dis-kussionsbeiträge zur Wirtschaftspolitik*, no. 27, April.

Blick durch die Wirtschaft, current issues, Frankfurt.

Boeing Commercial Airplane Company (1986, 1989), 'Current market outlook – world travel market perspective and airplane equipment requirements', Seattle, February.

Boeing Commercial Airplane Company, 'Setting the record straight', no year.

Boeing Commercial Airplane Company, 'International trade aspects of com-mercial aircraft programs', unpublished mimeo, no year.

Brander, James A. and Spencer, Barbara J. (1985), 'Export subsidies and international market share rivalry', *Journal of International Economics*, vol. 18, pp. 83–100.

Cain, Stephen A. (1987), 'The Defense Budget squeeze – will rapid R & D growth threaten spending choices?', Defense Budget Project, Washington, DC.

Commission of the European Communities (1986), 'The European aerospace industry – trading position and figures', Commission Staff Working Paper, Brussels.

Coopers & Lybrand, Certified Public Accountants (1988), 'The Airbus enterprise – a review of the public record', March.

De Jonquieres, Guy (1988), 'Too many pilots in the cockpit', *Financial Times*, 7 August.

Der Spiegel, 1989, Hamburg.

Economist (1988), 'All shapes and sizes – a survey of the civil aerospace industry', 3–9 September.

Economist (1985), 'The Big Six – a survey of the world's aircraft industry', 1 June.

Financial Times, current issues.

Finanz und Wirtschaft, current issues, Zürich.

Floßdorf, H. (1980), 'Stand und Chancen des Airbus-Familienprogramms', in Schulz, W. and Wilke, W. (eds) *Jahrbuch der Deutschen Gesellschaft für Luft-und Raumfahrt* e.V., Köln, bd. 1.

GATT (1980), 'Multilateral trade negotiations – agreement on trade in civil aircraft'.

Gerybadze, Alexander (1988), *Raumfahrt und Verteidigung als Industriepolitik?*, Frankfurt.

Gunston, Bill (1988), *Airbus*, London.

Handelsblatt (1988), 'Mit Staatshilfe zehn Prozent des zivilen Weltmarkts anpeilen', 27 September, Düsseldorf.

Handelsblatt, current issues, Düsseldorf.

Harbridge House Inc. (1984) 'Government support of the commercial aircraft industry', Boston.

Harvard Business School (1986), 'Turbulent skies: Airbus versus Boeing', Harvard Business Cases, 0-386-193, Boston.

Harvard Business School (1987), 'The aircraft industry's political profile', Harvard Business Cases, 0-387-190, Boston.

Harvard Business School (1987), 'Airbus update – the storm intensifies', Harvard Business Cases, 0-387-159, Boston.

Hochmuth, Milton (1986), 'The European aerospace industry', in Macharzina, Klaus and Staehle, Wolfgang H. (eds), *European Approaches to International Management*, pp. 205–25, Berlin.

Hofton, Andy (1987), 'Commercial Aircraft of the World', *Flight International*, 10 October.

Huffschmid, Jörg, *et al.* (1986), 'Neue Rüstung – Neue Armut: Aufrüstungspläne und Rüstungsindustrie in der Bundesrepublik Deutschland bis zum Jahr 2000', Köln.

International Herald Tribune, current issues.

Klepper, Gernot (1989), 'Entry into the market for large transport aircraft', Kiel Working Papers, no. 375, Kiel Institute of World Economics, May.

Majumdar, Badiul A. (1987), 'Upstart or flying start? The rise of Airbus Industrie, *World Economy*, vol. 10, no. 4, December.

McDonnell Douglas (1987), 'Outlook for commercial aircraft 1987–2001', Long Beach, Calif.

Mowery, David C. (1987), *Alliance Politics and Economics – Multinational Joint Ventures in Commercial Aircraft*, Cambridge.

Moxon, Richard W. and Geringer, J. Michael (1985), 'Multinational joint ventures in the commercial aircraft industry', *The Columbia Journal of World Business*, vol. XX, no. 2, pp. 55–62.

Nachrichten für Außenhandel, current issues, Eschborn.

National Research Council (1985), 'The competitive status of the US civil aviation manufacturing industry', Washington.

Rich, Michael *et al.* (1981), 'Multinational coproduction of military aerospace systems', A Project AIR FORCE report prepared for the United States Air Force, the Rand Corporation, Santa Monica.

Rodejohann, Jo (1985), 'Die Rüstungsindustrie in der Bundesrepublik Deutschland auf dem Weg in die Krise', Hessische Stiftung Friedens- und Konfliktforschung, Forschungsbericht 8/1985, Frankfurt.

Schneider, Hartmut (1980), 'Neue Politische Ökonomie und Technologiepolitik – Fallstudie am Beispiel der Luftfahrtindustrie', Frankfurt am Main.

Todd, Daniel and Humble, Ronald D. (1987), *World Aerospace: A Statistical Handbook*, New York.

Todd, Daniel and Simpson, Jamie (1986), *The World Aircraft Industry*, London.

United States Congress – Office of Technology Assessment (1988), 'The defense technology base: introduction and overview – a special report', OTA-ISC-374, Washington, DC.

United States Congress – Subcommittee on Trade of the Committee on Ways and Means (1985), 'Competitive conditions in the US civil aircraft industry and forest products industry', ninety-eighth Congress, second session, 9 July, 1984, Washington.

US Department of Commerce – International Trade Administration, 'U.S. high technology trade and competitiveness', manuscript, no year.

United States Department of Commerce (1986), 'A competitive assessment of the U.S. civil aircraft industry', Boulder.

United States Department of Commerce (1987), '1987 U.S. industrial outlook', Washington.

Weiss, Frank D. *et al.* (1988), 'Trade policy in West Germany', Kieler Studien, no. 217, Tübingen.

Wilke, Peter and Wulf, Herbert (1986), 'Rüstungsproduktion in der Bundesrepublik – Industrielle Überkapazitäten und staatliche Finanzierungsengpässe', *Aus Politik und Zeitgeschichte*, B2/86, pp. 26–39.

7

Electronic components and semiconductors

Harry P. Bowen

This and the next chapter are companion pieces. This introduction on the electronics industry refers to both of them. The full version contains a section which examines the strategies of the main companies individually. Copies can be obtained direct from the author.

Electronics are thought by many to be the global economy's main engine for growth and prosperity during the next decade. Europe, however, has been lagging behind. Much of Europe's demand for electronics is satisfied by imports and European-based firms are habitually late in introducing new technologies. The question has arisen whether Europe can achieve leadership in world markets or will it remain on the periphery of technological developments. The disappearance of the United States consumer electronics industry looms large in the minds of many Europeans and little comfort is afforded by the fact that Japanese firms have 95 per cent of the market in the most recent type of memory chip. The problem then is what is Europe doing in light of the 1992 initiatives, can these developments turn the tide, and what, if anything, can the Community do in a unified way to improve European competitiveness in electronics.

This chapter and the next address these questions with respect to two key sectors within the industry of electrical and electronic engineering (NACE 34): semiconductors and consumer electronics. The first section of this chapter overviews the status of the electronics industry as a whole and the second section examines the semiconductors sector. Chapter 8 explores consumer electronics. The study concludes with discussions of each sector in the light of the 1992 initiative for market unification.

The electronics industry in Europe

Overview

The electronics industry is operationally defined here as those manufacturing sectors comprising NACE Class 34 (electrical and electronic
engineering). This Class contains seven major industry groups (sectors),
each of which produces a diversity of products. Table 7.1 lists the major
industry groups and associated economic indicators for the Community in
1987.

Measured by value of production, electrical household appliances and
consumer electronics are the most important sectors. The Community
has an international comparative disadvantage in consumer electronics
and the sub-sector active electrical components (primarily semiconductors). On the basis of recent changes in world market share,
Community producers have improved their relative performance in
electrical machinery and held their position with respect to domestic
appliances, but have lost market share in electrical components (the
fastest growing sector in terms of value of sales). The following briefly
summarises each major sector of the electronics industry.

Table 7.1 Economic indicators for the Community's major electronics sector,
1987

NACE Group	Description	(1)	(2)	(3)	(4)	(5)
341	Wire and cable	39	8.6	4.0	0.5	1.6
342	Electrical machinery	30	4.5	na	na	na
343	Electrical apparatus	–	–	–	–	–
344	Telecommunications equipment	–	–	–	–	–
345	Electrical components:	–	–	–	–	–
	Active	20	6.2	4.6	7.0	0.7
	Passive	25	7.4	2.0	4.6	1.2
345.1	Consumer electronics	17	11.7	1.5	3.5	0.2
346	Domestic electrical appliances	54	16.2	2.0	1.5	1.9
347	Electric lamps and lighting	68	4.1	7.0	8.0	na

Notes: (1) = World market share (%)
    (2) = Production (billion ECU).
    (3) = Average annual market growth (%), 1984–87
    (4) = Forecast of annual market growth (%), 1988–90
    (5) = Ratio of exports/imports

Source: Panorama of EC Industry, 1989; Annual reports

Insulated wires and cables

The output of the insulated wires and cables sector is purchased primarily by the telecommunications sector. Community producers are world leaders in this sector with 39 per cent of the world market and are acknowledged world leaders in associated technology (R & D in this sector is estimated to be 5 per cent of sales). As a net exporter of the products of this sector, the Community has a large production base with which to meet both domestic and foreign demand. The Community's world strength in this sector is further evidenced by the fact that cables are exported by each member state. Despite the strength in this sector, the outlook for the medium term is not encouraging. Extra-Community exports are expected to decline as competitors in the Far East, the Middle East, Finland and Yugoslavia increase their export capability. In 1987, employment in this sector was between 15,000 and 20,000 people which represents less than 1 per cent of total Community employment in the electronics industry.

Electrical machinery

This sector produces electrical machinery, including electric motors, generators, transformers, switches and other basic electric plant. Employment in this sector was approximately 200,000 people in 1987 or 8.5 per cent of the Community's employment in the electronics industry.

Non-uniform standards have served to make the Community market for electrical machinery an accumulation of national markets. Community production accounts for 29 per cent of the world market compared to about 28 per cent for the United States. The United States has the largest national market with a per capita energy consumption 1.8 times that of other OECD countries. Japan also has a sizeable national market and is a dynamic exporter. Other major producers include the newly industrialised countries (NICs), India, Switzerland, Sweden and Canada. The relative competitive position of the two largest regions of production has remained largely unchanged since 1980.

The Community's weak competitiveness in this sector has been masked by the closure of national markets to external competition due to differing standards. Increased competition can be expected as 1992 reforms create more uniform standards across national markets. In anticipation, the European electrical equipment industry is beginning some restructuring, including international alliances and rationalisation of production facilities to improve profitability through economies of scale. These measures will improve Community competitiveness on international markets. However, whereas the opening of Community markets may be expected to accelerate industrial concentration, public procurement policies are likely to continue to pose a barrier to greater competition.

Consumer electronics

The consumer electronics industry has traditionally produced products for use primarily in the home. Whereas this still represents the bulk of the products produced by this sector, there is a trend for the distinction between personal and business products (e.g. personal computers, answering machines) to become blurred. The major products of this sector include the following:

1.   Traditional products:
   - *Audio*   Hi-Fi systems; compact disk (CD) players; portable audio equipment; in-car entertainment systems.
   - *Video*   TV receivers; video cassette recorders (VCR); compact disk video (CDV); video camera recorders (camcorders).
2.   New products (not in NACE 345):
   - *Communications systems*   Telephone and facsimile sets; CD-based information systems; portable communication devices.
   - *Personal computers*

In 1988, the Community market for consumer electronics was 30.6 billion ECU. Of this, audio products accounted for 8.1 billion, video products for 12.8 billion and 'new' products such as telephones and facsimile machines for 9.7 billion. In 1987 this sector employed some 262,000 people or 11.1 per cent of total employment in the electronics industry. (See Table 7.2.)

Table 7.2   Community production, consumption and trade of consumer electronics, 1980–87 (ECU m.)

	1980	1982	1984	1985	1986	1987
Consumption:						
Current value	11,350	13,487	12,925	14,304	18,550	18,395
Constant value	11,350	11,375	8,774	10,389	13,221	12,657
Index	100.0	100.2	77.3	91.5	116.5	111.5
Production	7,882	9,850	7,808	8,895	12,111	11,723
Net exports	−3,468	−3,637	−5,117	−5,409	−6,439	−6,675
Employment ('000s)	160.4	146.5	134.2	133.7	131.0	126.6

Source: Panorama of EC Industry, 1989

Between 1986 and 1987 the Community market for consumer electronics increased 13 per cent in volume (13.2 per cent for video, 12.5 per cent for audio equipment). Intense price competition, primarily from Korea and several South-East Asian countries (Malaysia, Thailand, Philippines and Indonesia) stabilised the market value of sales in 1987 at 18.4 billion ECU with audio equipment falling about 2 per cent and video equipment falling about 0.1 per cent. (See Table 7.3.)

The consumer electronics industry is increasingly affected by technological developments. R & D expenditures in this sector have increased steadily over the past decade and are now about 7 per cent of revenues. Continuing innovations in this sector are expected to bring about major changes in products and markets: for example, broader application of digital sound and image processing, the introduction of high-definition television (HDTV) and the development of communication networks. Current attention is focused on the transition from analog to digital and the development of high-definition television (HDTV). The transition from analog to digital is considered to be an irreversible technical change and implies a complete renewal of the existing product base. This change will also stimulate the appearance of a whole range of new products, including digital audio tape recorders and laser disk recorders.

The advent of HDTV has provoked competition for the establishment of production, broadcasting and reception standards. At issue is the potential replacement of the entire world's stock of television sets which includes Europe's 120 million operating receivers. This prospect has led Europeans to adopt a progressive attitude towards compatibility with existing equipment as evidenced by the MAC/Paquet standards. The D2 MAC/Paquet standard has been endorsed by European manufacturers who are now developing prototypes of high-definition digital equipment under the HDTV EUREKA programme.

Between 1985 and 1986 the market for colour televisions grew 16 per cent but fell to 4.5 per cent between 1986 and 1987 (15.6 million units sold

Table 7.3 Community consumption of audio and video products, 1980–87 (ECU m.)

	1980	1982	1984	1985	1986	1987
Video:						
Constant value (1980)	6,645	8,105	8,526	9.815	12,039	12,024
Index	100.0	122.0	128.3	147.7	181.2	180.9
Audio:						
Constant value (1980)	4,705	5,382	4,399	4,489	6,511	6,374
Index	100.0	114.4	93.5	95.4	138.4	135.5

Source: Panorama of EC Industry, 1989

in 1987). Demand is primarily for replacement and for secondary household sets. Community supply centres on large receivers (sets greater than 52 cm account for 42 per cent of the market) with the supply of small and mid-size TVs increasingly coming from imports: 27 per cent of the total market is covered by imports (20 per cent in 1986, 19 per cent in 1985). The share of imports from South Korea has increased steadily (7 per cent in 1987, 3 per cent in 1986, 0.7 per cent in 1985). In contrast, imports from Japan have been declining (3 per cent in 1987 compared to 5 per cent in 1986 and 6 per cent in 1985). Between 1986 and 1987, Community production increased by 1.5 per cent (5 per cent between 1985 and 1986) to 13.3 million units. The trend towards imports of small and mid-size receivers mirrors changes in the US market in the 1970s and reflects household preferences for inexpensive small and medium-sized TVs as secondary units.

European purchases of VCRs continue to grow, primarily in response to lower prices. Total purchases in 1987 exceeded 7.8 million units. Between 1986 and 1987 purchases increased 21 per cent while prices declined by 26 per cent. Imports of VCRs (assembled and unassembled) accounted for 64 per cent of the market in 1987 compared to 66 per cent in 1986 and 73 per cent in 1985. Purchases from South Korea increased 205 per cent between 1986 and 1987; South Korea's share of the Community market increased from 6 per cent to 16 per cent over the same period. Despite increased imports, European production and assembly rose to 4.2 million units in 1987, a 32 per cent increase over 1986.

Price declines have also bolstered purchases of CD players. Between 1986 and 1987 prices decreased approximately 20 per cent with purchases of CD players increasing 82 per cent (to 950 million ECU, 5 per cent of the total market). Imports of CD players accounted for 59 per cent of market demand in 1987 compared to 76 per cent in 1986. Increased imports of CD players from South Korea raised that country's share of the market to 4.5 per cent in 1987. Finally, increasing applications for CD players were an important factor in keeping the more traditional Hi-Fi sector from a marked slump.

Growth in the demand for mature products (current generation TVs, Hi-Fi) has been slight. Between 1986 and 1987 the Community market for colour televisions grew (in volume) by 4.5 per cent and is expected to increase only 3 per cent per year up to 1993. In contrast, demand for new products such as CD players increased over 80 per cent in volume between 1986 and 1987 and is expected to grow around 25 per cent per year up to 1993.

With the advent of optical and digital technology, magnetic tape players and recorders have moved to the list of 'mature' products. Between 1986 and 1987 the demand for tape products increased 21 per

Table 7.4 Community consumption and production of consumer electronics (1987 ECU m.)

	1979	1982	1987	1993
Real consumption	9,880	12,975	15,260	19,310
Average annual growth (%)		9.5	3.3	4.0
Production	8,460	8,210	9.065	11,405
Average annual growth (%)		−1.0	2.0	3.9

Source: National Statistics, forecast by BIPE, IFO, PROMETEIA

Table 7.5 Growth in Community demand for principal consumer electronics, 1987–93 (unit '000s)

	1987	1993	Expected Annual Growth (%)
Colour TV	15,630	18,770	3.1
VCR	7,830	10,610	5.2
CD	3,810	14,670	25.5

Source: National Statistics, forecast by BIPE, IFO, PROMETEIA

cent but by 1993 this growth is expected to slow to 5 per cent per year within the Community.

Finally, the product groups expected to show the most growth in demand in the medium term are as follows:

- Camcorders
- CD players
- Colour TV (large screen)
- VCR – both new and replacement demand
- Audio Products – primarily replacement demand

Electrical components

The electrical components industry produces a wide variety of devices whose sophistication ranges from simple switches to more exotic microprocessors. Figure 7.1 shows the major categories of components and sub-products.

In 1986, electrical components represented 13 per cent of the Community's total output in the electronics industry. By comparison, components accounted for 23 per cent of Japan's electronics industry and 16 per cent of the US electronics industry. In 1988, the European market for components was almost 17 billion ECU (23 per cent of the world

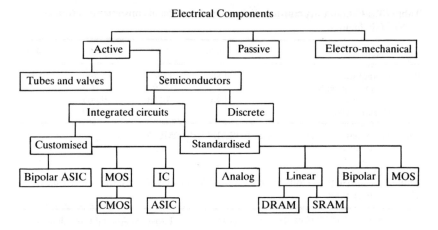

Figure 7.1 Electrical components family tree

market). In 1987, employment was 127,000 or 5.3 per cent of the Community's total electronics industry employment. As an intermediate goods supplier, the components industry is sensitive to cyclical changes in the level of economic activity. For example, between 1980 and 1985, the value of components production grew at an annual rate of approximately 12 per cent. Since 1986 the rate of growth has slowed co-incident with an overall reduction in the rate of growth of Community output. (See Table 7.6.)

By value of production, the Community's components industry ranks third behind that of the United States and Japan but was largest in terms of the value of consumption. Among the three, only the United States is a net importer. (See Table 7.7.)

The world market for components, particularly semiconductors, has been projected to grow as high as 20 per cent per year over the next decade, although accounting for the time lag between production and application of new products, market growth is more realistically expected to consolidate at around 13 per cent. The Community market is at present the fastest growing market in the world. Between 1987 and 1988 European purchases of semiconductors increased 31 per cent against 25 per cent in the United States and 13 per cent in Japan.

Electrical household appliances

The electrical household appliances sector covers the manufacturing of electrical appliances generally intended for home use. Until the mid-

Table 7.6 Community production of electrical components, 1988 (ECU bn.)

Active:	
IC	2,998
Tubes	2,157
Discrete components	1,442
Wound components	611
Passive:	
Connectors	2,670
PCB	1,794
Relays	556
Switches	527
Electro-Mechanical:	
Capacitors	1,134
Resistors	517

Source: BIS Mackentosh Limited

Table 7.7 Production, consumption and trade of components in the United States, Japan and the Community, 1986 (ECU bn.)

	US	Japan	EC
Production	28.0	28.0	13.6
Consumption	29.2	23.0	13.1
Net exports	−1.2	5.0	0.5

1980s, conditions of flat consumer demand, overcapacity and increased competition from imports created difficult conditions for Community producers. However, substantial restructuring since 1985 has largely returned the Community industry to profitability.

Community production of household appliances reached 16.2 billion ECU in 1986 but production fell in real terms by about 5½ per cent per year between 1980 and 1985. The production value of household appliances makes them a major subsector of the electrical industry. Although the degree of market saturation has increased sharply, steady growth in consumption is to be expected, particularly in product categories such as microwave ovens, home laundry machines and dishwashers. In 1987 this sector employed 219,000 people and accounted for 9.2 per cent of Community employment in the electronics industry.

Electric lamps and lighting equipment

Community production of electric lamps and other lighting is dominated by Philips Gloeilampen N.V. of the Netherlands who is also the largest supplier in the world, followed by General Electric of the United States. The second major European supplier is Osram, a division of Siemens. Market information is difficult to obtain for this sector owing to the small number of firms. However, the industry has clearly had steady growth, with compact, energy-saving fluorescent lamps and halogen lamps the major contributors to this growth.

Components and semiconductors industry

This section examines the electrical components industry, in general, and the semiconductor industry in detail. The electrical components industry is strategically linked to the consumer electronics industry since components are increasingly the critical determinant of the design and function of most consumer electronics.

Overview

As illustrated in Figure 7.2 in the case of semiconductors, the demand for electrical components derives fundamentally from the demand for the final products produced by the electronics industry (broadly defined).

The link between components and final products is critical for understanding the relatively weak position of Community firms, particularly in semiconductors. Present barriers to competition within the Community in final products (e.g. consumer electronics) whose value derives from the electrical components used in their production have restricted the possibilities for Community electrical components producers. Increasing competition in final electrical products would lead producers to greater demands on upstream component producers to provide more innovative products. Moreover, competition-induced price reductions would enable higher sales volumes of final products and would, in turn, increase the competitiveness of component producers via manufacturing cost reductions associated with scale economies.

The Community's position

Competition in the electrical components industry is at a global level with worldwide production and export activities increasing rapidly. In 1987, Europe produced 12 per cent of the world's supply of electrical components compared to 39 per cent for the United States and 47 per cent for Japan. In 1986, electrical components accounted for 13 per cent of the total value of Community production in the electronics industry. In Japan, components represented 23 per cent of the value of their

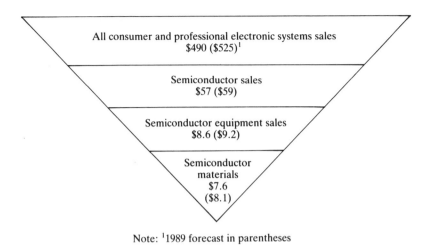

Note: [1] 1989 forecast in parentheses

Figure 7.2 Relationship of components to electrical end-products: 1988 sales, with 1989 forecast ($US bn.)

electronics output; the corresponding figure for the United States was 16 per cent.

Between 1980 and 1985, Community production of electrical components increased at an average annual rate of 13.4 per cent. From 1986 to 1987 the rate of growth of Community production slowed to 3 per cent to reach a total value of 14 billion ECU. In comparison, the 1987 values of US and Japanese production were approximately equal at 28 billion ECU.

Electronic components can be divided into three major groups: active, passive and electro-mechanical. In 1988, active components accounted for the largest share of the Community's production of components with integrated circuits the leading product category. (See Table 7.6.)

Among active components, semiconductors are the most innovative and strategic product group. Within semiconductors, the most important group of components are integrated circuits. Integrated circuits account for approximately 65 per cent of the Community's total output of semiconductors, 84 per cent of US semiconductor production and 78 per cent of Japanese. Within the Community, Germany is the largest producer and accounts for 29 per cent of total integrated circuit production. The United Kingdom is second with 24 per cent, followed by France with 21 per cent, the Netherlands with 11 per cent and Italy with 6 per cent.

Between 1986 and 1988 production of active components within the Community rose from 6.2 billion ECU to 9.1 billion ECU. Germany,

France, Italy and the United Kingdom accounted for more than 80 per cent of total output. Total demand for active components in 1986 was 8.7 billion ECU. (See Table 7.8.)

Foreign trade

In 1986, the Community had net export earnings from components of nearly 500 million ECU. However, the trend since 1980 has been a declining ratio of exports to imports. Between 1980 and 1986 the total value of extra-Community exports increased 57 per cent while the value of extra-Community imports rose 81 per cent. In addition, the overall Community surplus derives from sales of passive and electro-mechanical devices (relays, transformers, etc.) which represent older, more mature, technologies. There is some indication of an improving trend in the Community's exports of active components. (See Table 7.9.)

Table 7.8   Community production of active components, by type, 1987–90 ($USm.)

Type of active component		1987	1988	1989	1990
Integrated circuits		5,130	6,290	6,420	7,360
Discrete semiconductors		1,310	1,450	1,360	1,420
Opto-electronics		340	391	383	408
	Total	6,780	8,130	8,160	9,190

Table 7.9   Extra-EC trade in electrical components, 1980–86 (ECU m.)

Year		Active	Passive	Electro-Mech	Total
			Type of Component		
1980	Exports	897	953	2,907	4,757
	Imports	1,755	617	1,139	3,511
	Ratio (X/M)	0.51	1.54	2.55	1.35
1982	Exports	1,167	1,234	3,761	6,162
	Imports	2,154	735	1,434	4,323
	Ratio (X/M)	0.54	1.68	2.62	1.43
1984	Exports	2,760	1,270	4,104	8,134
	Imports	4,918	1,024	2,203	8,145
	Ratio (X/M)	0.56	1.24	1.86	1.00
1986	Exports	2,825	1,231	4,361	8,417
	Imports	4,481	1,107	2,331	7,919
	Ratio (X/M)	0.63	1.11	1.87	1.06

Source: Panorama of EC Industry, 1989

Imports of both passive and electro-mechanical components increased faster than exports: 58.4 per cent versus 22.5 per cent for passives and 71.6 per cent versus 40.5 per cent for electro-mechanical devices. Overall, the Community's international performance in passive and electro-mechanical components is eroding and the Community remains a net importer of active components despite the improvements in its ratio of exports to imports. Thus, although the Community's production of semiconductors is biased towards integrated circuits, its exports of active components are relatively concentrated in the technologically simpler discrete devices. In contrast, exports of both the United States and Japan are specialised in the more technologically advanced devices.

Semiconductors

The semiconductor industry is one of the most complex industries to analyse due to the variety of products and technical complexity of the manufacturing process. Semiconductors is a textbook global industry: product value is high in relation to weight and production is easily separated into discrete activities, many of which can move offshore at low cost. Semiconductor firms correspondingly adopt global strategies early in their development.

Unlike the growth phase of the 1970s, much of today's semiconductor industry is simply a 'commodity' industry. In earlier days, profitability was virtually guaranteed as entry into the market could be accomplished at a relatively low cost. New small firms proliferated as engineers with new designs would leave established firms, get venture capital and start production to serve an emerging niche market. However, once the market had increased, entry into the new market by larger existing firms would quickly reduce profitability. This trend continues, with almost every company announcing its intention to move into ASICs (application specific integrated circuits). Despite several quick fortunes in the industry's heyday, the accumulated value of global profits over the past forty years is effectively zero.

The structure of demand

The European market ranks third in terms of the overall world demand for semiconductors. Forecasts for 1992 suggest that 30 per cent of world demand will come from North America, 35 per cent from Japan, and 13 per cent from both Europe and South-East Asia. (See Tables 7.10 and 7.11.)

The distribution of semiconductor consumption by end-use varies by country/region. Approximately 70 per cent of the Community's

Table 7.10   Semiconductor consumption by country/region 1987–92 ($USm.)

	1987	1988	1992
US/Canada	12	15	23
Europe	7	8	13
Japan	14	17	27
South-East Asia	5	7	13

Source: Dataquest

Table 7.11   Growth rates of semiconductor consumption (%)

	Japan	US	Rest of World	World
1986–7	16.5	21.0	68.0	23.8
1987–8	20.5	23.0	41.4	23.7

Source: Dataquest

semiconductor consumption derives equally from industrial, communications and data processing sectors. In contrast, 75 per cent of Japan's semiconductor consumption derives from consumer goods and data processing industries with each sector representing about one half of this demand. In the United States, the largest share of demand comes from data processing, with remaining demand distributed evenly across the remaining sectors. Military uses account for roughly 15 per cent of US semiconductor consumption, 10 per cent of Europe's and effectively none of Japan's. (See Figure 7.3.)

The manufacturing process

An understanding of the manufacturing process is important in order to understand the nature of the semiconductor industry. The first and most important step is the design of the circuit. This stage requires highly skilled labour and is the most time consuming and costly. The importance of the design phase is one reason for the worldwide spread of semiconductor production. In the early days, an engineer with a new design could start a firm and then license the design to an established merchant firm in exchange for capital or access to a particular market. Aiding the spread of designs was limited patent protection. This permitted widespread copying of designs and led established manufacturers to cross-license their technology widely (often to avoid costly legal battles over proprietary designs). Licensing was easily accepted since the short life cycles meant that a licensee who copied a design would enter an already

Per cent

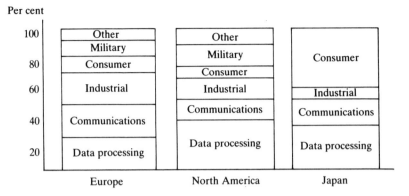

Figure 7.3 Global semiconductor consumption by end-use market, 1987

exploited market. In the mid-1980s firms began to move towards automated design tools such as CAD (computer-aided design) in order to reduce design times and labour costs. Efforts were also made to punish pirates and to strengthen laws in order to prevent further theft of designs.

Once a circuit design is created, actual production begins. The raw material is a silicon wafer with a standard size of six inches. Manufacturers have recently attempted to increase the size with some success. By 1987 most wafer fabrication plants were located in Japan. Only three companies in the United States produce wafers: Texas Instruments, IBM and Monsanto (recently purchased by Huels AG of Germany). Until recently, however, both Texas Instruments and IBM produced only for in-house use so that Monsanto is the only firm actually selling wafers on the external market.

The next step is to transfer the circuit design to a set of masks used in two lithography processes which imprint the circuit patterns, layer by layer, on to the wafer. This stage requires a dust-free environment and this requirement has become even more critical as the width between circuits has been reduced to under 1 micron. Costly clean rooms, utilising special air ducts, filters, water supplies, etc., are required to ensure control at this step.

Once the circuits are transferred to the wafer, testing is undertaken to determine defects. Each chip is then separated from the wafer and the chips packaged so that the circuitry can be connected to external outlets. The packaging process is low skilled and labour intensive. For this reason, virtually all US and Japanese firms have low-cost assembly and testing facilities located in low labour cost (developing) countries. The final production stage involves performing a series of computerised tests to ensure reliability.

In general, the complexity of the manufacturing process requires long lead times for plants to come on stream. As much as 18–24 months are required to build the plant, install the equipment and determine the quality and performance of the product.

The semiconductor product family

Figure 7.4 shows the relationship among the various semiconductor products and shows percentages of world consumption in each product group in 1987.

In contrast to the attention given by the popular press, memory devices are a relatively small part of the overall semiconductor market and represent only one-third of the market for digital semiconductors. Logic devices are the more important segment of the market. These devices are a critical input into many consumer and industrial end-products such as consumer electronics, telecommunications equipment, computers, professional machinery and industrial equipment.

Bipolar and MOS (metal oxide semiconductor) devices differ in their operational characteristics and method of manufacture. Bipolar technology is older but such devices generally operate at higher speeds. In contrast, the MOS technology generally results in devices that are slower

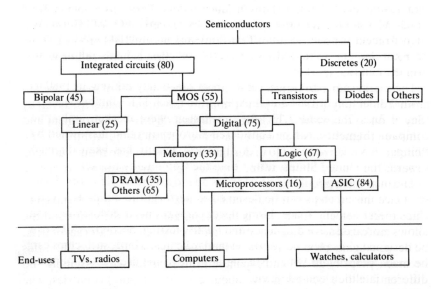

Figure 7.4   Family tree of semiconductor products, showing percentages of 1987 world consumption

but which require less power. Since the mid-1980s the lack of speed associated with the MOS technology has been improved with CMOS technology.

Both bipolar and MOS integrated circuits can be further divided into linear (analog) and digital. Linear integrated circuits accept and return signals over a continuous range whereas digital integrated circuits act as on/off switches. Digital integrated circuits can be further subdivided into memory and logic. Memory devices consist of DRAM (dynamic random access memory) and SRAM (static RAMs). Recently, SRAMs have been growing in popularity since they are faster. However, the cost of this greater speed is greater complexity and expense and less storage capacity than a DRAM of similar size.

Logic integrated circuits are capable not only of storing information but also of processing it. The simpler logic integrated circuits are preprogrammed to perform a specific set of functions and are used mainly in products such as watches and calculators. The more complicated logic circuits can be programmed to perform different tasks depending on conditions: for example, the air/fuel mixture of an automobile engine.

The fastest growing segment of the integrated circuit market is for semi-custom and custom devices known as ASICs (application-specific integrated circuits). ASICs can be divided into four groups: programmable logic devices (PLDs), cell-based integrated circuits, gate arrays and full-custom integrated circuits. Gate arrays and cell-based devices are typically designed jointly between the manufacturer and the user. Gate arrays, which can be designed in only 2–4 weeks, consist of fixed circuits (transistors, resistors and capacitors) which the ASIC designer interconnects to meet the user's application. Full-custom integrated circuits are the most efficient ASICs but also the more costly, with design taking up to twelve months.

The market for ASICs has grown from practically nothing in 1980 to around $6 billion in 1987 and is expected to reach $11.7 billion by 1992. (See Tables 7.12 and 7.13.) In this fast-growing market, only one company (Signetics) can be considered European in that it is owned by Philips, N.V. However, most of Signetics' activity has been directed towards the United States, rather than the Community market.

The increasing popularity of ASICs is due to a number of factors. First, such customised chips can be designed to perform the duties of several chips thereby saving space. Using fewer chips results in cost savings and allows more extensive diagnostic and quality testing. Second, ASICs can be designed to use less power than standard chips. Third, such chips can be made proprietary which is a big advantage for users attempting to differentiate their end-products.

The gate array is presently the most popular ASIC, since vast quantities of such chips can be manufactured in a semi-finished state and,

Table 7.12   Global ASIC consumption, 1987–92 ($USm.)

Type	1987	1988	1992
Programmable logic devices	417	583	1,616
Cell-based ICs	919	1,263	3,164
Gate arrays	2,407	3,164	7,832
Full-custom ICs	2,284	2,395	2,088
Total	6,027	7,405	11,700

Source: Dataquest, January 1988

Table 7.13   The ten largest ASIC vendors worldwide, 1986

Company	1986 Gross Revenues ($USm.)				% Growth 1985–6
	Gate Array	Cell-Based	PLDs	Total	
1. Fujitsu	309	50	–	359.2	43.0
2. LSI Logic	192	–	–	194.3	38.9
3. AT&T	–	183	–	183.1	26.8
4. MMI/AMD	–	–	172	176.7	19.3
5. NEC	145	–	–	151.2	55.9
6. Toshiba	120	–	–	132.6	152.3
7. TI	38	42	20	99.7	40.0
8. Motorola	92	–	–	94.7	20.9
9. Hitachi	79	–	–	78.8	34.6
10. Signetics	–	–	50	76.0	3.7
Total Top Ten				1,546.3	38.8

Source: Dataquest, 1987

thus, in advance of knowing the specific use to which the chip is intended. At the final stage of production, the previously unconnected logic gates of the chip are set open or closed thereby defining the pattern of the design and the function of the chip. The demand for gate arrays is forecast to growth to $8 billion by 1992.

Despite the current popularity of gate arrays, recent developments in the United States suggest that present methods for completing the last stage of production may soon be the relatively costly way to manufacture ASICs. At present, the final stage costs between $10,000 and $20,000 in non-recurring engineering costs and takes between two weeks and several months. During this time the designer does not know whether the chip will actually work as planned in his system.

In a recently invented process, the combination of new design tools (CAD) and a method called a 'silicon compiler' permits the most advanced gate arrays to be programmed in minutes at a cost of a few pennies, plus the price of the semi-finished blank gate array chip which itself costs only a few dollars to manufacture. The process has been developed by Actel Corporation in the United States who has over twelve patents pending. While still a young technology, the new process has important implications for the Community's Silicon Structures Project which, like Fujitsu of Japan, is trying to meet new design challenges with ordinary gate arrays and the currently more time-consuming method of customising the chips.

Structure of supply

In 1986, ten firms supplied 54 per cent of the total world demand for semiconductors ($30.6 billion). However, this masks an even greater degree of supplier concentration: 30 per cent of global production derived from only four companies: NEC, Hitachi, Toshiba and Motorola. Following these are a number of smaller companies specialising in customised chips. European enterprises are typically smaller than either Japanese or US firms, though they are trying to become major world suppliers.

The primary European suppliers (Philips, SGS–Thomson and Siemens) have not yet achieved their goal of being leaders in semiconductor technology. While they are global leaders in power integrated circuits, discrete and analog components, such products represent older technologies where market growth is expected to be no higher than 3 or 4 per cent per year. Even within their areas of strength, Community firms have been hurt by a variety of factors, including bad marketing. For example, it has been noted that in the United States the product strategies of Community firms are often unclear and that many potential customers have never seen a sales force. Signetics is also said to have suffered when no new strategy appeared after it was acquired by Philips. Overall, potential customers in the United States have limited beliefs about the ability of European firms to meet their needs.

In 1986 Japanese firms surpassed American firms as the main world suppliers of electrical components. In 1988, Japanese firms accounted for 95 per cent of world output of 1 megabit DRAMs. Much smaller than their US and Japanese competitors, the main European producers of semiconductors are Philips–Signetics, SGS–Thomson and Siemens AG. The Community's relatively weak position is also evident when one considers the number of Community firms in the list of the world's largest semiconductor producers. (See Table 7.14.)

Siemens ranked twentieth in the list of worldwide producers in 1988 but moved into fifteenth place in 1989. However, forecasts for 1993 suggest no improvement with respect to the Community's position as a consumer rather than a producer of semiconductors. (See Table 7.15.)

Table 7.14   Semiconductor producers ranked by value of world sales ($USm.)

1982		1985		1988	
1. [a]Motorola	1,310	[b]NEC	1,985	[b]NEC	4,534
2. [a]Texas Instr.	1,227	[a]Motorola	1,830	[b]Toshiba	4,302
3. [b]NEC	1,100	[a]Texas Instr.	1,767	[b]Hitachi	3,608
4. [b]Hitachi	800	[b]Hitachi	1,670	[a]Motorola	3,038
5. [a]Nat'l Semi.	690	[b]Toshiba	1,468	[a]Texas Instr.	2,741
6. [b]Toshiba	680	[c]Philips	1,070	[b]Fujitsu	2,368
7. [a]Intel	610	[b]Fujitsu	1,020	[a]Intel	2,350
8. [c]Philips	500	[a]Intel	1,020	[b]Mitsubishi	2,278
9. [b]Fujitsu	440	[a]Nat'l Semi.	940	[b]Matsushita	1,888
10. –		[b]Matsushita	900	[c]Philips	1,764
11. –		–		[a]Nat'l Semi.	1,700
12. –		–		[a]AMD	1,106
13. –		–		[c]SGS–Thomson	1,083

Note: [a]: US, [b]: Japanese, [c]: European

Table 7.15   Community production and consumption of semiconductors (1987 ECU m.)

	1979	1982	1987	1993
Consumption	3,220	4,300	5,070	9,000
Avg. annual growth (%)	–	10.1	3.3	10.3
Production	2,150	2,700	3,490	5,950
Avg. annual growth (%)	–	7.9	5.3	9.2

Finally, the relatively weak position of Community firms in the world market is to be contrasted with progress made against both Japanese and American firms in the Community market. (See Table 7.16.)

Competitive environment

Since 1988, the top three semiconductor producers in the world have been Japanese firms. This ranking is the result of a number of factors including higher quality of produced components, lower production costs due to a high derived demand from its own electronics industry, and past R & D efforts that have permitted them to move from the position of follower to leader in the manufacture of many semiconductor devices (most notably 'commodity' memory devices such as DRAMs).

The importance of the diverse set of electrical consumer goods produced by Japanese firms in permitting lower production costs and in fostering innovative designs of electrical components cannot be over-stressed. The dominant position of Japanese firms in many electronic

Table 7.16 Semiconductor producers ranked by value of sales in the Community market

1985	1986	1988
1. Philips	1. Philips	1. Philips
2. Tex. Instr.	2. Tex. Instr.	2. SGS–Thomson
3. Motorola	3. Motorola	3. Tex. Instr.
4. Siemens	4. Siemens	4. Motorola
5. Thomson	5. Thomson	5. Siemens
6. NAS	6. SGS	6. Intel
7. Intel	7. NAS	7. Nat. Sem.
8. SGS	8. ITT	8. NEC
9. ITT	9. Intel	9. Toshiba
10. NEC	10. NEC	10. AMD
11. AMD	11. AMD	
12. Hitachi	12. Tel. El.	
13. Tel. El.	13. Hitachi	
14. Toshiba	14. Toshiba	

consumer goods permits greater realisation of scale economies in component manufacture. Also, intense competition among Japanese firms also generate demand for more innovative components. In contrast, the lack of competition in consumer electronics within the Community deprives its component manufacturers of this critical link which can help lower production costs and raise creativity.

Competitive advantage in semiconductors is increasingly being determined in the design phase. As noted earlier, the trend in the industry is towards semi-custom and custom chips since these permit the creation of unique products and, thus, the possibility of leader advantages. Moreover, new design technologies involving CAD and silicon compilers are now giving the 'power' to the designer. In the past, whatever designs were thought up by designers or systems inventors would only get produced if executives of large fabrication plants could envisage a market for many millions of chips. But with the new design technology, the concentration of power in the hands of fabricators is rapidly eroding. In view of the increasing importance of the design phase, the outlook for the future appears particularly strong for US firms compared to either Japanese or Community firms. The reason? Over half of the world's supply of circuit designers are located in the United States.

Whereas design capabilities are becoming increasingly important, overall technological capability remains another important factor for success in electrical components. In this regard, the available data on spending for research and development (R & D) indicates that Community firms spend less, on average, than their counterpart US and Japanese firms. Lower R & D spending suggests less resources devoted for design and subsequent manufacturing innovations which results in weak product lines, non-existent or sub-standard manufacturing techniques and out-of-date products. (See Table 7.17.) In many instances, the lagging position of Community firms in technological development has led them to acquire technology by licensing it from Japanese or American companies (e.g. Siemens purchase of DRAM technology from Toshiba).

Manufacturing cost structure Until recently, a striking aspect of semiconductor production was that production costs would typically fall by 30 per cent for every doubling of cumulative volume. More recently, as the distance between circuits has narrowed, the expected cost reduction from such learning effects is more in the neighbourhood of 20 per cent. Such cost reductions are primarily due to the fact that any given production run produces more defective chips than good ones. For new products, yields can be as low as 10 per cent for inexperienced producers and 25 per cent for more experienced ones. For mature products, yields can be as high as 90 per cent. The comparison of US and Japanese loss percentages in Table 7.18 indicates the importance of learning effects in raising yields.

The enormous variation in yields makes it difficult to calculate minimum efficient scale (MES) for this industry. Estimates in 1987 calculated a MES of at least 1,000 wafer starts per week. At a cost of $25,000 per wafer start for a state-of-the-art one micron facility, this represents an initial capital expenditure for a facility of $40–50 million. Since a typical plant requires another $40–60 million in equipment, total costs range from $80–110 million.

Rapid obsolescence (equipment is outdated in 2–3 years) has led to huge ongoing capital investments. In the mid-1980s most large firms were building fabrication plants at a cost of $150 million. It was estimated that a firm would need a 3 per cent market share to justify building a plant in the late 1970s, while a 6 per cent share is needed in 1987. However, low-volume plants for specialised chips can be built for as little as $20 million.

Capital spending for semiconductors goes on production, testing and assembly gear. In 1987 the typical cost structure for the manufacture of

Table 7.17   R & D spending by Community firms – all activities (as % of sales)

Siemens	11.5
Signetics–Philips	15.0
SGS–Thomson	8.0
US (average)	18.0

Table 7.18   Semiconductor loss percentages for Japanese and US firms

	Test number	Average number of bad chips (%)	Range (%)
16 K RAM:			
Japan	1.	0.30	0.1–0.5
	2.	0.53	0.0–1.8
	3.	1.77	0.1–5.1
United States	1.	0.70	0.0–2.7
	2.	0.85	0.0–4.7
	3.	1.07	0.0–6.2
	4.	4.11	0.0–12.4
4 K RAM:			
Japan	1.	1.07	0.0–5.3
United States	1.	0.32	0.0–5.3
	2.	0.41	0.0–2.0
	3.	0.87	0.0–1.1

Source: OECD Report, The Semiconductor Industry, Paris 1985

semiconductors was around 30 per cent for capital equipment, 15 per cent for R & D and only 1–2 per cent for transportation and distribution. The remainder is, of course, allocated to labour and raw materials inputs. Since 1980, wafer costs have fallen considerably ($30 in early 1980s to $6–$10 in 1987) while labour costs have been falling due to a switch to automation. (See Table 7.19.)

Pricing   Given the relatively short life cycle of new products and significant scale economies in production, semiconductor firms typically adopt a 'forward pricing' strategy. Under this strategy the firm sets a low price in order to gain market share and achieve cost reductions through scale economies. This strategy also reflects the price sensitivity of buyers given a high degree of substitutability between new and existing products.

Many firms tend to build large plant sizes due to the importance of scale economies, although this may also reflect a strategy of investing in

Table 7.19   Semiconductor capital spending by country/region, 1987–92 ($USm.)

	1987	1988	1989	1990	1991	1992
North America	2,474	3,338	3,605	3,677	4,744	5,929
Japan	2,440	4,587	5,183	4,820	6,700	8,711
Europe	843	926	1,065	1,139	1,407	1,713
All Others	380	468	545	655	900	1,096
Total	6,137	9,319	10,398	10,292	13,751	17,449

capacity in order to prevent entry. Large capacities have led to aggressive price reductions in periods of slack demand. For example, considerable overcapacity was responsible for significant price reductions in 1985 to 1986. But even when the market improved in 1987, Japanese firms found that Korean firms had begun to exert considerable price pressure. The ensuing price reductions and excess capacity led, in 1989, to dumping accusations by Community firms against six Japanese firms. The outcome was an agreement between eleven Japanese firms and the Community to set floor prices of DRAMs within the Community.

The floor price agreement set a minimum price of $130 for the new 4 Mb DRAM which is ten times higher than the price floor agreed to regarding the older 1 Mb DRAM. A consequence is that the Community market for 4 Mb DRAMs is unlikely to show fast growth, which will, in turn, slow the adoption of this chip by Community firms into their end-products. In addition, the floor price system favours, and therefore raises the profitability of, leaders (i.e. the Japanese) relative to followers, since late entrants are limited in their ability to attract customers based on lower prices.

Product differentiation   There are thousands of integrated circuits that can be distinguished by function, speed of operation, size, power consumption and cost. However, the extent of meaningful product differentiation within categories of semiconductors varies considerably across categories of devices. For example, among 'commodity' memories, DRAMs can be distinguished from SRAMs in terms of speed but among DRAMs (or SRAMs) there is little differentiation. At the other extreme are logic integrated circuits which can be quite differentiated. For example, both the Intel and Motorola microprocessors provide similar functions but use entirely different operating languages. This illustrates a case in which switching costs can be quite high for consumers and tends to ensure brand loyalty. In general, the extent of substitutes within product categories is a central factor complicating rivalry among firms. As noted above, the growth in semi-custom and custom integrated circuits (ASICs), coupled with greater flexibility and power on the part of designers, implies much greater scope for differentiation among integrated circuits. In the industry as a whole, the development of product strategy, differentiation and promotion is different between standardised and customised chips. For standardised chips, differentiation is directed towards manufacturer–customer relationships to ensure supply, quality, etc. Among custom chips, differentiation is developing along more traditional lines with major differences occurring in design and associated speed, energy use and size characteristics of the chips. (See Table 7.20.)

Table 7.20 Characteristics of standardised and custom chips

Characteristic	Standardised chips	Custom chips
Type of product	memories and processors	full and semi-custom chips
Production differentiation	small	large
Price behaviour	low prices	'what market can bear'
Technological potential	very high	average or high
Scale economies	very important	minor importance
Vertical integration	highly or complete	none
Size of unit	large	small

Entry A primary entry-impeding factor in modern semiconductor production is capital costs. Capital costs have risen dramatically in the industry while cost-savings through scale economies have decreased. Initially, manufacturers could expect around 30 per cent reduction in manufacturing costs but this figure is now 20 per cent. Part of this is due to the greater complexity of chips which increases loss percentages from any given production run. Moreover, the scale of manufacturing and expenses associated with R & D has grown. Overall, these trends imply that only large companies are likely to survive as non-niche semiconductor producers in the future.

The creation and more vigorous enforcement of intellectual property laws is also making it harder for new companies to emerge. In the past, copying (reverse engineering) was widespread since there was little prospect of a pirate facing immediate legal retaliation. However, with increased competition and shrinking profit margins, innovating firms have increasingly turned to the courts to prevent entry.

On the other hand, there are effectively no barriers to entry with respect to design. In the past, many companies were started by mavericks who left successful companies when they developed a better design. Given the rapid developments in design noted above, the ease of entry due to design may overcome the capital barriers suggested above. However, with chips becoming more complex, the number of transistors on a chip and the amount of time required to design a chip have increased exponentially. The required CAD equipment that can reduce design time and design errors is currently a very expensive investment. For example, Intel invested over $100 million in CAD capabilities as part of its programme to design its new microprocessor, the 80486.

The above suggests an increasing trend in entry-impeding factors in semiconductors. However, the revolution in design tools as well as global excess capacity can be expected to reduce such pressures – start-up firms who have a good design can lease fabrication capacity in Japan or Korea and focus all their efforts on design and marketing.

Finally, the life cycle of many products is getting shorter. This makes it more difficult for firms to recoup investments in R & D and also places more emphasis on first-mover advantage. For example, if life cycles shorten to three years, being one year late implies one could never catch up. The new intellectual property laws reinforce the first-mover premium since latecomers cannot reverse engineer and so produce a marketable product in time to get a slice of the market.

Industry structure

Vertical integration and consolidation   The largest semiconductor firms are characterised by a high degree of vertical integration. This structure permits the realisation of scale economies, immediate feedback on design flaws, the possibility of new designs arising from spill-over effects, and risk reduction related to uncertainty concerning technological developments. Broadly speaking, the advantages of vertical integration are greater production and informational efficiency and reductions in uncertainty through risk sharing.

In semiconductors, two classes of firms can be distinguished: those who also produce consumer or professional electronic products and those who specialise in producing the custom chips for such applications. For custom chip producers, vertical integration is an unlikely form of organisation. For firms whose main activities are end-products, vertical integration is more likely, given the importance of proprietary designs in differentiating their end-products and spill-overs on to other product lines. Thus, despite the expected trend towards the growth of ASIC production, which favours small firm size and limited vertical integration, the evolution of the industry to date has been one of consolidation and increased vertical integration.

As shown in Table 7.21 the number of vertically integrated firms has increased over the past fifteen years. This integration reflects rapid increases in scale and attendant capital costs. Another indication of increased vertical integration among semiconductor producers is the percentage of production allocated for in-house consumption. (See Table 7.23.)

Increases in vertical integration among full-line producers reflects the increasing importance of the design and uniqueness of components as the major factor determining the value of firms' end-products. Vertical integration also helps to protect proprietary designs from theft.

Table 7.21 Vertically integrated semiconductor producers worldwide

1970	1976		1987
ITT	AEG-Telefunken	Bourns/PMI	Philips/Signetics
Motorola	Ferranti	Exxon/Zilog	Plessey
Raytheon	GI	Ferranti	Raytheon
RCA	Harris	Fujitsu	RCA
TI	Hughes	GE/Intersil	Rockwell
	ITT	GI	Schlumberger/Fairchild
	Motorola	Gould/AMI	Sharp
	NEC	Harris	Siemens
	Philips/Signetics	Hitachi	Sprague
	Plessey	Hughes	SGS–Thomson
	Raytheon	ITT	Thorn-EMI/Inmos
	RCA	Matsushita	TI
	Rockwell	Mitsubishi	Toshiba
	Sescosem	Motorola	TRW
	Siemens	NEC	
	TI	OKI	

Table 7.22 Non-vertically integrated semiconductor producers worldwide

1972	1977	1987
AMD	AMD	AMD
AMI	AMI	Intel
AMS	Electronic Arrays	National Semiconductor
Electronic Arrays	Fairchild	
Fairchild	Intel	
Intel	Intersil	
Intersil	MMI	
MMI	Mostek	
Mostek	National Semiconductor	
National Semiconductor	SGS-Ates	
PMI	Siliconix	
SGS–Ates	Synertek	
Siliconix	Zilog	

Table 7.23 Percentage of semiconductor production consumed in-house

NEC	20
Hitachi	28
Toshiba	31
Mitsubishi	34
Fujitsu	41
IBM	100

Source: OECD, The Semiconductor Industry

Co-operative agreements and alliances   Rising capital costs and
shorter life cycles imply that performance in the semiconductor market is
increasingly a question of economic strength. Big companies that show
good liquidity and wider product portfolios are more likely to survive
than are smaller companies.

However, the rising complexity of the industry and the rising scale of
R & D costs are making it difficult for even the largest firms in the world to
do everything in-house. Dataquest estimates that in 1980 $35 million in
annual sales was needed to justify building a fabrication plant but in 1987
that figure jumped to $175 million. By 1995 the figure is predicted to rise
to over $300 million, and by the year 2000 a fabrication facility could cost
$1 billion to build and would require over $600 million in annual sales to
justify. Consequently, firms are increasingly seeking co-operative
alliances to share increased risks and higher capital costs.

Recent developments surrounding IBM provide one example of the
role of increasing capital costs in necessitating alliances. Over 90 per cent
of the components used by IBM were traditionally produced in-house
and used exclusively in its own products such as computers and
telecommunications equipment, but were never sold on the merchant
market. However, with the advent of the 4 megabyte DRAM, and the
prospect of strong global competition, IBM recently decided not only to
expand its own DRAM production as a hedge against becoming
dependent on Japanese suppliers, but it also sought to begin development
of a 64 Mb DRAM based on X-ray lithography. Efforts to raise the
needed funds for the latter project were thwarted until IBM entered into
a co-operative agreement with Motorola.

Alliances between large firms can be expected to lead increasingly to
consolidation among market leaders. This consolidation will either be
accomplished explicitly through merger, such as National–Fairchild and
AMD/MMI, or implicitly through joint ventures such as Toshiba–
Motorola. The net result may be only five or ten fully integrated firms
over the next decade.

As part of the trend towards alliances, the main Community suppliers
(Siemens, Philips and SGS–Thomson) have sought out and found
partners in both the United States and Japan. Some of the major
co-operation agreements involving Community firms in the period
1980–86 are indicated below:

1.   Philips with:
   - Advanced Micro Devices (US)   Technology exchange in bipolar
      microprocessors (1981).
   - RCA (US)   Co-operation on integrated
      circuits (1982).
   - Control Data Corp. (US)   Joint venture (1982).

● Intel (US)	Technology exchange and co-operation – CHMOS circuits.
● Motorola (US)	Second sourcing of 16-bit processors (1981).
● Matsushita (JAP)	Joint venture (1986).
● Texas Instruments (US)	Build-up chip library (1984); exchange OMOS circuits.
● BULL (FR)	Joint manufacturing.
● Intel (US)	Agreement of 16-bit processor.
● Siemens (FRG)	Joint R & D on Megabit project, co-operative research.

2. Siemens with:

● Intel (US)	Co-operation on integrated circuits.
● Fujitsu (JAP)	Joint venture for assembly of integrated circuits.
● Toshiba (JAP)	Sub-micron exchange.
● General Elec. (US)	Sub-micron exchange.
● Matsushita (JAP)	Joint venture 75 per cent Siemens, 25 per cent Matsushita; in development of components Matsushita will extend its share to 50 per cent in 1991.

3. SGS–Thomson with:

● Toshiba (JAP)	Development of new integrated circuits (OMOS).
● Ericsson	Research co-operation and marketing collaboration.
● AT&T(US)	Joint venture, technology/marketing of AT&T chips.
● AMD, Gen. Instr., Gen. Elec.	Second source agreement.
● National Semicond. (US)	Joint venture with Saint-Gobain.
● Siemens, GCC, Philips and Plessey	Design of processor for military and civilian applications.

The emergence of ASICs implies that small firms will also have an incentive to form alliances in order to increase their design libraries since designs are a primary source of competitive advantage in ASICs. But small firms also need alliances to build their capital base. In this context, alliances between start-ups and Japanese or Korean fabrication firms will help diffuse technology and reduce barriers to entry for foreign firms that want to build distribution channels. Several US suppliers of custom chips have already entered the Community market with financing usually coming from Community-generated venture capital. The increased

Table 7.24   World distribution electronics production

	1984	1988	1993[1]
United States	55%	40%	35%
Japan	16%	23%	24%
Europe	18%	20%	20%
Rest of the world	11%	17%	21%
Value ($US bn.)	$275	$490	$740

Note: [1] forecast

Source: ICE

Table 7.25   Average wage for production workers in manufacturing, 1987 ($/hour)

Singapore	2.37
Taiwan	2.23
Hong Kong	2.11
South Korea	1.69
United States	over 11.00
Europe	5.00 to over 10.00

Source: US Bureau of Labor Statistics

sharing of designs and increased sources of venture capital suggest that the ASIC market will become more fragmented even as the number of large suppliers will be cut in half.

The location of production   As competition increases, major integrated circuit producers are increasingly locating production facilities around the world to take advantage of both skilled labour availability and lower labour costs. In this context, the fast-growing electronics business in the Far East together with its traditionally cheap labour continue to make the region a prime expansion site for component and system houses, particularly those of US companies. (See Table 7.24.)

Malaysia, Thailand and other South-East Asia countries are also attracting US, Japanese, Korean and Taiwanese investment in low-cost manufacturing and assembly sites. In the past, investment in South-East Asia was primarily the establishment of assembly and testing facilities using low-cost labour with final products destined for foreign markets. More recently, sales to local Asian markets have been of growing importance as many manufacturers seek to carve out long-term stakes in the rapidly growing Asia–Pacific market.

In general, the Asia–Pacific market is viewed by most foreign manufacturers as an enormous opportunity for sales of both components and finished products. Countries such as Malaysia, the Philippines and

Thailand currently offer the lowest wage rates in manufacturing. These countries are cheaper than the US and Europe for big volume semiconductor assembly and testing. They are also much cheaper than Japan and have been attracting many Japanese firms looking for low-cost production. (See Table 7.25.)

The country with the biggest future opportunities may be China, despite major stumbling blocks to developing the market. China expects to import more than $3 billion of electronic equipment in 1989 and is looking for production equipment to help modernise its own factories. The United States has a small share of the Chinese market, mainly due to tight export controls related to national security. Japanese electronic firms are estimated to have 60 per cent of import sales because of their government's more relaxed trade rules. Increasingly, American firms are setting up factories in China and Hong Kong with the intention of increasing sales to China. Most semiconductor makers see Hong Kong as a base from which to enter the Chinese market and surrounding regions. NEC, Toshiba, Hitachi, Texas Instruments and Motorola have opened design centres in Hong Kong.

Investment in production facilities in the United States and to a lesser extent in Europe is because of the enormous industrial potential in these areas. The United States remains the largest producer of computers, telecommunications equipment and other electronic equipment. The United States accounted for 55 per cent of worldwide electronic equipment production in 1984 (source: ICE) but its share is expected to fall to about 35 per cent by 1993. However, the United States will remain the largest producer. Investment by US firms in the Community reflects primarily the desire for market access.

Many foreign companies strengthened their position to participate in the post-1992 Community market by their decision to build plants in Europe. This is especially the case for wafer fabrication plants in view of the Community's rulings on chip production which requires that multinationals undertake wafer fabrication locally to avoid import duties. Examples of investment undertaken in reaction to this policy include Texas Instruments' investment of $250 million in a wafer fabrication plant in Avezzano, Italy and Fujitsu's decision to invest $680 million in a wafer plant in Newton Aycliffe, England. This is Fujitsu's first European manufacturing operation. Finally, Monsanto Corporation recently sold its US silicon wafer operation, the Monsanto Electronic Material Company, to Huels AG of Germany.

Establishment in Japan continues to be difficult for Western companies. There are a number of reasons for this difficulty. First, the size of Japanese companies requires a very high initial investment in establishing. Moreover, entry by acquisition is limited since merger or acquisition is uncommon and mostly unpopular. Second, hiring is more costly due to both the lifetime employment system and a wage system that rewards seniority. Third is the well-known nature of Japan's distribution systems in which suppliers and wholesalers have long-standing business relationships with retailers. Few Western companies have been able to penetrate this system.

Company strategies

In the full version of this paper the twelve companies whose focus is set out in Table 7.26 are explored in detail. Here, we only have space to summarise their main characteristics by country of origin. The companies vary markedly in size, with IBM as big as the four European producers put together. (See Figure 7.5.)

Japan

Japanese firms have become global leaders and low-cost producers of consumer goods and in the commodity segments of the semiconductor market, especially DRAMs and SRAMs. Japan was a late entrant into semiconductors who initially relied on American technology. Two events in the mid-1970s gave the Japanese an opportunity to gain a foothold in

Table 7.26   The importance of alternative electronic products to the major electronic firms

	Semi-conductors	Tubes and valves	Consumer electronics	Computers	Telecom.	Prof. systems
Japan:						
Matsushita	+	+ +	+ + +	+	+	+
NEC	+ + +	+	+	+ +	+ +	+ +
Hitachi	+ + +	–	+ +	+ +	+	+
Fujitsu	+ + +	–	–	+ +	+	+
Toshiba	+ + +	+ +	+ +	+	+ +	+ +
US:						
IBM	–	–	–	+ + +	+ +	+ +
Motorola	+ + +	+	–	+	+ +	+ +
Texas Instr.	+ +	–	–	+	+	+ +
Europe:						
Philips	+ +	+ +	+ + +	+	+ +	+ +
Siemens	+	+	–	+ +	+ + +	+ +
Thomson	+	+	+ +	–	+	+ +
Nokia	–	+	+	+	+	+

Note: (–) unimportant, (+) some importance, (+ +) important, (+ + +) very important

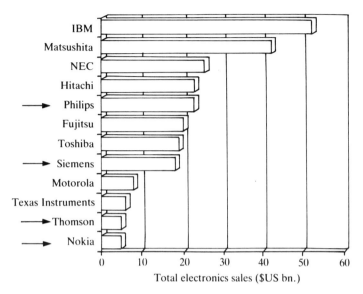

Note: [1] 1 April 1988 to 31 March 1989

Figure 7.5   Comparison of electronics firms by value of sales, 1988–89[1]

semiconductors. First, while US firms cut their plans for capacity expansion during the US recession of 1975, Japanese firms continued to invest. Second, Japanese firms took the risk of investing in large-scale commercial production of MOS circuits used in desk-top calculators at a time when US firms were committed mostly to bipolar technology. Higher capital spending and different factory management techniques combined to produce superior Japanese manufacturing capability. Japanese firms were generally more automated and had higher average yields.

The large Japanese manufacturers are highly diversified companies compared to US merchants. On average, 50 per cent of Japanese semiconductor production is sent to captive markets while semiconductor revenues average only 9 per cent of corporate sales. These vertically integrated firms include large integrated electronic manufacturers (Hitachi, Toshiba, Mitsubishi); computer and communications equipment manufacturers (NEC and Fujitsu); and consumer electronics companies (Sony and Matsushita).

In 1987 a rising Yen and intense competition from Korea accelerated the move of the leading Japanese companies away from volume products towards more creative research in artificial intelligence, new materials, and new system architecture.

Co-operative research

In Japan, the Ministry of International Trade and Industry (MITI) fulfils the role as co-ordinator and promoter of new developments, often by helping firms through the initial and most expensive stages of product development. Importantly, MITI not only subsidises projects but also supports them as a neutral co-ordinator and arbiter.

In semiconductors, support by the Japanese government began early in the 1950s in the form of financial assistance, R & D assistance and a liberal antitrust policy. MITI orchestrated the government support, beginning with the administration of a series of new laws, codified in 1957, that exempted the computer and semiconductor industries from antitrust prosecution. Government support of the industry continued throughout the 1970s and 1980s. It is estimated that between 1976 and 1982 the Japanese government provided at least $500 million in direct subsidies and loans to the semiconductor industry.

MITI also helps co-ordinate competitive strategies. In the mid-1970s MITI guided several of Japan's largest electronics companies into DRAM production, supporting the efforts of these firms with research grants, procurement contracts and a protected domestic market. By 1974, quantitative restrictions on semiconductor imports were eliminated and tariffs were reduced to zero in 1985. However, American firms believe that MITI continues implicitly to restrict market access.

MITI also tried to establish an Engineering Research Association (ERA). One effort was the VLSI (Very Large Scale Integration) project which involved the efforts of the five largest Japanese components suppliers (NEC, Toshiba, Hitachi, Fujitsu and Mitsubishi). Considerable government support came from NTT, the government telephone monopoly prior to privatisation in 1985. Between 1976 and 1980, NTT invested $350 million in VLSI research, the results of which were available to all Japanese semiconductor manufacturers.

The VLSI programme was particularly useful in enhancing related technological advances in specialised material supplier firms and specialised equipment manufacturers. Much of the success of the VLSI programme appears to have been due to the common threat felt by Japanese companies over the restrictive transfer policies of the leading US companies in the 1960s. Other reasons for the success of the VLSI project were: careful preparation of the project among the (future) participants leading to a very clear definition of the R & D objective; willingness to set up a separate joint laboratory under the leadership of a government scientist; and the administration of a MITI official.

MITI is working to co-ordinate and control the information explosion that has reached all sectors in Japan. In this context, MITI has outlined certain priorities for the information industry which include the following:

- Promoting the concept of an information university by establishing a nationwide liaison organisation for training information specialists to educate engineers and technicians.
- Promoting the use of computers in education institutions and adapting computers to the educational environment.
- Preparing for the smooth development and supply of efficient software.
- Expanding examinations of information-processing engineers.
- Promoting networks.
- Advancing information security.
- Promoting the local information industry.
- Assisting in comprehensive information utilisation in Asia.

To overcome problems in the area of software productivity, development and compatibility, MITI is attempting to apply proven automation techniques learned in manufacturing to the software design process. Its software Industrial Generalisation and Maintenance Aids project is an effort to automate software development and create standardised data structures.

In response to criticism that Japan's government-sponsored projects are not open, and typically help Japanese firms gain competitive advantages, MITI is also attempting to improve the image of Japanese industry by encouraging foreign investment and imports. These efforts include soft loans to foreign companies, tax incentives (worth some 30 billion Yen) and programmes to enhance consumer awareness of foreign products. In response, foreign firms have increasingly joined research projects under the sponsorship of MITI. Eight non-Japanese firms joined such projects in the first half of 1989. For example, in April, both IBM (Japan) and Thomson (Japan) began participation in an institute formed to develop software. The government expects that more foreign participation in such technology development projects will help reduce technology-related friction with other nations.

MITI's White Paper on Industrial Technology (December, 1988) recommended that Japan increase funding for basic research. The first areas designated are neural computers, optical computers, and high-temperature superconductors. For products with significant electronics content, the Paper concludes that Japanese technology remains behind only in rockets, jet engines, magnetic resonance imaging equipment, and databases. According to MITI, Japan will need to rely more heavily on their own research establishment to develop the technology for the next generation of products. MITI believes the government will have to step in and drastically increase its funding of basic research.

Despite its image, not all of MITI's efforts have met with success. An analysis of eighteen MITI projects concluded that ten could be considered failures. Moreover, the successful projects were mostly in the information technology field in which IBM (Japan) played a strong role. Overall, analysis of past MITI projects has suggested the following factors for success of such programmes:

- A fairly narrow and clearly defined R & D objective, even if this objective remains upstream to product development and, in this sense, is pre-competitive.
- An R & D association made up of a small number of firms faced, at least momentarily, with a situation where conflicts of interest are overshadowed by a perceived common threat.
- The establishment, on an *ad hoc* basis, of joint laboratories with locations distinct from member companies' R & D facilities.

Apart from MITI-sponsored projects are several private co-operative agreements among Japanese firms. For example, the 16 Mb DRAM project of Hitachi, Matsushita and Toshiba. In fact, Japanese sources have stated that private co-operation accounts for 90 per cent of all co-operation in Japan.

Summary

Japanese firms hold a strong position in the electronics industry. Their world market share of 51 per cent in semiconductors also benefits them in other areas of electronics such as consumer electronics. Non-Japanese companies are still the world leaders in computers, telecommunications and tubes and valves, but Japanese firms consistently show stronger growth. Among other things, the strength of Japanese firms is the result of governmental support and the relatively high degree of co-operation among companies.

United States

The three largest electronic companies in the United States are Texas Instruments, Motorola and IBM. Zenith is the only remaining US consumer electronics firm but is very small on a global scale. Zenith's profitable computer division was recently purchased by the French company Bull.

Co-operative research

Unlike the Europeans and Japanese, the US government has played a limited role in the direct development of either the semiconductor or consumer electronics industry. In semiconductors the US government played an early (negative) role by allowing industries very limited antitrust exemptions. This led the Semiconductor Industry Association (SIA) to establish the non-profit Semiconductor Research Cooperative in 1982 to fund basic research at American Universities. In 1983 a group of twenty-one firms created the Microelectronic and Computer Technology Cooperative (MCC) to sponsor long-term applied research. By the mid-1980s, however, neither effort had made a significant contribution to the competitive balance between Japan and the United States.

In 1986–87 the US government began to play a more active role. After apparent dumping of chips, the US retaliated against Japan in April of 1987 and in the autumn of 1987 Congress allocated $100 million to support a consortium (SEMATECH) of computer companies, chip makers and semiconductor equipment manufacturers. SIA firms made an equal monetary contribution while IBM and ATT donated proprietary chip designs for DRAMs and SRAMs, respectively. The goal of SEMATECH is to produce state-of-the-art manufacturing techniques to help US companies re-establish dominance in mass memory chip production.

The Defense Advanced Research Projects Agency (DARPA) is taking a larger, more public role by funding and overseeing SEMATECH and will award grants for the development of HDTV technology. DARPA's will devote half of its $1.1 billion budget for fiscal 1990 to direct research on weaponry, the remainder to be spent on basic research. This makes DARPA the biggest venture capital fund in the world. DARPA has turned its attention to the US electronics industry in an attempt to overcome the Japanese dominance in consumer electronics.

As noted, co-operative research is organised primarily within the MCC and SEMATECH. MCC is a co-operative research consortium designed to undertake co-operative long-term research in micro-electronics and computer technology leading to the development of generic technology and research and development goals that have commercial applications. Created largely in response to the threat of Japanese domination of the computer and electronics industry, MCC is a private sector consortium of nineteen shareholder or equity companies, fifteen associate members, and one government agency sponsor. Large-scale research projects carried out jointly by private companies are very important in the computer and semiconductor industry. MCC is unique in that it is purely a private joint venture. Previous joint research and development ventures in the US have involved only two or three companies, a relatively low level of effort, and firms that were not direct competitors. MCC's mission is as follows:

- To create a unique environment for leading US computer and electronics companies to co-operate and share in long-range, high-risk research.
- To generate new ideas and technologies that will significantly enhance the competitiveness of participating companies.
- To help its shareholders and the US maintain a competitive edge in the world marketplace.
- To remove barriers to achieving the full promise of artificial intelligence and to provide systems to make it practical for users.

MCC concentrates on applied research and has developed such technologies as new computer languages, computer-aided design software and a method of packaging semiconductor chips. MCC's problem thus far has been in transferring usable technology to member companies fast enough for them to maintain a competitive edge in international markets.

Other reasons why MCC members have not benefited to a greater extent are, firstly, the reluctance of firms to share information with competitors and, second, engineers who are hesitant to abandon older technologies. NCR Micro-electronics Inc. is the only company ever to develop a commercial product (Design Advisor) which is a $60,000 computer-aided design software system based on MCC technology. But after three years of research and over $200 million in funding by its nineteen member firms, the consortium (MCC) has produced 1,200 technical papers, six patents and only one commercial product.

SEMATECH is an industry- and government-sponsored research consortium which has flourished with funding from the US Department of Defence. All fourteen member companies in SEMATECH are competitors who hope that by co-operating to develop new techniques and capabilities they can all prosper. The stimulus behind SEMATECH is the US irritation of having lost the leading share in the semiconductor market to the Japanese.

Failure by the US to maintain leadership in manufacturing technology has been the primary reason for Japan's strength in the US semiconductor market. SEMATECH is working hard to recapture manufacturing dominance. Its door is open to smaller companies, but the entrance fee is approximately $2 million. Many firms find the cost of membership too high given perceived benefits, while others either distrust government involvement or worry about leaks of SEMATECH-developed technology via members' offshore manufacturing facilities, technology exchange or the departure of knowledgeable employees.

Yet the goal of SEMATECH is not to develop secret formulas but rather to achieve a closer relationship between semiconductor equipment manufacturers and chip makers. Although manufacturers selected for SEMATECH's fabrication line will gain advantages, opportunities also will exist for those not selected. SEMATECH is an example of how the US government is now actively and directly fostering industrial innovation, given that individual companies find it increasingly difficult to compete on a world scale without some form of co-operation.

Recognising that a larger scale is necessary to remain competitive, US antitrust laws have also been relaxed as have laws restricting the ability of national laboratories to push their technology into the private sector. The US Congress is considering further relaxation of antitrust laws so that companies can form consortia to manufacture HDTV sets. Robert Mosbacher, Secretary of Commerce, and some members of Congress have recently promoted consortia as the way for the US to enter into HDTV.

Summary

The strong position of the United States in computers, telecommunications and, to a lesser degree, electronic components (the US share in semiconductor production is 35 per cent) makes the US a very important supplier of electronic products. The US industry remains vulnerable, particularly in the lower technology and consumer-oriented product fields. IBM's decision to co-operate more fully on research and development suggests the possibility of a greater degree of co-operation among US firms in the future.

Europe

European firms have traditionally concentrated on discrete and opto-electronic devices although some European firms were making inroads into the custom design segment of the semiconductor market in the mid-1980s. The industry is comprised of a few large, vertically integrated, diversified electronic equipment manufacturers.

Co-operative research

In 1983 the twelve largest European electronic companies presented a dramatic view of the competitiveness of Europe's technology industries. Shortly thereafter, efforts were made to use co-operative research projects to funnel money into promising new technologies. The first was the European Strategic Programme for Research and Development in

Information Technology (ESPRIT). An example of pre-competitive co-operation on R & D, ESPRIT was patterned after the Japanese project on Very Large Scale Integration (VLSI). Participating firms and the European Commission each contributed 50 per cent of the cost of the project. In 1985 other projects were introduced including BRITE, RACE and EUREKA.

In addition to these activities, many electronic firms joined to establish common standards; eight electronics firms formed the Standard Promotion and Application Group (SPAG) in 1985. SPAG's goal was to unify European standards and to represent European interests in international standardisation. The Community's R & D subsidy was small compared to the total R & D budget of the large companies: total funding of ESPRIT, RACE and BRITE, together was less than, for example, the annual research budget of Siemens. None the less, the financial incentive has been sufficient for companies to participate, even if these projects have failed to produce a noticeable competitive effect.

Except for the BRITE project, the programmes are dominated by the large electronics companies. The most successful programme has been EUREKA, which has emerged as Europe's *ad hoc* industrial policy in high technology. Nearly 300 EUREKA projects worth $5 billion have been approved. One of EUREKA's goals is to help European companies compete in strong new markets. An example is the EUREKA 95 project for the development of HDTV. Since 1982, European firms have focused on the MAC standard which is compatible with existing television sets. The MAC standard has been accepted by the International Consultative Radio Committee and the rival Japanese standard (MUSE) has been rejected by the Federal Communications Commission. With the development of the MAC standard, the next step under the EUREKA 95 project is a $240 million project to develop HDTV.

European anxiety about the production of electronic components launched numerous subsidies but, thus far, these have done little to boost output. European consumption of semiconductors increased about 33 per cent to $8.5 billion in 1988, but this was twice as fast as semiconductor production. As the Megaproject draws to a close a new project, the Joint European Semiconductor Silicon Initiative (JESSI), is slated to begin. JESSI is subdivided into four areas: technology; equipment and materials; application and CAD-tools; and basic and long-term research. JESSI will cost about $4.5 billion over eight years with much of the finance coming from the companies themselves. In addition, Europe's three largest chip makers – Philips, Siemens and SGS–Thomson – have got together to share research and exploit synergies between semiconductor manufacturing and uses, since all are important consumers of semiconductors.

In addition to Siemens, Philips and SGS–Thomson, there is co-operation among a number of smaller companies. A main goal of JESSI is the development of 16 and 64 Megabit chips which should be marketed after 1995. JESSI is more or less the logical response to its predecessor, the Megaproject. As well as co-operation among European firms there has been the co-operation between firms in different geographical locations. Figure 7.6 indicates part of the network of international alliances that have developed in semiconductors. These alliances can be either an agreement on the development of semiconductors or the supply of certain semiconductors; nine of the relationships are micro-processor-related.

These alliances are not the complete picture since there are many agreements among smaller firms or between small and large firms. What Figure 7.6 does show is that in semiconductors the ties between Japan and Europe have not been close, except for Siemens' purchase of DRAM technology from Toshiba. Of course, much of this has to do with the success of the US firms Intel and Motorola in the microprocessor technology. But at the research level Europe remains an outlying area. This does not seem to be the case in other electronic areas such as telecommunications, where Siemens is the third largest producer in the world.

Summary

European electronics producers have been characterised as slow to react to the market and top heavy, and are said to be two or more years behind the US in technology and marketing. Yet SGS–Thomson, Philips and Siemens have spent $1 billion over the past five years to acquire technology and to gain a greater presence in the US market. But despite being present in the United States for more than ten years, these three companies have had limited success in semiconductors. European semiconductor companies have only 7 per cent of the US semiconductor market.

In ASICs, the European market is highly competitive and underpriced. The European ASICs market is growing at a healthy rate and the stakes for all players are high. The European ASIC market is estimated to be $600 million, with a large part claimed by non-European companies. European manufacturers have attempted to block further advantages by embracing US partnerships, enhancing customer service and playing their home-court advantage. The Europeans are doing battle with some of the biggest global players from both the US and Japan; however, they are not primed to win. While Europeans have superior knowledge of their territory, they are disadvantaged by their sluggish start in the ASIC market. Not only do Europeans fail to dominate their home ASIC market, but also none of the European companies is in the top ten

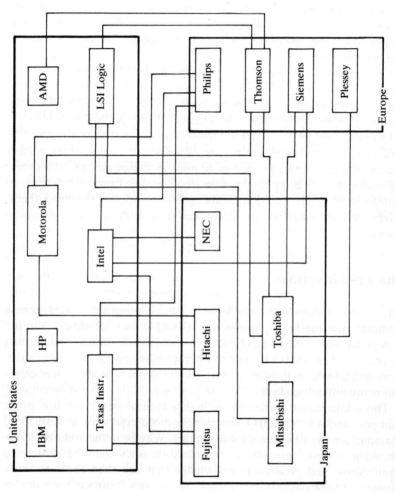

Figure 7.6   Co-operation agreements among major US, Japanese and European firms

suppliers of ASICs worldwide. The reasons are lack of competitive pricing, lack of cutting-edge technology, and not taking charge of marketing skills as their rivals from the United States and Japan have done.

In consumer electronics the trend appears to be for the two largest European companies, Philips and Thomson, to forge alliances with the Japanese, which partly reflects past animosities that have prevented these two firms from forming major collaborative agreements. The strategies of Philips and Thomson are similar, but Philips has the advantage in terms of size, product range and R & D capability. For each firm, as well as Nokia, the key to a future success in consumer electronics will lie in the development of more sophisticated products and product systems. In turn, the ability to develop such products is closely tied to capabilities for designing more sophisticated components and supporting software.

Overall, the position of European firms in electronics markets is relatively weak but there are signs of gaining strength. Their market shares in semiconductors and computers is minor compared to their Japanese and US competitors. The trend among European firms is to withstand fierce competition by increasing co-operation among themselves and to establish or strengthen ties with US and Japanese companies.

The 1992 initiative

The Community is relatively weak in semiconductors. The Japanese dominate the market in commodity DRAMs and SRAMs, while the Americans lead in MOS and EPROMs. Community firms are attempting to counter these facts through co-operative arrangements and acquisitions and they hope to be at the forefront of the new generation of chips, but many difficulties exist.

The semiconductor industry is highly cyclical with very low profit margins, and it is becoming increasingly more expensive to design and manufacture the next generation of chips. Why be in this industry? One reason is strategic importance, but mostly it is the gains to be derived from design and production knowledge that can then apply to other segments of the electronics industry. As we noted earlier, the value of consumer electronics is increasingly being determined by the components (in particular the design) and it is therefore clear that it is in the strategic interest of the major electronics companies to be 'in' semiconductors.

But it can be conjectured that a major factor determining the competitive strength of the Japanese in commodity chips, and the United States in both customised chips and advanced microprocessors, is directly related to national 'demand driven' factors. For example, dominance by the Japanese in commodity DRAMs and SRAMs was driven by the demand for consumer electronics, automobiles and telecommunications. Similarly, the US position in microprocessors and custom chips derives from its demand for computers, telecommunications equipment, and the technical requirements of both its industry and the military.

A combination of events in the 1970s, together with a shift in consumer demand towards Japanese products, positions Japanese firms in the market for commodity chips. The shift in consumer demand was widespread and included not only small-screen TVs but also automobiles and a host of other electronic products, all requiring commodity chips. The Japanese were to some extent ready for these events, partly because of MITI's planning and partly in spite of it, particularly regarding decisions to expand capacity at a time when US firms were holding back. But again, this capacity expansion was driven by the increased demand for Japanese electronic products. The resulting volumes that Japanese manufacturers were able to achieve to satisfy their own downstream uses was a primary reason for their subsequent cost advantages (on average, over 60 per cent of their commodity chip production was used in-house). Moreover, while much is (justifiably) made of the degree of co-operation among Japanese firms, it should not go unnoticed that a part of their success is also due to the intense competition that exists between Japanese firms in their own market (even though foreign firms are excluded). The same conditions can be said to characterise the US market in so far as consumer choice has dictated the trend of its semiconductor industry. And in this context we need to ask what factors have prevented European semiconductor producers from similarly benefiting from such demand-driven factors.

Since the demand for components is derived from the demand for the products using components, one need look no further than the fragmented and protected national markets within the Community, and its protection against imports of both industrial and consumer electronics. Protected and fragmented national markets have served to foster smaller, less efficient plant sizes, to increase design and distribution costs, and generally to reduce firms' incentives to serve the market. In addition, the higher price–cost margins made possible by protected national markets, together with import restrictions, dissuaded consumers from purchases that could have permitted the achievement of greater production levels, quality competition and marketing efforts. It is not, therefore, surprising to read that European firms fall short in marketing efforts and that, on average, the quality is somewhat higher for European products sold overseas. This latter observation is a direct consequence of the fragmented markets within the Community and the lack of effective competitive pressures to serve the market.

The difficulty now is that the requirements to achieve success in semiconductors are becoming increasingly more difficult. Rising scale and R & D costs suggest that only large companies will survive as non-niche players in the future. New intellectual property laws are making it more difficult to copy designs, and thus serve to increase barriers to entry. As chip densities increase and designs become more complex, the requirement for sophisticated and expensive CAD equipment is also making it more costly to enter the business. On the other hand, excess capacity in both Japanese and Korean fabrication plants can be leased, and CAD capabilities are available from specialised firms, so that many firms can focus their efforts on marketing and design.

Partly in response to 1992 initiatives, but mostly in response to the realities of the global market, European firms *are* attempting to counter the increased requirements of getting into, or staying in, semiconductors. A combination of national and international agreements on co-operation, cross-licensing, and outright acquisition or merger are all serving to 'globalise' European firms. In addition, the main Japanese, US and Korean firms are investing in production plants in the EC in an effort to position themselves for unification and consequent market growth. The relative size of companies such as Philips is likely to enable it to become 'global' and thus achieve production volumes that would allow it to be competitive in commodity chips, if it chooses to do so.

The emergence of ASICs has particularly encouraged alliances among firms since the main source of competitive advantage in this segment is in the design. Firms are swapping designs in an attempt to build large libraries and thereby attract customers. Competition in this segment is becoming more intense and there are signs that it, too, may become a commodity game; Toshiba has gone so far as to give away design tools for ASICs in an effort to get customers to use its fabrication facilities. Moreover, new design and manufacturing processes in this segment also hold the promise of substantially reduced entry costs and time to market (e.g. silicon compilers), making the market even more prone to low profit margins.

The current trend towards alliances implies the possibility of two outcomes in terms of market structure. Alliances between new start-ups and either Japanese or Korean firms would be likely to continue to diffuse technology and reduce barriers to entry, hence a more fragmented market. Alliances between large firms would lead to consolidation among the leaders, with the net result being perhaps five or ten fully integrated firms over the next decade.

Current Community policy in semiconductors is directed towards fostering alliances in R & D and, in general, co-operative behaviour among its firms. The implied co-ordination of activities is a positive step to the extent that it is not reduced to underwriting the cost of major programmes whose potential benefits to the Community have not been carefully evaluated.

The Community has also adopted a 'European-made' requirement for chips in an attempt to attract more 'high-tech' input into the Community. The European-made regulation specifies that the most critical operation in chip fabrication – imprinting the design – must take place within the Community. The origin regulation for chips is important for two reasons. First, by excluding chips whose patterns are printed offshore, the Community hopes to attract foreigners with chip knowledge and technology. Both Motorola and NEC have built chip production plants in Europe which satisfy the Community's rule. However, many other firms remain reluctant to settle in Europe and one may question the degree to which the policy serves as an employment policy, given the high degree of capital intensity of chip production. Second, the rule also determines import taxes for products containing chips. Aside from indirectly discriminating on imports from certain countries (e.g. Japan and Korea) the regulation may actually serve to foster increased competition within the Community (much to the future chagrin of local companies) since the net result is likely to be an increase in the number of Community fabrication plants which may, or may not, impart their production experience on locals. In addition, the larger local firms may begin to question the wisdom of such a restriction as they continue to acquire foreign operations, since the regulation presumably applies to any offshore chip, regardless of the parent company.

The above suggests that any policy must recognise the importance of demand-driven factors in fostering flexibility and innovation in the semiconductor industry. In this context, the harmonisation of standards, removal of administrative barriers, and overall integration of markets will serve to raise the possibility that demand factors will play an increasing role in guiding European firms. The major European firms are beginning to recognise this, and are attempting to reorganise their activities to reflect new realities. An example is the reorganisation by Philips into product divisions and the consolidation of its formerly autonomous subsidiaries.

One role for policy in this sector is to continue to function as a co-ordinator of pre-competitive co-operative activities among Community firms, and to disseminate resulting information to all concerned. Another is to continue to foster the environment for demand-driven innovation and flexibility through further removal of the internal barriers that have fragmented markets. Finally, reductions in external trade barriers should also be sought as the threat of market disruption is reduced through reorganisations and the altered strategies of local firms.

8

Consumer electronics

Harry P. Bowen

The consumer electronics industry

The consumer electronics industry encompasses video and audio equipment as well as blank video and audio tapes. In mature products such as colour television and video cassette recorders the Community faces stiff competition from countries such as Korea, Hong Kong and Taiwan. International competitiveness in such products requires large-scale production and the strategic response of many Community firms has been to close smaller plants and concentrate production in larger plants. Overall, the increased competition has reduced profit margins for all concerned. On the horizon are new products and applications related to optical compact disk technology, and the possibility of a new world standard for colour television: high-definition television (HDTV).

Structure of demand

Community demand for consumer electronics is expected to increase 4 per cent per year between 1987 and 1993. However, this average rate of growth masks widely varying rates of growth within main product categories. Little growth is expected for mature products such as current-generation TV and Hi-Fi. Between 1986 and 1987, Community demand for colour televisions grew in volume by 4.5 per cent and is expected to increase only 3 per cent per year up to 1993. In contrast, demand for new products such as CD players increased over 80 per cent in volume between 1986 and 1987 and growth of 25 per cent per year up to 1993 is expected. (See Table 8.1.)

Table 8.1   Growth in real Community consumption and production of consumer electronics (1987 ECU m.)

	Constant ECU value				Average annual growth (%)		
	1979	1982	1987	1993	1979–82	1982–87	1987–93
Consumption	9,880	12,975	15,260	19,310	9.5	3.3	4.0
Production	8,460	8,210	9,065	11,405	−1.0	2.0	3.9

Source: National Statistics, forecasts by BIPE, IFO, PROMETEIA

Video equipment

Video equipment accounts for two-thirds of total Community demand for consumer electronics with just over half of this demand being for colour television (CTV). (See Table 8.2.)

Audio equipment

Audio equipment accounts for just under 35 per cent of the Community's purchases of consumer electronics, primary purchases being car radios and Hi-Fi. Purchases of compact disk (CD) players increased sharply with demand rising from 150,000 units in 1983 to almost 4 million in 1987. Demand for CD players is expected to grow 25 per cent per year through 1993. Sales of CD players rose 59 per cent between 1986 and 1987 and were accompanied by a 20 per cent fall in prices. In 1987, imports of CD players accounted for 59 per cent of the market compared to 76 per cent in 1986. In 1987 South Korea held 4.5 per cent of the market. New applications for CD players have been important in keeping the Hi-Fi sector from a marked slump. (See Tables 8.3 and 8.4.) The advent of optical and digital technology has moved magnetic tape players and recorders on to the list of mature products. Between 1986 and 1987 demand for tape-related products increased strongly (21 per cent) but this

Table 8.2   Distribution of Community purchases of video equipment in 1987 (%)

CTV	53.1
VCR	32.6
Blank video cassettes	9.7
Cameras	2.9
B&W TV	1.4
Other	0.3

Table 8.3   Distribution of Community purchases of audio equipment in 1987 (%)

Hi-Fi	28.5
Car radios	27.9
Cassette radio	21.3
Blank cassette tapes	8.6
CD players	7.4
Other	6.2

Table 8.4   Percentage of households owning a CD-player

	1988	1989	1990	1991	1992
Japan	33	48	64	80	95
US	13	20	28	38	50
Europe	11	16	23	30	38
Switzerland	26	32	41	51	62
The Netherlands	21	30	43	57	70
United Kingdom	14	21	28	36	46
Italy	3	6	8	10	13

growth is expected to slow to around 5 per cent per year within the Community up to 1993.

Finally, the market for blank audio and video tapes is sizeable. For example, the UK market for blank audio tape in 1987 was 94 million units which is larger than either the CD players market (80 million units) or the personal stereo market (78 million units). The UK market for blank video tape is 223 million units which is larger than the market for Hi-Fi systems (209 million units). Sales of these products are dominated by a small number of companies, but mainly the Japanese companies TDK and Sony. The largest European company, BASF, has an estimated market share of 10 per cent.

Structure of supply

Community production of consumer electronics accounts for approximately 17 per cent of world production. Community manufacturers have engaged in extensive restructuring over the past ten years in the face of stiff competition from Japanese and South Korean conglomerates. Philips increased participation in its subsidiary North American Philips Corporation (NACP) as part of an international reorganisation of the Philips group which is continuing to transfer production units to Asian countries (video recorder factories in South Korea and Japan) and to expand in China and Asian countries through joint ventures.

Thomson acquired Ferguson (the consumer electronics division of Thorn-EMI) which was abandoning its production in order to specialise in renting, and by restructuring its activities in Germany, including relinquishing Dual and consolidating its subsidiaries Telefunken, Saba and Normende. Thomson's major acquisition was RCA, the consumer electronics division of General Electric. Thomson is now the second largest producer of colour televisions in the world and has opened the prospect of the US market.

In 1987 the Finnish group Nokia became the world's ninth largest producer of CTVs and the third largest producer in Europe through its part-acquisition of Oceanic, a subsidiary of Electrolux, and the consumer equipment activities of Standard Electric Lorenz (SEL), a subsidiary of Alcatel (part of the CGE group). Despite the apparent trend towards market domination by these three companies, the national market of most member countries is still supplied by small and medium-sized manufacturers, particularly in CTVs and top-end Hi-Fi components.

Japanese companies have accelerated the transfer of production and assembly units to Europe to deal with a rising yen, the saturation of certain markets, and increased competition from Korean manufacturers. Japanese production capacity in Europe has reached 2.5 million colour receivers, 3.2 million VCRs and over 500,000 CD players.

Tables 8.5 and 8.6 show the most important companies in terms of share of Community market and world sales of consumer electronics.

In 1989 the Community had a $6.7 billion trade deficit in audio/visual products. However, half of the VCRs purchased by the Community are made within the Community whereas in 1980 almost all VCRs were imported. The increase in local production largely reflects government trade policy, notably with respect to the Japanese and Koreans. In 1983 there were nine VCR plants in Europe. Of these, three were European-owned, three were Japanese and three represented joint ventures. In 1987 there were twenty-six VCR plants in Europe of which six were European-owned, fourteen were Japanese and four were joint ventures.

Although the market for consumer electronics appears to be increasingly dominated by a few large companies, the performance of Mivar and Seleco in Italy, Elbe in Spain, and Bang & Olufsen in Denmark proves that small companies can be both efficient (with low overhead costs) and profitable in their specific market. Such companies, however, have for the most part been sheltered by national markets. Their survival and growth are likely to depend more on ready access to technology and on new products, and less on the size of the market. In this regard, Community openness with respect to technology transfer and collaboration will be important.

Table 8.5 Market share of main suppliers of consumer electronics in the Community market, 1987

Firm	Market share (%)
Philips	15.0
Thomson	13.0
Matsushita	8.0
Grundig	7.0
Nokia	6.5
Sony	6.0
Bosch	4.5
Hitachi	4.0
JVC	3.5
Toshiba	3.0
Sanyo	3.0
Pioneer	3.0
Others	23.5

Table 8.6 Value of world sales of main suppliers of consumer electronics to the Community market ($USm.)

	1981	1982		1986
Matsushita	7.5	7.3	Matsushita	15.6
Philips	4.7	4.6	Philips/Grundig	10.2
Sony	3.5	4.0	Thomson (includes GE/RCA/Ferguson)	6.7
Hitachi	3.1	3.4	Sony	6.7
Toshiba	3.1	2.9	Hitachi	6.5
Sanyo	2.5	2.3	Toshiba	6.3
Thomson Brandt	2.4	2.2	Sanyo	5.1
RCA	2.3	2.1	JVC	4.2
Zenith	1.3	1.2	Sharp	4.0
Grundig	1.3	1.1	Mitsubishi	3.7
Pioneer	1.2	1.0		
ITT	0.7	1.0		

Competitive environment[1]

Given the diversity of consumer electronics products, the competitive environment is perhaps best understood by briefly considering the history of three major products: colour television, the video cassette recorder and the compact disk.

---

[1] This section is based on Cawson (1989)

Colour television

In the 1960s most European colour television manufacturers adopted the PAL system. Since PAL was incompatible with the Japanese and American systems and the PAL patents were held by Telefunken, European manufacturers were insulated from international competition. The French eschewed PAL and adopted their own system: SECAM. Access to the European market was therefore at the discretion of the patent holders and, not surprisingly, Telefunken refused to grant PAL licences to the Japanese.

The Japanese had adopted the American CTV system (NTSC) and by the late 1960s had begun to export high-quality, low-priced televisions to the United States. The Japanese were particularly adept at producing small televisions, and were thus in the right position to supply the US market with small-screen televisions just as the preferences of American consumers switched from large-screen to small-screen televisions. American producers were unprepared for this change in tastes since they had concentrated their efforts and production on large-screen televisions. Worse was the fact that they failed to react quickly to the change in consumer preferences with a competitive product. The end result was that most US firms closed and resources were released to find employment elsewhere in the economy.

Three factors prevented the Japanese from also penetrating the European market. First, as noted, patent holders refused to grant licences. Second was that fragmentation of national markets in terms of tastes and technical standards made it virtually impossible to enter these markets with a single standardised product. Finally, the preference for small and medium-sized televisions, as occurred in the United States, had not yet happened within Europe. Consequently, the overwhelming preference of Europeans for large-screen televisions meant high transport costs which limited profit margins. Not until the Japanese threatened to enter the European market with inexpensive 300-line sets which were not subject to the PAL patent did the Japanese receive licences to manufacture PAL-compatible sets. However, these licences only applied to small-screen sets since the market for such sets was thought to be small.

Like the Americans, the Europeans totally underestimated the market for small sets and by the early 1970s complaints of unfair competition and dumping were voiced by European manufacturers. Partly in response, Sony and Matsushita established manufacturing operations in Britain and Germany. At present, government policies such as a 14 per cent tariff on CTV imports, as well as rationalisation of the industry, have enabled Community producers to maintain a major share of the Community's CTV production. In 1986 the Japanese accounted for only 14 per cent of the Community market.

A new prospect has now risen, High Definition Television (HDTV), and efforts are being made by the Japanese and the Europeans separately to have their standard adopted as the world standard.

The Japanese MUSE system would require the complete replacement of every piece of current broadcast and receiving equipment. In 1986 the United States agreed to adopt MUSE, but attempts to have it adopted as the world standard failed due to the opposition of European firms. The latter were given until 1990 to develop their own system. The European system is based on the MAC standard for broadcasts by satellite (DBS) which has been adopted by major manufacturers and broadcast organisations, and backed by a directive from the European Commission. The proposal is for a system that is compatible with existing systems but would also allow permit HDTV broadcasts. The MAC system is claimed to offer better picture quality and several sound channels. But more important, the licensing of MAC equipment would be at the discretion of the Europeans.

HDTV proponents believe that consumers are willing to spend heavily to receive HDTV pictures, as they had been to purchase CTV and VCRs. However, this optimistic view must be tempered by the fact that both producers and consumers will need entirely new equipment and the price for HDTV is likely to be high. The European system does have the advantage of allowing existing sets to continue to operate but without receiving high-definition pictures.

The future of HDTV is highly uncertain. Thus far, no satellite TV company has the money to convert and many fear that the price to enter the world of MAC is too high to attract a mass market. Moreover, the high-definition version of MAC is not yet proven, and it is no longer obvious that a new transmission system is the best route to high-quality TV. In particular, the shift from analog to digital and the advent of the 4 Mb memory chip suggest it may be cheaper to process the existing signal to improve the definition of the picture and the quality of the colour. And if so, there seems little to recommend a change to an entirely different system and thus also little prospect that European firms would be able to dominate the market via monopolisation of the standard.

Video cassette recorders

The video cassette recorder's evolution is in marked contrast of that of colour television. In this case the VHS system developed by JVC of Japan was adopted as the world standard. JVC beat both Sony's Beta system and the Video 2000 system developed jointly by Philips and Grundig. Sony's failure resulted from its desire to maintain a firm hold on its technology and thus its refusal to license production or to offer its machines on an OEM (Original Equipment Manufacturer) basis. This limited both the spread of Beta machines and acceptance of the format. A key factor in the failure of the Video 2000 was that Philips rushed the system to market at the expense of quality control and extensive testing. The resulting reliability problems turned away potential customers.

A period of intense competition between the V2000 system and Japanese producers eventually led to a voluntary export restraint (VER) agreement between the Community and MITI in the spring of 1983. The VER established floor prices geared to Community production costs and not Japanese production costs. The effect of the VER was not to save the V2000 system but rather to increase VCR prices within the Community, and shifted profits to Japanese firms which they then used to increase their R & D investments. However, the VER did increase the rate of Japanese investment in VCR facilities in the Community. Over the period 1985–87 Japanese VCR capacity in the Community increased markedly and by 1986 Japanese firms held 71 per cent of the Community's VCR market and sourced from some 40 per cent of Community plants. The position of Philips/Grundig improved rapidly once it adopted the VHS system and it presently holds 15 per cent of the Community VCR market.

Since 1987 the policy emphasis has shifted from issues of Japanese import penetration to Korean import penetration and to the operation of Japanese plants within the Community. On the former issue, Philips and Thomson successfully induced the Commission to levy anti-dumping duties of around 30 per cent on three Korean and two smaller Japanese companies. As for the latter issue, controversy centres on local content requirements. Older plants such as the J2T joint venture claim up to 80 per cent Community content but firms such as Philips claim the opposite. In their defence, the Japanese insist that reliable suppliers of high-quality parts are difficult to locate within the Community.

Until recently, the Japanese dominated the VCR market but now the Koreans have started a concerted effort to gain a large share, based largely on their licensed Japanese technology. Goldstar is currently producing VCRs in Germany and is likely to open further factories. These factories are presently final assembly operations that operate below the scale needed for profitable manufacturing. As such, they could simply be viewed as ploys to diffuse any further trade tensions.

Compact disk

Philips invented the compact disk. But to avoid repeating its failure with the VCR, Philips chose to develop the final specification of the CD jointly with Sony. Since inventing the CD Philips has faced stiff competition from Japanese firms and has a Community market share of around 35 per cent (the Japanese dominate the rest of the world). However, unlike

CTV and VCR, Philips is forming a number of alliances with respect to further developments in CD technology. Although not principally developed by Philips, these new developments include CD-ROM, which enables vast amounts of data to be stored and then accessed using personal computers, and CD-I (CD-Interactive) which combines sound, high-quality graphics and text.

Philips has chosen to work with Sony on standards for CD-I but has not included such work under the umbrella of the EUREKA programme (Philips is leading two EUREKA projects, one for MAC-based HDTV and another to develop compatible standards for home automation). Philips' preference for pursuing a global network of alliances in CD-I appears in part as a reaction to the fact that no Community producer has chosen to produce CD players, and also Thomson's refusal to collaborate with Philips in the production of VCR components.

In addition to its joint work with Sony on CD-I standards, Philips has entered into three new joint ventures to produce both CD-I hardware and software: American Interactive Media, European Interactive Media and Japanese Interactive Media, as well as other joint ventures with publishers and computer firms in both the United States and Japan.

Philips' efforts with respect to the CD will provide a proving ground for determining if it can successfully form global alliances and enter the consumer electronics market on a global scale.

Industry characteristics

Firm size

The market for consumer electronics comprises both large and small firms. Large firms typically have diverse product lines outside consumer electronics and often design and produce their own components. Because of the strong technological link between the electronic components and consumer electronics, the large innovative firms display a high degree of vertical integration. The smaller firms typically specialise in some area of consumer electronics and typically purchase their components on the world market. Often there is greater profit in simply assembling components. However, many of the small assembly firms survive only as the result of Community import restrictions. If these restrictions were to be removed most of these operations would cease.

Because of their integration with respect to components and end-products, large enterprises often benefit from spin-offs as the result of R & D activities focused on products other than consumer electronics, such as semiconductors, telecommunication and computers. Small companies lack the opportunity for such spin-offs, but also have lower risks associated with R & D activities.

Consumer electronics rely heavily on standards with respect to formats such as PAL for colour television and VHS for video cassette recorder. Having a firm's own standard adopted as the world standard can mean significantly different levels of profitability. However, not having that standard adopted does not imply the demise of the firm. As noted, many firms operate quite well by purchasing components on the open market and assembling the final product for resale.

Cost structure

Since Philips and Thomson dominate the Community market for consumer electronics, details of cost are difficult to establish. What can be deduced, however, is the ease with which the assembly stage for most consumer electronics can be separated from the main production activity. This implies that labour costs are the critical factor determining the location of assembly and that it entails relatively low value added. Alternatively, for leading edge firms, costs associated with R & D and component manufacture represent the most important cost factors. The value of consumer electronics is increasingly in the components and helps to explain the high degree of vertical integration among the largest companies. Helping to offset the high R & D costs of large companies are significant economies of scope arising from the spill-over and synergy effects of R & D undertaken for one product group.

Unlike semiconductors, capital requirements in consumer electronics are relatively modest. In 1980 the minimum efficient scale for CTV production was estimated to be between 600,000 and 700,000 units per year and represented about 2 per cent of total world demand. Notable in this context is that the scale of Community VCR plants has been estimated to be sub-optimal compared to plants in Japan, and that Community-produced VCRs were up to 30 per cent more costly to produce compared to Japan. Evidence suggests that up to 20 per cent of the Community's cost disadvantage relates to extra costs incurred by Community firms through pensions, social security and other contributions.

As in most lines of manufacturing, both product and process innovations can be an important factor in reducing costs. For example, technological advances since 1984 have allowed Philips to reduce the number of parts in its CD players by 75 per cent, in its VCRs by 55 per cent, in its tuners by 45 per cent and in its amplifiers by 40 per cent. These reductions have meant improved rates of productivity in the assembly phase and decreased value added from assembly operations as a whole.

Delivery is also an important part of a firm's competitiveness. One study estimates that shipping a product six months late reduced life-cycle profits by approximately one-third.

Marketing factors

Production differentiation plays a major role in gaining a competitive advantage in consumer electronics. Such differentiation occurs not only in the product, but also in the design, quality, service and distribution. In this context, the importance of brand loyalty cannot be underestimated. Differentiation via brand names serves to focus attention on both differences and resemblances among products and also eases the introduction of new products. From the firm's perspective, brand loyalty also permits a range of pricing options for otherwise similar products. The importance of brand names is revealed when one considers that most firms have several brands with each brand covering a variety of products. (See Table 8.7.)

The constant opportunities for creating new products with uncertain markets imply that marketing is also an important factor in consumer electronics. Conversely, many examples exist of products which failed because of bad marketing. The importance of the marketing function is reflected by the fact that manufacturers usually conduct their own marketing activity whereas retailing activity is typically external to the firm. Thus, access to distribution channels is relatively free, with retailers stocking and selling competing brands. Although access to distribution is relatively easy, major firms nevertheless attempt to establish core relationships with certain dealer networks in order to provide point-of-sale and after-sale service in order to increase buyer confidence and increase brand loyalty.

The success of many consumer electronics products also depends on the design and marketing of accessories (mainly software). For example, the success of the compact disk, resulting in the CD player and prerecorded video tape, contributed to the success of the VCR. On the other hand, shortages of software (video-disks), coupled with severe shortages of prerecorded video tapes, led to low consumer popularity and weak market growth for CD-video hardware. This is the primary reason why the CD-video was only introduced in the US in 1987 and in Europe in 1988.

Table 8.7   Consumer electronics firms and their associated brand names

Company	Brands
Matsushita	JVC, Panasonic, National, Technics, Quasar
Philips GL	Philips, Grundig, Marantz
SGS–Thomson	Saba, Telefunken, Nordmende, Thomson
Sanyo	Sanyo, Samsung

The US consumer electronics industry

The globalisation of the consumer electronics industry and demise of the US consumer electronics industry became a fact when the television divisions of RCA and General Electric (GE) were purchased by Thomson–CSF. The takeovers left the unprofitable Zenith Electronics as the lone US-based supplier of TVs. Zenith, the only American consumer electronics producer at this time, had electronic sales of $2,873 million in 1988–89.

The demise of the US consumer electronics firms had many roots, but essentially it failed to meet the Japanese and European developments in this sector. In part, the lack of response was due to the priorities of the main electronic companies, the government and especially the Department of Defense (DOD). Most of DOD's research budget focused on basic research in components and computer technology in combination with telecommunications, reflecting the needs of military and space technology.

However, the US-based industry did not vanish because of lack of a home market. For the multinational leaders in the estimated $100 billion worldwide consumer electronics market, success or failure in the highly competitive American marketplace will be a decisive factor in an increasingly volatile global battle. Thomson's purchase of RCA/GE Consumer Electronics is seen as its US entry visa, giving it an estimated 23 per cent of the domestic colour TV market. Moreover, other firms operating in the United States such as Philips, Matsushita and Sony, are seeking to strengthen their foothold. Also Nokia, Finland's consumer electronics company, has shown an interest in Zenith. One reason for the all-American push is that the US is viewed as a critical launching pad for the next generation of TV products and systems (HDTV).

The 1992 initiative

The importance of demand-driven changes discussed earlier also applies to consumer electronics. In this sector the impact of market unification will be to generate greater efficiency in production, marketing and distribution, and more product innovation. These benefits of market unification are perhaps obvious, given that market fragmentation has involved multiple plants, multiple standards and attendant inefficiencies. In fact, market fragmentation explains the low rate of exploitation of economies of scale by European manufacturers and correspondingly why their production costs are often 20–35 per cent higher than those of their Japanese competitors.

Moreover, fragmentation resulted in greater product-base diversification for European firms that was not linked to fundamental market forces. The fragmentation by national markets not only raised production costs, but also necessitated that R & D expenditures be spread over lower output volumes which reduced its effectiveness. In addition, without demand-driven pressures for greater innovation, there was less pressure to seek upstream innovations (for example, in semiconductors).

The major European consumer electronics firms have recognised the past inefficiencies and are already consolidating their operations, and have entered into a plethora of arrangements with both Japanese and Korean companies. As the market broadens, we can expect greater stress on innovation in both product and production processes, a narrowing of product lines reflecting standardisation, a concentration of R & D expenditures on key products, the already occurring rationalisation of production facilities, and the rationalisation of distribution networks.

The rationalisation in distribution networks is likely to be the first and most pronounced change to sweep across the unified market. Harmonisation of standards and reduced barriers to the movement of goods will lead to a concentration of distribution activities, increased variety and competition, and lower prices.

The importance of the impending change in distribution channels has been noted by Buigues and Ilzkovitz (1988) and also by sources at Philips NV. An appreciation of the changes to come can be obtained by looking at the developments that occurred in the United States. Specifically, so-called 'power retailers' (volume retailers serving a wide geographical area) arose at the expense of traditional dealers. For example, the market share of such 'power retailers' in the United States market for colour televisions increased from 28 per cent in 1974 to 56 per cent in 1984 and is expected to rise to 70 per cent in 1990. In contrast, most European distribution channels are unconcentrated. In Italy, the share of the ten largest dealers in consumer electronics is 10 per cent of total sales and in France, only 3 per cent. However, in the United Kingdom the ten largest dealers have 60 per cent of domestic sales.

The benefits of the Single Market in consumer electronics will apply to many non-European firms as well as European firms. Many Japanese and American firms have either built, or plan to build, production plants within the Community. But at this point little can be said about how the benefits (and costs) will be distributed across firms. In a political sense, non-European firms have become a greater force since their production activities have significant employment implications for the Community. This makes their wellbeing as important to the Community as the wellbeing of strictly European firms. Two cases serve to illustrate these points.

First, the European revenues of IBM are four times greater than those of its nearest rival, Siemens. IBM is estimated to have a 70 per cent share of the European computer market and the company has 100,000 employees and fourteen production bases in Europe. Of course, one should recognise that the multiplicity of IBM operations within Europe reflects to some extent the same factors that have led European firms to fragment according to national boundaries. Accordingly, one would expect also IBM to rationalise some of its European operations.

Second, Japanese firms are taking countermeasures to cope with the pending Community unification in 1992. In 1988 Matsushita Electric Co. aligned with Matsushita (England) to create Panasonic Europe. Sony created Sony Europe in 1986 to achieve production, sales and distribution within the European Common Market.

European firms must become more efficient if they are to improve their performance on world markets. The consumer electronics industry is now going through a phase of development in which competition through innovation is important and R & D expenditures are consequently high. The potential for cost reductions through economies of scale are such that large firms should have a cost advantage. The prospect of major new standards, as for HDTV, portend enormous gains if a firm's own standard is adopted.

Despite the potential for gains in this sector from market unification, some Community firms are devoting significant time and resources to lobby for additional external protection rather than developing new products, increasing marketing efforts, and winning new markets. If policy makers cede to such demands one would expect the overall gains from the 1992 initiative to be shifted from consumers to producers with little increase in the competitiveness of Community firms. Policy must continue to focus on the overall gain from the liberalisation of commerce within the Community and not become preoccupied with issues of internal income redistribution. Policy must also not fail to recognise the added, and perhaps even larger, gains that could arise from further liberalisation of commerce with the rest of the world.

References

Buigues, P. and Ilzkowitz, F. (1988), 'The sectoral impact of the internal market', EC Brussels II/335/88-EN.
Cawson, A. 'Corporate strategies and public policy in european consumer electronics' in M. Sharpe and P. Holmes (eds), *Strategies for New Technology: case studies from Britain and France*, London: Philip Allan.

9

Office machinery, data processing and information technology

Isabelle Pouplier

The structure of the information technology sector and recent developments

The commercial and production activities that come under the heading of Information Technology (IT) are many and various, and can be grouped as follows:

- upstream: components (microprocessors, memories, etc.); hardware manufacture (computers, peripherals); distribution; leasing;
- downstream: information services and software.

The approach taken in this chapter will place great emphasis on the roles taken by manufacturers, IT services companies and leasing firms; other activities both upstream and downstream will only be examined in so far as they help to throw light on the problems encountered by the leading actors or on the strategies they have adopted; accordingly, discussion relating to components, computer printers and distribution is confined to specific sections of the study.

The objective is to identify the strategies specifically adopted, if any, by the information technology sector in order to prepare for the introduction of the Internal Market in 1993. These strategies are examined in the context of overall strategies adopted by the sector in recent years, especially in the European market, and by the major European and non-European firms that are active within it.

The first section gives a general introduction to the information technology sector, its structure and the overall trends discernible within the industry, while the second section attempts to examine the likely effects that the Internal Market will have, together with an examination of ways in which current strategies might be amended as 1993 approaches. The third and fourth sections look at the internal and external strategies respectively of individual firms, and attempt to identify which of these strategies have been introduced as a specific response to the imminent setting up of the Internal Market.

This study makes consistent use of a number of sources of information: various in-depth studies of the IT sector, company annual reports, and extracts from the international economics press and specialist magazines. It follows that the study cannot claim to be totally comprehensive: for example, the examples of strategies given in the third and fourth sections give little indication of their frequency or of their relative importance.

World supply and demand in IT hardware, software and all services

According to Datamation (see Table 9.1), the world turnover of the 100 top information technology firms (that is to say, all equipment, software and general services) rose from $209 billion in 1987 to $243 billion in 1988; these firms would therefore appear to account for approximately 80 per cent of the total world annual turnover ($255 billion in 1987).[1] The total European IT market was worth $86 billion in 1987,[2] about 34 per cent of the world market; by 1988, turnover had increased to $90 billion. A slightly different estimate comes from Electronics Industry Corporation: according to the EIC, the equipment side alone of the world IT market came to $165 billion in 1987.[3]

These figures relating to world turnover are probably overestimates because of some double counting. This comes about when the sale of a piece of equipment is registered first in the manufacturer's turnover and then in the turnover of the company which distributes it through an Original Equipment Manufacturer (OEM) contract.

Again, according to Datamation, the world leader, IBM, achieved a turnover of $55 billion in 1988, over four times more than its nearest rival, Digital Equipment, which reached $12.3 billion. There are only three European firms amongst the top fifteen, Siemens (8th), Olivetti (9th) and Bull (11th): the IT share of their annual turnover in 1988 came to $5.9, $5.4 and $5.3 billion respectively. An analysis, shown in Table 9.1, of the top 100 IT firms, grouped firstly by nationality and then by the countries where the goods will be sold, underlines the relatively weak position of European firms (they account for about 16 per cent of trade) given the size of their domestic markets (34 per cent).

The growth of demand for information technology in the United States has slowed down since the mid-1980s, only one or two years before the phenomenon appeared in Europe. Furthermore, the 8.4 per cent growth in the American market has been slower than in other markets; in

Table 9.1   IT sales breakdown of *Datamation*'s top 100 firms

(a) By geographical origin of firm

Firm based in	1987 %	1988 %
North America	64.0	61.3
Western Europe	16.4	16.5
Asia–Pacific area	19.6	22.2
Total	100.0	100.0
$ billions	208.9	243.1

(b) By geographical destination of sales

Destination	1987 %	1988 %	% growth 1988 over 1987
North America	41	38	8.4
Western Europe	34	34	14.5
Asia–Pacific area	22	25	29.0
Other	3	3	
Total	100	100	
$ billions	208.9	243.1	16.4

Note: [1]includes hardware, peripherals, software, IT services, IT leasing, point of sale technology, automatic teller machines (ATMs), and certain communications components systems such as Local Area Network (LAN), digital PABXs, multiplexors, modems and fax machines.

Source: *Datamation 100*, 15 June 1989

consequence, the US share has dropped and the gap between it and the European market has narrowed (see Table 9.1b). More recently, American firms have been energetically seeking new markets outside the United States, and particularly in Europe: in the main, this has been because the European market has been relatively dynamic and is due in part to the dollar's weakness in 1987, but it may also be explained by fears of impending European protectionism.

Information technology hardware and services: a world picture

Information technology hardware

World concentration of hardware production   Every year Datamation takes the information technology share of turnover of the sector's top 100 firms and publishes a breakdown under the headings: mainframes, minis, micros, peripherals, maintenance, software, services and data communication; the leading 15 companies in each activity are listed in

Appendix I. Table 9.2 shows how IT hardware activities have now achieved a higher level of concentration as measured by market share factors $C1^4$ (in which C1 represents IBM, the world leader in every activity), C5 and C15 of the world top 100 firms.

Production, apparent consumption and trade outside the EC   The data processing industry, that is, the manufacture of information technology, peripherals and office machinery (Nace 33), is a sector in which Europe has a chronic trade deficit (see Table 9.3). The annual rate of manufacturing increase by EC countries during the period 1980–88 was 14.1 per cent: this contrasts with the rate of growth in apparent consumption of 15.6 per cent, so much so that the trade deficit outside the EC deteriorated sharply, particularly during 1987 and 1988. The EC takes almost half its imports from the United States (48 per cent), a quarter from Japan (24

Table 9.2   Share of turnover by type of equipment: the top 1, 5 and 15 world leaders as a percentage of the top 100

	Mainframe	Minis[1]	Micros	Peripherals
C1	40.1	18.2	25.5	17.6
C5	79.5	48.9	52.9	38.5
C15	98.5	77.4	82.9	64.4
European firms:	8.3	6.5	7.9	3.7
	Bull	Olivetti	Olivetti	Siemens
	Siemens	Nixdorf	Amstrad	Memorex Telex
	STC	Bull		Bull
	Comparex			

Note: [1]includes work stations

Source: *Datamation 100*, June 1989 (Author's calculations)

Table 9.3   Information technology and office equipment (NACE 33): production and apparent consumption in the EC (ECU m.)

	1980	1985	1986	1987	1988	growth[1]
Apparent consumption						
EC–9	15.3	40.7	42.7	45.2	48.8	15.6%
EC–12				47.1	50.5	
Production						
EC–9	13.7	35.3	35.2	36.5	39.1	17.1%
EC–12				41.5	41.9	
Trading balance	−1.73	−5.15	−5.30	−6.72	−9.66	

Source: EC–9 – *Panorama of EC Industry 1989*
Source: EC–12 – *BIPE Europe in 1993 and 1994, Economic Outlook by Sector*, January 1989 and November 1989
[1]annual average growth rate

per cent), and nearly one-fifth from South-East Asia (18 per cent); exports go mainly to EFTA countries (40 per cent) and to the United States (28 per cent).

Supply structure in Europe   Table 9.4 shows the twenty-five leading suppliers in the European market in descending order of IT share of turnover, that is to say all equipment, software and services (*Datamation* (1 July 1989)). Of these twenty-five firms in 1988, thirteen were European, ten were American and two Japanese, and they represented approximately two-thirds (65.5 per cent) of European turnover; the non-European firms in the list are all manufacturers of hardware and peripherals, while four of the thirteen European firms concentrate on services and leasing.

Table 9.4   Main information technology suppliers in Europe in 1988 ($m.)

Name	Country	European IT turnover	European share of turnover[4]	IT share of turnover[5]
IBM	US M	20,520	37	
Siemens[1]	Ger M	5,296	89	17.6
DEC	US M	4,422	36	
Olivetti	It M	4,397	81	
Bull[2]	Fr M	4,025	76	
Nixdorf	Ger M	2,832	93	
Unisys	US M	2,639	29	
Hewlett-Packard	US M	2,331	37	64.0
Philips	Net M	2,208	79	9.9
ICL–STC	UK M	2,061	85	57.8
NCR	US M	1,757	33	
Alcatel	Fr M	1,647	96	13.1
Société Générale[3]	Fr S + L	1,174	96	23.4
Nokia Data	Nor M	1,165	100	22.4
Atlantic Computers	UK L	1,114	83	
Canon	Jap M	1,051	31	39.3
Apple	US M	931	21	
Prime	US M	909	57	
Wang	US M	892	29	
Hitachi	Jap M	825	10	17.6
Cap Gemini	Fr S	801	82	
Amstrad	UK M	783	93	75.9
Control Data	US M	781	22	
Inspectorate Intl	Swi L	726	59	73
Compaq	US M	723	35	

Notes: M = Manufacturer; S = Service and consultancy firm; L = Leasing company.
[1]excluding Nixdorf   [2]excluding Zenith   [3]two IT subsidiaries   [4]percentage of European turnover of the total IT turnover   [5]percentage IT turnover in the firm's total turnover (percentage below 80 per cent)

Source: *Datamation*, 15 June 1989 and 1 July 1989

IBM is far and away the leading supplier, but its share of the European market as a percentage of the twenty-five top firms has been declining steadily for several years – from 42 per cent in 1984 to 31 per cent in 1988. The European market is, nevertheless, of the utmost importance to IBM, as its sales to Europe are still on the increase, unlike its sales on the home market, and contribute a higher proportion to profit than to turnover. It should also be borne in mind that IBM's oldest and most important European subsidiary is in West Germany, and is responsible for about 20 per cent of its European turnover. However, the most dramatic strides have been made by IBM in Spain and Italy where sales increased by 16 per cent and 14 per cent respectively in 1989. Measured against the leader's market shares and calculated according to the performances of the ten and twenty-five leading firms, the concentration of all information technology firms within the European market continued to rise between 1987 and 1988 (Table 9.5).

A look at manufacturers active in the European market reveals a number of interesting factors:

- Broadly speaking, American manufacturers earn about one-third of their IT turnover in Europe; there are only three exceptions: Prime (57 per cent), Apple (21 per cent) and Control Data (22 per cent).
- European manufacturers have established themselves less successfully on the international market, usually earning less than 20 per cent of IT turnover outside Europe.
- American firms, with the exception of Hewlett-Packard, specialise much more in information technology than their European counterparts: IT accounts for more than 80 per cent of their total turnover. By comparison, the share of IT in the overall activities of Philips, Siemens, Alcatel and Nokia is small (9.9 per cent, 17.6 per cent, 13.1 per cent and 22.4 per cent respectively).

Table 9.6 sets out leading companies' market shares of product segments in Europe. The figures show a relatively high concentration in technical workstations and mainframes, with the four leading suppliers controlling 83.7 per cent and 21.7 per cent of the markets respectively.

Table 9.5 Concentration of information technology on the European market (Percentage market share of top 1, 10, 25 suppliers)

Percentage market share	1987	1988
C1	21.32	22.80
C10	50.55	56.37
C25	65.44	73.33
European total ($ billions)	86.00	90.00

Source: *Datamation*, 5 August 1988 and 1 July 1989

Table 9.6 Market shares by product segment: Western Europe, 1988 (percentage of the total market in each category)

Personal computers	
IBM	24.2%
Olivetti	8.2%
Apple	7.0%
Compaq	6.4%
Others	54.2%
Market size (million écus)	14,266
Technical work stations	
Sun	22.2%
Hewlett-Packard	21.6%
DEC	21.3%
Apollo	18.3%
Others	16.6%
Market size (million écus)	1,163
Mid-range computers	
IBM	22.8%
DEC	13.4%
Groupe Bull	8.7%
Siemens	5.8%
Others	49.3%
Market size (million écus)	11,893
Mainframe computers	
IBM	55.5%
Siemens	15.1%
Groupe Bull	7.0%
Unisys	3.7%
Others	18.7%
Market size (million écus)	7,848

Notes: 'Mid-range computers' comprise multi-user systems selling for up to $1 million; 'Mainframe computers' comprise systems selling above $1 million. The figures are for the total computer system as sold in the initial package. including peripherals and software; later add-on sales of peripherals and software are not included. The figures are in end-user values, i.e. they include distribution mark-up. Groupe Bull's figures include Honeywell Bull

Source: Dataquest in *Panorama of EC Industry 1990*

An analysis of the total information technology turnover of the twenty-five leading suppliers on the European market makes it possible to classify them according to their areas of specialisation (see Appendix II): mainframe manufacturers may be divided into generalists making a wide range of other IT goods (IBM, Unisys and, to a lesser extent, Bull and Siemens) and specialists (Hitachi, ICL and Control Data); the list of specialists could also include Comparex and Memorex, manufacturers of plug-compatible mainframes. Manufacturers of mini-computers (for example, Digital Equipment) are frequently specialised by comparison with mainframe producers, and Hewlett-Packard and Philips have been amongst those to have also succeeded in building up expertise in the microcomputer branch of IT; Nixdorf and NCR, by contrast, are the only manufacturers of minis to have made any impact in both the mainframe and micro segments. Other mini manufacturers include the Norwegian Norsk Data and the German firm of Mannesmann. Micro-computer information technology continues to be an area of considerable specialisation, although Olivetti and Nokia are exceptions in that they have a presence in both minis and mainframes; other, much smaller, European firms specialising in this branch include the British Apricot, the Dutch firm of Tulip and the French companies, Goupil and Normerel.

The proportion taken up by peripherals, maintenance and software in IT turnover is relatively high, although it varies considerably from firm to firm: for example, companies specialising exclusively in micros such as Apple, Amstrad and Compaq have no maintenance revenue whatsoever, while only Apple lists peripherals and software in its turnover.

Information technology services and software

Measurement of activities   Information technology services cover a wide range of activities including standard software, customised software, IT consultancy, third-party processing, training, maintenance, systems integration and activities linked to data communication. This focuses on the part of the IT services sector working for firms as clients rather than for households, and, moreover, only when third parties are invoiced for the services rendered. Certain activities are then excluded from this: for example, software written by the firm for internal use. Other activities normally excluded from the statistics include equipment value and services revenue earned from service work done for the Head Office.

World demand   The world market for software and information technology services was estimated to be worth 112.4 billion ecus in 1988; the American market accounts for over half of that and the EC market for about 24 billion ecus. The Japanese market is as yet undeveloped (see Table 9.7).

International trade   There are no reliable statistics covering world trade in software and services. International trade in software is recorded by using the value of the carrier such as floppy disks, but it is even more difficult to measure the volume of the trade in services except by means of a geographical breakdown of company turnover and a careful study of those sections of annual reports dealing with the activities of subsidiaries abroad. According to the European Computing Services Association (ECSA), among European companies the French and British are the most active abroad, the IT service and consultancy leaders in these countries exporting about 10 per cent of turnover.[5]

Table 9.7 Estimated world market by region for software and services[1] in 1987 and 1988

	1987	1988	1987 Market share	1988/87 growth
	Billion écus		%	%
Western Europe	27.6[2]	32.3[2]	28.8	17.0
United States	53.2	62.1	55.4	16.7
Japan	7.8	⎫ 18.0	8.1	⎫ 18.4
Rest of World	7.4	⎭	7.7	⎭
Total world	96.0	112.4	100.0	17.0

Notes: [1]As far as possible, market estimates exclude the revenues for the hardware elements of systems [2]The size of the Community market is estimated at 24 billion écus – 25 per cent of the world market

Source: *Panorama of EC Industry 1990*

The share of the European information technology service and software market occupied by American manufacturers and service companies went up to about 40 per cent in 1988 (see Table 9.8): if the market is broken down, American penetration into the standard software market is seen to be in the order of 55–60 per cent, although their control of customised software and consultancy work is much lower at about 20 per cent.

European demand for services by product segment The consultancy firm of INPUT has produced a useful breakdown of information services throughout Europe, showing relative market share and growth rates (see Table 9.9). The majority of turnover covers software and professional services (mainly custom software), and both areas are experiencing a sustained growth which is outstripping the European and world averages; processing services, however, a more traditional activity, are undergoing a much slower growth which is lower than the average for the whole

Table 9.8 Market share of American firms on European markets in 1988

Product segments	
Standard software	55–60%
Custom software and consultancy	19–20%
Third-party processing	35–40%
Average for all segments	40%

Source: *Panorama of EC Industry 1990*

Table 9.9   Software and service revenues in the Community (EC–11) and Western Europe in 1987 and 1988, and a forecast for 1993

	1987		1988		88/87	93/88
	Billion écus	Market share %	Billion écus	Market share %	Growth %	Forecast CAGR %[6]
Software products	7.1	29.5	8.6	30.4	21.2	22
Professional services[1]	8.1	33.6	9.7	34.3	19.5	20
Turnkey systems[2]	2.6	10.8	3.0	10.8	17.3	17[7]
Systems integration[3]	0.6	2.5	0.8	2.8	33.0	26[8]
Processing services[4]	5.0	20.7	5.2	18.4	4.6	6
Network services[5]	0.7	2.9	0.9	3.2	35.6	28
Total (EC–11)	24.1[7]	100.0	28.2	100.0	17.2	
Total W Eur (EC–11 + EFTA–5)	27.6		32.3		17.0	19
memo: US	53.2		62.1		16.7	17

Notes: [1]Includes custom software (76%), consultancy (12%), training (11%) and facilities management (1%)   [2]Includes (standard) systems and application software; excludes hardware (assumption: 50% of systems value)   [3]Includes software products and professional services; excludes computers, communications hardware, etc. (assumption: 40% of system value); only contracts above $1 million   [4]Includes transaction, utility and other processing services   [5]Includes managed network services (VANs), network (e.g. ED1) applications and electronic information services   [6]Compound annual growth rate. Dollar-based forecast   [7]INPUT's adjusted sector aggregate for EC–11 compares with IDC's sector total of 23.7 billion écus for EC–8   [8]The forecast relates to the total of the system

Sources: INPUT/CEC; *Panorama of EC Industry 1990*

sector. Two new segments, systems integration and network services, boast exceptionally good growth rates but as yet occupy a tiny part of the overall market.

The structure of European supply   Estimates from IDC and the European Computing Services Association (ECSA) suggest there are 13,000–15,000 IT service and consultancy companies within the European Community, with a total workforce of approximately 287,000;[6] it follows that it is a very fragmented sector, with the majority of firms being very small and employing an average of only 19–22 people. In fact, the only segment anywhere in the world where there is any marked concentration is in the very narrow one of horizontal standard software (word processing and spreadsheets); here, the five leading companies in the world are all American and are responsible for 65–75 per cent of sales worldwide.

Measured by the market share taken by the world's leading suppliers of services and software in the European market during 1987, concentration was 21.7 per cent (C10) and 32 per cent (C25);[7] however, services and software seem to be substantially less concentrated than information technology activity as a whole: when hardware is added to services and software, the levels of concentration are 50.5 per cent (C10) and 65.4 per cent (C25).[8] The degree of concentration in the services and software sector among independent operators (i.e. not subsidiaries of a manufacturer or of a client) measured by C10 varies considerably from one EC country to the next (see Table 9.10).

Companies market very different combinations of information technology services and software, and apart from those manufacturers which sell software and some services, it can be difficult to classify most firms according to their main line of activity in IT services and software. When the supply of services and software is analysed by the main type of business the operator is in, it can be seen that there is a clear preponderance of software houses active not only in standard application software but also in customised application form (see Table 9.11). If the breakdown is limited to software, manufacturers score more heavily because of their sales of standard software, particularly of system software such as operating systems.

Main suppliers on the European market Table 9.12 classifies the twenty-five leading suppliers on the European market by turnover in services and software: they include ten manufacturers, who account for over half of the 32 per cent of the total market produced by the twenty-five. Some of this classification is now out of date as a result of

Table 9.10 Market share of the ten leading independent suppliers of services and software in the member states of the EC during 1987

Country	C10 %
Germany	18.5
France	28.2
United Kingdom	28.8
Italy	28.2
Netherlands	35.6
Belgium	25.3
Denmark	54.0
Spain	30.2

Source: IDC/CEC in *Panorama of EC Industry 1990*

Table 9.11 Percentage breakdown of 1987 turnover on the European market (EC–8) by type of supplier

Supplier	Services and software	Software only
Manufacturers	35.9	53
Systems houses	18.5	16
Software houses	45.6	31
	100.0	100

Source: IDC/CEC in *Panorama of EC Industry 1990*

Table 9.12 Vendor rankings and market shares in computer software and services in Western Europe in 1987

Rank	Company	Market share %	Estimated revenues ($ millions)
1	IBM (M)	8.3	2,950
2	Nixdorf (M)	3.0	1,055
3	Unisys (M)	2.0	725
4	Cap Gemini Sogeti	1.5	525
5	Siemens (M)	1.5	520
6	Digital (M)	1.3	475
7	Finsiel	1.2	415
8	Reuters	1.1	400
9	Transpac	1.0	355
10	Olivetti (M)	0.9	330
11	Bull (M)	0.7	250
12	Datev	0.7	245
13	Sligos	0.6	225
14	GSI	0.6	210
15	McDonnell Douglas	0.6	200
15	Scicon	0.6	200
15	Volmac	0.6	200
18	Sema Metra	0.5	195
19	CISI	0.5	190
20	Andersen Consulting	0.5	180
20	Computervision (M)	0.5	180
22	Computer Associates	0.5	170
22	ICL (M)	0.5	170
24	Télésystèmes	0.4	155
24	Thorn Software	0.4	155
26	Microsoft	0.4	150
27	Logica	0.4	145
28	CCMC	0.4	140
29	CAP Group	0.4	135
29	Intergraph (M)	0.4	135
	Others	68.0	24,320
	Total Market	100.0	35,700

Note: (M) = Manufacturer

Source: INPUT

recent mergers. For the list of the main European IT firms see Appendix III.

While Reuters, Transpac and Télésystèmes are strongly specialised in data communication, European firms active in the services and software sectors have undergone a number of recent mergers; they can now be divided into the following three groups:

Cap Gemini Sogeti (Fr)	Turnover 1987–88:
SD-Scicon (UK)	over $400 million.
Sema Cap Group (UK–Fr)	3000–5000 employees;
Finsiel (It)	marketing in Europe
	and the USA.
Datev (Ger)	Turnover 1987:
Sligos (Fr)	over $200 million.
GSI (Fr)	
Volmac (Neth)	
CISI (Fr)	Turnover 1987:
Thorn Soft (UK)	over $150 million
Logica (UK)	
CCMC (Fr)	

Service and consultancy firms' captive revenue Many service and consultancy firms started off as information technology subsidiaries whose Head Offices were also major clients (in industry, the banks or the local or national state). In so far as some of such a service company's turnover is achieved in tandem with Head Office, and falls therefore outside a conventional market analysis, it is extremely interesting to identify which these firms are, the importance they have within the sector and the proportion of captive turnover.

It is noteworthy that the world's leading service and consultancy company by turnover is a captive firm: EDS, a subsidiary of General Motors. In 1987, EDS had a turnover of $4436 million, of which $1550 million of turnover was achieved with GM.[9] The ECSA 1986 annual report shows that in every member country of the EC there are service and consultancy firms benefiting to varying degrees from captive revenue. In Italy, in particular, two of the main national operators, Enidata (No 2) and Cerved (No 4), are captive firms by over 50 per cent of turnover.[10]

Current trends: The main product segments

Computers and peripherals

Mainframes Mainframe super-computers are now well established in the more highly sophisticated information systems. The super-computer market is very small and as much as 85 per cent of it is owned by American and Japanese firms; the firm of Cray Research alone is thought to control about 60 per cent of the market. R & D of that market segment is very dynamic in parallel architecture. There is also plenty of European research in this field: the European firms of Siemens, ICL and Bull are participating in a research project which it is hoped will produce a European super-computer.

The traditional mainframe segment has been going through the maturity stage of a product life cycle since the 1980s, although profits have been reduced by a variety of factors including the slowdown in sales, the overall fall in prices, and increased R & D costs aimed at lengthening hardware life span. Furthermore, rapid progress in the semiconductors industry has compelled manufacturers to bring out ever more powerful machines that are price-competitive. Mainframes face most competition from below: one reason for this is the attractiveness of minis and work stations, whose increased capacity has won business away from mainframes; the other principal reason is the movement towards decentralised information technology systems, such as departmental processing and, more recently, local network services involving the use of personal computers. The future of mainframes is thus somewhat in doubt, particularly as there are very few activities which are specific to it; on-line transaction processing is one of the small number of exceptions.

To make matters worse, the leading European mainframe manufacturers are beset by a number of serious structural handicaps which will be very difficult to solve in the short term. The clear division of Europe into individual nations allied to the strategic importance of advanced technology at one time favoured the development of national leaders. These firms depended significantly on orders from the state and were subsidised by the government. The new scenario is one of worldwide competition: many European manufacturers are too small to take advantage of economies of scale in production, and above all in research, and there are even some that hardly market their products outside their own countries. However, the future for the European mainframe computer industry is not all bleak; the moves towards more open architectures, common operating systems and network systems are already testing American domination of the markets.

Minicomputers Minicomputers are computers with capacities for local and decentralised processing, and have been thus developed for small groups of users without the need for teams of computer specialists: the biggest markets are business management, scientific research applications with CAD–CAM (computer-aided design/manufacturing) and some data communications applications. Minis were at their most marketable in terms of price and performance in the 1970s, although they are now facing hard competition again both at the top of the market segment (superminis and mainframes) and lower down (top-of-the-range personal computers and work stations). The unquestioned world leader, DEC, is active in both management systems and workshop CAM applications. European firms have long had a successful niche strategy here, but now face keen competitive pressure; IBM has recently entered the minis market with the AS/400 in an attempt to take advantage of a weakness in product range.

Faced with such competition, some manufacturers have tried to improve the performance of their products by means of technological advances in semiconductors (like Unisys and DEC) or by the introduction of a higher performance architecture (for example Hewlett-Packard and its Reduced Instruction Set Computers (RISC) architecture). Other manufacturers have opted for a strategy of specialising in a specific area of application; examples of this policy include Prime with CAD, and Wang with image processing for business use. European minis manufacturers include Nixdorf, Norsk Data, Bull, Philips and Olivetti.

Work stations and CAD–CAM Work stations are essentially high-performance personal computers which have been developed for scientists and engineers. Technical advances in components have made it possible for work stations to be increasingly used on applications requiring power and good graphic quality like CAD–CAM, or molecular design. This has been accompanied by a rapid fall in computing power prices, and firms are watching for opportunities to enlarge their market share. The market has been growing very quickly for several years now, partly because of new marketing opportunities in business and finance via the improvements in graphic quality. Current world leaders are Sun, HP-Apollo, DEC and IBM with 85 per cent of the market between them. This sector can look forward to a period of consolidation as it passes from low production volume and high profits to high production levels and limited profit margins; this will entail restructuring at all levels including distribution, and could even mean a move from direct sales to marketing through dealers.

The world CAD–CAM sector carried out several mergers and acquisitions in the late 1980s: Hewlett-Packard bought Apollo, Daisy bought Cadnetix, and Prime bought Computervision (engineering), Calma and Versacad (micro applications) and made an unsuccessful takeover bid for MAI Basic Four. The market for CAD–CAM still has considerable potential in industry and among subcontractors. But the suppliers of traditional turnkey systems are facing competition upstream from manufacturers of minicomputers and downstream from producers of simple, personal computer-based systems solutions aimed at small and medium-sized companies. So, many firms that specialise in CAD–CAM have ceased developing their own hardware, opting to strike preferential agreements with manufacturers like Sun or Apollo. Those firms concentrate exclusively on the CAD work – the development of application software. Intergraph is an exception to that strategy and is making strenuous efforts to control all supply stages, from its own hardware to its software.

Computer manufacturers like IBM, DEC and Hewlett-Packard have been active in this work station sector for many years, but the actual market prospects suggest a rosy future for the application of information technology to the industry when, indeed, much of the work of these manufacturers that has been carried out on the application of computing to management systems is now coming to market maturity. In many cases, their position in the CAD–CAM market is partly attributable to a partnership or a commercial contract with small specialist firms. Many firms, French ones in particular, use this as a way of entering foreign markets and of marketing their application software more widely: examples of this trend include agreements whereby IBM takes responsibility for marketing the software of Cadam (a subsidiary of Lockheed), Catia (Dassault Systems) and IOMS (Steria). Similarly, Digital markets products of Matradatavision (Fr), Schlumberger (US–Fr), McDonnell Douglas (US) and SDRC, and Silicon Graphics markets the software produced by Cisigraph (Fr). An example of a move in another direction is the sales agreement made by SGS–Thomson (It–Fr) to buy software from Cadence Design System (US), and a technical agreement with the same firm to develop new CAD software tools.

Manufacturers have not been alone in finding the CAD–CAM market attractive. The amount of know-how that any firm must now have often makes it essential to reach agreements with specialist service firms: there have been many examples in France of generalist service firms in IT taking over specialist service and consultancy companies. In the field of research, the ESPRIT programme includes the CIM-OSA project, active in the field of open systems architecture in CAM, a line-up of nineteen European firms.

Microcomputer information technology Microcomputers can be divided into two large groups: IBM and IBM-compatible computers mainly using Intel microprocessors on the one hand, and non-compatible machinery like Apple computers which use Motorola microprocessors on the other. Apple is a rarity in that it for a long time produced non-compatible computers and has yet succeeded in establishing itself strongly in the microcomputer market.

However, IBM and IBM-compatible machines are themselves divided over a problem of architecture which is of great significance to the sector in general: in 1987, IBM lauched a new microcomputer, the PS/2, with a completely new system architecture, the MCA microchannel; it was IBM's hope that the PS/2 would earn them large royalties which would enable them to regain ground in the microcomputer market lost to producers of clones. Moreover, the new architecture does not seem very compatible with the earlier MS–DOS which was adopted by the majority of manufacturers. This crisis is taking place within the context of an important technological evolution towards 32-bit personal computers: the gross power of this machine is equivalent to that of a minicomputer, and gives personal computer users access to multitasking and multi-user functions. Computers capable of such performance are top-of-the-range personal computers aimed at the professional and business markets, both of which are expanding rapidly.

The top microcomputer technology manufacturers such as IBM, Apple, Compaq and Hewlett-Packard are increasing their sales to Europe. Many of them already have production units in Europe, or are expanding. Firstly, they have a number of things going for them: the arrival on the market of 32-bit computers allows them to restore their old profit margins; yet a further advantage enjoyed by the leaders is that they benefit from a consumer preference for well-known reliable brands – the bewildering choice of brands currently on the market ironically works to their advantage. Small, bottom-of-the-range computers like home computers can be marketed off the shelf, without much customer counselling or after-sales service, through computer chain stores, but the situation is different for more sophisticated technology. Dealers are keenly aware of the difficulties involved in guiding customer choice and in ensuring that the customer receives increasingly complex support systems; this encourages them to limit the number of brands they sell, and is therefore to the detriment of clones and small manufacturers, many of which are European.

European manufacturers of microcomputers like Tulip, Goupil and Apricot are relatively well established in their home markets. Tulip could even overtake IBM at the head of the Dutch microcomputer market: government orders, particularly from schools, have contributed to their expansion in the national market, although it has to be said that they have made little headway outside the Netherlands. All of these firms need to establish themselves abroad as urgently as possible: as the development of a distribution network using subsidiaries takes a long time, the leading European firms are seeking ways of gaining access to networks that are already up and running.

Unlike large computers, most personal computers are not built around in-house components such as microprocessors. Thanks to its sales to IBM, Intel leads the world in microprocessors but, generally speaking, relationships with components suppliers remain problematic for European microcomputer manufacturers. Basically, the Europeans are too small, and therefore are not in a position to negotiate prices effectively; they are also the first to suffer from component shortages when they have not fixed long-term contracts on supply quotas or have not made anticipated purchases. In the search for competitive prices, therefore, they look for suppliers outside the EC: the United States for microprocessors and Japan for memories. During 1987–88, Amstrad had a major shortage of DRAMS (dynamic memories) and is now trying to establish long-term agreements with suppliers.[11]

Prices of microcomputers continue to fall steadily, and manufacturers are now concentrating on a strategy of quantity based on the size of the distribution network and marketing. The undeniable advantage that American computer trade marks have in Europe is a well-established distribution network: this enables them to benefit from a number of economies of scale in the distribution network: the major micro manufacturers, for example, operate a system of indirect sales using several categories of retail outlet. In the hierarchy of modes of distribution used in microcomputers, the leading manufacturers exert a powerful control over distributors who sell nothing but their brand, although they face keen competition from those that sell a variety of brands. Such a problem was faced by Compaq when promoting the EISA group's merchandise in the USA: they are thought to have run into difficulties with a multibrand distributor who gave what they felt was undue prominence to the IBM MCA-based microcomputer.[12] There is, on the other hand, a demand-led trend towards global system solutions (i.e. including a substantial amount of IT services); a number of manufacturers like Apple are now insisting on such conditions with exclusive dealers.[13]

Peripherals: printers   Two technologies currently dominate the computer printer market: the matrix printer (impact) and the laser printer (non-impact). The former is more popular, particularly with small, bottom-of-the-range, eight-pin models which are marketed with personal computers. Matrix printer manufacture is dominated by Japanese firms (Epson, Brother, Nec and Fujitsu), although there are a number of European producers as well: Olivetti, Philips (through its German subsidiary PKI), Groupe Bull (through Compuprint, Bull HN's subsidiary in Italy) and Mannesmann Tally. There is greatly improved printing quality with 24-pin models, and some manufacturers are now thinking of bringing out a 48-pin model. As far as other printing technologies go, lasers are very fast and the printing quality is good, but they are also expensive: the leader might be Hewlett-Packard with 40 per cent of the market; ink-jet printers are also coming through fast in competition with the two dominant technologies: the leaders here include Hewlett-Packard, Canon and Epson. According to IDC, sales of matrix printers will fall away after 1991, although it is thought that 24-pin models will continue to do well. Generally speaking, though, this development will leave the field open for non-impact technology: ink-jet, laser and thermal printers.

Several Japanese and American firms have manufacturing plants in Europe – Epson in the UK and France, Star in Wales, Fujitsu in Spain and QMS in the Netherlands – and some of them have difficulty in passing the minimum threshold of local value added required by the EC for foreign firms. All of them market most of their merchandise by means of indirect sales, about 30–40 per cent of their sales being concluded through Original Equipment Manufacturer (OEM) arrangements with European producers: for example, Star with Victor, Commodore with Goupil, and Fujitsu with Olivetti; most sales, though, are effected through a network of licensed retailers – in France, for instance, QMS uses the distribution firms of Tekelec and Japy. Direct sales and sales through a partnership with a specialised firm are confined to special application printers and are only used for major orders.

Software and information services

Information services cover a wide variety of different activities. They include:

- Supply and development of software ranging from standard software to fully customised software.
- IT consultancy, project development and systems integration.
- Third-party data processing.
- Maintenance.

Other activities that could also be added include leasing, and even more recent developments such as those information services that are linked to data communication (e.g. network development and network management services). Although leasing is a financial service, IT leasing has close links with IT services.

Many services like software supply, training and maintenance have been traditionally supplied in part by the manufacturers themselves or by their distributors. However, IT service firms and consultancies have established themselves in a number of service areas, and they characteristically choose one as their area of specialisation: thus, one can identify software, systems and consultancy, data processing, third-party maintenance and leasing firms. The smaller such firms are, the more likely they are to specialise: they do so vertically (matching all the IT needs of either a limited client group or even a single economic sector like banking, distribution or medicine) and/or horizontally (concentrating on a particular area of technical IT application like word processing or bookkeeping software), and meeting the needs of a wide range of users. It is now widely accepted that there will be sustained growth in the software sector, particularly in packages, and in systems advice and project development, to the detriment of classic services activities like third-party data processing.

According to the report *Costs of non-Europe*, information technology services do not face barriers to trade or to the establishment of subsidiaries, and nor will they be directly affected by legislation associated with the opening of the Single Market. So far, though, most firms in the sector are achieving a relatively small part of their turnover in a second EC country, and even less outside the Community.

Among the reasons mentioned in the report, one finds the time small IT firms need to set up viable subsidiaries, but also the fact that they demonstrate a disturbing lack of awareness of the potential. This attitude has been accentuated by two factors: satisfactory growth within the major home markets, and, for some of them, the ability to achieve a substantial proportion of turnover in a captive market with the parent enterprise or as a result of privileged relations with the local state (a phenomenon widespread in Germany and Italy); the overall effect has been a false sense of security.

The setting up of the Single Market will bring with it the likelihood that home markets will be increasingly penetrated, mainly by American and Scandinavian firms. To fight off this challenge, European service firms will need to establish their activities on an international footing. To achieve this firms can do a number of things: set up subsidiaries; negotiate mergers with, or takeovers of, foreign firms that are already in business; and, as far as software is concerned, sign trade agreements or even technical agreements leading ideally to the development of common products.

The software sector   In the world of information technology, it is not enough to sell the customer some hardware and a programming language: indeed, the fact that the vast majority of users do not develop their own applications is fundamental to the software industry's spectacular success.

Recent advances in the field of software are so striking that the whole sector now has a decisive influence on the future of the whole information technology industry. For example:

- The successful development of software compatible with a new piece of hardware is now essential if the hardware is to be effectively marketed. Equally, technical progress in hardware, such as higher and greater speed, means that there is a need for special software to operate it to best advantage.
- Thanks to the availability of an even greater variety of software, the whole IT industry is now able to penetrate even further into the economy, sometimes by performing tasks that had not previously been attempted through data processing, by entering new industrial and commercial sectors and by developing new activities linked to data communications.

Standard software needs to be distinguished from the tailor-made variety: the greater efficiency and flexibility of software in general, not to mention the cost of custom software, go some way towards explaining the relatively steep growth in demand for standard software. There are three main categories of standard software; they are as follows:

1. Close to the machine language software – operating systems and programming languages.
2. Application software – this category has the biggest market share and is sub-divided into two types: horizontal technical applications (e.g. spreadsheets, word processing and data base management systems (DBMS) and vertical applications developed for a specific business or commercial sector.
3. Development tools – fourth- and fifth-generation programming languages, software design tools and software testing tools.

Software houses and service companies concentrate more on application software than on any other aspect of the business, but it is important to acknowledge in this context that American software houses have a strong competitive edge with their general horizontal packages (spreadsheets and word processing), particularly for microcomputers, and they have achieved good penetration into the European markets. Leaving to one side the software emanating from the major software producers and even from computer manufacturers themselves, software supply is very fragmented. Most firms supplying software, particularly the small independent software houses, have adopted niche strategies in application software, but horizontal application software specialisation, for example, does not exclude any adaptation by the service firm to suit the customer's specific needs.

In the foreseeable future, the software sector is going to be strongly influenced by developments in three important areas: a move towards the standardising of open operating systems, the more frequent use of software development tools, and research into more sophisticated languages and artificial intelligence. In this sense, the opening up of the Common Market will force the sector to respond even faster to the new challenges.

Consultancy and systems integration firms Firms in this category concentrate on specific IT project development: functional analysis, choice of hardware and software, programming, installation, training and maintenance.

The markets are perceived vertically according to the customer's line of business rather than horizontally, and geographical proximity to the client is often deemed to be the justification for a decentralised structure. The major service firms in this segment have a key role in the important matters of writing standard software in vertical application and adapting packages to the customer's needs; nevertheless, programming revenue on its own is diminishing as consultancy work shows healthy profits, thanks to the development of the software sector and to the consequent variety of choice.

Another area showing good growth is systems integration. This has been assisted both by technical advances in IT and by the increasing complexity of users' needs, as follows:

1.   Users no longer have a single hardware supplier; they increasingly need a single service agent who will be able to ensure the system's coherence.
2.   Information technology continues to invade the workplace, and is discovering ever more complex problems to solve.
3.   There is a growing need for data communication between users, and for identification of links between the various IT applications within the firm.
4.   Advances in telecommunications, such as electronic data interchange, will make it possible for highly sophisticated material to be communicated between different sites; this further underlines the need for companies to prepare for the setting up of the European Single Market.

Third-party processing This sector is closely linked to the large computer market: now that minis and micros are widespread and the cost of much information technology has fallen, firms are subcontracting this type of work less and less. Service firms will need to re-organise in order not to rely so much on that activity.

Third-party maintenance   Service firms active in this field are independent companies which carry out maintenance and repairs on computers,
terminals and other peripherals. In Britain and France, such firms control
6–10 per cent of the maintenance market: British firms in this sector
include Granada, Advanced Technology Maintenance and Computer-
aid; French firms include Metroservice, Spectral and MIS.

The development of this sector has been assisted by two factors in the
development of the information technology sector:

1.   The increasing diversity of hardware used in firms where there are
large concentrations of computers coupled with users' growing concerns
that the multitude of maintenance contracts should be rationalised.
2.   The large number of microcomputers in a given firm which have been
sold without an after-sales service agreement.

The companies carrying out this type of work operate exclusively on
small and medium-sized computers, mainframes remaining within the
domain of the manufacturers themselves; the microcomputer maintenance market in particular is expanding very fast. TPM companies' main
selling points are the ability to deal with a firm's problems as a totality, the
capacity to maintain all makes of computers, and a flexible structure
which makes it possible for them to respond quickly to a crisis and that
enables them to charge less than the manufacturers.

However, as far as the small and medium-sized computer market is
concerned, small maintenance firms are now beginning to face competition from dealers and manufacturers. The latter are faced with the
problem of the product maturity of their hardware and are of course keen
to hang on to maintenance revenue, so they employ their normal strategy
of either tying the customer to a service agreement or building in new
technological developments which are beyond the small service firms.
And increasingly, the manufacturers are beating the small maintenance
firms at their own game by signing maintenance contracts covering whole
computer populations, even to the extent of contracting out some of the
follow-up work. Moreover, independent maintenance firms depend on
manufacturers as suppliers of spare parts and of technical documentation.

Maintenance firms will have to get substantially bigger if they are to
keep abreast of the ever-increasing corpus of know-how and thereby see
off the competition. Some of them have already started: Granada, which
is the leading British firm with a third of the market, has bought
Computer Field Maintenance and DPLE, two firms which are themselves
amongst the leaders in the British market. While the manufacturers, who
are their biggest competitors, are well established on the international
scene, the independent maintenance firms have only achieved a national
standing, for the moment keeping close to their clients.

Leasing

About a third of all large information technology systems in Europe are acquired by means of leasing; indeed, Europe boasts several leasing firms of international stature: Atlantic Computers (British Commonwealth Group), ECS (Fr – Société Générale), Inspectorate Intl (Swi) and Econocom (Neth). Leasing firms have normally specialised in mainframes but, given the slump in that sector, they are now developing policies of both diversification and concentration. The latter policy is rapidly taking shape on an international level and is particularly well advanced in France: in 1988, the five top French leasing companies controlled 81 per cent of the market as against 63 per cent for the previous year.

Likely changes in the information technology sector following the setting up of the Internal Market

The information technology sector consists of activities that range from hardware (for example, manufacturers of computers and peripherals) to services and software. Most segments of the sector dealing with hardware operate essentially on the international stage; whereas non-hardware segments, with the exception of certain activities associated with standard software, have so far been developed within a particular country, and even within a particular region of a country.

The opening of the frontiers and the ushering in of the Internal Market – in practical terms, it will not happen until 1993 – are only two of a number of important economic changes taking place in Europe, and it is therefore difficult in most cases to tell from the ways in which companies are behaving exactly what is being done as a direct response to 1993.

The only direct impact on the IT sector that we can foresee during the period leading up to 1993 is the application by member countries of the regulation dealing with orders placed by public authorities. However, current world trends will gradually affect the whole industry inside Europe, and in particular the services sector, and in consequence the Internal Market will probably bring additional influences to the movement: increased pressure from private customers, the adoption of international standards, and the effects of deregulation in related sectors. Perhaps the major impact will be that 1993 will simply speed up the whole process. At the same time, and independently of the setting up of the Internal Market, European industrial policy relating to strategic technologies such as information technology now encompasses collective pre-competitive R & D programmes which all the main firms will be participating in. It should also be borne in mind in this context that the indirect effects of a unified market (e.g. the pulling down of non-tariff barriers) have an impact on all businesses, whether they are European or not.

The influence of private customers

The possible effects of the Single Market on demand for information technology

The numerous mergers and acquisitions observed in many economic sectors in preparation for the 1993 Internal Market could result in mergers and rationalisation of the various information systems of the participating firms, or in the requirement to ensure the standardisation of the information systems departments when not merged, and, consequently, in the decrease in the number of orders simultaneously with the increase in their size.

The fact that clients are rapidly internationalising their activities will place national information technology manufacturers and service firms in competition with their opposite numbers in those countries where the client is extending his activities; it could even act as a spur to encourage these local firms to seek new markets abroad. It will also speed up the development of all IT activities (ranging all the way from hardware to services) that are associated with telecommunications.

The setting up of the Single Market will encourage the major clients to make more serious demands on information technology; it will even call the manufacturers' classic strategies into question: clients will wish to be able to connect up different brands of hardware, to have them communicate on a network basis, and to preserve previous software investment by their compatibility. It is also likely that they will want products to be standardised: the more IT penetrates a company, the more management will see standardisation as synonymous with cost-cutting, flexibility and communication capability.

Local markets facilitate market growth

Information technology has by no means spread to all corners of the economy. Taken as a whole, the US market is less dynamic than the whole of Europe, and many American and Japanese firms are only now beginning to make a growing proportion of their profits in Europe. IT is growing at a remarkable pace in Spain and Italy; while American firms are well established there, other EC countries are now moving in rapidly to set up commercial bridgeheads and service subsidiaries.

The effects of the opening up of public sector markets on information technology

Public sector orders for information technology packages are traditionally for large, complex systems and more recently for personal computers for school use and it has also been traditional for home-based manufacturers to be awarded such contracts. IBM is the European leader in the private sector markets, and national manufacturers are usually leaders in the public sector markets, but where there is no home-based producer it is IBM that dominates the public sector as well. It is even the leader in the public sector in Italy because the home-based manufacturer, Olivetti, is not a mainframe producer. Changes in public purchasing procedures might have a major impact on the policies of IT firms.

Firstly, the right established in April 1988 for foreign suppliers to be able to put in bids for all public sector orders worth more than $100,000 will probably continue to favour firms that are already well established in the home markets; this will be particularly those firms that already have production units in place, although the Single Market is likely to replace the idea of a national value added with a European version.[14] Seen in this light, IBM seems well placed by comparison with European producers, as it already has manufacturing bases in several EC countries. European manufacturers may benefit, however, from their long experience in dealing with the public authorities, or more simply from the public sector's inertia when it comes to changing supplier.

Secondly, it will be mandatory for contract specifications to conform to European standards, or international standards if there are no others. These standards place the emphasis on the need for compatibility and connectivity, and they are an expression of the European authorities' wish to arrest the process whereby the IT market has fragmented as a result of each manufacturer having its own technology, a fragmentation that could conceivably spell the end of the European manufacturing industry. The new regulations within the Single Market formalise growing tendencies among consumer requirements. They should then be seen as a challenge to all firms in the sector, whether European or not, and they will help to accelerate the adoption and spread of the new standards.

The public sector, finally, is in the process of reorganising its budgeting structure and will spend an increasingly large proportion on software and services, and correspondingly less on hardware.

According to the study on costs of non-Europe, the opening up of the public sector markets is unlikely in itself to bring about a substantial fall in prices in the IT sector, given that the public sector accounts for only 30 per cent of market openings. Indeed, the marked dependence that home-based manufacturers have had on the public sector could rather place them in considerable difficulties.

The impact of European Directives on sectors with which information technology works very closely

Both the current deregulation of national telecommunications networks and the Europe-wide harmonisation of standards will lead to the widespread development of transnational data communications applications. Upstream in IT, in the domain of components, integrated circuits whose European value added is insufficient will not receive the EC seal of approval and will be heavily taxed. This measure may protect European components manufacturers, but it will in no way satisfy actual consumers: small firms producing microcomputers who have long turned to foreign suppliers, particularly the Japanese, for cheaper goods.

The world dimension

In any study of business strategies, the development of the new economic community in Europe necessitates a careful look at what they are doing outside the member countries. Once again, it is difficult to tell how much companies are changing their policies simply because the Single Market is due to open in 1993, or to what extent might firms be amending their strategies towards non-EC countries anyway? How far are any changes due to the gradual internationalisation of the sector which is taking place quite separately?

In fact, the setting up of the Single Market could well encourage the formation or strengthening of large, thoroughly European IT firms. They would unquestionably be powerful actors on an enlarged domestic stage, well established in several EC countries, capable of extending their strategies beyond the EC boundaries into other markets, and thereby be in a better position to compete with non-EC firms, both within the domestic European market and in overseas markets.

Many recent surveys have revealed that preparation for the Single Market in 1993 is raising the spectre of 'Fortress Europe' amongst American and Japanese businessmen. This fear feeds on elements of current EC policy relating to non-EC firms, such as external customs duty, minimum local value added, and anti-dumping taxes. One consequence of this policy has been to make the Japanese move their businesses even more rapidly into external markets, and into Europe in particular.

The role of standards in information technology

The world of information technology is slowly bracing itself for the establishment of common standards which will enable all systems to be completely open. It is a development that has been taking place worldwide for some time, but EC regulations regarding norms and certification which will come in with the Single Market are serving to accelerate this process. At first, the industry developed in several segments as each manufacturer sought to establish his own technology; this led to closed architectures and made the consumer a prisoner of a single brand of computer, sometimes of a particular model. Market forces then led first to the *de facto* emergence and then the co-existence side by side of several standards which the vast majority of small manufacturers, software houses and service companies were more or less obliged to adopt.

There are very powerful arguments in favour of common standards, as follows:

- The consumer saves money and avoids the extra expense caused by the existence of a number of different environments. What this means, in effect, is that it will be possible to use applications on any machine with sufficient capacity without having to bother about the make, and it will also be possible to communicate with other equipment.
- There will be more competition as the market becomes less technically partitioned. This will give small IT firms an opportunity to develop in specialist areas – European firms in particular will have the chance to challenge American might by breaking free of their *de facto* standards. The adoption of common standards could ultimately make it possible for European manufacturers to work more closely together, and eventually form new European companies to rival the world giants.
- The adoption of common standards has an indirect influence on competition in the software and services sectors. With the elimination of the costly exercises which are necessary in order to adapt software to different types of hardware, the existence of common standards encourages a further spread of applications and a markedly faster growth in innovations. These reasons supporting the introduction of common standards are putting a lot of pressure on both the EC and the major private sector customers to put their authority and economic weight behind the campaign to persuade manufacturers to adopt them.

Amongst all the international work around the definition of completely open systems, two major development projects stand out: Unix as the standard selected for operating systems and OSI (Open System Interconnection) for network communication. The Unix operating system was not originally linked to any specific hardware; indeed, the company which initially developed Unix, AT&T, gave exploitation rights to any firm that asked. Its success is no less due to the fact that it runs on all kinds of machine from mainframes to personal computers, with the result that the base operating system of AT&T has been adapted under licence by many manufacturers, and this has led to a multiplicity of different Unix versions. The current trend is towards a consolidation of these versions; there are effectively only two groupings left, Unix International (backed by AT&T) and Open Software Foundation (backed by IBM), with most of the European manufacturers, with the exception of Olivetti, favouring the latter. It is likely that products from both of these groupings will become closer and closer as time passes. The proportion of the information system population using Unix is still small, but most manufacturers, particularly European ones, intend to offer machines that will use Unix in addition to their own operating systems. It is limited to minis and mainframes for the time being, but should extend to portable computers before long.

There are now several other initiatives aimed at unifying standards: in addition to the independent Unix and OSI developments, an American consortium called X-Open is attempting to harmonise their pooled results within a completely open system. There are also European agencies at work on promoting and testing the conformity of European standards: these include SPAG (Standard Promotion Application Group) which gathers together IT distributors. The EC has gone even further by setting up the European Telecom Standards Institute: since 1990, it has been the sole point of approval for all telecommunications terminals sold in Europe.

Internal strategies

Manufacturers' product strategies

Mainframes and minicomputers

As sales of minis and micros have continued to rise, many traditional mainframe manufacturers have moved to broaden their product range, but on the whole they have failed to take into account consumer needs in respect of such matters as connectivity and integrated applications. IBM, Unisys, Bull, Siemens and Hitachi are amongst those mainframe manufacturers that have expanded their range to include minis and micros; in the very recent past, IBM and Hitachi have both added a mini to their ranges, and Siemens has moved into portable computers and work stations; also, the merger of Bull HN and Bull SA and the purchase of Zenith will enable the Groupe Bull to cover the entire computer range.

There is now a trend for companies to make a feature of an expanded product range and carefully controlled compatibility. IBM is working towards software harmonisation across its entire range with the introduction of its System of Architecture and Application (SAA); other manufacturers, like Hitachi which has brought its own version called HAA, are following in their footsteps.

Certain manufacturers, particularly manufacturers of minis like DEC and Olivetti, are expanding their range without developing new products: DEC continues to be a specialist in minicomputer technology and is systematically following through a strategy of working closely with other microcomputer manufacturers with a view to building an integrated IT system. Olivetti, on the other hand, has enlarged its product range in microcomputers towards the top of the market by introducing minis, and has incorporated elements from outside firms, notably AT&T and Stratus; it also markets Hitachi mainframes in Italy and Spain and Japanese printers. Finally, DEC and Olivetti have announced the setting up of integration systems architectures, Application Integration Architecture and Open System Architecture respectively: the objective in each case is the ability of their hardware to be integrated into open systems (i.e. into heterogeneous systems).

Comparex, the European leader in IBM plug-compatible mainframes, is now re-orienting its service activities towards systems project development, consultancy, training and user support in software.[15] Comparex was formed in 1987 out of the plug-compatible activities of BASF and Siemens: 50 per cent of its business is currently in the German market but it is rapidly increasing its sales elsewhere in Europe.[16]

The major European manufacturers of minis are Nixdorf, Norsk Data, Bull, Philips and Olivetti; all of them have already announced, or are about to announce, that their products will be Unix-compatible and most of them are trying to develop services and systems integration side as well. Both Norsk Data and Nixdorf are experiencing economic difficulties and are taking the opportunity to carry out restructuring exercises: Norsk Data has depended for too long on its home market and on public sector orders, and has not responded in time to the demand for open systems; it has not looked seriously beyond its own technology and has therefore lost several public sector contracts to Apple and IBM and, more recently, to Bull. By contrast, Nixdorf depends much less on its home market: as much as 60 per cent of its turnover is produced outside Germany, and it is well established in the banking and distribution sectors, and small and medium-sized firms, although it failed to foresee the downturn in demand and is still having to pay off heavy investments; its principal areas of activity are Unix-compatible personal computers, services, the development of an ISDN terminal and close working relations with other firms. After being the subject of innumerable rumours, Nixdorf was finally bought by Siemens in early 1990.

Like Siemens, Philips devotes a relatively small part of its turnover – 10 per cent – to computers and data communication. It has developed its IT products (minis, personal computers and office machinery) towards interconnectivity and open systems.

As a general rule, manufacturers of mainframes and minis are also seeking new ways of making profits outside hardware: this may take the form of adding application software to standard software production; alternatively, it may involve putting new resources into services, maintenance, systems integration, network services and other services linked to data communication.

In both the main areas of diversification, software and services, manufacturers are signing a large number of trading agreements and partnership projects, or are proceeding directly to takeovers.

Microcomputer technology

At the other end of the computer range, manufacturers of microcomputers are moving rapidly away from the home computer to more powerful microcomputers; the 32-bit professional personal computer; and portable computers. Despite the fact that it first specialised in home computers, only 22 per cent of Amstrad's 1988 turnover came from that market, compared with 54 per cent for professional micros. Firms like Compaq which are manufacturing 32-bit computers using the 80386 microprocessors have already announced computers using 80486s; they are quite as powerful as minis.

The strategies of open systems

Given the current trends towards standards in operating systems and open architectures, manufacturers can no longer rely on their own technologies to guarantee a captive market. The success of IBM-plug-compatibles made by Amdahl and certain Japanese firms like Hitachi makes it quite clear that the hardware market is becoming more sensitive to price than to specific technical advances.

As far as minis and work stations are concerned, the potential of decentralised IT and the appearance of personal computers at the workplace have given greater urgency to advances in connectivity and open systems. Most manufacturers, above all those based in Europe, are keeping faith with their own technologies but are also adopting Unix and are beginning to sell a line of products which are compatible with it. They have responded to this particular challenge in different ways: Siemens has developed Unix work stations, while in 1988 Groupe Bull set up X3S, a Bull HN/Bull SA subsidiary, with the aim of developing and manufacturing Unix products. Bull was among the first firms to achieve conformity to X/Open specifications; meanwhile, ICL has based its departmental system on Unix and, by means of a takeover, has expanded its range to include Unix-compatible, fault-tolerant computers.

Internal reorganisation of manufacturing firms

A number of manufacturers are carrying out, or have even completed, major internal reorganisation plans. The reasons for these plans are sometimes related to new plans to diversify upstream and to strategies aimed at establishing the company on an international footing; other reasons include a rationalisation of costs, or more simply the integration of recent takeovers. The first of these restructurings took place in the United States where the slowdown in growth was felt much earlier: first at NCR, then at Unisys after the merger between Sperry and Burroughs in 1986, then IBM and finally at Control Data in 1989.

The reorganisation plans carried out by the big mainframe manufacturers, IBM, Bull and Siemens, and by microcomputer manufacturers like Olivetti, aim to design product departments to be more adaptable and flexible so that they can respond better to customers' needs. These objectives seem to have been achieved by granting greater autonomy to these newly formed product divisions, and by decentralising decision-making processes and areas of responsibility.

European manufacturers

The products of Groupe Bull are shared between its two units, Bull HN in the United States and Bull SA in France.[17] Each of these units is responsible for all stages of the process – from product development and manufacture to sales – but they are headed up by a central management team which defines and co-ordinates the firm's world strategy. The ways in which the two firms work in tandem ensure that Groupe Bull now has better geographical coverage of the world markets, and one of the main reasons is that they each have established themselves in different geographical zones. As far as marketing goes, the Bull logo has been kept for all activities carried out in its name; this has necessitated a publicity campaign in the North American markets to establish Bull's name in place of the better-known Honeywell.

In 1989, Siemens started the first major structural reorganisation in Germany since 1969, and initially it covered the five central departments and then the individual divisions.[18] According to Datamation, the company will probably end up with 15–20 divisions, instead of the present ten, all of them specialised and empowered with considerable autonomy.[19] The 1988 Annual Report shows the Components division already broken up into two distinct units, and there is also the likelihood that the Communications and Information Technology division, which accounts for no less than 17 per cent of the company's activities, will also be cut up into several sections. Finally, thought is being given to the possibility of combining some or all of this division with Nixdorf,

Siemens' new subsidiary. The objective of this fundamental reorganisation is to ensure that the firm has the flexibility, dynamism and competitiveness needed to take it into the 1990s. It is being made very clear that this will be achieved by maximising the productivity of the new divisional structure, keeping in step with technological developments and organising new sales networks.

Olivetti's reorganisation was announced at the end of 1988, and to take charge of it they called back V. Cassoni, a senior manager who had been lent to AT&T. Olivetti's activities have since been broken down into four divisions, each corresponding to a market-product: office equipment, IT systems, services and software, and specialist IT technology. Head Office has overall control and takes all broad policy decisions, while each division deals with all functions from research to sales; they will all eventually be turned into subsidiaries.

Unlike IBM and Bull, Olivetti and Siemens are not solely manufacturers of information technology, but show that IT will end up having a much higher priority as a result of their current reorganisations. Their internal and external strategies demonstrate the growing importance already attached to IT.

The Americans

The primary purpose of the restructuring exercises currently being carried out by Unisys and IBM is to shape their products and services into global solutions (hardware, software and user support) to meet the needs of the customer. As a first stage, IBM decided to place heavy emphasis on the trading side of the business, and moved a substantial proportion of staff into sales and customer care.[20] These activities were broken down into five new lines all linked with a new-look marketing division; the reorganisation resulted in a more decentralised decision-making process and product responsibility. However, in late 1989, IBM announced a new series of draconian restructuring measures: these will be a cut of $1 billion in annual production costs, a reduction of 10,000 jobs in the United States by the end of 1990 and a repurchase of shares valued at $4 billion.[21] The share repurchase programme was launched in 1986, and in four years topped $10.5 billion, or 15 per cent of capital; the objective could be to reduce the risk of a hostile takeover. Analysts expect factories to close and subsidiaries to be sold off in consequence, and the measures overall have needed provisions on a scale that reduced IBM's net profit for 1989 by 35 per cent against the previous year.

Of the other American firms in the sector, Unisys has invested equally in training, sales teams and its Industrial Skills Centres, particularly in Europe where the company says it is making special preparations for the Single Market in 1993.[22] In 1989, Control Data launched a restructuring programme costing $490 million and decided to prune a number of its commercial activities:[23] in April 1989 it closed down its super-computer subsidiary, ETA, and in June sold Imprimis Technology, its data storage subsidiary, to the American firm of Seagate; then, in the same month, it announced the sale to the French company Thomson of a large part of its European maintenance activities. It is also thought that Control Data might be ready to sell off its training section.[24]

Manufacturers' commercial strategies on the European market

The internal organisation of marketing

In 1988, ICL (UK) divided its commercial activities into two, ICL Europe and ICL International, the division forming part of the STC group's voluntary strategy for entry into the Single Market.[25] Meanwhile, although the international sales of Apple (US) continue to rise (turnover up 28 per cent in 1987 and up another 33 per cent in 1988), the company reorganised twice during 1988; in April, marketing was divided into three (Asia, Europe and the United States), and in August four independent divisions were set up (Apple Products, Apple Europe, Apple Pacific and Apple USA).[26]

Distribution strategies

Apple has recently announced that, as part of the preparation for the Single Market in 1992, all the company's products will henceforth be distributed according to the same procedures throughout the European Community, involving the same system of trade discounts, price calculations and services, so that any client having subsidiaries in more than one member country would be able to rationalise its purchasing and maintenance policies accordingly.[27] Apple now proposes to extend its sales network, and it is also in the process of redefining its retailer's profiles.

Amstrad has opted for organic growth by means of expanded markets and the development of new products.[28] As part of this policy during 1988 and 1989, Amstrad replaced a number of existing distributors by setting up new subsidiaries in several countries including West Germany, Belgium and the Netherlands; it also bought up some of its distributors in the United States and Spain.

The strategy of international customer service

Siemens has already anticipated the internationalising of the world IT market. In response to client demand to respond to problems worldwide,

Siemens set up its 'International Corporation Program', a planning, policy implementation and customer care programme that operates throughout the world.[29] This is an important first step in the field of international customer care, particularly in the context of the Internal Market.

Japanese commercial and distribution strategies on the European and American markets

Growth in demand and the development of Japanese product ranges (from office machinery and photocopiers, towards printers, fax machines and, more recently, micros and lap-top computers) has forced Japanese businesses to look again at their sales networks on the international markets.

One example of a Japanese firm responding to these new pressures is Nec which has reorganised all its regional sales networks in the United States, and bought shares in a marketing agency and in two distribution firms; in Europe, it has opened subsidiaries in France, and in Sweden it has announced a complete rationalisation of its European marketing strategy.[30]

Toshiba is reorganising its American strategy by giving more autonomy to local staff: all divisions of Toshiba America are now subsidiaries, and TAI (Toshiba America Inc) has become the holding company co-ordinating all activities.[31] The company is pursuing the same objectives in its European structure, and is setting up three marketing subsidiaries here, each with product responsibilities: Toshiba Information Systems Gmbh in West Germany (office equipment and customer service), Toshiba Information Systems in Spain (IT and communication equipment)[32] and Toshiba Electronics in the United Kingdom (electronic apparatus). In 1989, Toshiba announced that it was opening a London office where the company would ultimately take all decisions that related to the co-ordination of European activities leading up to 1993.[33]

Fujitsu has a subsidiary in Malaga, Spain, and in 1984 bought Secoinsa, a Spanish firm specialising in the sale of professional microcomputers.[34]

Location of sites manufacturing products for the European market

European and American manufacturers

European manufacturers have located most of their production sites making goods for the European market within their own countries. Many American manufacturers, too, which are active in the European market produce a large proportion of their goods on this side of the Atlantic:

IBM, for instance, has factories in most EC countries, achieving one-third of its total turnover in Europe, and 90 per cent of that comes from goods that are designed and manufactured here in twelve factories and nine R & D centres. Several other manufacturers, mainly Americans, have production units in Ireland and Scotland: the Irish government, in particular, has been conspicuously successful in attracting IT multinational firms by offering them fiscal advantages, and investment and employment/training subsidies.[35] Today, most of the top twenty-five world manufacturers have factories in Ireland; at the outset, they may have been interested in the advantages referred to above, but they now stay in Ireland because of the presence of a highly skilled workforce. As for Scotland, Compaq has increased its production capacity there in order to ensure that the plant was able to sustain all its sales in Europe (60 per cent of the total turnover).[36] Similarly, Amstrad, which had relocated some production to South-East Asia, decided to bring some of that back to Scotland to sites belonging to GPT, a subsidiary of GEC and Plessey: the production affected is keyboards and IT systems; screens will continue to be imported.[37]

By contrast, Olivetti has gone to Japan to produce portable computers for the European and Japanese markets: it has set up a joint subsidiary with the Japanese firm of Y-E Data.[38] Examples relating to large and medium-sized computer manufacturers, on the other hand, include ICL (UK) which opened a factory in West Germany in 1986 to assist its penetration into European markets,[39] and the American company Commodore which has announced that it will build a factory in Europe but has not yet decided on the exact location.[40] South European countries like Spain and Greece do not seem able yet to get IT companies to relocate there, especially when the firms have already established plants elsewhere in Europe. However, the US firm of Dataproducts will soon open a factory in Portugal for the production of printer ribbons, which will be in addition to the factory it already owns in Dublin.[41]

Japanese strategies on foreign markets

The Japanese are in the process of developing a worldwide strategy, and since the mid-1980s have been siting production units close to their export markets. This policy of delocalisation first took them to the United States in 1987 when customs tariffs were imposed; today, the policy is still in place and the company now has Europe in its sights because of fears that more commercial restrictions will be placed on both markets. The thinking behind the Single Market in 1992 and EC external policies in general continue to raise the spectre of 'Fortress Europe' in Japanese minds.

Japanese manufacturers are expanding the capacities of production units located abroad, and are also adding new product lines and even building new factories. Delocalisation initially affected peripherals (particularly printers), electronic office machinery, photocopiers and components; it has now been extended to include micros, lap-top computers and fax machines.

A completely different strategy has been adopted for large computers. Here are some recent examples of delocalisation to Europe for the purpose of setting up production units and/or enlarging capacity:

Firm	Country	Products
NEC[42]		
3 factories	UK (2), Ireland	
enlargement of capacity	UK, Ireland	semi-conductors
new products	UK	fax machines and mobile phones
Epson[43]		
2 factories	France, UK	
enlargement of capacity	France	printers
Fujitsu[44]		
new factory announced	Europe	ASICS components
Canon[45]		
3 factories: including a joint venture with Olivetti	France, West Germany Italy	photocopiers
enlargement of capacity	France, West Germany	photocopiers
new products	France, West Germany	fax machines, electronic typewriters, laser printers
new factory	UK(?)	laser printers, fax machines
Toshiba[46]		
factory joint venture with Rhone-Poulenc	France	
enlargement of capacity	France	photocopiers,
new factory	West Germany	portable computers

Rationalisation of production costs and economies of scale

After the acquisition of Bull HN, Groupe Bull made it known publicly that its increase in size would enable it to benefit from economies of scale in both purchasing and production, and that production economies would be made by making the factories specialise.[47] Moreover, the leading mainframe and minicomputer manufacturers are, or will soon be, rationalising production costs by means of laying off staff; these firms include IBM, Siemens, Control Data and Unisys, in addition to Bull. Behind Comparex's intention to buy up NAS's European activities lies another wish to benefit from new economies of scale: both Comparex and NAS manufacture and sell the Hitachi PCM (Plug-Compatible mainframe).[48] According to Panorama of EC Industry 1990, intra-firm trade for firms which have factories in different member countries has increased for the very reason that many of them are rationalising their production throughout the Community and are making their factories specialise in particular products.

Strategies of firms supplying information technology services and consultancy

Diversification

The types of services companies need now to diversify are all linked to traditional IT. These services are suffering particularly badly as a result of the hardware crisis, because some service firms have opted to specialise in them: for example, office services, third-party maintenance and leasing.

Companies attempting to market office services like agency data processing are now having to face up to the fact that fewer and fewer firms are subcontracting computer work. They are responding to the challenge in different ways: some of them are expanding the services on offer to their existing clients, for example by adding hardware distribution, while others have moved into facilities management (i.e. they put their own staff in to manage the client's IT work). There are even some services firms with an eye to the establishment of the Single Market which are making use of their computing power to set up as videotex providers.

A specific example from the United States concerns Automatic Data Processing (ADP) which was one of a number of aggressive office services firms in the 1970s; today, it has diversified into information technologies that have been developed for the finance and business sectors, and has further rationalised its office services work by replacing its forty-three regional centres with ten mega-centres.[49]

European firms have not been idle.[50] Several French firms have opted for highly sophisticated office services as a way of staying in business:

CCMC, for instance, has moved up from customised processing for accountants to take in microcomputer distribution and sales of global IT solutions for the commercial sectors where its expertise is already established; GSI has developed the same way from its specialist payroll software, but has opted to stay out of distribution; Facilities Management are just starting up in Europe, and the French firms of Segin and Sligos are already well placed as videotex providers.

Third-party maintenance firms have two problems to deal with: firstly, in the mini and medium-sized computer markets they are running into more and more competition from the manufacturers, and from distributors who are fighting to hang on to maintenance revenue; then there is the problem of the falling prices of hardware as maintenance revenue is closely linked to the value of the equipment being serviced. However, developments in IT are opening up new areas for maintenance firms to exploit, such as software recovery, network services, electronic communications and fault-tolerant systems; a major problem is that these new areas call for different and very complex know-how. A few small firms will survive either because they are highly specialised or because they have signed contracts with micro manufacturers; for the rest, the big maintenance groups marketing more value-added services will have the market to themselves.

Many maintenance firms are diversifying into new skills within the areas in which they have built up experience and expertise, but also are going for upstream services such as systems integration and network installation, thereby giving themselves an opportunity to enter a market dominated by companies marketing classic IT services. Taking the United Kingdom and France, for example:[51] Computer Aid (UK) has diversified into support systems, network planning and systems integration; Metroservice (Fr) into testing systems integration and systems installation; and MIS (Fr) into installation of computer rooms and of communications networks for large computer systems.

Computer leasing firms are badly overspecialised in mainframe work, and must diversify. They are approaching the problem in two main ways: by seeking new areas within the leasing market itself and moving into IT services, software or computer distribution. In practice, few leasing firms have remained single-product or single-brand (such as IBM mainframe): ECS, for example, has expanded its range by adding Compaq, Toshiba and Bull personal computers to its IBM mainframe. A number of leasing companies have shown a preference for diversification into quite new areas: one such is Inspectorate which is moving into software development and systems project development; another is ECS which is seeking new markets in services and in distribution through specialist subsidiaries: ECS Diffusion (micros), ECS Maintenance, ECS Bureaucratique (training), ECS I (systems integration) and ECS Technologies

(CAD–CAM applications). Compared with other leasing firms, ECS has made little effort to move into the takeover market, whether domestic or international, as a means of external growth.

A wide range of services or specialisation?

The range of operations offered by a service firm develops in response to various types of market pressure. From the demand side, customers are veering sharply in the direction of having a single consultant who will solve all their IT problems nationally and internationally. Furthermore, service firms are having to deal increasingly with problems of connectivity which are being thrown up by the growing use of decentralised, multibrand technology; the solution is usually to be found in the application of systems integration techniques.

Such demand-led pressures are met both by offering the customer an across-the-board range of services and by limiting the number of client sectors having different IT user profiles. The priority of internal and external growth strategies currently being employed by service companies appears to be the consolidation of the old specialist work by means of completing the range of services marketed to the current client sectors; when the time comes to expand the firm's expertise in order to take in a new client sector, the objective will normally be that the skills demanded by this and the existing sectors should overlap to a greater or lesser extent.

Diversification takes many forms these days: some service firms are opting for industrial information technology, while others are diversifying upstream from IT services into management consultancy activity which is very much part of the overall strategy of providing a global IT service; a third category of company is expanding activities to include services linked to data communication and telecommunications.

All these trends have lives that are independent of the opening of the Internal Market, although they will unquestionably continue to be strongly coloured by demand-led indirect effects of the Internal Market. Only the strategy involving expansion into services linked to telecommunications will directly benefit, and this will come about as a result of a number of factors including the liberalisation of the telecommunications industry, the installation of ISDN networks and the adoption of international standards throughout the European Community in preparation for 1993.

Despite the continued search for larger company size throughout the sector – and there are many good reasons for this trend – there will always be a place for small software houses and services firms which are innovative and specialised. Commercial dynamism and the capacity for innovation will continue to be trump cards in the hands of small firms, but their survival will also depend on their ability to get sound basic contracts and track down effective marketing channels, particularly abroad. Two examples of successful strategies adopted by small European service firms are: the British firm of Systematica, which has signed a project-study contract with the European Space Agency in software design and an agreement with DEC for the marketing of some of Systematica's software on DEC's scientific work stations aimed at the European market; and the Danish firm of Uniras, which, alternatively, has specialised in graphic programmes for the petroleum industry and has succeeded in producing a graphics visualisation tool for use in scientific research on work stations and mainframe terminals. This latter firm also sells direct to universities in Britain, France, Germany and Scandinavia.[52]

Smaller service companies, working, for instance, in consultancy, installation, training and maintenance, are developing sectoral and local niches; they tend to have a regional catchment area, and their strongest selling points are geographical proximity to the client, quick response to problems and a sound understanding of the client's line of business.

Product strategy in software

All the evidence suggests that an increasing number of European software producers are concentrating on Unix-compatible applications, thus following the lead of those computer manufacturers who have also thrown in their lot with Unix: in the field of standardised operating systems, the Open Software Foundation has set up a software house specifically to develop a common operating system based on the IBM version of Unix. The effect of adopting such a standard will be sharper competition between software producers, but there will also be a reduction in the amount of time spent on making a package 'portable', so that it can cope with a large number of systems. By contrast, in the field of microcomputer technology, many software houses have chosen to write software applications which will run on the operating system of the new IBM personal computer.

In the period leading up to the opening of the Single Market, the most important tasks for software houses will be the adaptation of their products to the demands of other member countries (e.g. language and local laws) and the placing of their affairs on a more international and far-sighted footing. When a product is adapted for use in another country, it does not simply mean that it can be marketed in that country, but also that it can be used by a client firm which has branches in several countries. The objective of the firm of Concept with its accounting software is to get that software working in different national accounting systems and legal contexts.[53]

Service and consultancy firms are establishing themselves abroad

The strategy of establishing abroad is based on a large number of notions ranging from the exporting of goods and services to foreign revenue. The internationalising of the software industry, particularly in the case of packages, involves the exporting of the software, that is to say selling it abroad. To do so, it has either to open trading subsidiaries; or to find its way in through some existing channel of distribution. IT services and consultancy work characteristically involves two ways of internationalising services activities. On the one hand it can export services, resulting in invoicing of fees and charges from one country to another. The only other way of achieving this end is to earn the money in the country of the client by means of establishing subsidiaries or taking over existing firms: this has the decided advantage of enabling the company to remain abreast of local trends and guaranteeing a close working relationship with the client.

We have here a sector that has long been traditionally national or even regional in character, but the need to acquire an international base has never been felt more keenly than now. The national markets are turning out to be too narrow for firms to derive sufficient profit from the specialised know-how that the company has to develop, for example in software project development and project management, and this stands in the way of them retaining niche leadership. Moreover, decisions taken by certain clients to expand into foreign markets is forcing service firms to do likewise, particularly in view of the fact that their competitors are already relatively better placed in the international arena.

It seems clear that the Internal Market's challenge will be for these firms to strengthen their market positions in Europe and the United States, provided they have established themselves sufficiently on their home markets. The American market appeals to the largest European service companies because they are keen to establish worldwide, but it also has attractions for certain small service companies which have secured highly specialised niches for themselves.

There are three main ways in which firms establish themselves abroad: by the setting up of subsidiaries (internal growth); by takeovers; and by the signing of co-operation agreements (the second and third are both means of external growth). It would appear that international co-operation agreements, particularly in the exchange and adaptation of products, are actions of small and medium-sized service and consultancy companies; sadly, information relating to this trend is very thin and it is not possible to say how widespread it is. By contrast, there is plenty of evidence to demonstrate that the larger firms in the sector are increasingly seeking to expand abroad by means of takeovers rather than by the setting up of subsidiaries.

External strategies are examined in the final section; in the meantime, it is instructive to take a look at some examples of international growth being achieved through subsidiaries. Firstly, Finsiel, the leading Italian service and consultancy organisation, has completed building up its subsidiary network in Italy, and since 1987 has been implementing its overseas expansion programme by opening subsidiaries in the United States, Cyprus, Greece and Spain; Finsiel also exports its services to the USSR.[54] French firms, too, have been active in this area: according to a survey referred to in 01-Informatique, thirteen service companies including Sesa and Sligos, have recently set up subsidiaries in Spain.[55] Furthermore, the leading French leasing companies, ECS and Promodata, have established subsidiaries abroad, most of them in other European countries: ECS opened up in Belgium, Britain, West Germany, Italy and Japan in 1986, and in Spain and Switzerland in 1988;[56] Promodata established subsidiaries in Spain and Switzerland in 1988.[57]

Growth management

The IT service sector can already claim above-average growth compared to the world economy as a whole, and, in this context, the current frenetic round of mergers and takeovers is making it even more difficult to manage the expansion effectively. Given that mergers and takeovers are likely to continue to snowball for some time to come, it is by no means certain in every case that the firms making the acquisitions have planned the moves as judiciously as they might have done. Moreover, rapid internal or external growth in the field of services places very considerable strains on human resource management: firms have sometimes to recruit or redeploy numbers of workers despite the fact that the sector is already noted for its high staff turnover. The firm of Cap Gemini Sogeti, for instance, runs a decentralised network of 250 agencies, and to promote company loyalty ('Cap Geminisation') the agencies are controlled by a management system which is characterised by detailed reporting, and synergy is best developed by means of formal exchanges of methodological know-how; CGS is also developing an in-house 'university' for agency managers.[58]

Research and development by service and consultancy firms

As a result of increased demand for application software and a sharpening of competition in supply, many firms are seeking to upgrade the tooling used in software design in an attempt to improve designer productivity. Through the Esprit II programme, the EC is about to launch a new scheme called the European System and Software Initiative (ESSI) with the objective of raising software productivity; it will have a budget of 500 million ecus over five years and will oversee a wide range of organisations including research centres, the major European manufacturers, approximately twenty European service and consultancy companies, and some of the major software users.

External strategies

Worldwide developments in mergers and takeovers in IT and IT services: 1988–89

Mergers and takeovers in software and IT services in 1988

It is estimated that there were as many as 358 mergers and takeovers in the IT software and services sector worldwide during 1987, and this figure, which represents an increase of 17 per cent on the previous year, seems to suggest that the sector is opting in the main for development by external growth.[59]

With a view to examining developments in Europe during 1988, we have taken the list of merger and takeover operations registered in the DOME data bank and targeting European IT service companies. Tables 9.13a and 9.13b show that the countries that are most active in both the national and the international arenas are Britain and France, and a breakdown of national operations by percentage of shares acquired demonstrates that fifty of the sixty-nine operations were takeovers involving a minimum of 50 per cent of the shares. Furthermore, the number of operations registered for the two countries demonstrates that British firms generally opt for takeovers whereas French companies have a preference for majority shareholdings.

If we move to transnational operations for 1988, however, and leaving to one side those mergers and takeovers which British companies have carried out in France and vice versa, we can see that Britain and France again have quite different aims: Britain favours countries like Germany, the Netherlands and Ireland while France is building a sound base in the countries of southern Europe, and Spain in particular. According to the information registered with DOME, Britain and France are almost the only EC countries active transnationally.

Some transnational operations are carried out via a subsidiary that is already established in the target country: for example, in 1988 the American firm of MAI used its German subsidiary to buy up its sixth software house in that country.[60] We have identified a number of operations of this type, and we have the impression that their frequency

Table 9.13 Targeted service and software firms: mergers and takeovers in 1988

(a) Mergers and takeovers within the same country

	Percentage of shares acquired					
Country	Total	100%	50–100%	25–50%	up to 25%	Mergers
France	26	4	16	4	2	–
United Kingdom	20	15	3	1	–	–
Netherlands	6	3	1	2	–	–
Germany	5	1	3	1	–	–
Italy	4	–	2	2	–	–
Belgium	4	–	–	2	–	2
Portugal	2	–	–	2	–	–
Spain	1	–	–	–	1	–
Ireland	1	–	–	1	–	–
Total	69	23	25	16	3	2

Source: DOME DG IV, CEE, sector 737

(b) Transnational mergers and takeovers

	Target countries										
	Fr	UK	Swi	Swe	US	Sp	It	Ger	Neth	Ire	Total
France	–	3	–	–	–	3	1	–	–	–	7
United Kingdom	2	–	–	–	–	–	–	2	1	1	6
Switzerland	–	1	–	–	–	–	–	1	–	–	2
Sweden	–	–	–	–	–	–	–	1	–	–	1
United States	–	2	–	–	–	–	–	–	–	–	2
Totals	2	6	0	0	0	3	1	4	1	1	18

(c) Transnational mergers and takeovers transacted through the medium of subsidiaries in the foreign country

Nationality	Target country
United States	West Germany
Switzerland	West Germany
Austria	West Germany
France	Spain

(d) Takeovers of overseas subsidiaries by local companies

Purchaser	Vendor	Site of subsidiary
France	United States	France
United Kingdom	United States	United Kingdom
Belgium	France	Belgium
Italy	France	Italy
Germany	Finland	Germany

Source: DOME DG IV, CEE, sector 737

may have been underestimated: however, taking all transnational operations into account, it would appear that Britain and Germany are still target markets much sought after by IT services firms.

One last type of transnational operation concerns the purchase of the subsidiary of a foreign firm by a firm from the country where the subsidiary is set up; this type of disengagement is counted as external growth on the home market.

Mergers and takeovers in the office machinery and information technology equipment sectors in 1988

The DOME data bank has logged twenty-six European operations for 1988 clearly involving the office machinery and IT equipment sectors (Table 9.14): Table 9.14a shows that eighteen of these were national operations carried out by only three countries – France (seven), Britain (six) and Germany (five) – while the Netherlands was also responsible for three operations in EC member states. As was the case with services, nearly all merger and takeover operations involve holdings of more than 50 per cent of the shares.

Table 9.14 Office equipment and IT equipment (target sector): mergers and takeovers in 1988

(a) National and transnational breakdown

| | Target companies | | | | | | | |
	UK	Ger	Fr	US	Den	Ire	Bel	Totals
United Kingdom	6	–	1	–	–	–	–	7
Germany	–	5	–	–	–	–	–	5
France	–	–	7	1	–	–	–	8
Netherlands	–	1	1	–	–	–	1	3
United States	–	–	–	–	1	1	–	2
South Africa	1	–	–	–	–	–	–	1
Totals	7	6	9	1	1	1	1	26

(b) Target product segments

Office equipment	3
General computers	6
(micro-computers only – 5)	
Specialised IT systems	8
(industrial IT, CAD–CAM, CIM only – 4)	
Peripherals	9
(graphic and optical equipment only – 5)	
Total	26

Source: DOME, DGIV European Commission

A breakdown of operations by segments reveals that the vast majority take place in the field of information technology, and most of them in three sub-segments: microcomputer technology (five), graphic and optic peripheral systems (four) and CAD–CAM industrial systems (five). An overall analysis of the motivation behind these moves is out of the question as press reports fail to list systematically either the activities of the purchaser or the nature of the target activity, for example in terms of production or distribution.

Mergers and takeovers across frontiers in Europe in 1989

Electronics and information technology[61] The rate of mergers and takeovers in all industrial sectors in Europe accelerated throughout 1989 – 259 in the first 3 months, 341 in the second and 377 in the third. Amongst the sectors most heavily targeted, electronics and information technology accounted for forty-two operations in the third quarter of the year, exactly the same number as for the whole of the previous six months: this increase in the electronics and IT sectors clearly represents a more rapid acceleration than in industry as a whole.

It is difficult to analyse the value of the various transactions, as the agreed prices were not divulged in 530 cases out of the 953 instances that are registered for the first 9 months of the year. During the first six months, the average size of operations in the electronics sector was lower than that for all sectors (474 million ecus against 56 million); by the end of the third quarter, the total value of transactions in the electronics sector had risen to 2479.2 million ecus against 947 million ecus for the first six months. It should be borne in mind that the rise during the third quarter includes Siemens' participation in the purchase of Plessey in Britain: only Siemens' contribution of 1.8 billion ecus is registered in the tally of transnational takeovers; if it is excluded, operations in the electronics sector for the third quarter come to only 697 million ecus. None of the top thirty mergers and takeovers for the third quarter affect purely IT activities.

Office machinery, information technology and IT services in 1989 For an assessment of mergers and takeovers in the office machinery, information technology and IT services sectors, we have made use of a detailed list of transnational operations in Europe compiled by DGII and covering the first seven months in 1989 (Table 9.15). Between January and July there was a total of twenty-one operations affecting these sectors and leasing combined, and of these fifteen involved EC member states (Table 9.15a). The most active purchasing countries were again Britain and France: they were responsible for eight out of the thirteen operations carried out by EC countries. The country most frequently at the receiving end within the

Table 9.15 Office equipment, IT and service sector: transitional mergers and takeovers in Europe during the first seven months of 1989

(a) Number of mergers and takeovers

Month	Mergers/ takeovers in IT only	All sectors
January	1	64
February	2	83
March	2	99
April	3	113
May	6	116
June	3	127
July	4	145

(b) Transnational breakdown

	Target countries										
	Ger	Fr	UK	It	Neth	Bel	Sp	Den	Nor	Swe	Total
West Germany	–	1	–	–	–	–	–	–	–	–	1
France	1	–	–	1	–	1	1	–	–	–	4
United Kingdom	2	1	–	–	1	–	–	–	–	–	4
Italy	–	–	–	–	–	–	–	–	1	–	1
Netherlands	1	–	–	–	–	–	–	–	–	–	1
Belgium	1	–	–	–	–	–	–	–	–	–	1
Denmark	–	–	1	–	–	–	–	–	–	–	1
Sweden	–	–	–	–	–	–	–	1	3	–	4
Switzerland	1	–	–	–	–	–	–	–	–	–	1
United States	–	–	–	–	–	–	–	–	–	3	3
Totals	6	2	1	1	1	1	1	1	4	3	21

(c) Commercial activities as declared by firms involved in mergers and takeovers

Target sector	INFO	DIST		SERV	LEAS	Total
		INFO	OFF			
Purchaser						
OFF	3[1]	1	–	–	–	4
INFO	1	2[2]	–	3[2]	–	6
DIST	–	3[3]	–	–	–	3
SERV	–	–	–	2	–	2
LEAS	–	–	–	–	2	2
Other	–	–	1	3	–	4
Total	4	5	2	8	2	21

Notes: INFO = IT equipment and peripherals;   OFF = Office equipment;   DIST = Distribution of IT or equipment;   SERV = Software and IT services;   LEAS = Leasing
[1] All targets are in the printer sector   [2] Of the three shareholdings acquired by IBM in Sweden, two were in service firms and the other was in a distribution firm   [3] Three takeovers in different EC countries transacted by the French distributor CDME

Source: Listing mergers and takeovers about EC 1992 for EC internal use.

EC was Germany: of the fourteen operations concerning eight different member states, Germany was targeted on six occasions (Table 9.15b).

North European countries such as Norway and Sweden were involved in eight operations all told: the three takeovers in Sweden took the form of IBM acquiring minority (10 per cent) shareholdings in two service companies and one distribution firm: Sweden itself was responsible for four transnational takeovers, of which three were in Norway.

Taking the 21 operations as a whole, the commercial operations most frequently targeted are services and software (eight operations) and distribution (five operations); as for the main commercial activities of the purchasing firms, there are four companies which are not part of the sector: they have invested in services in three cases and in the other case they invested in distribution (Table 9.15c).

The external strategies of information technology manufacturers

Recent mergers and takeovers carried out by the major European manufacturers

Since 1988, most of the main European IT manufacturers have launched external growth programmes or speeded up programmes that were already up and running. In the systems and equipment sectors, these takeovers have had a double purpose: on the one hand, they take place outside national boundaries and therefore give the firms concerned a more secure international footing; on the other, they are the implementation of a strategy aimed at expanding product range or strengthening the firm's market position either in a specialist area of IT or in communications systems.

Bull Group In December 1988, Groupe Bull increased its share in Honeywell Bull Inc, a joint American subsidiary, from 45.5 per cent to 65 per cent by buying Honeywell shares; the two other shareholders were Honeywell, which moved down to a 20 per cent holding, and Nec which kept its 15 per cent share. The subsidiary was renamed Bull HN, but each part remained a legal entity.

The overall objectives of the new firm include the development of a world strategy to deal with many activities ranging from R & D to production and marketing. As far as trading and marketing are concerned, Bull has substantially increased its presence outside France (61 per cent of turnover in 1988 against 37 per cent in 1987), and it has increased its control of the European market by moving successfully into the British and Italian markets, previously Honeywell preserves; Groupe Bull has also improved its market prospects in North America (21 per cent in 1988) by making use of the new Honeywell–Bull links: the two entities share the various geographical markets on an agreed basis. Bull hopes to be able to market a full range of products, and is already expanding its own range together with Honeywell's. Finally, with regard to production and R & D, the takeover of Bull HN should undoubtedly enable economies of scale to be made.

In October 1989, Bull bought up from Zenith Electronic Corp the American firm, Zenith Computer Group, and two of its subsidiaries, Zenith Data Systems and Zenith Health, for $630 million; Zenith Electronic has decided to revert to its High Street activities, in particular high-definition television.[62] The final agreement was expected to be signed in December 1989. Zenith Computer Group's activities will strengthen the microcomputer technology segment of Bull's already enlarged product range: Bull's presence on the US markets will be all the stronger for Zenith's participation, and the microcomputer technology share of Bull's turnover is now likely to rise from 10 per cent to 30 per cent.

Siemens   This company has launched into a whole series of takeovers and mergers in a move to strengthen its market position outside West Germany. Siemens is somewhat narrowly based on the German market where 74 per cent of turnover is accounted for by large and medium-sized systems and 61 per cent by communications products and peripherals.[63] Within Europe, the British and French markets are fairly undeveloped (only 5 per cent of turnover for information systems), but, according to Datamation, as much as 89 per cent of Siemens IT activity is probably now in Europe in 1988 and 10 per cent in the United States.[64]

In March 1989, Siemens bought a 52 per cent interest in the French firm of IN2 from Intertechnique for 346.6 million French francs. IN2 is a manufacturer of small IT systems, and eventually Siemens will have to buy 30 per cent of the public shares; for the time being, Intertechnique retain 18 per cent of the holding. Siemens' objectives then were to produce small Pick and Unix systems and to move into the French public sector market.

In the meantime, it has been active with other takeovers: in 1988, Siemens bought 51 per cent of the shares of the Norwegian firm of Tandberg, a manufacturer of terminals,[65] and in early 1990 bought 51 per cent in Nixdorf, the German manufacturer of minicomputers, although this awaits approval from the Bundeskartellamt, the German monopolies office; it is anticipated that Siemens will sooner or later increase its capital stake in Nixdorf.[66] Siemens, for its part, can offer Nixdorf its position in IT and communications; indeed, they complement one another very effectively in a number of different segments: the turnover of Siemens Information System and Nixdorf put together is probably equivalent to that of Bull and Zenith combined.

Siemens also linked up with GEC to bring off the biggest transnational takeover in Europe during 1989: in the third quarter of the year, Siemens and GEC bought Plessey for 1800 million ecus and 1100 million ecus respectively.[67] The two main aims are, firstly, access to the UK electronics market and defence contracts, and secondly, access to the UK telecommunications market through GPT, a subsidiary of GEC and Plessey.

With regard to its policy of developing its software business, Siemens has bought into a number of service and consultancy organisations, mainly outside Germany; these include the takeover of the Hungarian firm of PSI and minority shareholdings in four Italian companies.[68] The takeover of Plessey brought with it the British IT service firm, the Hoskyns Group: it is thought that Siemens and GEC might be ready to sell off Plessey's 70 per cent holding in Hoskyns.[69] ICL is the information technology subsidiary of STC, and during 1988 carried out several takeovers on the American and European markets. In the spring of 1989, 85 per cent of ICL's turnover was estimated to be produced in Europe, and 60 per cent of that in Britain.[70] According to the magazine *Tribune de l'Expansion*, ICL is likely to continue prioritising external growth and benefiting from financial backing from its holding company:

Date and price	Target company and its activity	Objectives
Feb 1988 £5 million	IT and communications system activities of Northern Telecom (Canada).	Access to European market; close working relation– ship in telecoms
Dec 1988 $168 million	Intelligent networks and work stations of Computer Consoles.	Access to USA market and expansion of product range.
Dec 1988	Control of Datachecker (USA), part of National Semiconductor; instore retail systems; electronic point-of-sales technology.	Access to USA market; market position, No. 3 in the world in retail systems.
Sept 1988 £6 million	Regnecentralen (Denmark) (50–50) joint venture. Fault-tolerant systems; Unix-based.	Access to Danish market; expansion of product range.

Olivetti In 1989, the composition of Olivetti's capital was drastically modified when the US firm of AT&T handed over the 22 per cent share of

Olivetti's capital it had held since 1986 to CIR, the holding company of De Benedetti.[71] CIR thus became the leading shareholder with 40 per cent, and AT&T exchanged its Olivetti shares for shares in CIR. Olivetti will undoubtedly seek to increase its capital in order to finance further development, and CIR's involvement is likely to have a key impact as it heads up a wide range of activities which overlap significantly with Olivetti's. Most observers are convinced that there will soon be a rash of takeovers. Olivetti's shareholdings and takeovers to date cover a total of 240 companies throughout the world, including Acorn Computers (UK), Bunker Ramo (USA) and Triumph Adler (West Germany); more recent forays into the stock market in 1988 and 1989 have been aimed at moving into software and services in Italy, developing trading activities in Scandinavia and strengthening the US market position in banking automation.

Operations in Italy have included a dramatically increased sharehold-ing (from 51 per cent to 100 per cent) in the European activities of Decisions Data, and if the takeovers of Ibmaint and Ciesse in 1987 are included, it makes Olivetti one of the leading firms in Italy in the field of IBM mid-range mainframes. Olivetti has also taken a 100 per cent holding in O Group, an Italian IT services company: Olivetti already owns G4S, the sixth-largest service firm in Italy, and this takeover will further fuel its ambition to become one of the European leaders in IT services.[72] Other stock market operations in Italy which have been part of this strategy include takeovers of Delos S.p.A. (systems experts), STS S.p.A. (banking sector IT consultancy), Sikonia S.p.A. (a service and consultancy firm active in public administration) and Sistemi 90 S.r.L., and minority shareholdings in Infosistel S.p.A. and Quercia Software S.p.A.[73]

Recent Olivetti operations outside Italy start with the takeover of the Norwegian firm of Scanvest Ring in 1988; this was done with a view to stepping up the company's presence on the Scandinavian markets, and above all in Norway. The following year, Olivetti announced a takeover bid of $174 million for ISC System Corp: this firm specialises in banking automation and, with 20 per cent of the market, is No. 2 in the United States behind IBM which has 30 per cent.[74] Olivetti's ultimate aim is to amalgamate Bunker Ramo (which has 8 per cent of the market) and ISC, and thereby become No. 2 on the American bankteller automation market with a 28 per cent share. This strategy will also serve to increase Olivetti's US turnover by a substantial margin.

Philips This company is hoping to buy up the whole of its German subsidiary PKI (Philips Kommunikations Industrie) through Adelphi, which controls all of Philips's German subsidiaries and owns 70 per cent of PKI. PKI markets a number of office-based machinery, in particular Philips's own printers and telecommunications systems.[75]

Comparex   In 1988, Comparex attempted to buy the European activities of the US firm of NAS, which markets a wide range of products including Hitachi plug-compatible mainframes. The objectives were both to rationalise costs and to benefit from economies of scale by expanding the market (50 per cent of turnover in Germany); the proposed takeover may well have run into problems with Hitachi.[76]

Nokia Corp   In 1988, Nokia Corp acquired a majority shareholding in Data Division which belonged to Ericsson Information Systems, a subsidiary of the Swedish telecommunications group L. M. Ericsson. The aim was to gain access to Ericsson's IT clientele in Scandinavia, and it was felt that this was a much faster way of achieving the objective than by building up Nokia's own sales network.[77] Ericsson's IT division and Nokia's IT subsidiary have amalgamated to form Nokia Data, with Ericsson retaining 20 per cent of Nokia Data's shares.

Withdrawals from microcomputer technology

1989 saw a major defection from the European micro-computer technology sector when the Thomson–CSF group decided to pull out and concentrate on its other activities which include the High Street electronics market.

There are many obstacles facing a company attempting to break into this branch of IT: the overall quality of distribution networks is poor, there has long been a difficulty in selecting a non-IBM-compatible microprocessor, and the product is very expensive for what it achieves; Thomson–CSF are still important, though, in the field of third-party maintenance through their subsidiary, Thominfor.[78]

Early in the same year another firm withdrew from the minis market when Matra closed down Matra Datasysteme, a company which used to market Sun stations, Norsk Data and Encore Computer minis, and also manufacture specialist terminals. Matra handed over the latter work to ETC and the maintenance contracts attached to computers were sold to a French maintenance firm, but it is still in specialist IT through its work on space technology, business communications and CAD–CAM.[79]

Manufacturers' strategies for co-operation

In the view of some observers the major IT manufacturers have recently opted for fierce competition in their main (domestic) market while they simultaneously and quite deliberately work out a less frenetic strategy – and even forms of co-operation – elsewhere. The Americans and the Japanese are keen to be their own masters at home, and the Europeans are trying to dominate their own home markets and the overall European market. However, outside the geographical markets, the main companies are likely to be more adaptable when they come up against quotas, taxes and the like, and it may well be that the big firms will begin to see products and sectors of activity in the same light – that is to say, that competition on identical products will continue to be keen, but they will develop forms of co-operation when it comes to marketing complementary products or moving into new know-how.

Trading agreements   The European manufacturers who are currently going in for trading agreements in the field of microcomputer technology are mainly manufacturers of minis and micros, and they are pursuing quite different objectives from the other firms that are party to these agreements.

Any company having a product marketed by another company seeks above all to enlarge the distribution potential by gaining access to existing networks. The trouble is that, although small European micro firms like Apricot (UK), Tulip (Netherlands) and Goupil (France) are well established on their home markets, they urgently need to expand abroad: they acknowledge that the setting up of an independent distribution network takes an extremely long time, and that is why they are looking to reach trading agreements. For example, Goupil signed an agreement two years ago with the German firm of Leuwico which was already distributing Philips microcomputers, and shortly afterwards acquired a majority stake in the same firm.[80] As for Tulip, its subsidiaries are getting under way slowly but surely, but it is likely that Tulip itself is looking for a partner to facilitate access to a distribution network abroad.[81]

The present climate is one in which there is widespread acceptance of the view that urgent advances need to be made in the field of interconnectivity, and it follows that some of the trading agreements conceal different ambitions. When the contract is one between manufacturers, it means that the protagonists have come to an agreement on technical compatibility on the equipment they produce, and they will effectively be setting up a captive market for one another. The trading partner also gains from the fact that the product range will be enlarged by the inflow of complementary goods and services.

In April 1988 Olivetti signed an agreement with DEC to distribute 40,000 of its own personal computers via DEC's European commercial network. The two firms had had an agreement covering technical co-operation since the previous year and DEC will continue to specialise in minicomputers, although it seeks to be able to market more global IT solutions introducing micros made by other manufacturers in the IT networks it sells. Two manufacturers have been selected to develop this compatibility – Apple and Olivetti – and Olivetti in particular has long experience of being involved in trading agreements: for example, it markets fault-tolerant computers made by the American firm of Stratus, with which it has recently started developing Unix-based products.[82] After withdrawing its capital investment in Olivetti, AT&T remains one of Olivetti's trading partners but the relationship is now on quite different terms: Olivetti will continue to sell personal computers in the US through AT&T, but in smaller quantities than before in view of the fact that the North American firm has already signed agreements with other companies; in return, under an agreement signed in August 1989, Olivetti will market AT&T memory boards in Italy.

Another firm with a reputation for having a dynamic approach to trading agreements is Nokai Data, a subsidiary of the Finnish Nokia Group: it sells its terminals and monitors on the European markets through DEC and IBM, while in Finland it distributes Bull, Tandem and NAS products which are complementary to its own.[83]

External strategies adopted by service companies and software houses

The reasons behind mergers and takeovers: service and consultancy firms

In recent years, the service and consultancy sector has had to rely increasingly on external growth as a means of meeting strategic objectives; indeed, during 1986 and 1987 it was the opinion of most experts that external growth served to mitigate both the shortage of specialist firms and the absence of major innovations coming from the leading European firms.[84] When the big companies began to take over the smaller dynamic firms, they increasingly saw it as a way of solving these two problems: on the one hand, given the high demand for those particular skills, the shortage of software specialists sent salaries through the roof, with the result that it actually became easier to get hold of qualified staff by buying a company that already existed; on the other hand, it was often the case that the most innovative products originated in small firms, and the purchase of such companies gave the market leaders the right type of environment for further technical advances to be made. Since 1988, and particularly in 1989, there have been even more mergers and takeovers, and the reasons underlying this trend have begun to reflect the imminent setting up of the Internal Market.

Diversification It would appear that the aim of takeovers is initially to strengthen the company's basic range of goods and services, and then to broaden specific areas of expertise with a view to moving into a particular client sector later on. To take the example of systems integration, this area of expertise is partly developed in-house, but inevitably begins to become an aspect of external growth as the company struggles with the fact that it is still too small to survive; by contrast, many generalist service and consultancy firms move quickly from Management Information systems to information technology for scientific and technical purposes. It is widely accepted that one way of avoiding starting from scratch is to buy existing specialist service and consultancy firms, and examples include the following: CGI (Compagnie Générale d'Informatique) bought CR2A a firm specialising in the design and production of automated applications in 1987,[85] and has since acquired a controlling interest in L'Informatique Scientifique[86] and Technique et Production Systeme; Sema has bought Cerci[87] and in 1987 Sligos took a 53.5 per cent interest in CMG (France's third biggest company dealing in industrial IT), following that up two years later with a successful bid for 74.6 per cent;[88] finally, CGS has bought Sesa and Itmi,[89] and Dataid has bought AS&I.[90]

The trend is by no means over: service and consultancy companies like SD–Scicon and the Sema Group have announced that they intend to strengthen their base in information technology for industrial and military purposes.[91] Similarly, service firms which diversify upstream from IT services in the direction of management consultancy and strategy work often find themselves adopting external growth policies. An example of this is CGI, which now has a 51 per cent controlling interest in the management consultancy firm of Eurequip.[92] Conversely, it should be noted that there are also major management consultants like Arthur Andersen which are moving downwards from management into IT services.

A policy of diversifying by means of buying in existing expertise grants the firm a considerable breathing space during which in-house skills may be developed; it also guarantees immediate credibility in the new segments or with the new client sector. For this strategy to work, it is essential that the technological services and areas of expertise have proved themselves in the market place: this is standard practice in industrial information technology and in associated services. However, in the newer and less sharply defined areas of information technology like data communications and Electronic Data Interchange (EDI), most technical difficulties which have been brought to the surface by 1992 are being dealt with in-house or through contracts of co-operation with other firms.

It stands to reason that external diversification should be realistic (clear objectives, adequate finance and so on), but that does not in our view explain the current craze for external growth: a much broader range of pressures is forcing service companies to grow – and grow fast.

Facing up to competition The first aim of service and consultancy organisations nowadays is to win shares on the home, European and American markets so as to be in the best position to take on the competition. This competition is growing rapidly within the European Community, mainly between the largest IT service firms, and it will be sharpened still further by the increased presence in Europe of the major American firms.

An example of this trend is EDS which is a GM subsidiary and is the biggest service and consultancy company in the world: a few years ago, it attempted to buy the British firm of Logica but instead bought the IT subsidiary of the French company, Pechiney. Additionally, it is well established in Spain and has recently decided to open a teleprocessing centre in France.[93] Another example is provided by Computer Science Corp, another major American firm, which has bought CIG–Intersys: the largest company in Belgium and No. 10 in Europe, it is established on the Belgian, Luxembourg, Dutch and French markets.[94]

Another threat comes from the main manufacturers, and from IBM in particular, because they are diversifying their activities specifically in the direction of software and services. For a year and a half now, IBM has been busy acquiring holdings in software specialist firms (image processing, IT for scientific research and Unix-based networks) mainly in the United States but also in Europe; however, IBM has also been buying into service companies specialising in systems integration, thereby strengthening its interests in application software for specific commercial and industrial sectors.

It is equally true that growth opportunities in IT software and services are attracting new entrants: a very real threat to service companies now comes from the major consultancy firms, the Big Eight. Some of these companies are already active in the IT business, and they are helped in this by the fact that they have branches all over the world, to add to their redoubtable reputations and management expertise. Arthur Andersen, for instance, now occupies fourth place in the list of the top fifteen world IT services firms listed by Datamation, and the merger between Ernst & Whinney and Arthur Young turns them, too, into a major competitor. This merger will trigger others amongst the Big Eight – Deloitte, Haskins & Sells with Touche Ross, and maybe Arthur Andersen with Price Waterhouse – but this type of concentration will initially affect only their auditing activities.[95] According to *The Financial Times*, Arthur Andersen's IT expertise could be more celebrated in accountancy circles throughout Europe, than in the United States:[96] as much as one third of the turnover of Arthur Andersen's French subsidiary is thought to come from IT work,[97] Andersen's consultancy division having already established itself in the business of selling the software products that had been specially developed for clients.[98]

All these firms adopt aggressive stances, but for different reasons: the manufacturers need to restore their profit margins, the Big Eight are well along the road of developing areas of complementary expertise, and

American service and consultancy companies, having established a stranglehold on their domestic market, are now looking for pastures new. The European market is expanding apace: the prospects for 1992 are such that there are already abundant opportunities and they are forcing the main actors to take urgent strategic decisions.

Side by side with this real competition is a type of potential competition which may turn out to be more specific than other forms encountered so far. It stems from service sectors outside information technology and involves firms like Saatchi and Saatchi, Reuters and Dunn and Bradstreet: Saatchi and Saatchi, one of the world's leading marketing firms, has taken control of the Gartner Group, an American IT consultant,[99] while Reuters is making its way in the international financial services market via external growth in Europe and the United States; Reuters has also bought the Imstinet Group (in 1987) and I.P. Sharp Associates.[100]

The Japanese have no significant presence in IT services outside their own country yet. In Europe, they delegate software development and problems relating to mainframe systems integration to their distributors, who are themselves manufacturers; in other niche areas, they are coming under increasing competitive pressure from producers in South-East Asia and, like the Americans, are now obliged to increase their value added. It is for this reason that some analysts see the joint purchase in the United States of NAS by Hitachi (80 per cent) and EDS (20 per cent) as an expression of Japanese willingness to co-operate in the field of IT services.

Escaping the predators   One of the aims of rapid external growth is to make takeover bids more difficult or less attractive. Many service firms started life when the IT divisions of industrial firms or banks were turned into subsidiaries so that they were better placed to specialise in the burgeoning field, and to this day many of them, like EDS, have managed to hold on to much of their captive turnover. Others have opted to turn their independence into some sort of professional selling-point, and will go to any lengths to preserve that independence. In this context, the threat comes not only from the major customers like banks and industry but from IT manufacturers. In practice, the growth and profitability levels of software and services firms hold out considerable appeal to foreign firms which are still outside the IT sector but are keen to diversify into it, either because it could bring immediate practical advantages or because it is a financial investment in a promising sector. Examples in Germany include AEG's takeover of GEI and Thyssen AG's holding in IKOSS;[101] meanwhile, in France, banks have been investing consistently in IT services since the end of 1987.

Appendix I

Top 15 companies in 8 IT sectors

The Top 15 in Mainframes

	DTM 100 rank	Company	Mainframe revenues		% change*	Market share[†]
			1988 ($mil.)	1987 ($mil.)		
1	1	IBM	12,138.8	11,193.0	8.45	40.1
2	3	Fujitsu	4,184.9	3,318.2	26.12	13.8
3	4	NEC	4,033.1	3,082.0	30.86	13.3
4	6	Hitachi	2,507.3	1,850.4	35.50	8.3
5	28	Amdahl	1,225.2	926.2	32.28	4.0
6	5	Unisys	1,175.0	1,322.0**	(11.12)	3.9
7	11	Groupe Bull	901.0	844.0**	6.75	3.0
8	8	Siemens	683.4	695.5	(1.74)	2.3
9	22	STC	658.4	596.8	10.32	2.2
10	64	Cray Research	632.9	588.3	7.58	2.1
11	16	Control Data	465.0	510.0	(8.82)	1.5
12	25	Nihon Unisys	384.8	226.9	69.59	1.3
13	51	National Semiconductor	372.0	362.0	2.76	1.2
14	73	Comparex	239.7	133.0	80.23	0.8
15	10	NCR	218.3	200.3	8.99	0.7

*In local currency. Fujitsu's mainframe revenues were up 11.8% to ¥536.3 billion. NEC's were up 16% to ¥516.8 billion. Hitachi's were up 20.1% to ¥321.3 billion. Groupe Bull's were up 5.8% to Fr5.4 billion. Siemens' were down 4% to DM1.2 billion. STC's were up 1.4% to £370 million. Nihon Unisys' were up 50.3% to ¥49.3 billion and Comparex's were up 76.2% to DM421.0 million.
**Restated figures for 1987.
[†]Percentage share of DTM 100 mainframe revenues.

The Top 15 in Minis

DTM 100 rank		Company	Minicomputer revenues		% change*	Market share[†]
			1988 ($mil.)	1987 ($mil.)		
1	1	IBM	4,400.0	4,000.0**	10.00	18.2
2	2	Digital Equipment	3,735.6	3,248.4	15.00	15.5
3	7	Hewlett-Packard	1,500.0	1,221.0	22.85	6.2
4	37	Sun Microsystems	1,096.2	566.9**	93.37	4.5
5	13	Toshiba	1,092.1 ·	919.6	18.76	4.5
6	5	Unisys	1,080.0	1,125.0**	(4.00)	4.5
7	3	Fujitsu	991.2	804.3	23.24	4.1
8	17	Wang	912.1	909.3	0.31	3.8
9	25	Nihon Unisys	658.5	400.1	64.58	2.7
10	34	Prime	626.7	387.0	61.94	2.6
11	9	Olivetti	614.3	603.9	1.72	2.5
12	38	Tandem Computers	557.0	472.8	17.81	2.3
13	44	Mitsubishi	490.5	403.3	21.62	2.0
14	18	Nixdorf Computer	484.1	466.6	3.75	2.0
15	11	Groupe Bull	477.0	446.8**	6.76	2.0

*In local currency. Toshiba's mini revenues were up 5.2% to ¥139.9 billion. Fujitsu's were up 9.2% to ¥127 billion. Nihon Unisys' were up 45.8% to ¥84.4 billion. Olivetti's were up 2.1% to L799.6 billion. Mitsubishi's were up 7.8% to ¥62.9 billion. Nixdorf's were up 1.4% to DM850 million. Groupe Bull's were up 5.8% to Fr2.8 billion.
**Restated figures for 1987.
[†]Percentage share of minicomputer revenues.

The Top 15 in Micros

DTM 100 rank		Company	Microcomputer revenues		% change*	Market share[†]
			1988 ($mil.)	1987 ($mil.)		
1	1	IBM	7,150.0	6,500.0**	10.00	25.5
2	12	Apple	2,950.0	2,069.0	42.58	10.5
3	24	Compaq	2,065.6	1,224.0	68.76	7.4
4	9	Olivetti	1,427.5	1,176.0	21.39	5.1
5	29	Tandy	1,232.2	1,132.2	8.83	4.4
6	39	Zenith	1,220.4	936.0**	30.38	4.4
7	4	NEC	1,204.7	933.2	29.09	4.3
8	13	Toshiba	1,083.4	800.0	35.43	3.9
9	5	Unisys	1,050.0	732.0**	43.44	3.7
10	59	Amstrad	784.0	685.3**	14.40	2.8
11	7	Hewlett-Packard	670.0	499.0	34.27	2.4
12	21	AT&T	630.0	540.0	16.67	2.2
13	54	Commodore	601.1	514.3	16.88	2.1
14	3	Fujitsu	595.3	463.3	28.49	2.1
15	14	Matsushita	585.0	436.8	33.93	2.1

*In local currency. Olivetti's micro revenues were up 21.8% to L1.9 trillion. NEC's were up 14.4% to ¥154.4 billion. Toshiba's were up 20% to ¥138.8 billion. Amstrad's were up 5.1% to £440.6 million. Fujitsu's were up 13.8% to ¥76.3 billion. Matsushita's were up 18.7% to ¥75 billion.
**Restated figures for 1987.
[†]Percentage share of DTM 100 microcomputer revenues.

The Top 15 in Peripherals

DTM 100 rank		Company	Peripherals revenues		% change*	Market share[†]
			1988 ($mil.)	1987 ($mil.)		
1	1	IBM	10,700.0	9,661.0**	10.75	17.6
2	6	Hitachi	3,917.6	3,036.2	29.03	6.5
3	2	Digital Equipment	3,166.2	2,764.7	14.52	5.2
4	4	NEC	2,828.4	2,270.1	24.59	4.7
5	3	Fujitsu	2,728.5	2,164.0	26.09	4.5
6	7	Hewlett-Packard	2,250.0	1,735.0	29.68	3.7
7	10	NCR	1,872.0	1,808.4	3.52	3.1
8	20	Xerox	1,725.0	1,560.0	10.58	2.8
9	14	Matsushita	1,582.9	1,185.1	33.57	2.6
10	8	Siemens	1,566.1	1,502.3	4.25	2.6
11	15	Canon	1,382.1	878.0	57.41	2.3
12	40	Seagate Technology	1,351.0	1,075.7	25.59	2.2
13	12	Apple	1,350.0	900.0	50.00	2.2
14	23	Memorex Telex	1,339.1	681.6	96.46	2.2
15	11	Groupe Bull	1,325.0	1,241.2**	6.75	2.2

*In local currency, Hitachi's peripherals revenues were up 14.3% to ¥502 billion, NEC's were up 14.3% to ¥362.5 billion, Fujitsu's were up 11.7% to ¥349.7 billion, Matsushita's were up 18.3% to ¥202.8 billion, Siemens' were up 1.8% to DM2.7 billion, Canon's were up 39.5% to ¥177.1 billion, Memorex Telex's were up 91.7% to G2.6 billion, Groupe Bull's were up 5.8% to FF7.9 billion, Nixdorf's were flat at DM2.2 billion.
**Restated figures for 1987.
[†]Percentage share of DTM 100 peripherals revenues.

The Top 15 in Maintenance

DTM 100 rank		Company	Maintenance revenues		% change*	Market share[†]
			1988 ($mil.)	1987 ($mil.)		
1	1	IBM	7,347.0	7,691.0	(4.47)	25.7
2	2	Digital Equipment	3,882.3	3,086.8	25.77	13.6
3	5	Unisys	1,971.0	1,952.0	0.97	6.9
4	10	NCR	1,678.6	1,556.0	7.88	5.9
5	11	Groupe Bull	1,374.7	1,290.8	6.50	4.8
6	3	Fujitsu	1,006.3	799.9	25.80	3.5
7	7	Hewlett-Packard	980.0	800.0	22.50	3.4
8	8	Siemens	968.1	1,001.5	(3.33)	3.4
9	9	Olivetti	929.6	820.4	13.31	3.3
10	17	Wang	829.4	822.3	0.86	2.9
11	6	Hitachi	742.3	639.6	16.06	2.6
12	31	Prime	560.0	318.7	75.71	2.0
13	42	Data General	450.2	435.0	3.49	1.6
14	19	NV Philips	417.3	385.1	8.36	1.5
15	23	Memorex Telex	417.1	198.0	110.9	1.4

*In local currency. Groupe Bull's maintenance revenues were up 5.6% to Fr8.2 billion, Fujitsu's were up 11.5% to ¥128.9 billion, Siemens' were down 5.6% to DM1.7 billion, Olivetti's were up 13.7% to L1.2 trillion, Hitachi's were up 2.8% to ¥95.1 billion, Philips' were up 5.8% to G825 million and Memorex Telex's were up 105.6% to G824.6.
[†]Percentage share of DTM 100 maintenance revenues.

The Top 15 in Software

DTM 100 rank	Company	Software revenues		% change*	Market share†
		1988 ($mil.)	1987 ($mil.)		
1	1 IBM	7,927.0	6,836.0	15.96	38.5
2	4 NEC	890.4	676.0	31.72	4.3
3	5 Unisys	875.0	875.0**	0.00	4.2
4	2 Digital	794.6	691.1	14.98	3.9
5	55 Computer Associates	705.4	497.6	41.76	3.4
6	3 Fujitsu	676.1	515.9	31.05	3.3
7	8 Siemens	626.4	550.8	13.73	3.0
8	66 Microsoft	610.8	397.3	53.74	3.0
9	6 Hitachi	602.1	448.8	34.16	2.9
10	11 Groupe Bull	583.0	546.1**	6.76	2.8
11	7 Hewlett-Packard	500.0	415.0	20.48	2.4
12	82 Lotus	438.5	380.6**	15.21	2.1
13	90 Oracle	424.6	198.0	114.44	2.1
14	18 Nixdorf	418.6	405.8	3.15	2.0
15	9 Olivetti	414.4	347.9	19.11	2.0

*In local currency. NEC's software revenues were up 16.7% to ¥114.1 billion, Fujitsu's were up 16.1% to ¥86.6 billion, Siemens' were up 11.1% to DM1.1 billion, Hitachi's were up 18.9% to ¥77.2 billion, Nixdorf's were up 0.8% to DM735 million, Olivetti's were up 19.5% to L539.4 billion.
**Restated figures for 1987.
†Percentage share of software revenues.

The Top 15 in Services

DTM 100 rank	Company	Services revenues		% change*	Market share†
		1988 ($mil.)	1987 ($mil.)		
1	27 Electronic Data Systems	1,907.6	1,440.5	32.43	9.7
2	26 TRW	1,805.0	1,780.0	1.40	9.1
3	33 Automatic Data Processing	1,617.0	1,467.0	10.22	8.2
4	45 Computer Sciences	1,253.4	1,133.8	10.55	6.3
5	49 Arthur Andersen	1,158.5	705.9	64.12	5.9
6	16 Control Data	1,114.2	896.4	24.30	5.6
7	53 Cap Gemini	976.5	682.3	43.12	4.9
8	1 IBM	935.0	850.0	10.00	4.7
9	31 NTT	847.0	565.6	49.75	4.3
10	5 Unisys	825.0	800.0	3.13	4.2
11	43 McDonell Douglas	791.0	825.4	(4.17)	4.0
12	65 Martin Marietta	743.4	685.7	8.41	3.8
13	80 Emhart	508.9	404.8	25.72	2.6
14	68 General Electric	495.0	450.0	10.00	2.5
15	86 American Express	446.9	383.0	16.68	2.3

*In local currency. Cap Gemini's services revenues were up 41.9% to Fr5.8 billion and NTT's were up 32.7% to ¥108.5 billion.
†Percentage share of DTM 100 services revenues.

The Top 15 in Data Com

DTM 100 rank		Company	Data com revenues 1988 ($mil.)	1987 ($mil.)	% change*	Market share†
1	1	IBM	1,600.0	1,507.0	6.17	10.1
2	8	Siemens	1,338.3	1,402.1	(4.55)	8.4
3	21	AT&T	1,250.0	1,010.0	23.76	7.9
4	15	Canon	1,132.3	742.9	52.42	7.1
5	4	NEC	963.8	842.1	14.45	6.1
6	14	Matsushita	929.1	680.2	36.59	5.9
7	56	Northern Telecom	900.0	865.0	4.05	5.7
8	30	Ricoh	850.3	590.9	43.90	5.4
9	3	Fujitsu	816.7	674.4	21.10	5.2
10	13	Toshiba	762.4	615.4	23.89	4.8
11	31	Alcatel	721.9	1,039.3**	(30.54)	4.6
12	61	Motorola	565.0	528.0	7.01	3.6
13	77	Racal Electronics	491.8	488.7	0.63	3.1
14	19	NV Philips	460.3	518.3	(11.19)	2.9
15	7	Hewlett-Packard	400.0	330.0	21.21	2.5

*In local currency. Siemens' data com revenues were down 6.8% to DM2.3 billion, Canon's were up 35.1% to ¥145.1 billion, NEC's were up 1.4% to ¥123.5 billion, Matsushita's were up 21% to ¥119.1 billion, Ricoh's were up 27.5% to ¥109 billion, Fujitsu's were up 7.3% to ¥104.7 billion, Toshiba's were up 9.8% to ¥97.7 billion, Alcatel's were up 32.2% to ECU610 million, Racal's were down 7.5% to £276.4 million, Philips' were down 13.3% to G910 million.
**Restated figures for 1987.
†Percentage share of DTM 100 data com revenues.

Source: *Datamation 100*, 15 June 1989.

Appendix II

Turnover in (world) IT by principal manufacturers present in Europe, 1988 ($mn.)

	IT total	Mainframes	Minis	Micros	Peripherals
IBM	55,003	12,139*	4,400*	7,150*	10,700*
Hitachi	8,248	2,507*	82	190	3,918*
Unisys	9,100	1,175*	1,080*	1,050*	1,039
Bull	5,297	901*	477*	318	1,325*
Siemens	5,951	683*	285	313	1,566*
ICL	2,425	658*	399		814
Control Data	3,254	465*	15		1,146
Digital Eq.	12,285		3,736*		3,166*
Hewlett Pack.	6,300		1,500*	670*	2,250*
Wang	3,074		912*	220	569
Prime	1,594		624*		313
Nixdorf	3,045	131	484*	205	1,280
NCR	5,324	218*	454	388	1,872*
Philips	2,795		415	308	903
Apple	4,434			2,950*	1,350*
Compaq	2,066			2,066*	
Olivetti	5,428	119	614*	1,427*	1,000
Amstrad	842			784*	
Nokia Data	1,165	19	66	338	299

	Services			Other IT	
	Maintenance	Software	Other	Data communication	Other
IBM	7,347*	7,927*	935*	1,600*	2,805
Hitachi	742*	602*		206	
Unisys	1,971*	875*	825*	30	755
Bull	1,375*	583*	318		
Siemens	968*	626*	171	1,338*	
ICL	227	232		95	
Control Data	385	100	1,114*		29
Digital Eq.	3,882*	795*	216	225	215
Hewlett Pack.	980*	500*		400*	
Wang	829*	227	220	96	
Prime	560*	97			
Nixdorf	313	419*	34	179	
NCR	1,678*	140	419	173	
Philips	417*	184		460*	106
Apple		134			
Compaq					
Olivetti	930*	414*		233	690
Amstrad					
Nokia Data	167	60	36	58	123

*In top 15 in the world in this activity.

Source: *Datamation 100*, 15 June 1989
   Datamation 100, 1 July 1989.

Appendix III

Principal European IT firms in 1988

Rank	Firm	Country	IT turnover $mn
Manufacturers (computers and peripherals)			
1	Siemens	Germany	5,951
2	Olivetti	Italy	5,428
3	Groupe Bull	France	5,297
4	Nixdorf	Germany	3,045
5	Philips	Netherlands	2,795
6	STC/ICL	UK	2,425
7	Memorex Telex	Netherlands	2,078
8	Alcatel	France	1,716
12	Nokia	Finland	1,165
15	Amstrad	UK	842
16	Mannesmann	Germany	779
17	Comparex	Germany	614
18	Racal Electronics	UK	554
20	Norsk Data	Norway	450
IT Services (S) and leasing (L)			
9	Atlantic Computers (L)	UK	1,342
10	Inspectorate Intl (L)	Sweden	1,230
11	Société Générale (L+S)	France	1,222
13	Cap Gemini Sogeti (S)	France	976
14	Econocom (L)	Netherlands	897
19	Finsiel (S)	Italy	545
21	Sema Cap (S)	UK	375
22	SD–Scicon (S)	UK	366
23	Sligos (S)	France	343
24	Logica (S)	UK	270
25	GSI (S)	France	263

Source: *Datamation Top 25*, 1 July 1989.

References

BIPE–IFO Institut–Prometeia (1989), *Europe in 1993: Economic Outlook by Sector*, January.

BIPE–IFO Institut–Prometeia (1989), *Europe in 1994: Economic Outlook by Sector* (preliminary draft), November.

Buigues, P. (1989), *Les redéploiments stratégiques en cours dans les enterprises européennes*, CEE–DG II, II/184/89–FR.

Buigues, P. and Sananes, C. (1989), *Les enterprises et 1992*, CEE–DG II, II/60/89 – FR.

Buiges, P., Jacquemin, A. and Ilzkowitz, F. (1989), 'Concentration horizontale, fusion et politique de concurrence dans le communauté européenne, *Economie européenne*, no. 40, CEE–DG II, May.

Datamation (1987), *Datamation 100*, 15 June.

Datamation (1988), *Datamation 100*, vol. 34, no. 12, 15 June.

Datamation (1989), *Datamation 100*, vol. 35, no. 12, 15 June.

Doz, Y. L. and Pralahad, C. K. (1987), *The Multinational Mission*, New York: The Free Press, Macmillan.

Emerson, M., Aujean, M., Catinat, M., Goybet, P. and Jacquemin, A. (1988), '1992: La nouvelle économie européenne', *Economie européenne*, no. 35, CEE–DG II, March.

European Computing Services Association (ECSA) (1986), 10th Annual Survey of Computing Services in Europe.

European Computing Services Association (ECSA) (1988), 12th Annual Survey of Computing Services in Europe.

Humbert, M. (1988), 'Etude globale sur l'électronique mondial', Onudi (ed.) (version préparatoire), September.

Information Services Association (INSEA), *Guide pratique des services informatiques en Belgique*, vols I and II.

Nomura Research Institute (1988), *Investment Opportunities in Europe: 1992 and beyond*, autumn.

Porter, M. E. (1980), *Competitive Strategy*, New York: The Free Press, Macmillan.

European Commission (1988), *Research on the 'Cost of Non-Europe'*, vol. 2 (studies in the economics of integration), vol. 5 (on public procurement), and vol. 8 (on business services)

01 Informatique (1987), *Dossier spécial, Top 500*, September.

01 Informatique (1988), *Dossier spécial, Top 500*, September.

01 Informatique (1989), *Dossier spécial, Top 500*, September.

Notes

1. Estimates by A.D. Little quoted in *Datamation 100* (July 1989).
2. IDC estimates quoted in *Datamation 100* (1 July 1989).
3. Figures quoted in *Panorama of EC Industry 1990*.
4. The expressions C10, C25, etc., refer to concentration ratios showing the proportion of total output coming from the 10, 25, etc., largest firms in the industry.
5. Quoted in *Panorama of EC Industry 1990*.
6. *Panorama of EC Industry 1990*.
7. Author's calculation based on INPUT data quoted in *Panorama of EC Industry 1990*.
8. Author's calculations based on *Datamation* Top 25 of 1987 (August 1988).
9. According to Pierre Audoin Conseil, quoted in *L'Usine Nouvelle* (11 May 1989).
10. Report of the European Computing Services Association 1986.
11. Amstrad Annual Report 1987–8.
12. Profile of Compaq in *Datamation 100* (June 1989).
13. *Open Apple* magazine (1989), published by Apple.
14. *Datamation 100* (June 1988).
15. *Financial Times* (22 March 1989).

16. *Datamation 100* (July 1989).
17. Groupe Bull Annual Report 1989.
18. Article on Siemens in *Datamation* (July 1989).
19. Siemens Annual Report 1988.
20. Profile of IBM in *Datamation 100* (July 1989).
21. *Echo de la Bourse* (6 December 1989 and 18 January 1990).
22. *Echo de la Bourse* (23 February 1989).
23. *Echo de la Bourse* (20 June 1989).
24. *Le Monde Informatique* (July 1989).
25. STC Annual Report 1989.
26. Profile of Apple in *Datamation 100* (July 1989).
27. *Open Apple* magazine (1989).
28. Amstrad Annual Report 1987–8.
29. *Datamation* (1 February 1989).
30. NEC Annual Report 1989.
31. Toshiba Annual Report 1989.
32. *Agence Europe* (17–18 April 1989).
33. *Echo de la Bourse* (5 October 1989).
34. *01-Informatique* No 1044.
35. *Irish Times* (28 October 1987).
36. *Tribune de l'Expansion* (1 June 1989).
37. *Echo de la Bourse* (22 February 1989) and *Financial Times* (27 April 1989).
38. Olivetti Annual Report 1988.
39. ICL Annual Report 1986.
40. *Agence Europe* (23 February 1989).
41. *Agence Europe* (23 February 1989).
42. Nec Annual Report 1989.
43. *Agence Europe* (19 July 1989).
44. *Japan Company Handbook 1989.*
45. Canon Annual Report 1986, *Agence Europe* (20 March 1989) and *Financial Times* (14 March 1989).
46. Toshiba Annual Report 1989.
47. Groupe Bull Annual Report 1989.
48. *Financial Times* (22 March 1989).
49. *Financial Times* (23 January 1989).
50. *01-Informatique* Top 500 (September 1988).
51. *01-Informatique* Top 500 (September 1988).
52. *Financial Times* (5 April 1989).
53. *Tribune de l'expansion* (27 February 1989).
54. Profile of Finsiel in *Datamation 100* (June 1989).
55. *01-Informatique* No 1044 (1989).
56. Profile of Société Générale in *Datamation 100* (June 1989).
57. *01-Informatique* Top 500 (September 1989).
58. *L'Usine Nouvelle* (11 May 1989).
59. According to Broadview and quoted in *Business Week* (July 1988).
60. *Agence Europe* (27 October 1988).
61. European Deal Review – figures quoted in *Echo de la Bourse* (26 July and 5 December 1989).
62. *Echo de la Bourse* (3 October 1989) and *Libre Belgique* (December 1989).
63. *01-Informatique* (6 March 1989).
64. Profile of Siemens in *Datamation 100* (15 July 1989).
65. Siemens Annual Report 1988.

66. *Echo de la Bourse* (11 January 1990) and *de Standaart* (13–14 January 1990).
67. *Echo de la Bourse* (5 December 1989).
68. *01-Informatique* (6 March 1989).
69. *Echo de la Bourse* (22 January 1990).
70. *Tribune de l'Expansion* (1 March 1989).
71. *Agence Europe* (17–18 July 1989).
72. 'L'Europe du sud' in *01-Informatique* (23 January 1989).
73. Olivetti Annual Report 1988.
74. Olivetti Annual Report and *Financial Times* (9 February 1989).
75. *Agence Europe* (19 May 1989).
76. *Financial Times* (22 March 1989) and *Le Monde Informatique* (28 August 1989).
77. *Datamation 100* (15 June 1989).
78. *Echo de la Bourse* (7 February 1989).
79. *Les Echos* (7 February 1989).
80. 'Au delà de l'Europe' in *01-Informatique* (6 March 1989).
81. *Tribune de l'Expansion* (5 June 1989) and *Les Echos* (7 June 1989).
82. *Le Monde Informatique* (28 August 1989).
83. Profile of Nokia in *Datamation 100* (15 June 1989).
84. *Financial Times* (15 October 1987).
85. *Les Echos* (19 January 1988).
86. *Les Echos* (19 January 1988) and *Tribune de l'Expansion* (18 January 1989).
87. *Les Echos* (19 January 1988).
88. *Le Monde Informatique* (28 August 1989).
89. *Les Echos* (19 January 1988).
90. *Le Monde Informatique* (7 March 1988).
91. *Tribune de l'Expansion* (18 January 1989).
92. *Le Nouvel Economiste* (19 February 1988).
93. *Les Echos* (19 January 1988) and *L'Usine Nouvelle* (18 February 1988).
94. *Agence Europe* (2–3 May 1989).
95. *Echo de la Bourse* (7–8 July 1989) and *Le Monde Informatique* (28 August 1989).
96. *Financial Times* (29 June 1988).
97. *La Tribune* (3 April 1989).
98. *Financial Times* (23 January 1989).
99. *Tribune de l'Expansion* (20 June 1989).
100. *Computer Weekly* (7 January 1988).
101. *Panorama of EC Industry 1989.*

10

The chemical and pharmaceutical industries

Elisabeth de Ghellinck

The general approach to 1992

The chemical and pharmaceutical industries cover a huge span of productive and commercial activities ranging from the transformation of an aggregate of basic materials (oil or minerals) to the production of semi-finished products; these in turn will end up in a variety of industries (e.g. textiles, paper, printing, rubber, transformation of plastic, food) and finished products (e.g. medicines, hygiene products, inks, paints and varnishes, fertilisers). The sector therefore covers a diverse range of products and services, each with its particular technology and clientele.

The basic products, or commodities, have the following characteristics:

- A highly capital-intensive production process.
- Growing automation of this process – this is leading towards a fall in employment.
- Intensive use of raw materials (e.g. oil, salt, potassium) which encourages the siting of production units near ports (in the case of potassium), refineries (in the case of oil) and salt mines.
- High energy consumption (electricity, gas, coal or oil) – this encourages the siting of production units near sources of cheap energy.

For these basic products, economies of scale are important but profit margins are small. Decisions over exactly where these production units are sited are a compromise between taking advantage of economies of scale and the importance of transport costs (which already have a bearing on small profit margins).

For certain sectors, the demand in developed countries is saturated (e.g. fertilisers). Generally speaking, the technology is being acquired by many more countries and price competition is being stepped up by developing countries which control the raw materials and want to acquire market leadership for them; European producers have responded by producing in these developing countries, either on their own or in association with local firms, and by attempting to control energy costs through investing in research and in energy-saving equipment.[1]

The prospects for growth in demand in other sectors like plastics remain good, but the importance of investment linked to the dependence on oil prices leads to large fluctuations in price and profits. These diverse characteristics have encouraged the producers of the main basic products to try to control price rises in European markets (e.g. action by the European Commission in the polypropylene, low-density polyethylene, PVC and soda ash sectors).

The fine chemicals, or specialities, are distinctive products adapted to a specific market demand. They rely on heavy investment in R & D and marketing. The quantities are more limited – but growth prospects are high – and they produce a bigger profit and increased stability for the makers. An estimate of the share of base products by comparison with differentiated products is given in Table 10.1.

Organics, inorganics, artificial fibres, fertilisers and plastics constitute 51 per cent of European production, while other products mainly include pharmaceuticals, dyes, paints, detergents, perfumes and cosmetics. This distinction by product class is far from satisfactory,[2] in the sense that in sectors like paints, for example, decorative paints are characterised by standardised production; by contrast, the development in the direction of greater added value in basic chemistry tends to increase the share of differentiated products. It is estimated that the share of differentiated products in plastics is as high as a quarter. The evolution in the share of basic products is still conditioned by thoughts on how new materials will develop. The decline in demand for basic materials (e.g. chlorine, ethylene and ammonia) cannot be explained solely by slower growth since 1973–4; it is also due to their entering a phase of maturity.

Two contrasting scenarios can be posited regarding the threats of substitution hanging over basic materials:

1. Amongst all the new materials bursting on the market, some will be significantly more important. In such circumstances, competition will continue to lean heavily on the mass production of crude materials for multiple application.
2. The list of available materials will be constantly improved with specifications that are better adapted to end needs. In this case, what is critical is the ability to integrate a range of materials to a range of potential final outlets, which would imply a shift towards the quality

Table 10.1 Distribution of European chemical production according to
production and end-use markets

Product	%	End-use markets	%
Organics	19	Construction	5.7
Inorganics	8	Services	19.2
Fertilisers	7	Consumer goods	27.4
Fibres	4	Agriculture	10.3
Plastics	13	Food industry	3.1
Pharmaceuticals	15	Metal industry	6.5
Dyes	2	Mechanical engineering	2.4
Paints	4	Electrical and electronics	3.8
Detergents	4	Automotive industry	3.6
Perfumes and cosmetics	5	Textile and clothing	6.6
Others	19	Paper and printing	3.9
		Other industries	7.5

and plurality of the materials offered. It would also imply a powerful vertical integration, the sole gauge of a rigorous control of the cost and quality of a new material. The general tendency would then be for firms selling new materials to move away from specialising.

With the exception of the aeronautical industry, the future of European producers as far as new materials are concerned is handicapped by the absence of European leaders in those industries (like electronics) which stimulate the development of new materials. This reinforces the need for firms to be established in Japan and the United States if they want to be part of the development of new materials.

The chemical industry is heavily concentrated in developed countries, with Western Europe and America responsible for 60 per cent of world chemicals production. In 1987, European, American and Japanese firms made 98 per cent of the sales of the 200 major chemical companies in the world (45 per cent by European firms, 38 per cent by American and 15 per cent by Japanese),[3] and of the ten top companies judged by turnover from chemicals, seven are European and three are American. Other important producers are the countries in the Middle East, the Arabian Gulf and Eastern Europe. The two most significant developments in recent years have been the growth of petrochemical activity in Arabian Gulf countries and the entry of new industrialised countries like Korea into the field of basic chemicals.

What is most striking about the industrial structure of chemicals is that it is dominated by big multinational companies. In the area of basic chemicals this is explained by the need for massive investment in production machinery and by the huge transport costs which oblige firms to build factories locally in order to take advantage of foreign markets.

Also, multinationals are present in parachemicals and medicines because of the importance of research and development costs. Lastly, small and medium-sized firms have a moderately large role both in sectors of differentiated products and in segments of basic chemicals where their production is aimed at very specific orders.

The chemical industry is subject to considerable fluctuations because it is very sensitive to the following factors:

1. Variations in the price of oil (both a source of energy and a basic material for a whole range of chemical products).
2. The exchange rate of the dollar (the American market is of considerable importance and the price of oil is quoted in dollars).
3. A certain rigidity in supply (the production process is capital intensive).

The two oil crises had a profound effect on the chemical industry, particularly in those parts of the world that have no oil resources (e.g. Europe and Japan). Furthermore, competition in fertilisers from Eastern European countries and in petrochemicals from Arabian Gulf countries was felt very keenly in Western Europe.

The consequence was a sharp downturn in the financial results of European chemical firms in the early 1980s and a significant restructuring of certain sectors of basic chemicals. Since 1986, demand has quickly returned to its earlier levels and companies are enjoying good profits: the average rate of return of the sixteen biggest firms in 1987 was 10 per cent. This covers a huge disparity: the large chemical firms take 6 per cent on average while the chemical subsidiaries of the large oil companies take 15 per cent.

Vertical integration has favourable effects when the prices of raw materials are low and when factories are working at full capacity. The situation was, however, different between 1982 and 1985 when the prices of raw materials were high and demand weak: the chemical sectors of oil firms were in severe disarray, while the companies in the chemical industry were able to emerge from their difficulties.

The chemical industry is equally sensitive to the development of industries which use chemical products. Among the firms which use chemical products are the consumer goods industry, which absorbs 27.4 per cent of European chemical production, and the services sector which absorbs 19.2 per cent. The demand in these sectors is mainly determined by prospects of growth throughout the economy. The achievement of the Internal Market, and the potential for economic growth which it will bring about, therefore opens up favourable prospects for the European chemical industry in the medium term.

It should also be pointed out, however, that certain segments of the industry are suffering from the fact that their clients are losing competitiveness. For example, the crisis in the artificial fibres sector is linked to a serious decline in the European textile industry as it faces imports from developing countries.

The main companies in the chemical, pharmaceutical and artificial fibres sectors in Europe

Several large firms deal in all aspects of these sectors and dominate supply at world level. They are the three German firms stemming from IG-Farben (BASF, Hoechst and Bayer), ICI in Britain, Akzo in the Netherlands, Rhône-Poulenc and Elf-Aquitaine in France, Montedison in Italy and Solvay in Belgium (see Table 10.2). In each commercial area these firms are in competition both with other companies whose base activities are outside chemicals (e.g. oil, consumer goods or textiles) and with firms that specialise in a clearly defined segment.

The companies can be separated into the following groups:

- *Chemical firms* These companies operate in all sectors and normally maintain a strong presence in their basic activity (e.g. Solvay in products derived from chlorine, Bayer in dyes). Some of these firms already do operate globally. ICI is a firm with a high degree of integration ranging from oil exploration in the North Sea to manufacturing pharmaceuticals, paints and seeds; it is also noted for its 'harmonious' distribution of factories around the world, in line with the study by the consultants Nadoulek. BASF, Hoechst and Bayer are also established in many countries round the world, but concentrate most of their production and productive investment in Germany (52 per cent of Hoechst's investment in equipment and production units was placed in West Germany in 1989) and in the rest of Europe. Production and marketing are therefore largely carried out on an international level, but the technological base of these firms is still firmly concentrated in the home country. In 1989 Bayer invested 59 per cent of its R & D budget in West Germany in spite of the fact that Germany supplies no more than 22 per cent of its turnover; ICI placed 70 per cent of its R & D investment in the United Kingdom with home sales of only 24 per cent of turnover, although there are plans to transfer more resources abroad.[4]
- *Oil companies* These companies have diversified downstream by moving into basic petrochemical products (e.g. the Belgian firm of Petrofina and the Anglo-Dutch firm of Shell) or into fine chemicals (e.g. Elf-Aquitaine which has moved into pharmaceuticals with its subsidiary Sanofi). The comparative advantage which these firms enjoy lies in the control over the prices of oil by-products: the supply

Table 10.2 The top chemical firms in the world

			Turnover ($ billion) 1987	Turnover ($ billion) 1981	World position 1981
1	BASF	WG	25,636	12,211	4
2	Bayer	WG	23,664	14,977	2
3	Hoechst[1]	WG	23,545	14,928	3
4	ICI	GB	20,989	10,565	5
5	Du Pont[2]	USA	17,601[4]	15,791	1
6	Dow Chemical	USA	13,377	8,733	6
7	Ciba-Geigy	Switz	12,422	7,260	9
8	Montedison	It	11,920	5,755	15
9	Shell[2]	Neth-GB	11,707[4]	7,544	8
10	Rhône-Poulenc	Fr	10,564	6,200	12
11	Akzo	Neth	8,804	5,867	14
12	Mitsubishi Kasei[3]	Jap	7,965	3,150	26
13	Elf Aquitaine[2]	Fr	7,961	3,158	25
14	Monsanto	USA	7,639	5,894	13
15	Exxon[2]	USA	7,177[4]	8,449	7
16	Sandoz	Switz	7,075	–	–
17	Union Carbide	USA	6,914	6,581	11
18	Solvay	Belg	6,784	4,087	18
19	Roche Sapac		6,071	–	–
20	EniChem	It	5,324	–	–
21	Norsk Hydro[2]	Nor	5,266	–	–
22	DSM	Neth	5,088	4,008	19
23	Merck & Co	USA	5,061	2,930	31
24	Pfizer	USA	4,920	3,000	29
25	BP[2]	GB	4,640[4]	2,968	30
26	Showa Denko[3]	Jap	4,516	–	–
27	Grace, WR	USA	4,515	3,042	28
28	L'Air Liquide	Fr	4,413	–	–
29	Sumitomo	Jap	4,262	2,670	37

Notes: Unilever, Procter & Gamble, Henkel and Colgate have not been included in this classification although they are important chemical firms   [1]Companies owned less than 50% are excluded   [2]Only chemical activities   [3]Consolidated data   [4]Inter-firm turnover excluded

Source: *Chemical Insight* (September 1988, for 1987 turnover)

of these by-products is dictated by the demand for the main products (fuel for cars and central heating) and does not necessarily respond to the needs of the petrochemical industry. Supply of certain basic materials in petrochemicals goes through periods of overproduction and shortage. This has encouraged chemical firms to integrate upwards (e.g. ICI, BASF and Solvay),[5] although they have been known to abandon some of these arrangements after a few years.[6] In 1988, chemicals contributed for the most part to the profits of oil companies, and this has continued to influence their investment strategy: for example, chemicals represented less than 15 per cent of Shell's turnover in 1988 but contributed a third of its profits.

- *Firms operating in the consumer goods market* These organisations have been diversifying into health products (e.g. Unilever).
- *Textile firms* Some of these companies diversify upstream into the manufacture of artificial fibres (e.g. Courtaulds).
- *Firms in the paper industry* Some of these companies have diversified into the manufacture of chemical products for use in their own industry (e.g. the Finnish firm Metsa-Serva).
- *Firms which specialise in certain sectors of the chemical industry and are highly internationalised* For example, the British firms Glaxo in pharmaceuticals and MacPherson in paints, and the German firm Benckiser in detergents.
- *Firms which specialise and have a limited geographical market* These firms' market limitations may be national or even regional, and they are most often to be found in pharmaceuticals, cosmetics and inks, although some are active in basic chemicals too. In the fertilisers sector, for example, the Engrais Rosier firm has a production and marketing base that enables it to supply goods more or less to order; unlike most large companies operating worldwide and bound to a system of standardised mass production, this firm is not integrated on the supply side, preferring to scour the market for the suppliers who offer the best conditions.

Some of the major European firms have been established in the market for many years (e.g. ICI, Solvay, Akzo and the three German leaders), but others are the result of fairly recent restructuring: the Italian firm of Enimont came into being in 1989 following a regrouping of chemical activities carried out by Montedison and ENI; the restructuring of the French chemicals industry in 1982 resulted in the setting up of three giants (Rhône-Poulenc, Atochem – a subsidiary of the oil company, Elf-Acquitaine – and CDF-Chimie) and discussions are currently taking place about the possibility of grouping the activities of EMC and SNPE around these three and maybe ending up with only two major firms; the Spanish firms of Explosivos Rio Tinto and Cros both came under the control of the Kuwait Investment Office through the holding company Torras Hostensh during 1987, and were regrouped in 1989 to form a new company active in fertilisers, petrochemicals, petroleum, plastics, paints and defence.

The evolution of the strategy of chemical firms

Five major tendencies in the evolution of the strategy of chemical firms stand out, as follows:

1. A move towards products with higher added value within basic chemicals in order to be able to face up to competition in fertilisers

from Eastern European countries and in plastics from Middle Eastern countries; furthermore, by differentiating production and by establishing an atmosphere of trust with customers, they become less dependent on economic cycles by making sure of a captive market for basic products.

2. A shift in R & D practices towards production methods that save on energy and cause less pollution.

3. A move downstream, even if these sectors do not always appear more profit-making than the companies' basic activities; they do, however, ensure outlets which are stable (as in the transformation of plastic) and/or less cyclical than basic products (such as health products). This often comes about as a result of external growth. ICI has made 100 acquisitions since 1982 – 25 of them in 1985, 40 in 1986 and 30 in 1987 – and the vast majority have taken place downstream. At Solvay, plastics transformation went from 10 per cent to 20 per cent of turnover between 1963 and 1987 as a consequence of takeovers in France and Spain during the 1980s, while the health division rose from 3 per cent to 12 per cent following the takeover of Duphar in 1980. With heavy petrochemicals and commodity plastics now producing profits again, some companies might decide to put a brake on the flight into speciality chemicals, as shown by the wave of investment in commodity plastics announced in 1990 by the main suppliers striving for cost leadership. Specialities can be very profitable, but the necessary R & D costs are substantial and product lifetimes can be short.

4. Renewed concentration on core activities, a development which can be observed very clearly in American firms, particularly in the pharmaceutical sector, but is also to be found in European companies. Here are some examples:

- Bayer's withdrawal from the marketing and technology of polyethylene (they explained that they wanted to concentrate on polymers with higher added value) and halt on the production of cellulose acetate.
- BASF's decision to stop production of acrylic fibres resulted in their factory in Williamsburg being handed over to the American firm Mann Industries (they blamed cyclical problems and competition from foreign imports); they only produce nylon and rayon in the US, and this has been kept on.
- ICI's withdrawal from petrochemical activity in the United States.
- Hoechst's decision to pull out of fertilisers from 1990.
- Solvay's transfer of its bottle-making activities (30 per cent of

turnover of its subsidiary BAP) to Carnaud, the leader in the plastic packing sector.

Faced with this downstream development on the part of the chemicals giants, small and medium-sized firms have often had no alternative but to specialise in a segment where they can concentrate their resources. The German firm Benckiser put this form of concentration into practice with considerable vigour. It brought its share of detergents and hygiene products from 20 per cent of annual turnover in the mid-1960s up to 90 per cent in 1988, and geographically extended its operations at the same time (by 1988, over 90 per cent of turnover was realised outside West Germany). This double-pronged movement was achieved by means of taking over firms and also by getting rid of those divisions of the newly acquired firms that no longer had a role in their strategic portfolio. The sum of all the operations carried out since the mid-1980s consists of takeovers to a value of DM1.2 billion (compared with a turnover of DM1.4 billion in 1987) and sales amounting to DM200 million.

5. A geographic expansion by developing basic products in developing countries (in collaboration with local partners in those cases where governments insist) and products with higher added value in the United States and Japan. Establishment abroad is usually achieved by means of direct investment, but also by granting licences, by the creation of joint ventures with local partners (frequent in Japan and in those developing countries where the authorities demand it) and by buying up local firms. Further examples include BASF which spent $2.2 billion on takeovers in the United States in 1985, ICI which acquired companies in the United States during 1986–7 for $3 billion, Hoechst which spent $2.8 billion in 1986–7 on buying Celanese, and Rhône-Poulenc which laid out $1.1 billion during the same period also for acquisitions in the United States.

These trends have had a significant impact on the market for corporate control. In 1985, there were 914 takeovers worldwide, in 1986 1,359 and in 1987 1,153 (source: Chemtrak); and although it is true to say that the majority of these operations take place in the United States (836 in 1986, and 643 in 1987), they are multiplying significantly in Europe (285 takeovers in 1985, 371 in 1986 and 381 in 1987). Japanese firms rarely figure in this trend but they are changing their strategy. Pharmaceuticals and specialised chemical products are concerned in 37 per cent of these takeovers.

In view of the fact that the sector is dominated by a small number of large integrated firms, it is hardly surprising that a sizeable percentage of reorganised product portfolios and market portfolios take the form of exchanges of divisions or plants or of mutual participation between the firms. For example, in 1987 ICI bought Stauffer Chemical, an American agrochemical group, from Unilever[7] for $1,925 million; it immediately resold the specialities businesses to Akzo for $625 million, and a year later it sold the basic chemicals to Rhône-Poulenc for $522 million and various other small parts to other firms, so that, in the end, the cost of the acquisition had come down to $700 million.

This shift from bulk chemicals towards specialised products implies a shift in the chain of added value. In the traditional industry, it is standard to devote 5–8 per cent of turnover to production investment, and only 1–2 per cent to research and training; in specialities chemicals, production investment attracts much less (2–8 per cent of turnover) while research (5–15 per cent) and training (2–5 per cent) are much more important.

The likely impact of 1992

It is widely thought that this sector, with the exception of the pharmaceutical and cosmetic industries, will be little affected by the setting up of the Internal Market.[8] This view is supported by a number of factors:

1. The sector is dominated by large companies which compete for world markets, and the setting up of the Internal Market will have little effect on the competitive climate in which they operate; the European market is already their 'national' market, to quote the most recent annual report published by Bayer and BASF.
2. Given the nature of the sector's operations, the direct influence of the non-tariff barriers will be limited.

It should not be construed from this that chemicals firms will not be affected by the establishment of the Internal Market, but either the direct impact will be limited (for example, the reduction of transport costs) or it is far too uncertain to be evaluated (for example, the harmonisation of energy policy and of prices in pharmaceuticals).

Commodities

The production of these goods is dominated by a tight group of big European firms. The likely impact of 1992 seems rather limited in the short run.

Likely benefits

Transport costs have been reduced as a result of simplification of frontier administrative formalities and by liberalising road transport; this can be observed when road haulage is not carried out by the manufacturing companies, and the transport firms pass on to their customers the profits derived from integration. An important effect of this cost reduction is to increase the geographical size of the market which is served by a plant and hence to modify the optimal geographical distribution of plants. If changes do come about, they will be cautious,[9] as the impact of transport charges on total costs is low[10] and the cost of adjusting productive capacity is high.

Indeed, it is estimated that multinational firms like ICI[11] will make negligible savings in distribution and in administrative costs associated with the Single Market: such firms already boast marketing structures that cover the various European markets and look to European sources for financing.

None the less, there is one area where the establishment of the Internal Market may well lead to substantial savings and that is in the integration of the energy markets, because the share of energy consumption in the cost price of basic chemicals products is very large. National policies in the energy market vary from one country to another whether it is by means of taxation or an obligation to buy highly priced domestic products. We can therefore expect the single energy market to lead to a drop in prices as a consequence of competition amongst suppliers in the member countries. However, it is still difficult to predict exactly how these prices will fall because the protagonists have not yet started to discuss how the new energy market will work. Furthermore, there is little indication, at least in the short term, that chemicals firms will turn in large numbers to new foreign suppliers. One reason for this is that they will balance the new suppliers' attractive prices with less reliable deliveries; another is that the huge disparity between official prices which are currently charged by domestic energy distributors reveals nothing whatsoever about the effective prices which are asked of the big chemical firms.

Harmonisation of regulations should also link profits to a rationalisation of production, as long as the harmonisation is strictly observed. At present, the barriers seem to be staying up even where there has been a mutual recognition of national standards in respect of certain products (e.g. on the diameter of polyethylene tubes).[12]

One last issue concerns the customers of the producers of basic chemicals products. The growth of small and medium-sized firms has been slowed down by the fragmentation of the European internal market, and the establishment of the Single Market will enable them to achieve faster growth, something which their suppliers will benefit from as well. It should be pointed out, however, that this growth potential will vary from one firm to the next because of differences in the ranges on offer and in the choice of target customer. The markets most likely to be affected are plastics, inks and varnishes. In the meantime, the various policies of customers, national operators and European operators could well force the manufacturers of chemicals products to modify their marketing strategy away from a decentralised operation in each country towards a single centralised European one.

Likely costs

In the context of the establishment of the Internal Market, one of the anxieties faced by manufacturers of basic chemicals products is the abolition of import quotas, particularly in the fertilisers sector. To quote an ICI internal memorandum, 'it is feared that the UK market, served by an efficient distribution network and easily accessible from convenient coastal ports, could be very attractive to non-European producers.'[13] Another anxiety concerns the harmonisation of regulations relating to the protection of the environment. In a general climate of fighting industrial pollution, the chemical industry is faced with the need to modify certain production processes (e.g. the control of organic solvents in paint manufacture) and certain products themselves; this could even entail having to withdraw products which are considered to be too harmful to the environment (e.g. products containing fluorine gases which destroy the ozone layer). Any harmonisation that forced the adoption of the very strictest regulations frightens producers in those countries with a poor record of enforcing standards: they fear that they start from a disadvantageous position by comparison with those producers who have to abide by strict enforcement because they have already had to find the investment necessary for reconversion.[14]

Specialities

As far as differentiated products are concerned, the likely impact of the establishment of the internal market will probably be more important in that some of the existing markets are still reliant on national markets. In the case of pharmaceuticals and cosmetics, it has been the regulations currently in force that have confined the producers to their home markets. By contrast, in the inks, home gardening products and plastics sectors, it has been demand that has prevented the manufacturers from seeking foreign markets. Changes to the regulations open up new possibilities for companies in the health field; similarly, the impact of the unification of the Internal Market on the purchasers of specialised chemicals products will bring about major modifications to the practices of those selling them (see below – Paints and solvents and Fertilisers, agrochemicals and seeds).

Specific markets

Paints and solvents

General characteristics

Production within the European Community represents 75 per cent of all European production, two-thirds of American production and over twice Japanese production. High transport costs inevitably lead to the building of factories over a wide area, in addition to joint ventures and the granting of licences. European supply is more fragmented than in America. Because of high production costs, this leads to even smaller profit margins than in the United States.

Production is divided into two equally important segments of the market:

1. *Decorative use* Paints for decorative use are produced in considerable volume and are marketed hard to consumers. Demand is growing weakly. The market has been driven by a retailing revolution similar to the one which has transformed the grocery trade. The number of Do-It-Yourself specialist stores is shrinking and superstores' sales account nowadays for 65 per cent of all sector sales in the United Kingdom (see Table 10.3). This has transferred the decision power away from producers to retailers. Price competition has intensified and margins have tightened. Barriers to entry are considerable in that only two manufacturers succeed in selling their brands in a given supermarket alongside the retailer's own-brand products. Any expansion in a particular geographical market depends on having acquired the brand that is established there. Two firms (Akzo and ICI) have pursued active takeover policies, not only in Europe but also in North America (see Table 10.4).
2. *Industrial use* The paints for industrial use are sophisticated products which respond to an increasing specialisation in demand for more important properties than mere decoration: for example, protection from corrosion in automobile and marine markets, antifouling paints in the marine market, and ability to withstand high temperatures in the aeronautics sector. This type of demand induces suppliers to adopt a strategy of specialising in a particular area and to broaden their geographical base. The manufacturers of the products requiring the highest technology in their coatings – cans, cars, ships, aeronautics – operate globally. They therefore want global suppliers, or at least global standards of supply.

This development is illustrated by the decisions of Hoechst and the Swedish firm of Beckers to leave the decorative paint market and concentrate on industrial paints. The only way in which firms can increase

Table 10.3   UK paint and coatings market

Sector	Volume by millions of litres	Average price £/litre	Value £m	Leaders (10% and above)
Decorative–retail	158	1.57	248	ICI, Crown, Macpherson
Decorative–trade	152	1.34	204	ICI, Crown, Akzo, Macpherson
Marine	9	2.66	23	International, Jotun
Offshore	2	2.35	4	Ameron, International Hempel
Protective	15	2.18	33	Becker, Crown, Croda, Sigma
Automotive	28	1.86	52	ICI, PPG, BASF, Herberts
Vehicles refinish	27	3.34	90	Herberts, ICI, BASF
Commercial vehicles	9	2.93	25	J Mason, ICI, PPG, Croda, Herberts
Aviation	4	2.04	8	ICI, PPG, Herberts
General industrial	39	1.95	76	Trimite, ICI, International, Macpherson
Cans	20	1.38	28	ICI, BASF, International
Powder	16	1.78	28	Evode, Macpherson, International
Coil coatings	11	1.95	21	Crown, ICI, Becker Herberts, Macpherson
Agricultural	12	1.35	16	Macpherson, Croda, International
Wood	20	1.33	27	Macpherson, Granyte, Manders, Sonneborn & Rieck
Electropheretic	3	3.19	10	PPG, ICI

Source: *Financial Times*, 10 March 1989

profits[15] is by charging higher prices which involves a large number of takeovers and disposals: the most active companies over the last five years have been ICI, International Paint (a subsidiary of Courtaulds), BASF and the American firm of PPG. This has led to an increased concentration at the world level. The top ten paintmakers controlled 20 per cent of the world market in 1980; by 1987, this figure was 30 per cent. According to ICI, the ten leading manufacturers will have half of the world market in 1995 (see *Financial Times*, 10 March 1989).

Table 10.4 Acquisitions by leading companies in the paint industry

Company	Acquisition	Year	Sector
Akzo	Wyandotte (US)	1983	Automobiles
(Neth)	Levis (Belg)	1984	Decorative/Automobiles/ industrial
	Bostik (US)	1984	Aircraft
	Blundell-Permoglaze (UK)	1985	Decorative
	Sandtex (UK)	1986	Decorative
	Procolor (Sp)	1986	Decorative/industrial
	Brink Molyn (Neth)	1986	Decorative
	Ypiranga (Brazil)	1987	Decorative/industrial
	Reliance Universal (US)	1989	Wood/Plastics/Metal
BASF	Valentine (UK)	1984	Automobile refinishing
(Ger)	Inmont (US)	1985	Automobiles/Refinishing/ Can coatings
	Mobil Coatings (Neth)	1985	
	Lusol (Argentina)	1988	Can coatings Automobiles/industrial
DuPont	Ford Motor Paints (US)	1986	Automobiles
(US)			
	SFDUCO (Fr)	1988	Automobiles
	IDAS (j-v with ICI)	1988	Automobiles
Hoechst	Renault paint (Fr)	1986	Automobiles
(Ger)	Ault & Widborg (UK) part	1986	Automobiles/refinishing/ Industrial
	divested part (Ger)	1984	Decorative
	divested Berger (UK)	1987	Decorative
ICI	Holdens (UK)	1982	Can coatings
(UK)	Valentine (Fr)	1984	Decorative/refinishing
	Ault & Wiborg (UK) part	1985	Can coatings
	HGW Paints (Irl)	1985	Decorative/Refinishing/ Industrial
	Knopp (Ger)	1986	Powder coatings
	Glidden (US)	1986	Decorative/Can coatings Powder
	Bonaval (Ger)	1986	Finishing
	Attivilac (It)	1988	Can coatings
	DuPont (Sp)	1988	Powder
	Berger (Australasia)	1988	Decorative/Industrial
	IDAC (j-v with DuPont)	1988	Automobiles
	Bapco (Can)	1988	Decorative/Automobiles
International	Silap (Fr)	1982	Powder
Paint (UK)	Litoverti (Brazil)	1982	Can coatings
	Oxyplast (Australia)	1985	Powder
	Porter Paint (US)	1987	Decorative/Yacht
	Extensor (Sweden)	1987	Marine
	La Minerva (It)	1988	Powder
	Suministros (Sp)	1988	Powder
	Epiglass (NZ)	1988	Yacht/Marine
PPG	Cipisa (Sp)	1982	Automobiles
(US)	IVI (It)	1984	Automobiles/Refinishing Industrial
	Wulfing (Ger)	1984	Automobiles
	International (UK) part	1985	Automobiles

Source: *Financial Times*, 10 March 1989 (updated by the author)

Development

Between 1977 and 1987 there was a drop of 40 per cent in the number of European paint producers; the number now stands at 1,600. However, the last four years have seen an increase in large-scale takeovers and disposals, either of whole paintmakers or of part of their portfolio of products. Faced by the weakness both in demand and in margins, companies are now trying to improve their technical and geographical structures and eliminate weak points.

The impact of growing pressure on environmental issues is part of the reason for the development of new products which are less rich in organic solvents: powder coatings (containing no solvents, just pigments and resins) and water-based paints. It needs to be borne in mind that these new products demand not only heavy investment in R & D and in promotion on the part of the manufacturers, but also significant investment by users (e.g. new paint installations in the motor car sector). That customers are increasingly demanding improved quality in fact triggers higher spending on R & D (4 per cent of turnover in 1986) and promotion. Furthermore, a higher degree of specialisation of demand means firms have to keep in stock a larger and more flexible range of materials, which favours big companies. The rationalisation process can now be expected to continue, with the disappearance of small and medium-sized firms that have not specialised, thus benefiting large integrated companies.

The main organisations

The five big international chemical firms (BASF, Bayer, Hoechst, ICI and DuPont) play a decisive role in the paints and coatings sector, both as producers (BASF, Hoechst, ICI and DuPont) and as suppliers of resins, solvents, pigments and other materials used in production. Of the ten top paint producers in the world, four – ICI (No. 1 in the world), BASF and the American firm of PPG (joint No. 2), and International Paint (a Courtauld's subsidiary at No. 7) – can claim a truly global spread. Indeed, the last named built its worldwide status on the niche of marine paint where it acquired expertise in international marketing which it then applied to powder paints. These four have also been the most active in the takeover market over the last five years (see Table 10.4): in 1985 BASF bought up the tenth biggest firm in the world (the American firm of Inmont), in 1986 ICI bought the eighth biggest (the US firm of Glidden), while PPG and International Paint have built up their growth on taking over smaller companies.

When Akzo took over the American firm of Reliance Universals in 1989, it acquired a good base in the US market and simultaneously reduced its dependence on the European market; it has now climbed to third place in the world rankings. The others, like the Japanese firms of Kansai and Nippon Paint and the American company Scherwin Williams, are regional players. Small and medium-sized firms can only survive in high-technology niches (e.g. the German Grebe Group and the British firm of Beckers in the coating of sheet metal, and Sonneborn & Rieck in plastic coating) or in local markets.

The impact of 1992

The establishment of the internal market is looked upon by the big firms more as a threat than as an opportunity because they have already diversified geographically under their restructuring programmes over the last five years. They are now restructuring the firms that they have taken over on a world or European level according to the sectors in which they operate.[16] The threat looms from the stricter environment restraints that will accompany the harmonisation of regulations, particularly in the field of industrial paints; such a phenomenon could favour firms like BASF that are already confronted with restrictive national regulations.

In decorative paints, distribution firms have been regrouping at a European level and this could in turn lead to changes in the big firms' marketing strategies, with the possibility of the establishment of European brands. Small and medium-sized firms have opted for specialised technology and the Internal Market may well offer them easier opportunities for growth in a unified market, or for working together on centralised purchasing and then closer co-operation later on. Those small and medium-sized firms that have not specialised, however, will experience difficulty in fighting off price competition from the big companies.

Fertilisers, agrochemicals and seeds

General characteristics

The first distinction that needs to be drawn in this grouping of sectors is between the upstream (fertiliser production – extremely intensive in its use of capital, raw materials and energy, and producing standardised goods for sale) and the downstream (agrochemicals – more specialised, high-added-value products and highly innovative).

The *fertiliser* industry had to undergo a massive restructuring in the 1980s in order to build up its ability to compete with developing countries (which are on the point of capitalising on their huge natural resources of gas and phosphates) and with East European countries (which offer low selling prices in order to obtain foreign currency). The volume of imports in the European Community doubled between 1980 and 1987 at the same time as the value of exports fell dramatically following a supply surplus on world markets. With 15 per cent of world production, the EC is in third place after the USSR and the United States.

The fertiliser sector accounts for 7 per cent of all chemicals sales in Europe. Its difficulties are equally related to supply and demand: on the supply side, production processes are capital-intensive and continuous production is essential, whereas demand is concentrated on a period of two months; demand is exclusively agricultural and has dropped in the face of agricultural surpluses in developed countries and financial problems in developing countries. Despite restructuring programmes that have been carried out in the sector (see Table 10.5), profitability is still not satisfactory;[17] BASF, the second largest European manufacturer, is planning a reduction of 930,000 tons by 1990. According to a study by Credit Commercial,[18] the solution to the problems of the fertiliser sector involves reducing the number of producers in each country to two per country; the companies which are going to survive are those which are already well advanced in their restructuring processes and which have been able to consolidate their share of the market.

The future for the *agrochemicals* sector is no less heavily dependent on the way agricultural markets progress. Throughout the world, some forty producers are responsible for 90 per cent of the market, and there is even a tendency to concentrate even further because of the growing importance of R & D in product development. The same can be said for pesticides, a sector which is highly specialised and characterised by high added value; here, R & D plays a key role partly because organisms can sometimes develop immunity to the pesticides and partly because better environment protection standards mean that some older products can no longer be put on the market. In 1987, the investment needed to launch a new product was estimated at $30m and the development period at 5–7 years, but the impact of biotechnology on the development of new products is urging most companies to acquire a base in this science.

Table 10.5   Main takeovers in the fertilisers sector

Company	Acquisition	Year	Capacity
Kemira	Esso (Neth) part	1984	450,000 tons
(Fin)	Carbochimique (Belg)	1987	350,000 tons
	DSM Rotterdam factory	1987	350,000 tons
	UK Fertilisers	1987	400,000 tons +
	(British subsidiary of DSM)		200,000 tons
Norsk Hydro	NSM (Neth)	1982	1,300,000 tons
(Norway)	Cofaz (Fr)	1985	
DSM	Geleen	1987	Purchase of 33% held by
(Neth)			Kemira (via Carbochimique)

The main companies

Fertilisers The principal companies in the restructuring of the European fertiliser sector are the Norwegian firm Norsk Hydro and the Finnish firm Kemira. Since 1982 they have both been involved in a series of takeovers with the aim of being able to take advantage of economies of size at the level of production and of raw materials (in the case of ammonia, the optimum output is probably in the order of 2m tons per year). In addition to Norsk Hydro and Kemira, the main producers are ICI (only in the UK and in Ireland via Irish Fertilisers, a subsidiary jointly held with the Irish firm NET), BASF (in France and Germany), Orkem (in France), DSM (in the Netherlands) and Cros-ERT and Enfersa (in Spain).

Agrochemicals A series of rationalisations has taken place in the agrochemical sector in the United States, which had 30 per cent of the world market in 1986 and only 22 per cent in 1987. It was a period marked by some most striking events: DuPont's purchase of Shell Oil's pesticides interests, Rhône-Poulenc's takeover of Union Carbide's activities in this sector (at a cost of $575m) and ICI's acquisition of Stauffer Chemical (for a net price of $700m after disposals of various other activities). In 1987, the main operators on the world stage were:

Company	Agrochemicals turnover ($billions)	Market share
Bayer	2.35	13%
Ciba-Geigy	1.78	10%
ICI/Stauffer	1.4	8%
Rhône-Poulenc/ Union Carbide	1.4	8%
Monsanto	1.07	7%
DuPont/Shell	1.03	7%

The impact of 1992

Fertilisers The establishment of the internal market is likely to favour restructuring programmes in the various national fertiliser markets (e.g. the elimination of small units of production facilitating the profitability of larger firms). The unification of the energy markets could at some stage influence thinking (in an industry where energy is a decisive cost factor[19]) about where production units should be sited. Stricter environmental standards may well favour those producers who have already had to deal with even stricter national regulations. The European Community's position on external commercial policy is no less decisive a factor in the competitive pressure coming from the Arabian Gulf and Eastern Europe: current political developments in these areas must be followed very carefully.

Agrochemicals This sector encompasses a whole series of different markets. Besides all the customary factors such as the harmonisation of environmental regulations, the main thrust of the internal market will take different forms according to the characteristics of end-user markets.

Consider, for example, the home gardening sector. The big European firms dominate their home markets – ICI (Fisons) in Great Britain, Bayer and BASF in Germany and Rhône-Poulenc in France – and remain marginal elsewhere. The marketing of these products is undergoing a major review, with large-scale distribution taking over a growing share of sales at the expense of specialist retailers: in France, for example, 75 per cent of turnover comes from self-service stores. The sector will probably face growing competition as a result of the opening of the market, when European distributors adapt their strategies to the unified market.

Pharmaceuticals

The pharmaceutical sector is subdivided into two segments with very different characteristics, as follows:

1. Drugs sold on prescription (88 per cent of the market in the EC). These medicines need to be further subdivided into the following categories:

    -   ethicals: i.e. drugs based on R & D and protected by patent;
    -   out-of-patent generic products.

2. Those medicines that can be sold over the counter without prescription.

Ethicals

Two important factors tell us a lot about this market: the fragmentation of the market and worldwide expansion of competition. Fragmentation of the market has the characteristic that each product is in competition only with other products in the same clinical area, and within each area it is effectiveness that is the chief factor in determining competitive edge. Investment is so steep in both R & D and marketing that firms are compelled to specialise in a restricted number of clinical areas so as to be able to control the individual markets. No product conquers more than 1–2 per cent of the pharmaceutical market in each country and the world leader has a market share of only 4 per cent; within certain clinical areas, some firms are able to hang on to dominant positions in certain distinct sub-segments.[20]

The market is also powerfully influenced by the globalisation of competition: well over half of production worldwide comes from a small number of companies which are established in the developed world,[21] particularly in Europe and the United States, and are striving to break into Asia, especially Japan. The European Community, the United States and Japan account for 81.5 per cent of demand.

Characteristics of the sector

The role of *R & D and innovation* is of striking importance; on a world average, the share of turnover devoted to research and development is 11 per cent and in some cases approaches 15–20 per cent, compared with 4 per cent for the chemical sector as a whole. This percentage has been rising since 1980 (in the United States it has gone from 11 per cent to 16 per cent) although the number of new products appearing annually on the market (58 in 1987) has remained stable since 1964: this slowing productivity is explained by the fact that there has been an increase in R & D costs as a result of extra expenditure on clinical trials. It is worth noting that only 30 per cent of R & D costs go to research (see Table 10.6). The total cost of bringing out a new active substance, including all delays and setbacks, comes to about 75 million ecus and this sort of investment can only be turned into profit by access to the world market. Research and development can be very profitable when it works: Glaxo has moved, thanks to Zantac (42 per cent of Glaxo's turnover), from sixth to third place in the world table in 1987.

Research is capital-intensive and risky, and this will continue to keep small and medium-sized firms out of the market in the long term. However outstanding their innovations, they cannot run the risk of failure; nor can they develop a grand marketing strategy, because of the huge capital necessary for clinical trials and promoting their products to prospective prescribers – unless they fall back on licensing agreements. Stable market structures going back to the 1960s have their origin in these challenging barriers to entry; periodic clinical breakthroughs by particular firms and various mergers and takeovers lead to some mobility among the group of dominant firms.

In the future, research productivity is likely to rise, thanks to developments in bio-technology; indeed, firms that have developed out of bio-technology could be potential entrants into the pharmaceutical market as long as they are not absorbed by pharmaceutical companies (Rorer has a majority stake in Biopharmaceuticals; Hoffman-LaRoche has a collaboration agreement with Cetus and Genentech, two leading American bio-technology firms).

Table 10.6   Distribution of R & D costs in the pharmaceutical sector

Stages	Percentage of R & D costs
Synthesis and detection	17.0
Detection of biological substances	11.3
Toxicology	10.9
Metabolism and pharmacocinetics	8.2
Analysis	4.5
Effectiveness and harmful effects on humans	20.2
Active ingredients	6.4
Technology and production	10.7
Other costs	11.3

Source: Dafsa

Marketing, too, is of prime importance: the differences between the national registrations regarding authorisation to sell a given medicine, the segmentation of the market into specific clinical areas and the need to influence prescribing doctors are together throwing the sector back on to local sales forces. Companies in the sector are very keen to move quickly into a new geographical market or clinical area, and they are also seeking to grow sufficiently big to be able to support the costs and risk of innovation and the need to be established in the main developed countries. To achieve these aims, pharmaceutical firms are relying on a variety of weapons, ranging from research or marketing agreements to the granting of licences, joint ventures and mergers (see Table 10.7).

Table 10.7   Main agreements reached by pharmaceutical firms

1. *Mergers*
   Smithkline (US) – Beecham (UK)
   Dow Chemicals (US) – Marion Laboratories (US)
   Nova (Dk) – Nordisk (Dk)
2. *Joint ventures*
   Solvay (Belg) – Meiji (J): promotion of Solvay's products in Japan
   Takeda (J) – Rousel-Uclaf (Fr) – Abbot (US): R & D agreement
   Sanofi (fr) – Daiichi Seiyaku (J): reciprocal commercialisation agreement
3. *Acquisitions*
   Kodak (US) has acquired Sterling Drugs (UK)
   AHP (US) has acquired A. H. Robins (US)
   Sankyo (J) has acquired 74% of Luitpold-Werk (Ger)
   Baxter Travenol (US) has acquired Don Baxter (It) which commercialised the products
      of the American group in Italy
4. *Co-operation agreements*
   Solvay (Belg) – Theratech (US): R & D agreement
   Hoffman-La Roche (Switz) – Cetus Corp (US): worldwide co-operation in the field of
      medical diagnostics

Development

As far as *demand* goes, there is going to be fierce competition in a stagnant market. Developed countries today account for 86 per cent of demand, a percentage that has been rising since the 1970s; in certain areas, for example in the field of diagnosis, the American market alone represents 45 per cent of world demand – it is obviously essential to get established there. The average growth rate between 1982 and 1987 was 5 per cent in the United States (it was 2.5 per cent in Japan and 2.8 per cent in Europe); government pressure to cut back on health expenditure together with the development of generics will in all probability encourage this tendency in the future.

When we turn to *supply*, we see that the markets are (as a result of government pressure) generally stocked up by local production; in fact, a third of all world consumption is supplied by the local affiliates of multinational firms, the EC market being more open (both to American and to European firms) than the American or Japanese markets.[22] Establishments converting active ingredients into dosage forms are both too numerous and too unspecialised: it has been estimated that the firms that now have seven or eight establishments in Europe will probably have no more than two or three by the year 2000 (Burstall, 1988). The production of active ingredients is confined to a limited number of sites and exchanged between subsidiaries.

Research and development is normally concentrated in the firm's home country (ICI spends 70 per cent of its R & D investment in Britain) but there is sometimes government pressure to keep laboratories open in different countries in the wake of takeovers; for example, Solvay has four laboratories, in the Netherlands (Duphar), Germany (Kali), France (Sarbay-Latema) and the USA (Reid Howell). There is also a trend towards decentralising R & D, particularly in the field of bio-technology where the Japanese and Americans have taken a lead.[23] The big European firms devote a much larger proportion of turnover to R & D than the major American or Japanese companies and average annual growth of these costs is also higher, but this research seems to be less effective by comparison with Japanese research, which has been responsible for 15 per cent of pharmaceutical innovations since the 1980s and 20 per cent of bio-technological innovations.

Japanese pharmaceutical firms faced with a stagnation in their home market may well rethink their strategy: up to now, they have largely relied upon import substitution and the penetration of foreign markets by various means like licensing, research agreements and the setting up of joint ventures. When seeking to penetrate foreign markets in the future, they are now more likely to adopt a more aggressive strategy. Ajinomoto, for example, bought the Belgian firm of Omnichem in 1988 and in the same year had a total turnover of FB146 billion: its aim for the year 2000 is to have total foreign sales of FB123 billion. In January 1990, Sankyo, Japan's second largest pharmaceuticals company, bought a 74 per cent interest in a West German drugs maker, Luitpold-Werk, and intends to use it as a springboard for selling its own products in Europe.

Generics

Generics do share one major characteristic with drugs protected by patent: as they are sold on prescription, they have to get the same authorisation to be put on the market. On the other hand, they do not rest on huge research investments because they are copies of medicines that no longer enjoy the protection of a patent. It follows that the firm producing them does not need to be large; indeed, most pure generic manufacturers are small and medium-sized firms, and they compete mainly in price. Barriers to entry into this sector are in the field of distribution, with pharmacists refusing to stock more than a limited number of varieties of a given product (characteristically, the brand product and a maximum of two other versions).

Seventy per cent of out-of-patent products are made by companies other than the inventor that manufacture ethical pharmaceuticals and are sold under different brand names. Their brand names and reputation as ethical manufacturers enable them to break down distribution barriers more easily than a small or medium-sized firm could. Price competition is therefore less fierce, although marketing counts for more than in the ethical sector. Firms like Glaxo and Smithkline which thought that research was one of their major assets have sold off their generic interests; other firms like Rhône-Poulenc, Fisons and Hoechst have invested by means of takeovers.

The extent to which generics penetrate a market depends heavily on the prices charged in that market and on how much encouragement the authorities have given them: penetration is 8 per cent in Britain and 10 per cent in Germany and the Netherlands, compared with 20–25 per cent in the United States and Japan – and almost none at all in Spain. The growth in sales of generic products is likely to be particularly fast in Germany, the Netherlands and Britain, all countries where drugs are expensive and whose governments have said they wish to cut back on health expenditure.

The main actors

There are several firms co-existing in the sector but which are different both to the extent they have entered international markets and to the extent they have specialised in pharmaceuticals and health in general.

Several firms like Sandoz, Pfizer, Abbot and Roche started off as chemical firms but have become essentially pharmaceutical producers (see Table 10.8). By contrast, there is sometimes a very high rate of diversification among pharmaceutical firms outside prescription drugs and over-the-counter products (see Table 10.9). However, in the last few years some firms, particularly in the United States, have reconsidered their strategy of diversification and have decided to concentrate on pharmaceuticals or more broadly on health matters, like lightweight medical instruments, animal nutrition, diagnosis and food additives.

The impact of 1992

The two most important strategic issues for firms facing up to 1992 are the admission of new products into the market and pricing policies.

The *registration systems* for authorising the introduction of medicines into the market are being harmonised. The purpose is to reduce the time and cost spent on developing new medicines, and thereby to prolong effectively the period of patent protection and accelerate the recovery of capital invested. These factors are likely to give further encouragement to innovate. Two options have been considered: a centralised authorisation system or a systematic use of the principle of mutual recognition introduced in the multistate procedure (Directive 83/570/EEC).

Given the problems encountered in setting up the mutual recognition system[24] and the difficulty in getting a centralised system off the ground quickly, the Commission has gone for an optional system whereby the

Table 10.8 Proportion of pharmaceuticals in turnover of chemical companies, 1986

Companies	Turnover US$mn.	% Pharmaceuticals
Bayer	18,762	14.9
Hoechst	17,503	17.4
ICI	14,858	10.3
Montedison	9,437	.6.1
Ciba-Geigy	8,872	32.1
Rhône-Poulenc	8,157	20.3
Monsanto	6,879	9.7
Akzo	6,374	14.3
Solvay	4,841	9.0
Sandoz	4,649	46.4
Roche	4,349	40.7
American Cyanamid	3,816	25.0
Schering	2,147	45.4
E. Merck	1,469	38.3
Fisons	1,030	35.5

Source: Dafsa

Table 10.9   Diversification of leading pharmaceutical firms, 1986

Firms	% of turnover in non-pharmaceuticals
Merck (US)	16.7
American Home Products (US)	40.5
Glaxo (UK)	0.0
Bristol-Meyers (US)	48.3
Pfizer (US)	50.0
Eli Lilly (US)	43.0
Smithkline Beckman (US)	44.8
Abbott (US)	46.0
Warner Lambert (US)	34.2
Takeda (J)	43.3
Upjohn (US)	26.5
Rhône-Poulenc Santé (Fr)	0.0[1]
Schering Plough (US)	35.1
Squibb (US)	14.8
Sankyo (J)	15.1
Sterling Drug (US)	29.4
Wellcome (UK)	15.4
Boehringer Ingelheim (Ger)	14.2
Sanofi (Fr)	44.7
Fujisawa (J)	8.3
Syntex (US)	18.1
Shionogi (J)	28.0
Rorer (US)	0.0
Roussel-Uclaf (Fr)	46.3
Astra (Swed)	2.9
AH Robbins (US)	14.4
Erbamont (It)	7.4

Note: [1] Health products subsidiary of Rhône-Poulenc

Source: Dafsa

firm can choose between a national authorisation scheme (with the possibility of extending it to other markets through the multistate procedure) and a European-wide authorisation system (something that already applies to bio-technology).

The importance of this choice, according to P. Claessens of the Association Belge de l'Industrie du Medicament (Belgian Association of Medicine Manufacturers), is that small and medium-sized firms would find the cost of a Europe-wide system prohibitive as the most likely outcome is a combination of the most severe elements of each national agency. What is more, such a scheme would open up the twelve markets equally, but if a product were to be rejected all twelve markets would be automatically closed.

The view of F. Sauer, DGIII, is that the centralised system which would facilitate the entry on the market of products seeking the world market would cover no more than fifteen bio-technological products and five high-technology specialities a year. According to this view, another 50 chemical products and 300 other products looking for the European market could choose between the centralised procedure and the decentralised one, while a thousand or so products aiming at local or regional markets would be covered by national regulations.

Only a tiny fraction of products currently on the market would therefore be affected by changes to the authorisation procedures. On the other hand, new chemical products should benefit from a reduction in the amount of time and money devoted to development which either a centralised procedure or an efficient mutual recognition procedure could offer. The firms most concerned by this are the most innovative, that is to say American, Japanese, German, British and Swiss firms. Small and medium-sized firms, though, will benefit from being able to make use of the multistate procedure more easily. In consequence, there will be more agreements to co-operate on marketing strategies aimed at combining available sales resources.

Pricing policies are directly dealt with by the Directive on transparency of pharmaceutical pricing. The objective of this Directive is to ensure that all national measures to control the price of pharmaceutical products, manufacturers' profits and access to reimbursement systems of health insurance operate on a fair and transparent basis with objective and verifiable criteria. A fundamental harmonisation of national systems seems to be unrealistic because of the huge diversity of control systems operated by member states, and has therefore not been proposed.

Unlike the existing regulations which explicitly or implicitly look forward to a link between price or price–cost margin and the intensity of indigenous activity, the objective of the Directive is to ensure that a given firm's European dimension is properly recognised, so that production can be rationalised with a view to decreasing the number (and increasing the degree of specialisation) of establishments formulating active ingredients into dosage forms.

As far as price levels are concerned, the BEUC study[25] shows that, in the case of 51 per cent of the 125 medicines looked at, the price in the most expensive country was 2–5 times higher than in the cheapest country. The countries with the highest prices are Germany, the Netherlands and Denmark, while the cheapest medicines are to be found in Greece, Spain and Portugal although, given the level of development and importance of its pharmaceutical industry, France, too, has low prices.

Changes to German law covering the reimbursement for medicines would appear to be an important factor in price convergence. The Health Reform Act which came into effect in the late summer of 1989 establishes the progressive introduction of a system of a maximum reimbursement amount fixed for various therapeutical classes of drugs having the same active ingredients. Experience shows that the producers of ethical drugs reacted to this new system by lowering their prices when the fixed amounts become effective to the latter's level. The spirit of the German legislation could well be extended to other countries[26] given that many governments are seeking to reduce health costs.

This overall drop in European prices may handicap European R & D, as research and development in the pharmaceutical sector is financed almost exclusively from own proceeds. Europe as a research site can only survive in competition with the United States and Japan – where pharmaceutical prices are remaining high – if the ability to carry on expensive research, which is linked to the firms' profitability, is fostered. In this context, discussions about an extension of the length of patent protection for medicinal products are of vital importance.

In practice, the large firms in the EC do not expect that the impact of 1992 will be so very great in the short term, because it is their view that the transparency and convergence of prices are riding on the backs of a harmonisation of social security systems. Foreign firms, however, seem to be responding by buying up the companies which were responsible for the production and marketing of their products in Europe; here are some examples:

- The American firm of Baxter Travenol has bought the Italian firm which used to exploit its brand rights in Italy and distributed its products there, and has merged two of its subsidiaries in Germany.
- Dow Chemicals has increased its share in the Italian firm of Hammer from 49 per cent to 100 per cent.
- Rorer has now bought up from Rhône-Poulenc, Pharmindustrie, which used to work exclusively for Rorer.
- Ciba-Geigy is rationalising its production units in the EC and, according to a company representative, this has led to the closure of a factory in Lyons.

Large firms also think that the integration process will not impact a lot on product development or marketing because advice and information available locally are more useful and clinical tests can be carried out more easily through a local contact (see an evaluation of the benefits expected from the Smithkline-Beecham merger by P. Marsh in *The Financial Times* of 11 April 1989).

In addition to a restructuring of activities by American and Swiss firms, the sector is spreading into southern European markets through takeovers or partnerships on the part of EC firms, American firms or firms from other European countries, including those from northern Europe (e.g. Norway and Sweden); there is also an increase in the number of co-operation agreements between Japanese and EC companies.

Over-the-counter products

Medicines available over the counter without prescription accounted for about 12 per cent of the market of the twelve countries of the EC in 1984, but it is difficult to pin down the real importance of this segment of the market because regulations dealing with prescriptions and distribution circuits vary between one country and the next. The supply side is undertaken by the subsidiaries of large companies and by small and medium-sized firms, many of which produce specialised products of limited local or regional interest (this is particularly prevalent in France).

Product registration procedures are similar to those applied to medicines sold on prescription, and their harmonisation should have the same beneficial effect for large firms and for the small and medium-sized firms selling truly innovative products. Those small firms whose products respond mainly to cultural consumption habits could well find that the Single Market makes little difference to them.[27]

Unlike special pharmaceutical products which are only sold on prescription, over-the-counter medicines are bought directly by the consumer; marketing is therefore fundamentally different, and advertising plays a decisive role. Changes to the distribution system (the French supermarket chain – Centres Leclerc – is fighting to obtain the right to sell pharmaceutical products) and the harmonisation of regulations dealing with publicity should sharpen price competition and encourage firms to step up marketing investment.

It is already possible to see the entry of new firms – or a tougher position being taken by old firms – which have no background in chemicals but which do have marketing expertise. For example:

- Kodak has ousted Hoffman LaRoche in its purchase of Sterling Drugs, and has taken over Pharma Investi in Spain.
- Unilever has taken over Glyco Yberica, a Spanish manufacturer of raw materials for the pharmaceutical industry, and has moved into the marketing of pregnancy tests.

However, there have also been some pharmaceutical firms that have withdrawn from the market producing over-the-counter medicines because they felt their expertise lay in research and development and not in marketing. Examples include the following:

- Glaxo has disposed of Evans Medicals and Farley Health Food.
- Merck has sold its subsidiary Merck Consumer Pharmaceuticals to Johnson & Johnson.

- ICI is negotiating with Ciba-Geigy over the disposal of its subsidiary Care Laboratories; in October 1989, it sold its rights on various products sold without prescription in the United States to the Johnson & Johnson–Merck Consumer Pharmaceuticals group.
- Hoechst has sold its Optrex division to Boots.

Some pharmaceuticals firms have, by contrast, been established in this market for a long time, or else are seeking to develop by acquisition; Bayer, the Aspirin leader, is one of the main organisations in the over-the-counter market; Ciba-Geigy and Sandoz (both new entrants) have expanded by means of takeovers; and Rhône-Poulenc Santé (the Health division of Rhône-Poulenc) has taken over the pain-killer activities of the Monsanto group and aims to become world leader in this field.

The impact of 1992

This will depend on the harmonisation of the registration procedures and of regulations pertaining to publicity. It will also be affected by changes to distribution systems and the extension of price competition. This could lead to an acceleration of rationalisation processes (particularly in France) and increased concentration – especially if marketing is in the ascendant. Demand could also go up and the range of products on offer could widen, but only if price competition proceeds and there is harmonised access to the various national markets.

Perfumes and cosmetics

Characteristics of the market

This is a stable sector which has experienced an annual growth in real terms of 4 per cent, the market of the twelve EC countries (12 billion ecus in 1986) being marginally bigger than the American market (11.8 billion ecus) and twice the size of the Japanese market (6.1 billion ecus). Within the European Community, supply in high-revenue countries is in the hands of a small number of large firms, whereas it is divided amongst a large number of small and medium-sized firms in low-revenue countries.

Only those Mediterranean countries that joined the Community late have a procedure for authorising the marketing of perfumes and cosmetics; for the most part, these authorisations are granted, but they do delay the arrival of goods on the market by several months. Systems and types of distribution vary from country to country because the structures (and the customs) are quite different: in some countries, the products are sold in big stores (although not much in Germany or Mediterranean countries where there is still little large-scale distribution), in others, by specialist dealers like hairdressers and small operators in perfume retail, and in yet other countries they are on sale in pharmacies. Clearly, marketing is of paramount importance.

Development

The perfumes and cosmetics sector is underpinned by two key trends, developments in marketing and in health. In addition to the ever increasing importance of marketing, new firms are entering the market, together with older-established firms which are in the process of strengthening their positions: they come from the soap and detergent sector (as a result of takeovers), and they are moving into perfumes and cosmetics in order to complement their mass-market product portfolios with high-added-value products. For example, Unilever bought Cheeseborough-Pond, failed in its attempt to take over Fabergé, but did succeed in buying up Rimmel International, Chicogo and 90 per cent of Glyco Iberica (a Spanish producer of raw materials for pharmaceuticals and cosmetics); it also hopes to take over Beecham's interests in this field.

Developments in cosmetics have brought it into the realms of skin care, and thereby placed firms in this segment of the industry at the frontier between pharmaceuticals and cosmetics: L'Oreal, a French leader, has a pharmaceutical subsidiary, Synthelabo, which bought up the Roche-Posée laboratories; the French firm, Sanofi, a subsidiary of Elf-Aquitaine, is now established in pharmacy (40 per cent of turnover) and in perfumes and beauty products (31.6 per cent of turnover).

New regulations dealing with product quality and authorisation to put goods on the market will affect perfumes and cosmetics in the same sort of way as they will affect over-the-counter medicines: they are likely to lead to a substantial increase in foreign trade.

The main companies and the impact of 1992

The main companies in this market are divided into three groups:

1. The big multinational firms (Unilever, Henkel, L'Oreal and Evans) whose affairs are already conducted on an international basis and for whom the establishment of the Internal Market will bring but minor modifications (for example, to transport costs). For around fifteen years, they have been improving their concentration of production capacity, to the point that they are now in a position to exploit economies of scale in both production and R & D (e.g. a laboratory specialising in hair products in one place, another specialising in skin products in another).

2. Medium-sized firms which usually have only one production unit in
    the EC (probably in France or Germany), but whose business is
    decidedly international.
3. Local manufacturers or importers, characteristically small or
    medium-sized firms, who have more to fear from the unification of
    the market because increased competition could put their survival in
    doubt.

During the 1970s, a number of pharmaceutical firms bought companies
that manufactured cosmetics since they intended to extend their R & D in
that direction; during the 1980s, their policy of refocusing has led some of
them to sell off their cosmetics subsidiaries. Takeovers that took place
between January and July 1989 demonstrate how the sector is growing
more and more internationalised. Betrix Cosmetics (Germany) bought
by Revlon (US); Goldwell (Germany) bought by Kao (Japan); and
Parfums Charles Jourdan (France) bought by 4711-Gruppe (Germany).

Conclusion

The chemical industry accounts for 10 per cent of the added value of all
European manufacturing industry. The firms in it are very well established on the world stage: of the ten most important firms in the world (on
the basis of 1987 turnover in chemicals), seven are European and three
are American.

The group of sectors dealt with in this chapter start with the
transformation of a wide range of basic materials (oil and minerals) and
end with the production of finished and semi-finished goods. These come
under two headings:

1. *Commodities*   Mass-produced goods with small profit margins –
    here, economies of scale play a strategic role, investment is large, the
    manufacturing firms are big and the market concentration is relative-
    ly high.
2. *Speciality chemicals*   Niche products – here, R & D and marketing
    are the decisive factors, and small and medium-sized specialist firms
    operate in the same arenas as the major chemical giants.

The share between these two groups of products at the moment is more or
less even, but the general movement towards a higher proportion of
specialities is influenced by the development of new materials and by the
relative profits prospects in these two groups.

The principal tendencies in the strategies of the large chemical firms are
as follows:

●   Development towards products with higher added value.

- Increased emphasis downstream.
- Concentration on a more restricted number of activities.
- Expansion into developing countries for basic products, and into the USA and Japan for goods with higher added value.

The result has been a period of intense activity in the market for corporate control. Since the late 1970s, there has been an unending cycle of mergers, takeovers, R & D and marketing co-operation agreements, and exchanges of shares, divisions and equipment, but it is difficult to see which of these activities have taken place in response to setting up of the Single Market in 1992.

Surveys suggest that it is not felt that the chemical sector will be greatly affected by the establishment of an Internal Market, with the exception of the pharmaceuticals and cosmetics. This view might be explained thus: the establishment of the internal market will not substantially change the competitive environment of the large firms because they are already involved in competition worldwide and the European market is already more like their 'national' market (this is how Bayer and BASF see things, according to annual reports). As for firms in sectors which are hamstrung by statutes which restrict their national markets, there is a feeling that harmonisation will not have any effect for several years and therefore the protagonists do not need to have any worries in the short term.

None the less, there are undeniably some factors connected with the setting up of the Internal Market which will have an impact on company strategies.

In the case of *commodities*, the integration of the energy markets could lead to sharper competition among suppliers and harmonisation of standards could enable production to be further rationalised. The effect of the Single Market on some of the downstream markets could encourage some manufacturers to modify their marketing strategies away from a country-by-country organisation and more in the direction of a product-by-product European organisation. Meanwhile, the development of the external commercial policy (e.g. the abolition of national import quotas and anti-dumping actions) must be giving the leading chemicals manufacturers grounds for anxiety. Similarly, harmonisation of regulations dealing with environment is fuelling the fears of producers in the most lax countries that they are suffering from a disadvantage compared with their competitors sited in markets with strict regulations.

As for *specialities*, changes in the regulatory climate open up new perspectives for firms in the health field. Harmonisation of registration procedures and transparency of price-fixing procedures should facilitate some rationalising in establishments converting active ingredients into dosage forms and improved productivity in research. Furthermore, price convergence could encourage the transfer of production units to countries with lower production costs.

Strategic movements recorded in 1989 suggest only an increase in the number of American firms (frequently as a consequence of taking over production units and the marketing of their products) and of firms from northern Europe, together with a decided interest on the part of European manufacturers in the Mediterranean countries. The European giants seem much more worried about the need to get established in the United States and Japan than in the effects of the Single Market. Stronger competition from generics, and the drop in pharmaceutical prices which might follow this, pose the problems of the profitability of R & D investments and of a disadvantage which European producers would face against American and Japanese manufacturers. In this context, the discussions about the creation of a supplementary protection certificate for medicinal products assume increasing importance. The impact of the Internal Market on consumers of specialities will, in turn, cause the suppliers to adapt themselves in ways similar to those followed by the producers of commodities.

Notes

1. The Finnish firm of Kemira Oy which bought Carbochimique (a fertilisers subsidiary of Société Générale de Belgique) invested FB 4.5 billion in it with several objectives in mind, including the modernisation of the engineering used in the production of nitric acid.
2. According to an article in *La Tribune* of 15 March 1989, 'commodities' in the broad sense accounted for 61 per cent of the activities of the major chemical firms in 1970 and 'specialities' 39 per cent. By 1985 the percentages had moved to 53 per cent and 47 per cent respectively.
3. 'L'Industrie Chimique Français dans la perspective de 1992', Commissariat Général du Plan (June 1989), p. 2.
4. A new laboratory has been set up in Arizona to look at advanced materials (an investment of $20 million) and in Japan to study advanced materials and electronics (an investment of $30 million).
5. In its most recent annual report, Bayer acknowledges the importance of captive production in view of the acute shortage of ethylene in 1989.
6. An example of withdrawal includes that of Solvay and ICI from the American firm CCPC. In exchange, Solvay got a contract which guarantees the supply of ethylene to its American subsidiary until 1992.
7. In 1985 Unilever had itself taken it over at the time it bought Cheeseborough-Pond for $1.25 billion, and has resold the seeds subsidiary to Sandoz.
8. See the results of polls of firms concerning the expected effect of the establishment of the Internal Market.
9. Based on an interview with a Solvay representative.
10. ICI internal memorandum on the implications for 1992.
11. *ibid.*
12. According to Petrofina representatives.
13. ICI internal memorandum, *op. cit.*

14. As part of a move to anticipate the likely introduction of tougher European anti-pollution regulations, ICI raised its own environmental standards (*Financial Times*, 21 February 1989).
15. The rate of profit over turnover of International Paint (a subsidiary of Courtaulds) is one of the best in the paint industry: it was 5.6 per cent in 1987.
16. ICI has regrouped its activities in can coatings (i.e. Holden, Edward Marsden, Wiederhold and Attivilac).
17. In 1986 agriculture contributed 17 per cent to ICI's turnover but only 2 per cent of its profits.
18. Quoted in ECN Special Report (13 June 1988).
19. In 1988 Carbochimique found that natural gas accounted for 86 per cent of the cost price of ammonia; in some countries (for example, the Netherlands) home producers benefited in the 1980s by anything up to a 27 per cent reduction.
20. In the treatment of cardiovascular disease (18.1 per cent of the market in all countries with market economies) there is a sub-class of treatments of hypertension (45 per cent of cardiovascular treatment, 8.5 per cent of the total market) which is dominated by approximately ten firms, all of which figure in the three main categories of products: *beta blockers* – 70 per cent of sales constituted by three products (sold by Ciba-Geigy Astra and Fujisawa, ICI and AHP, and ICI); *calcium antagonists* – 70 per cent of sales accounted for by four products (manufactured by Bayer and Takeda, Marion Laboratories, Pfizer and Yamanouchi); *ECA inhibitors* – a recent type of molecule, sold exclusively by Squibb, Merck, and Sankyo.
21. According to Scrip, 50 firms account for 50 per cent of world production, 150 firms for 75 per cent.
22. The penetration of foreign firms into the French pharmaceutical market during 1986 was 46.9 per cent; of these firms, 47 per cent were American.
23. Regulatory obstacles which are encountered in certain countries (e.g. by Hoechst in Germany) are slowing down the development of activities based on bio-technology in these countries.
24. The vice-president of Astra (Sweden) is of the view that not a single product has benefited from the mutual recognition procedure without an objection. This supports the opinions of a Ciba-Geigy representative and the head of the pharmaceutical division of Hoechst that the system has only worked two or three times in West Germany (*Financial Times*, 6 November 1989). According to F. Sauer in a CEPS document dated 3 November 1989, the European Commission acknowledges that there are problems with the working of the mutual recognition procedure. Proposals to improve the efficiency of the multistate are: to render the opinion of the advisory committee binding and to enforce the delays at the various stages of the procedure.
25. 'Drug prices and drug legislation in Europe', BEUC/112/89 (March 1989).
26. This system was already under discussion in 1988 in the Netherlands under the name 'ijkprijsvergoeding'.
27. *The Cost of Non-Europe in the Pharmaceutical Industry*, a study produced by the Economists' Advisory Group, in *Research on 'The Cost of Non-Europe'* (European Commission, 1988), vol. 15.

11

The steel and metal industry

Gernot Klepper

Introduction

This chapter analyses strategies of firms in the metal sector. The statistics distinguish two industry groups:

1. The production and preliminary processing of metals (NACE 22), hereafter simply called *the steel industry*.
2. The manufacturing of metal articles – except for mechanical, electrical and instrument engineering and vehicles (NACE 31), called, for simplicity, *the metal industry*.

Whereas the steel industry covers a group of companies with a relatively homogeneous set of activities, the metal industry as defined by the statistical nomenclatures covers a diverse set of firms. Companies in the different branches of the metal industry seem to have little more in common than the metal input. Companies in the metal industry are further classified as follows:

- Foundries (NACE 311).
- Forging; drop forging, closed die forging, pressing and stamping (NACE 312).
- Secondary transformation, treatment and coating of metals (NACE 313).
- Manufacture of structural metal products (including integrated assembly and installation) (NACE 314).
- Boilermaking, manufacture of reservoirs, tanks and other sheet-metal containers (NACE 315).
- Manufacture of tools and finished metal goods, except electrical equipment (NACE 316) (e.g. heating appliances, metal furniture).

● Other metal workshops not elsewhere specified.

The structure of the industries under consideration is shown in the upper branch of Figure 11.1 while the industries using metal are shown in the lower branch. The first three metal industries are still relatively similar to the steel industries in that they perform additional processing of steel. In the remaining industries the use of metal as a primary input is substantially reduced. They also differ widely with respect to the markets in which they sell.

In many cases there are only a few links between the steel industry and the metal industries, take the domestic heating and kitchen appliances industry, or the steel furniture industry, for example. In other cases steel companies have diversified into the manufacture of metal articles. But this diversification is not confined to activities under the statistical heading of NACE 31 and covers most areas with a heavy metal content.

In a sense NACE groups 314 to 319 are a conglomerate of industries which do not fit into other two-digit industries. It will become apparent as this chapter develops that these industries often have little in common with the core of the steel and metal industry.

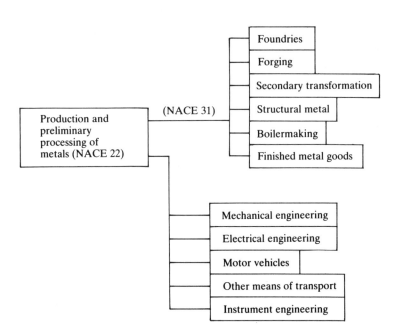

Figure 11.1 The steel and metal sector

Industry structure

Determination of the industry structure in steel and metals is made difficult by the fact that this industry is not well demarcated by technological or market characteristics. Large firms in the industry are quite active in other sectors, like shipbuilding and production of machinery. At the same time, there are quite a few firms which have some of their activities in the steel and metal sector, but their main business is in other sectors. This is especially true for companies specialising in the production and processing of aluminium. Aluminium is an important input in the production of the sectors 314 and 319, hence quite a few aluminium firms can influence the allocation in these markets.

The main players in the steel and metal industry are large conglomerates with widespread activities. The list of the largest steel and metal firms in the EC shown in Table 11 includes firms which often have only a minor part of their turnover in the industry under study. In terms of the sheer size of steel and metal activities this list may be misleading. Although large conglomerates have a strong financial basis due to their diversified structure, they may not, however, dominate the market when their steel and/or metal activities are relatively small.

Most companies have in common a concentration on raw materials of all sorts or on metals and metal products. Traditional iron and steel firms and traditional metal producing firms do not constitute the largest firms in the market any more. Furthermore, there are specific markets – especially in the metal processing sector – which are served by a different set of firms with a structure quite different to that of the large conglomerates.

Production of iron and steel

The basic industry in the metal sector is the iron and steel industry. It was the first industry which was subject to a European integration agreement, the ECSC in 1952. The industry is highly concentrated. A small number of large integrated companies coexist with smaller companies which specialise in certain activities.

The integration firms account for about 70 per cent of EC production of iron and steel. They belong to the largest iron and steel producers worldwide. Thyssen, Usinor-Sacilor, and Krupp belong to the top five companies (see Figure 11.2). Through the acquisition of one British and two German foundries, Thyssen has, in the mean time, also become the largest European company in the foundries sector. It will also buy Otto Wolff AG, another steel company specialising in special steels, trading, and mechanical engineering. Salzgitter, which has been a state-owned

Table 11.1   The fifteen largest steel and metal companies in the EC, 1987

Rank	Company	Country	Turnover (mn. FF)	Major activities
1	IRI	I	247,755	Diversified conglomerate
2	Thyssen	GER	88,812	Trading services (38%) Raw steel (27%) Capital goods (25%) Special steel (10%)
3	Usinor Salicor	F	67,114	Steel products (52%) Trading services (18%) Special steels (11%)
4	Metallgesellschaft	GER	44,587	Non-iron raw materials (65%) Processing (13%)
5	RTZ Corporation	UK	41,415	Engineering products (24%) Specialty minerals and chemicals (17%) Steel (9%) Other metals (23%)
6	Pechiney	F	38,947	Aluminium (43%) Special products and packaging (32%) Trading services (16%) Electrometallurgy and heavy carbon products (9%)
7	British Steel	UK	34,053	Steel (78%) Special Steel (10%) Tubes (9%)
8	Salzgitter	GER	33,148	Trading and transport (34%) Steel (25%) Shipbuilding (10%)
9	Hoesch	GER	24,547	
10	Cockerill Sambre	B	23,701	
11	EFIM	I	20,599	
12	Krupp Stahl	GER	18,320	Special steel (42%) Crude steel (32%) Steel processing (17%)
13	Hoogovens	NL	17,356	Steel (55%) Aluminium (23%) Trading services (8%)
14	VAW	GER	14,876	
15	Kloeckner-Werke	GER	13,162	

company, was privatised and sold to the Preussag on 1 January 1990. The then Preussag–Salzgitter became a conglomerate, with activities ranging from iron and steel, non-ferrous metals and energy to all types of engineering activities and trading services. With a combined turnover of DM28 billion, it will be among the top two or three iron and steel conglomerates in the world.

The largest crude steel producing country in the EC is Germany with 28.8 per cent of Community production, followed by Italy (18.2 per cent), France (13.6 per cent) and the UK (13.6 per cent) (see Figure 11.3). In other steel categories the situation is similar.

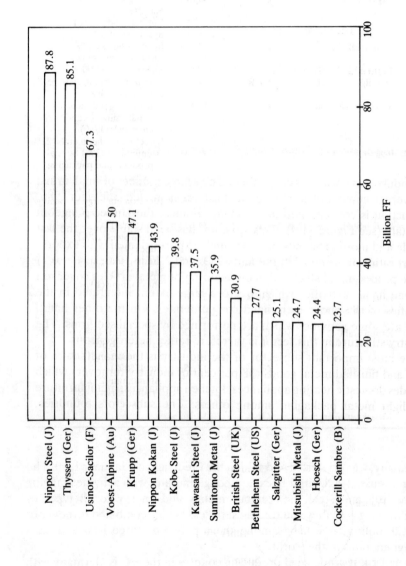

Figure 11.2   The largest iron and steel companies by turnover in 1987

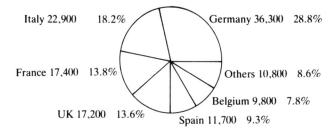

Figure 11.3   Raw steel production in the EC in 1987 ('000 tons)

Processing of steel and manufacturing of metal articles

The industry as a whole is characterised by a large number of small firms; the average number of employees per firm was estimated as fifty for 1986. Production is concentrated in Germany, France, the United Kingdom and Italy (see Figure 11.4). This structure has been stable over the last decade and more. The industry is strongly export oriented with export–import ratios of around 3 in the mid-1980s and 2.12 in 1988.

The processing of steel and manufacturing of metal articles cover, on the one hand, activities which are to a large extent integrated in the activities of the above-mentioned conglomerates. On the other hand, there are some activities which are performed by specialised firms. The industry structure in this sector is therefore rather heterogeneous.

The most important subsector of the industry is the manufacture of tools and finished metal goods (38 per cent of industry turnover) which includes domestic heating appliances, kitchen appliances, metal furniture and light metal packaging among others. The subsectors foundries,

Figure 11.4   Metal industry production by EC member state in 1987

secondary transformation and coating of metals, structural metal products (including assembly and installation) and boilermaking each
account for around 14 per cent of total industry turnover.

Most foundries belong to the iron and steel conglomerates, but steel
forging seems to be a more specialised activity. The main customer is the
automobile industry which buys 50 per cent of production. Firms have to
be flexible to meet the needs of their customers. Compared to the number
of automobile companies, the number of forging firms is large, but among
the many small firms each country has a few large ones. In the United
Kingdom Engineering & Forging (formerly GKN) accounts for 50 per
cent of UK production. In France three groups dominate the market:
Ascometal, Forge Stephanoises, and Forge de Courcelles. In Germany
there is a larger number of big firms.

The boilermaking industry consists of three types of firms:

1. The system integrators who perform all activities from design to
    installation. (As medium-sized firms they are subsidiaries of the iron
    and steel conglomerates.)
2. The product specialists who produce parts which are then integrated
    into larger production processes, such as vessels, exchangers or
    boilers. They have lower value-added content than system integra-
    tors.
3. The activity specialists who produce special items which require
    special skills. These are small firms acting as subcontractors.

Ninety per cent of domestic heating appliances are produced by
twenty-five companies in the EC. Except for Italy the number of firms in
each country is very low (Germany 2, United Kingdom 6, France 6, Italy
85). Around 50 per cent of total production is handled by a small number
of vertically integrated firms – again, usually belonging to the iron and
steel conglomerates.

The light metal packaging industry uses tinplate and aluminium to
produce containers for food and other consumptions goods. The sector
comprises two distinct types of firms. So-called 'made to measure'
products are supplied by small and medium-sized firms. Standardised
products which are produced in high volume come from large companies
operating internationally. American firms like American Can, Continental Can, Crown Cork, and National Can used to dominate the industry.
Recently the British (Metal Box) and the French (Carnaud) have merged
to create a large European conglomerate, called CMB. Also Pechiney,
one of the largest European aluminium producers, is bidding for
American National Can. Production sites are well dispersed over the EC
since transportation costs are high due to the high volume relative to its
value.

Demand trends

The demand for iron and steel is very sensitive to the business cycle. Since production capacities cannot be changed in the short run, slack demand in the automobile industry and the investment goods industry directly affect the iron and steel industry. Heavy price competition in times of recession is the consequence.

This dependence on the business cycle does not seem to be as strong in the metal industry. Demand follows more structural trends of the economy. For example, the boilermaking industry in France has specialised in producing boilers for nuclear reactors and has, therefore, been adversely affected by the reduced construction of new facilities. Light metal packaging, domestic heating appliances, and steel furniture will probably all face a demand which is less dependent on business cycles.

The medium-term perspective is that demand will grow at about the rate of GDP growth. There do not seem to be any special regional developments which could affect the regional structure of the industry.

Regulation of the industry

The iron and steel industry has a long history of regulation. It was the first industry to be under the regulatory authority of a European institution, the European Coal and Steel Community (ECSC). The ECSC was founded in 1951 and given supra-national authority. The steering mechanisms of the High Authority/Commission can be categorised as:

- instruments concerned with steering the market; and
- instruments concerned with structural policies.

The ECSC can aid structural adjustment through subsidies for investment programmes, for R & D, for laid-off workers, and to prevent plant closure. It also has the right to obtain company-specific data on price and market movements.

Market steering can take on several forms. Article 58 of the Treaty, which empowers the Commission to establish a system of production quotas, has the most far-reaching potential. In the area of pricing the Commission also has powers of intervention. It can fix maximum or minimum prices and for exports both maximum *and* minimum prices can be set simultaneously. These powers are also extended to traders in iron and steel. In trade policy the competence of the Commission encompasses regulatory measures in the following circumstances:

- Dumping by third countries.

- Practices distorting competition (e.g. public subsidies).
- Excessive (sic!) imports from third countries of products which are available in large quantities on the home market.

The overall effective rate of assistance for the European iron and steel industry is not published. Some numbers for Germany could, however, indicate a lower limit, as subsidisation in other member states was higher than in Germany. In the 1970s the iron and steel industry had slightly negative effective tariff protection and a small positive effective subsidisation. The negative protection comes through the intermediate price effect of highly protected coal inputs for the industry.

This picture has dramatically changed with the introduction of the quota system in 1980. If the tariff equivalent of the quotas is included, effective tariff protection was 40.8 per cent in the mid-1980s and effective subsidisation was 24.4 per cent, giving an overall effective rate of assistance of 65.2 per cent. Extra-Community barriers are still relatively high due to import quotas; not so much through tariffs, which are only around 5 per cent nominally (Weiss *et al.*, 1988).

These numbers have changed with the removal of the quota system and the banning of subsidies. Internal assistance for the steel industry in the late 1980s has probably returned to a relatively low level. Only the Italian steel industry is still paid government subsidies.

Apart from the protection against imports from outside the EC, competition among European companies in the iron and steel market is practically free.

Since part of the agreement for a quota system was the reduction in production capacities in all member countries, the industry underwent drastic structural change. Companies specialising in iron and steel were forced to shrink or to expand into other non-regulated activities. It is not clear whether this has induced the process of vertical diversification or whether it has only amplified it. Nevertheless, today's company structures are at least partly a result of the regulation of the 1980s.

The metal sector is not regulated more than the manufacturing sector in general, while its external protection may still be slightly negative through the high protection of coal as well as iron.

Company strategies

The creation of the Internal Market does not directly change the institutional structure of the markets for steel and metal products. There are no measures in the programme which specifically address these markets. Since the European regulation of the steel market has been removed, no deregulation is necessary. Some impact will come from the general measures such as the removal of border controls, the freedom of establishment and they will influence the competitive position of firms to some extent. Indirect effects will come through changes in the system of public procurement and the deregulation of the transport industry.

One can only speculate about the importance of these changes. *De facto*, the steel and metal industry will experience the potential of an internal market just like other industries where there are no sector-specific provisions in the internal market programme. The competitive environment and industry structures which have grown up may, however, result in a different reaction to the Internal Market from that in other industries.

The impact of the internal market programme can only be seen today to the extent that companies anticipate 1992 in their company strategies. Such anticipation depends on the expected changes of the European market, but also on the importance of these expected changes relative to other current developments in the industry.

This is especially true in the case of the iron and steel industry, because in the 1980s a dramatic restructuring of the industry has been taking place. The establishment of the quota system and its removal last year have dominated company strategies. These changes require a concentration of entrepreneurial efforts, but they also offer opportunities for an integration of institutional features of 1992 in company strategies. This process of restructuring is described in the next section and some speculations about the impact of 1992 are presented.

Restructuring of the large iron and steel producers

Since the steel crisis in the early 1980s and the subsequent heavy subsidisation and protection of the iron and steel industry, the industry structure has changed dramatically. Faced with the quota system for the production of raw steel and the requirement of capacity reductions, companies had to restructure internally and externally.

Previously large steel producers reduced capacity and at the same time increased productivity. Employment in the steel industry dropped by almost 40 per cent between 1980 and 1988. Production remained about constant, not counting seasonal variations. Production capacity was reduced by 40 million tons to around 140 million tons today. Half of this reduction took place in Germany.

German iron and steel companies have therefore been the first to look for activities outside the regulated sectors. All large iron and steel producers started to diversify into downstream activities, mostly in the metal industry. Today, the largest German iron and steel companies' business is not dominated by iron and steel any more. These companies are organised as holdings with rather independent subsidiaries. The vertical structure of activities seems to make this form feasible.

This vertical diversification was accompanied by an increasing internationalisation of activities. For example, Thyssen now has cast-iron subsidiaries outside Germany in Brazil, United Kingdom, and South Korea. Its elevator subsidiaries reside in sixteen countries throughout the world. Other European firms have also diversified internationally, but to a somewhat lesser extent.

It is, however, remarkable that the foreign activities often go beyond EC boundaries whereas foreign markets inside the EC are not contested. It may be that the quota system and the regulation of the industry have led to a cartel-type behaviour in which national markets are not contested by foreign companies. Consequently, companies have not focused on acquisition and expansion into EC markets in the 1980s. Under the quota system this would not have been a rational strategy, since output could not have been expanded anyway. It is too early to say whether in the new quota-free environment and the prospect of 1992 companies will change their national focus of activities to a European focus.

If one looks at the reasons for the vertical diversification of company activities, two major causes emerge. One comes from the fact that the reduction in raw steel capacity had left underutilised know-how and human capital in companies which could be used in related activities. Also restrictive firing laws in Germany and costly 'social' requirements (non-wages labour costs) made it worth while to engage in new activities. Because of the specific know-how of the labour force and since management is probably more familiar with downstream activities than with other non-steel-related industries, the retreat from the core steel business resulted in new ventures in many different metal sectors.

The other reason for diversification is rooted in the nature of the iron and steel markets. Demand for iron and steel varies strongly with the business cycle. At the same time, the production of iron and steel requires large investments in fixed capital. The resulting economies of scale have a strong impact on competition in times of weak demand. Since capacities cannot be reduced and a reduction of output in one firm increases its average costs relative to those of other competitors, competition drives prices close to average costs and, in a recession, even below. In order to escape these risks it is rational to invest in activities which react in less volatile fashion to the business cycle.

Whether investments in downstream activities completely relieve companies from the variations in demand can be called into question. At least, variations will be slightly reduced. However, given the constraints in technological and managerial skills, the observed strategy of the large iron and steel holdings may be optimal.

None of the acquisitions and mergers which have taken place lately in the EC among iron and steel producers indicates that it has been induced by the internal market programme. One cannot exclude the possibility that 1992 may have had some influence, but it was almost certainly not decisive in these decisions. The relatively minor integration of companies within Europe and their extra-EC focus gives particular support to this conjecture.

The metal industries

The situation in the metal industry is more differentiated than in the steel industry. We have already mentioned that the metal industry encompasses several groups of activities often with little relation to each other. Market and industry structures differ widely in these subsectors.

Consequently, the extent and the form in which companies design strategies with respect to the internal market differ widely. It is not possible to discuss the specific situation in all the different subsectors separately. Instead some important factors will be mentioned which might influence the industry.

The metal industry is already strongly export-oriented. Trade barriers as well as entry barriers are low. In markets with relatively small transport costs exports can achieve an efficient international division of labour. Theoretically, the Internal Market and free trade describe similar situations. There are, however, cases for which this is not true.

The metal packaging industry faces large transport costs, such that production sites have to be near the customer (mainly the food industry in this case). Several mergers have recently taken place in this industry. The most prominent is the emergence of a large European producer, CMB. Metal Box (UK) and Carnaud (France), both producers of metal packaging material, joined to become one of the large producers on the international stage. It may be that this merger has taken place in the expectation that consumer demand for canned food and beverages in different member states will be further assimilated in the Internal Market and marketing as well as production will become more harmonised. However, there is no direct evidence for this conjecture.

A considerable part of the metal industry, especially steel forging, relies on close subcontracting relationships. With the advent of just-in-time manufacturing methods these ties have become even closer. Proximity of production sites seems to be necessary in these cases, although modern communication and management techniques might reduce this need. It is therefore an open question as to whether a more international orientation will take place in the Internal Market. European mergers have so far not taken place in this subsector.

The metal industry depends to a large extent on standards and technical norms. The more such standards become harmonised, the easier it is to exploit economies of scale by exporting. Small and medium-sized firms in particular might gain from such harmonisation, whereas large system firms may find it easier to overcome the additional costs of different designs and informational and administrative requirements. Since small and medium-sized firms will benefit most from such harmonisation, this explains why anticipatory strategies are not observed today.

There are two possible reasons for this. First of all, small firms usually lack the funds and size to anticipate institutional changes like large firms. They react to these new opportunities by expanding at the time when the opportunity for further sales (i.e. exports) occurs. The other reason is simply that the many activities of small firms are not well recorded in the press. They can only be found in official statistics at a much later date.

Overall, one can say that the metal industry does not reveal any obvious and clearly observable company strategies with respect to the Internal Market. On the contrary, for example, representatives of the German association of the tools and finished metal goods industry complain about the little attention which their member companies pay to the 1992 programme.

Industry structure after 1992

It is virtually impossible to make a prediction about the structure of the iron, steel, and metal industry after 1992. The reason has already been mentioned: the diversity of the industry in terms of markets, products, and firm size is too large to generalise. A few trends in potential developments can be discerned in some cases. They do not seem to be reflected in current company strategies, however.

The iron and steel industry still seems to be focused on adjustment strategies to the turbulent 1980s. Once the restructuring of company activities has been put in place, these companies will probably pay more attention to the opportunities of the Internal Market than they seem to have done so far.

For the metal industry few changes are expected, although in some special activities or smaller markets the industry structure might change. Currently, there is not enough evidence to isolate such subsectors. One indirect effect which one would expect to be important for the industry is the deregulation of transport markets. An essential part of the activities of the iron and steel conglomerates is trading services. Some subsectors in the metal industry also face high transport costs. Yet the accessible information does not reveal that companies react to the expected lower tariffs. It may be that they do not consider this to be important for their business; it may also be that they have so far simply ignored the potential of a deregulated transport market. The conclusion can be summarised briefly. There is no clear evidence that 1992 influences company strategies to a noticeable degree; while in the news about the industry the Internal Market is hardly ever mentioned, suggesting that companies do not consider it to be important at the moment.

References

Grunert, Thomas (1987), 'Decision-making processes in the steel crisis policy of the EEC: neocorporatist or integrationist tendencies?', in Yves Mény and Vincent Wright (eds), *The Politics of Steel: Western Europe and the Steel Industry in the Crisis Years (1974–1984)*, Berlin, pp. 222–307.
Weiss, Frank D. *et al.* (1988), *Trade policy in West Germany*, Tübingen.

12

The machine tool industry

David G. Mayes

Introduction

For reasons which are not always clear there have at various times been attempts to define the heart or core of the economy, in which lie the activities which are central to economic development. For some it is the private sector, for the others, productive industries. Some feel it should be manufacturing or even engineering, shrinking down to an ever smaller definition, but for no one does it exclude the machine tool industry because it is that industry's products and technologies which enable production of most of manufacturing industry. Even in chemicals, which may seem further away, the equipment for production, whether of traditional or specialised items, requires machine tools for its construction. By any definition, therefore, the impact of the 1992 programme on the EC machine tool industry is a central component of the success of the single market as a whole.

The continuing vitality of the European machine tool industry, despite the size of that in the US and the strong efforts of the Japanese to increase their market share, gives substance to the view that whatever the distortions of the current trading world it is possible to find a viable basis on which Europe can compete. A third of the world's output comes from the European Community, nearly half as much again as Japan, the world's largest single producer (see Table 12.1). Just over half that output comes from one country, West Germany, which alone exports a quarter of the world's trade (see Figure 12.2). The study of machine tools is thus an illustration of the impact on a position of strength and may give pointers to the wider prospects for the mechanical engineering industry as a whole.

Much of the reason for this strength stems from the sheer variety of

Table 12.1 World machine tool production, trade and consumption

Rank	Country	Production Total	Cutting	Forming	Trade Export	Import	Balance	Apparent consumption
1	Japan	8.6	6.8	1.9	3.4	0.4	3.0	5.6
2	W. Germany	6.8	4.9	2.0	4.1	1.2	3.0	3.8
3	USSR	4.5	3.6	0.9	0.4	1.9	−1.6	6.1
4	Italy	2.8	2.1	0.7	1.3	0.7	0.6	2.2
5	USA	2.4	1.6	0.9	0.6	2.0	−1.4	3.8
6	Switz.	1.9	1.7	0.2	1.6	0.4	1.2	0.7
7	E. Germany	1.5	1.2	0.3	1.3	0.3	1.0	0.5
8	UK	1.4	1.2	0.2	0.7	0.7	0.0	1.4
9	France	0.8	0.6	0.2	0.3	0.9	−0.6	1.4
12	Spain	0.7	0.5	0.2	0.3	0.3	0.0	0.7
23	Belgium[1,3]	0.2	0.0	0.1	0.3	0.3	0.0	0.2
27	Denmark	0.1	0.1	0.0	0.1	0.1	0.1	0.1
29	Neths[1]	0.0	0.0	0.0	0.2	0.3	−0.1	0.1
33	Portugal	0.0	0.0	0.0	0.0	0.0	0.0	0.0
	EC as shown above	12.8	9.4	3.4	7.3	4.4	2.9	9.9
	(% of total)	34	32	38	42	30	104	28
	Rest of world[2]	25.2	19.6	5.6	10.0	10.1	−0.1	25.3
	Total	38.0	29.0	9.0	17.3	14.5	2.8	35.2

Notes: [1] Exports > Production indicates significant re-export trade [2] 35 leading producers only, hence exports exceed imports for the 'world' [3] approx.

Source: *American Machinist*

machine tools. The specialist uses are such that although there is a strong market for multipurpose computer-controlled tools, at which the Japanese excel, for many operations they are inappropriate either because of excessive cost or because they cannot provide the particular specialised technique. We therefore observe an extremely fragmented industry with around 1,500 companies producing the vast majority of the output, with an average size of not much over 100 employees (see Table 12.2). The average firm sizes in Germany and Japan are only 240 and 300 respectively, even excluding all the firms with less than 50 employees in the latter case.

In the circumstances it is relatively difficult to observe the impact of the European Single Market. First of all, it is difficult to see how much trade has been inhibited, because there are many European companies that are world leaders in the industry despite the barriers that exist. Secondly, it is difficult to be precise about the extent of competition, because many parts of the market offer little scope for substitution between products or producers. Thirdly, many of the non-tariff barriers to trade, although clear and measurable, do not constitute serious obstacles in practice. Machines tend to be special orders. Frontier delays are not important

Table 12.2   Number of firms and employment, 1988

Country	No. of producers	Total employment	Average firm size
Austria[1]	25	3,500	140
Belgium	29	2,450	85
France	150	9,190	60
W. Germany	380	94,000	250
Great Britain[1]	200	23,000	115
Italy	450	31,000	70
Netherlands[1]	22	1,060	50
Portugal	20	1,000	50
Spain	148	7,850	50
Sweden	33	3,000	90
Switzerland	115	14,000	120
Total	1,572	190,050	120

Note: [1]1987

Source: CECIMO

when it can take several months to build a large machine. Many machines have a very high value added against which the costs of the barriers are small. Although technical differences in the requirements of countries can be irritating, the industry has been developing common standards for a long time and small differences are often required in any case by purchasers because of the specific use to which they want to put the machine.

The major characteristic of the European industry in many of the countries, particularly Germany, France, Italy and Spain, is its strong national (or regional) flavour. Although cross-border linkages, particularly in the case of France, are important, they are just as likely to be with non-EC suppliers as with companies in other member states. The national emphasis stems from the system of support for firms within the various industry associations and local areas, including banks, research institutions and governments. The arrangements in Germany are particularly thorough and comprehensive. The Italian industry puts forward its *Systemi per Produrre* as a major reason for its competitiveness from what would otherwise seem an unpromising basis.

Because Europe has been a major market for the consumption as well as production of machine tools, taking 30 per cent of total output, there has long been an incentive for firms in the industry to adopt a business strategy on a European or wider international basis. While much machine tool production is too specialised to warrant production in more than one location, in areas where sales are much larger, Japanese producers, such as Yamazaki, and US producers, such as Cincinnati–Milacron, have set up manufacturing plants in the Community. While 1992 may have heightened that incentive, there has not been any substantial surge to reorganise. This is perhaps aided by the fact that the market for machine tools has been extremely buoyant in the last three years, growing in value by three-quarters between 1985 and 1988. Manufacturers have therefore been at full stretch and there has been less incentive to reorganise than there would be in industries with spare capacity. Since demand is highly cyclical it remains to be seen how attitudes change as the investment boom peaks and competition becomes harder.

The sections which follow discuss the structure of the industry and the main firms within it, the forces that the 1992 programme brings to bear on the market and the impact they are having on all the stages in the value-added chain, from research and development and training through component suppliers, producers, distribution, service and finance. The next two sections discuss the 'internal' and 'external' strategies that are being employed by firms in the industry in response to these pressures. Internal strategies involve changes such as reorganisation and restructuring of the product market focus, while external changes involve links with other firms, ranging from licensing agreements to outright takeovers.

The structure of the machine tool industry

The nature of machine tools and their market

Machine tools are capital goods and as such form part of investment in equipment by their purchasers. They are thus subject to the fluctuations in demand stemming from the cycle in investment, which is much wider than that for economic activity as a whole. The main users of machine tools are in engineering, principally mechanical and transport, who are themselves often capital goods producers (see Table 12.8). They are thus also subject to such fluctuation, emphasising the impact on the machine tool industry. Over the period 1978–86, while GDP growth in the seven main Community countries slowed almost to zero in the years 1981–2, output of metal products fell by 12.5 per cent and was still 10 per cent lower in 1986. Demand by mechanical engineering fell 10 per cent and had still not recovered by the end of the period, while output of transport equipment has continued to grow, reaching a level some 10 per cent higher than in 1980 by 1986. This recession was a worldwide phenomenon and hence, by the beginning of the Single Market programme the industry had had to endure a very difficult period. Since then the picture has changed, world demand has accelerated and hence the demand for capital goods and machine tools among them has been striking. The industry has therefore been at full stretch over 1988–9 and any restructuring in the face of the Single Market has to be viewed in that context. Pressures for change are very different in downturns compared to upturns in activity.

There is no shortage of detailed data on the machine tool industry. In some respects this is almost a disadvantage as many of the sources are not compatible and, indeed, contradictory. The industry can be divided in two in at least three different ways. The first is by form of operation, distinguishing cutting from forming. Cutting includes lathes, boring, drilling, sawing, and grinding, while forming includes bending, folding, shearing, punching, forging and wireworking (more exact definitions are set out in Table 12.3). This may seem a great deal of detail but these activities are distinct and not readily substitutable. Cutting itself can be subdivided into lathes, where the part rotates and the tool is stationary,

Table 12.3   Main classification of machine tools, EC trade, 1987

Type	ECU m.		
	Exports	Imports	Balance
Total	5,293	3,469	1,824
Cutting Total	3,368	2,556	812
Nuclear Retreatment	0	0	0
Physical and Chemical Erosion	76	185	−109
Lathes	729	607	122
Boring	217	166	51
Planing	3	2	1
Sawing, Cutting Off	170	97	73
Milling	535	345	190
Drilling	132	153	−21
Grinding, Polishing	792	495	297
Jig Boring	182	228	46
Gear Cutting	98	52	46
Tapping, Screwcutting	19	18	1
Machining Centres	57	61	4
Transfer Lines	301	35	266
Other	56	111	−55
Forming Total	1,600	850	950
Presses	490	210	280
Bending, Folding	209	129	80
Shearing, Punching	283	211	72
Forging, Stamping	55	33	22
Drawing	93	28	65
Threadrolling	12	6	6
Other working flat products	42	13	29
Wireworking	82	49	33
Other	336	171	165
Other metalworking	325	63	262

Source: CECIMO

and other operations where the part is held fixed and it is the tool which moves (in bending operations, of course, one facet of the part moves relative to the others). Secondly, machines can be distinguished by their control methods, where computer and numerical control machines are distinguished from the rest. Despite the rapid rise in computer control, CNC machines represent only half of production although the proportion is much higher in Japan where 78 per cent of orders in 1988 were for NC machines. Lastly we can distinguish between machines designed for specific tasks and those which can be adapted for many uses. While, by and large, the more adaptable machines are more expensive and usually numerically controlled, this is not always the case.

The position of the EC in the world market

The machine tool industry in the European Community represents only a quarter of 1 per cent of GDP (and a similar proportion in Japan); however, machine tool production is almost twice as important in the German economy although this in turn is small compared with the 1 per cent in Switzerland (see Table 12.4). In the last ten years German production has been more important than the whole of the rest of the Community put together (54 per cent) (see Figure 12.1). Italy, the United Kingdom, France and Spain are the other producers of any consequence with 18.6 per cent, 11.5 per cent, 8.7 per cent and 4.2 per cent of total production respectively (see Table 12.1). Germany is a substantial net exporter, to the tune of 44 per cent of production, while Italy is also in surplus (22 per cent), the United Kingdom and Spain in deficit, 5 per cent and 8 per cent, and France substantially so (70 per cent). However, it is

Table 12.4   Shares of machine tool production in GDP (%), 1987

Belgium	0.1
Denmark	0.1
France	0.1
West Germany	0.6
Great Britain	0.2
Italy	0.3
Netherlands	0.0
Portugal	0.1
Spain	0.2
EC[1]	0.3
Japan	0.3
US	0.1
Switzerland	1.0

Note: [1]eight largest only

Source: CECIMO

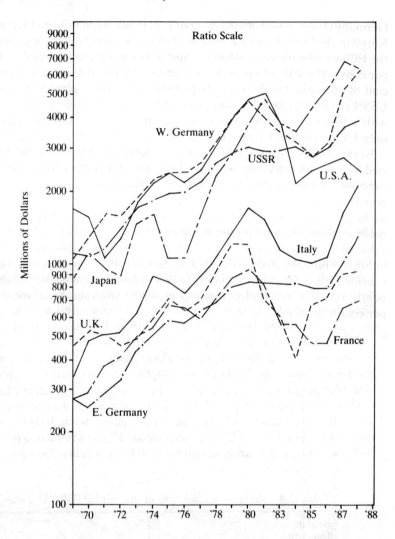

Figure 12.1 Machine tool shipments of eight leading nations (Source: NMTBA, 1988)

really rather misleading to ignore Switzerland, whose output is the third largest in Europe and three-quarters of which is exported to the other European countries.

The European industry is very important in the world as a whole (see Table 12.1). While Japan is the largest producer (20.5 per cent),

Germany is very close behind (19.9 per cent), and, since Italy, the United Kingdom and France are the fourth, eighth and ninth largest producers, the EC as a whole produces over a third of the world's machine tools (34 per cent). The EC is even more important in trading terms with 42 per cent of the total. This is largely because although the United States and USSR are the fifth and third largest producers they are largely concerned with satisfying domestic demand and have shares of export demand of only 4.4 per cent and 2.1 per cent.

Because of the degree of specialisation in the industry it is characterised by intra-industry trade. Germany, despite being the world's largest exporter, imports nearly a third of its requirements and the United States imports over half of its requirements, making it a net importer by as much as 58 per cent of its total consumption (see Figure 12.2). Taking the balance divided by total trade as a measure of intra-industry trade gives a value of 0.2. This ratio would be 1 if there were no specialisation in the industry and zero if specialisation were total; 0.2 thus indicates very considerable intra-industry specialisation. The EC as a whole imports nearly a third of its requirements and has a net export surplus of some 30 per cent of its needs.

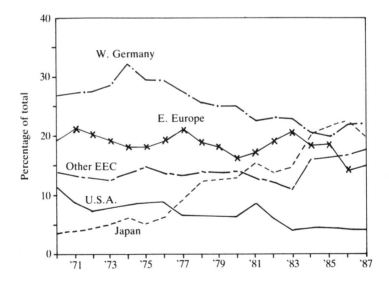

Figure 12.2 Machine tool exports as a percentage of world exports (Source: NMTBA, 1988)

The evolution of the market in recent years

During the early 1980s demand and production in the EC were stagnant in total terms, reflecting the general downturn in world activity and the reduction in the amount of equipment needed to manufacture (see Table 12.5). As a result employment fell by a quarter and the number of firms also declined (see Table 12.6). Since 1984 demand has picked up again and remains strongly increasing. There is a clear distinction between the behaviour in the component countries. In Spain and Italy the number of firms is increasing, while employment is fairly constant; so there is a slight fall in firm size. In the remaining countries the number of firms has fallen but the path of employment has varied from a rise in West Germany to a fall of a third in France. We must therefore look at the picture for the various countries separately.

The German industry has weathered the Japanese challenge and after a period of relative difficulty seems to be re-establishing market share. The Italian industry continues to improve. The UK industry after a major collapse in the 1970s and further difficulties in the 1980s is recovering steadily, while the French industry has yet to turn the corner. The Spanish industry, on the other hand, continues to grow. Within those totals the importance of larger firms has continued to increase in West Germany (see Table 12.7) while the reverse is true in Italy. The structure of the industry is also changing as is described by CECIMO (1989) in their follow-up to the BCG study:

> To a more [sic] or greater extent in all countries, but always within normal proportions, machine tool companies have dropped out of business by bankruptcy or closure. Takeovers and, especially in the UK, management buyouts have also led to significant changes in the structure of the industry. Remarkable are not only the takeovers by Japanese companies in France and by Korean companies in Germany, but also the same activity by Swiss and Austrian companies in EC countries. Though in some countries such as France and the UK a certain concentration process in relatively small groups occurred, it cannot be seen that larger groups consisting only or mainly of machine tool manufacturers are being created in Europe. The larger multinational or foreign-owned groups to which a number of EC machine-tool manufacturers belong obviously do not intend to expand their activities at this moment. Intra-EC co-operations are still an exception. Such co-operations take place at national levels and then chiefly between machine-tool manufacturers and electronics/software companies.

This increase is largely unrelated to the European Single Market except in so far as this is a product of investment in consequent structural change. This surge in demand dwarfs any reallocative forces which may be present, as almost all firms are doing well and with little spare capacity. As is shown very clearly in the work of Grinyer, Mayes and McKiernan

Table 12.5 EC output and trade, 1980–87 (EC 10^1 values: 1980 = 100)

	1981	1982	1983	1984	1985	1986	1987
Production							
Value	102.5	99.2	95.8	99.7	117.0	136.2	145.4
Volume	93.4	83.7	76.8	75.9	85.0	95.8	100.0
Imports							
Total	103.3	101.5	86.8	100.9	127.5	162.8	167.4
Intra-EC^2	107.5	104.0	84.8	94.4	113.2	143.9	165.2
Extra-EC^2	98.7	89.1	108.2	143.7	184.1	169.9	–
Exports							
Total	108.2	103.0	97.8	102.4	119.2	137.7	133.2
Intra-EC^2	105.6	99.2	92.4	94.9	116.9	143.8	155.4
Extra-EC^2	109.5	104.8	100.3	105.9	120.3	134.8	122.7
Import Penetration							
(%)	45.1	44.9	41.2	44.1	45.7	47.7	43.6
Export/Imports	2.0	1.9	2.1	1.9	1.8	1.6	1.5

Notes: ^{1}excluding Greece, Ireland ^{2}EC12

Source: CECIMO

Table 12.6 Number of companies and employees in the EC, 1983–87

(a) Companies

	1983	1984	1985	1986	1987
Germany	435	425	400	390	390
Italy	400	380	420	430	430
UK	166	150	210	210	200
France	166	161	148	146	148
Spain	128	122	120	139	144
Total EC5	1,295	1,238	1,298	1,315	1,312

(b) Employees

	1983	1984	1985	1986	1987
Germany	83.7	83.0	88.0	93.0	93.5
Italy	30.8	28.5	28.2	28.7	30.5
UK	24.5	23.0	24.2	22.8	23.4
France	15.5	13.4	12.1	11.5	10.0
Spain	7.6	7.3	7.3	7.6	7.7
Total EC5	162.1	155.2	159.8	163.5	165.2

(c) Employees per company

	1983	1984	1985	1986	1987
Germany	192	195	220	238	240
Italy	77	75	67	67	71
UK	148	165	150	114	117
France	93	83	81	77	68
Spain	59	59	61	54	55
Total EC5	125	125	123	124	126

Note: The jump from 150 to 210 firms in the UK in 1985 is implausible and disagrees with such UK information as there is. It looks like a change in definition. This gap should therefore be treated as a discontinuity, which therefore also applies to the total

Source: CECIMO

Table 12.7 Structure of the German and Italian industries

Size of establishment (employees)	Number of companies (%)		Number of employed (%)		Production (%)	
	Germany					
	1983	1987	1983	1987	1983	1987
0–50	37.7	39.7	3.0	2.2	2.2	1.9
51–100	19.1	19.0	7.1	4.7	5.7	4.2
101–250	19.3	20.0	16.9	13.7	16.6	12.7
251–500	12.9	11.1	24.0	18.2	21.6	17.7
501–1000	8.0	7.6	27.8	33.5	27.3	33.3
1001–	3.0	2.6	20.8	27.7	29.6	29.2
	Italy					
0–20	40.7	41.9	7.1	8.4	6.1	7.7
21–50	29.2	29.9	14.9	17.2	13.3	15.4
51–100	14.2	14.9	16.8	19.4	18.7	19.5
101–200	10.6	8.8	23.5	21.5	21.2	19.0
201–500	4.9	3.9	25.7	20.3	24.2	24.7
501–1000	0.0	0.3	0.0	3.7	0.0	2.4
1001–	0.4	0.3	12.0	9.5	16.5	11.3

Source: CECIMO

(1988) the major impetus for structural change by companies, whether externally by takeover, merger or other linkage or internally through reorganisation, comes at times of adverse pressure. Indeed, some have argued (see Slatter, 1984) that substantial change can only be achieved by a crisis. Patently this does not exist for the machine tool industry. It is only when the current cycle falls away that we shall see how the industry acts in adversity. It is then that rationalisation is likely.

Perhaps some indications of what may happen are given by history. Fortunately, the industry was subjected to a close study by the European Commission in 1985, undertaken by the Boston Consulting Group, so their assessment of the position in the early 1980s and the strategic issues then presented forms a useful basis for considering the developments in the transition to the European single market. This involved several interviews with firms which revealed data not normally available in the published surveys by the NMTBA and others. In particular, they formed a view of the structure of demand which shows that a quarter of total demand for cutting machine tools comes from the road vehicle industry (see Table 12.8). Regrettably, the same analysis was not extended to metal forming, where again the motor industry forms a major part of demand, with the pressing of car bodies, etc. The transport industry also provided around a further 10 per cent of total demand through aircraft.

Table 12.8   Distribution of demand by machine types and industries in metal cutting, 1983[1]

	Lathes	Milling	Drilling	Boring	Machining centres	Grinding	Total
Autos and trucks	7.0	3.5	1.5	2.0	4.0	5.0	23.0
Agri. and const. equipt	3.5	2.0	0.5	1.0	2.5	1.0	10.5
Machines	5.5	3.5	0.5	1.5	2.0	2.0	15.0
Heavy engineering	3.5	1.5	–	1.5	2.5	1.0	10.0
General engineering	8.0	4.0	1.0	1.0	1.5	1.5	17.0
Precision engineering	1.0	1.0	–	–	0.5	1.0	3.5
Electrical and electronics	4.0	2.5	1.0	–	1.0	1.0	9.5
Aircraft	4.0	2.5	0.5	1.0	2.0	1.5	11.5
Total	36.5	20.5	5.0	8.0	16.0	14.0	100.0

Note: the estimates presented in this table should be considered as orders of magnitude only   [1] 4 major EEC countries

Source: National Statistics, market surveys, BCG analysis (1985)

Machine tool demand comes naturally from engineering, with a third from the major categories, and 15 per cent from the construction of machinery. This leaves 10 per cent in the agricultural and construction sector and a similar amount in electrical and electronics. The central role of machine tools in the major manufacturing sectors – largely one form of engineering or another – is clear. Although this machinery relates to metal working rather than the much smaller wood working sector (also the subject of a direct study by the Commission) much of it also extends to newer materials such as plastics, ceramics and composites which are becoming more widely used. The aircraft industry (see Table 12.9) is the dominant user but road vehicles (see Table 12.8), electrical/electronics and precision sector are also of important consequence.

The role of technology in the strength of the European industry

Much of the European industry's success depends on it maintaining a technical lead. While some of this relates to production methods it also relates to the ability to handle new materials. While the trend towards increasing use of NC and CNC machines is continuing (see Figure 12.3) there are clear limits to its applicability. Numerical control relates to the larger operations and larger firms. Whereas firms with less than 300 employees tend to have about half their tools numerically controlled (in 1983), this proportion had risen to three-quarters at around 1,000 employees and almost total penetration in larger scale enterprises. It is thus important to realise that half of demand in fact comes from the

Table 12.9 Substitution of metal by new materials: expected impact on the amount of machining (in %)[1] – cumulative 1984–89

	Plastics		Composites		Ceramics	
	MC	MF	MC	MF	MC	MF
Automotive and trucks	5.0	5.0	3.0	6.0	5.0	–
Agric. and const. equipt.	1.0	–	–	–	–	–
Machines	0.5	0.5	2.0	–	–	–
Heavy engineering	–	–	6.0	1.0	1.0	–
General engineering	1.0	1.0	3.0	2.0	–	–
Precision engineering	7.0	15.0	2.0	2.0	–	–
Electrical and electronics	3.0	3.0	2.0	16.0	–	–
Aircraft	9.0	13.0	14.0	15.0	–	–
Total	4.5	5.0	4.0	6.0	1.0	

Note: [1]Number of firms weighted by machining department size. Each column must be read independently. MC and MF refer to the cutting and forming processes respectively

Source: BCG (1985): Large end-user (with over 100 employees) questionnaires

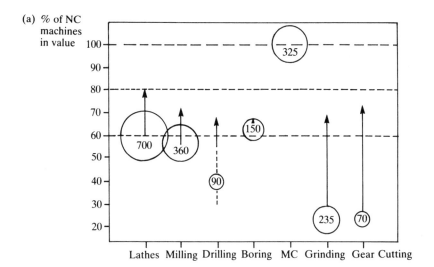

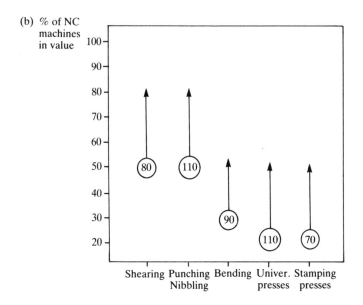

Notes: The size of the circle is proportional to total demand in each
machine type (NC + conventional) in 1983 (actual demand) in
1983 $ m. MC = machining centres
[1]major EEC countries

Figure 12.3   Penetration of NC in Europe[1] at the end of the 1980s: (a) in metal
cutting, (b) in metal forming (Source: BCG, 1985: end-user questionnaires)

smaller companies (see Table 12.10), that is, those with less than 100 employees. Thus it is clear that, with the exception of the motor and aircraft industries, there are few dominant purchasers. Because of specialisation many individual suppliers are very strong in individual sectors, but there is strong competition in the volume markets.

There are three main sorts of automated systems in the use of machine tools, as follows:

1. *Flexible machining cell* A group of one or more computer-controlled machines which are linked automatically by a parts-handling system and can change their own tools.
2. *Flexible manufacturing system* A more sophisticated arrangement, where the control computer can handle variable sequencing, optimal scheduling, etc.
3. *Flexible transfer line* Where a set of machines handles a sequence of operations under computer control. This is an extension with computer control of long-standing transfer line arrangements.

Of course, the cells can be introduced relatively readily to replace existing operations, as, indeed, can be the computerisation of lines. Systems, however, require a much greater transformation and sophistication for their adoption and operation. As a consequence, their rate of market penetration has been lower. There are two major problems in implementing FMS even if it is clear that when implemented the system will improve a firm's competitiveness (see the report from the Advanced Manufacturing Systems Task Force, National Economic Development Office, London, 1987). The first is simply cost. The size of the investment required is too great for many independent companies to tackle at one time, especially if part of the incentive for the investment is a fall in profits. FMS has to be phased in via FMC in a series of stages, each of

Table 12.10 Demand by end-user size, 1983

	Number of employees					Total demand (in value)
	<20	20–100	100–500	500–2,000	>2,000	
Germany	5	8	20	28	41	100
France	5	10	15	18	52	100
UK	5	10	32	17	36	100
Italy	10	25	24	18	23	100
US	20		25	20	35	100
Japan	15		35	15	35	100

Source: BCG (1985)

which improves profitability. Secondly, an FMS requires a very different and very highly skilled team to operate it. Problems in the system cannot be solved in the short run by manual adjustment of bringing in spare old capacity. The computer control system itself needs to be altered and this is not usually best served by bringing in support staff from the machine tool manufacturer.

Despite the rapid rate of increase in automation there are limits to its applicability as is clear from even the Boston Consulting Group's suggestions which are quite optimistic (see Figure 12.3). In the case of the United Kingdom, for example, where penetration of NC machines has been quite high (7 per cent in 1987), the vast majority of the stock of machine tools is not merely conventional but half of it is over 10 years old and over a quarter over 20 years old. Many conventional operations neither require nor can justify the purchase of more up-to-date machinery and for their limited range of operation would not require numerical control.

The industry is subject to two sorts of technological change. The first is in the tools themselves and their control systems, with the extremely rapid rise in numerically controlled machine tools – the growth rate in the UK was 44 per cent *a year* over the decade 1977–86 (Sixth Survey of Stock of Machine Tools) – and the increases in other areas such as lasers, electrical discharge (EDM) machines. These changes actually mean that the stock of machine tools in industry is tending to fall, as new machines have the ability to work considerably faster. The second is in the purchasing industries themselves. The faster the product and process development, the more likely it is either that new machine tools will be required or that the tools used will have to be more adaptable. This contributes to the popularity of numerical control. However, the changes in the purchasing industries also include changes in the nature of the product, which may involve changes in materials as well as the means of machining (see Table 12.9). It is in this context that we now have to examine how the completion of the European Internal Market will affect the industry and the strategy of firms within it.

The impact of the Single Market

The scope for economies of scale

Machine tools have been classified by the Commission (Buigues and Ilzkovitz (1988) in a study of the structure of European industry as being one of the forty sectors of European industry which are most 'sensitive' to the changes stemming from the Single Market programme, in the sense that they are likely to be most affected. In the case of machine tools this conclusion emerges because at present the industry is fragmented, characterised by small firms, where there is the possibility, in technical terms, of exploiting substantial economies of scale in production. Prima facie, therefore, one might expect that the removal of barriers in Europe would permit substantial rationalisation, increased scale and lower costs. However, this view is not borne out by a more detailed study of the industry, as its fragmented structure is not primarily due to intra-European barriers but to factors which will not be so substantially affected by closer economic integration. This, of course, is not to say the industry will not be much affected by the 1992 programme. We have already noted that since an increase in the rate of European investment is expected, particularly in the early part of the response by companies, the machine tool industry should be a major beneficiary.

The machine tool industry is differentiated, as the substantial size of intra-industry trade indicates. Hence, although there are substantial economies of scale in volume products, whether numerically controlled or conventional, this does not apply to most of European production which, to use the terms of the BCG study, is either 'fragmented' or 'specialised'. The four terms, explained in Figure 12.4, disaggregate the market in two respects: first, into the size of gain available, and second, into the number of routes available to achieve that gain. Thus, if the size of gain is expected to be small and there are only a few ways to achieve it, it is unlikely that any individual company will be able to find a profitable avenue forward. On the other hand, volume production is a means of proceeding if there are large gains to be had but few routes to achieving them. The best opportunities occur where not only is the potential market large but many routes can be used to exploit it. Fortunately, this describes the specialisation which characterises much of the European industry. Even in 1983 (see Figure 12.5) only 18 per cent of production was in the most unpromising sector, labelled 'stalemate'.

The degree to which benefit from economies of size can be obtained thus depends on the degree to which European firms decide to pursue the 'volume' end of the market, where the Japanese have shown their major strength and Taiwanese and South Korean firms also appear to be gaining market share. This is not the whole picture because economies of size can also be obtained with related products through standardisation of components, economies of marketing and sharing of other overheads. This can be true because of the technological development of machine tools themselves. Machine tools are extensively used in the production of machine tools. Increasing flexibility means that a wider variety of parts can be produced by a single machine and that the costs of the machine itself is higher, thus increasing the importance of keeping the machine in production. There may, therefore, be considerable economies of scope.

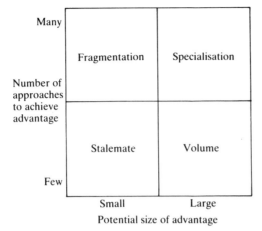

Figure 12.4   Competitive environments (Source: BCG, 1985)

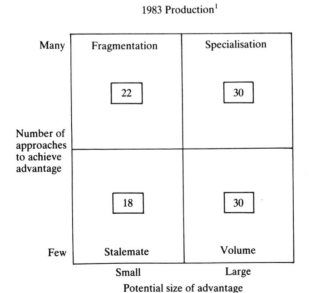

Note: [1]France, Germany, Italy, UK, USA, Japan

Figure 12.5   Structure of machine tool production by competitive environment (Source: BCG, 1985)

However, except where the products are closely related it may be difficult to exploit them. The smallness of the companies makes takeovers difficult because owners are concentrated and have substantial equity holdings which they do not wish to sell as they enjoy running the company. Linking largely independent firms, particularly across national borders, will have much more limited effect, especially in so far as production remains fragmented. 'National' purchasing patterns are not common and firms tend to have had considerable success in crossing the borders within Europe already.

Other sources of impact

If we run down the list of barriers that may be eliminated by the Single Market programme, those at the frontier have relatively little significance. With the exception of delivery of crucial replacement parts, for which special arrangement would be made, machine tools are not subject to the fine deadlines of components in just-in-time production or problems of a very short life in a marketable condition. Since they are high-value-added items the costs of border delays and paperwork are small in relation to the total. The competitive advantage for EC companies from their removal will tend to be small. Important Japanese companies like Yamazaki, and others with third-country owners, which already have substantial production facilities within the Community, will be able to benefit from these changes in just the same manner as European-owned firms.

Fiscal barriers have little relevance, except in so far as they relate to the mobility of capital. Capital mobility will have twin impacts. First of all, if the cost of capital falls among the EC countries this will stimulate investment and hence the demand for machine tools. Second, it will help producers restructure, particularly across borders, which will also stimulate investment and machine tool demand. Regrettably, it is very difficult to strip out how much of the recent surge in demand is due to the Single Market programme. In the first place the demand increase is widespread, occurring outside as well as inside the EC. While demand rose by 12 per cent in the EC it rose by the same percentage in the world as a whole, and by as much as 55 per cent in Japan, although it fell in the United States. These increases may be stimulated by a common world upturn. There is no specific survey of demand available which seeks to examine the impact of the Single Market programme on investment and the major survey of purchases undertaken in the United Kingdom last year (Sixth Survey of the Machine Tool Industry) does not place any special emphasis on the effects from 1992.

One might be forgiven for expecting that technical barriers would be important in a high-technology industry which is also undergoing rapid technical change. There are clear instances where they do, particularly in regard to safety. The problems with regard to wood-working machinery are well documented (GEWIPLAN, 1988) and similar considerations apply to metal-working machines. For 'standard' machines this can present a problem as it fragments the market. Since there is a substantial element of customisation in many tools, this further source of difference merely makes an existing problem harder. None of the firms or producer organisations interviewed put much emphasis on this barrier. What may be more important is the impact of the removal of technical barriers on customer industries, which may reduce the range of different products required, hence lowering the number of machine tools needed to produce them. Thus other industries' efficiency gains may actually entail a loss for machine tool makers – not that there are any signs of this happening as yet with the rapidly increasing demand.

One problem which companies do face is shortage of skilled labour. With firms operating at full capacity and demand rising it is not surprising if constraints are being encountered, especially as the labour force is tending to shrink, particularly with smaller numbers of young people entering the labour market. The question at issue is, does the removal of barriers to the movement of labour do anything to help alleviate this? In theory the answer to this is 'yes', because these shortages lie in areas where qualifications form an important component of the ability or willingness to employ. However, the problem is only resolvable if there is a surplus in some areas and a deficit in others. Unfortunately, the shortage is general. Hence, the incentive for labour movement across borders is relatively muted compared with the incentive for the various countries to increase the amount of such skills through training and retraining.

It is instructive that in many respects Switzerland ought to be regarded as being part of the same labour market. It is geographically next to the main Community producers, West Germany and Italy and, given that German and Italian are official Swiss languages, this make labour rather more interchangeable than might normally be the case with the barriers to labour movement in both directions. A slight drawback to this neatness is that the Swiss machine tool industry has its major concentration in the north-west of the country rather than the German north-east or Italian south.

This Swiss connection applies more widely to the impact of the 1992 programme and is of some significance as Switzerland is the world's sixth largest producer of machine tools, second only to West Germany and Italy in Europe. Swiss machine tools are already subject to a free trade arrangement with the Community and hence enjoy a competitive margin over other major producers in Japan or the United States.

Furthermore, technical harmonisation in the Community is largely a matter for CEN and Switzerland is also a member of CEN along with the other EFTA countries. This larger community also applies to the European trade association CECIMO (Comité Européen de Coopération des Industries de la Machine Outil) which is based in Brussels.

The weakness of influences on the Community industry therefore have their corresponding impact on Switzerland, namely, that there is no strong adverse pressure from increases in European Community competitiveness. The links between German and Swiss companies are at least as important as the links between companies across the various member states. Tornos-Bechler, for example, has substantial German capital while Make Holding owns a number of German companies. These links and the pressures to forge them pre-date the Single Market programme. They stem not only from desires for Swiss companies to have a foothold within the Community and for Community companies to have access to the Swiss market but from the needs for technical links, both to improve products and to extend the product range, given the high degree of specialisation of the machine tool industry.

Further discussion of these issues is reserved for the next two sections which discuss the response of the firms in the industry to the pressures placed upon them. It is, however, worth summarising the conclusions on the impact of the Single Market at this point before moving on to the response. The European machine tool industry is already highly competitive, particularly in the more specialised products, despite the size of the Japanese industry and its strong position in volume markets, especially those involving computer control. The measures in the Single Market programme will generally be advantageous for the industry, reducing the technical fragmentation of the market, lowering costs and encouraging the exploitation of economies of scope, including those involving linkages between small specialised producers in areas such as marketing and technical co-operation. The scope for technical economies of scale in these specialised areas is limited by the size of the world market rather than by existing barriers in the European market. The current surge in investment and further enduring increases in demand will be helpful in expanding scale, but since demand has been strongly cyclical in the past there will be limits to the response.

The strategic response by firms

While the single market is expected to increase the efficiency of European firms by reducing costs to the purchaser it is also expected to raise welfare both by increasing the value added that accrues to Europe in the production of the various goods and services and by increasing the rate of growth of production itself. We have noted thus far that the impact on costs from the reduction in barriers proposed is likely to be fairly limited, first because they are minor, by comparison with the total value of the product, and second because, with a highly specialised industry characterised by small and medium-sized firms, the scope and usefulness of takeovers, mergers and the exploitation of economies of increasing size are limited.

There is an important distinction to be made between the volume side of the market where foreign producers, particularly the Japanese, are important players and the majority, specialised markets, where European companies are already world leaders. However, we can best proceed by exploring the means of exploiting competitive advantage open to European firms. These are usually characterised by economists under three headings: 'competition', 'co-operation', and 'control'. While many advocates of the single market put the emphasis on the first of these categories it is by no means clear that it is the dominant feature of the response of the machine tool industry, nor that it would be in the interests of either European machine tool producers or consumers if it were.

In highly specialised markets it may not be possible to sustain more than a handful of producers operating at an efficient scale. An increase in competition would imply new entrants and, in the longer run, not an increase in competition but a change in the players, as some existing firms are driven out of business. This should entail an increase in competitiveness as the surviving firms will tend to be more efficient than those that leave. This is not, however, a necessary condition, as Baden-Fuller (1989) has shown in the castings industry; the ease of exit varies by company. Those that exit may very well be those who can most readily transfer resources to other users, not necessarily the least efficient firms. Indeed an efficient company will switch fairly rapidly out of industries where the rate of return is low.

What we see in Europe in general is a continuing reduction in the number of companies as time passes. By and large this does not represent an amalgamation of enterprises into larger companies, with the exception of France where concentration has been encouraged, in part by the 'Plan Machine – outil' in 1982 which was aimed at encouraging the leading firms to concentrate their efforts on strategic sectors; Matra and CGE were the main beneficiaries and CADCAM, robotics and process control, the areas of focus. The adoption of automation, 'Development de l'Automisation de la Production' and 'Robotic Billion' programmes assisted purchasers in the first half of the 1980s, followed by the 'Plan Productique' in 1984–8 which envisaged large-scale intervention in industry to achieve the adoption of new production technologies.

Average company size in Europe as a whole remains small and firms are increasing their competitiveness by increases in productivity. The declining number of firms is, in part, because the pressures for exit continue but the opportunities for entry are relatively limited. Specialist manufacture requires a substantial R & D base and experience. New companies are relatively unlikely to build this up. 'New entry' comes either from foreign companies entering a new market or existing companies expanding their product range. 'Fortunately', most new entry comes in the more standard and volume categories of machine tools where Europe has already contracted, as it is here that low labour costs can offset technological sophistication and that new countries can enter the market, less efficient ones such as the USSR and East Germany maintain a position and rapidly improving countries, such as Spain, develop one. It is thus not completely clear how genuinely contestable the specialist machine tool industry has become and the extent to which it enjoys natural protection from the costs of knowledge required to enter a subsector successfully.

Given that it is difficult for European companies to generate any competitive edge through lower prices, clearly their main competitive influence comes through non-price factors. The German industry prides itself on quality, the Italian industry stresses flexibility, the Swiss industry is well known for precision and long working life for its products. The 1992 programme assists some of these non-price factors of competition by easing delivery and after-sales service, repair and maintenance. This should help strengthen the position of European companies with their customers.

However, any pressure on non-price competition will tend to elicit a response from overseas competitors, principally the Japanese. This response can be in either price or non-price terms. In price terms, Japanese producers still have a margin by which they can squeeze costs in order to secure bids. However, this in many respects is an attempt to buy market share as the result of stronger power in the labour market. It is thus very difficult to support any hypothesis which suggests that European firms have a strong competitive edge in flexible CNC machines. The greater non-price competition is likely to be beneficial for the European consumer and, on the whole, a benefit for the better producers which succeed on this criterion. European firms have the advantage of nearness and existing non-price competitive strength to exploit. Such evidence as there is suggests that they are, indeed, exploiting this position.

The Japanese can improve both price and non-price competitiveness with Europe by setting up capacity there, thus getting inside the tariff barrier and being able to get closer to customers. If experience in other industries such as brown goods, cameras, cars and motorcycles is considered, the Japanese have made their initial inroads into the market in cheaper, volume products. Having got that bridgehead, their products have become more sophisticated and diversified, allowing them to move up-market and into more specialised areas, thus also managing to colonise the two niche directions down which European producers have retreated. Despite the resilience of European industry this must continue to be a worry.

CECIMO (1989) argues that the reduction in Japanese market shares was a temporary phenomenon largely due to the initial impact of the strength of the yen. Makino already have a German subsidiary Heidenreich and Harbech, and Amada make products in France. Other companies such as Hitachi-Seiki are rumoured to be close to setting up European plants. As the CECIMO study states:

> The Japanese machine tool manufacturers will probably continue to develop production on European soil by buying up local companies or setting up subsidiaries of their own. Even if they will not be able to enjoy the same cost advantages as elsewhere, the Japanese have sufficiently proved their ability to organise real competitive production under European conditions. This is all the more true as they are very flexible in the integration of parts made in Japan. (CECIMO, 1989, p. 11)

In many respects the main thrust to competition, particularly in the volume sectors, comes not from the EC companies themselves but from excluded companies, principally outside EFTA. But even within EFTA pressures for competitive improvement are increased, with consequent pressures for EC producers.

Hence, given the weakness of the competitive route and the large number of small independent companies, it is not surprising to see that considerable use continues to be made of co-operative responses to competition. This co-operation occurs both through the efforts of national trade associations in supporting research, training, common standards, marketing, export fairs, finance, etc. and through more specific linkages between groups of firms. This co-operative strategy also involves the state, particularly at the more local level. Although EC restrictions on subsidisation of industry by member governments inhibit the assistance which can be given the opportunities which remain are very considerable.

The exploitation of external linkages

Links in the supply chain

There are two main forms of co-operation between firms which are available and being used, normally referred to as 'vertical' and 'horizontal'. Horizontal co-operation involves firms involved in the same stage of the production process agreeing on common action, while vertical co-operation involves agreements between those responsible for different stages of production. Many examples are, of course, combinations of these two, where, for instance, companies co-operate in setting up a joint sales and service organisation or a joint research facility as mentioned in Spain below.

The single market is encouraging both forms of linkage to exploit market power. The tighter the supply chain, the more difficult it is for other companies to gain entry. The most important link is that between producer and purchaser. The more the purchaser can be tied in the better from the point of view of the producer. Thus, the more machine tools are linked by computer systems and the less compatible one manufacturer's computer systems are with others, the more any purchaser becomes tied into having to make further purchases only from the same manufacturer in order to achieve compatibility. Otherwise, the purchaser either has to put up with heavy costs of linkage or has to replace much of the system of machines and not just a particular element in the sequence. The Fatronik grouping in Spain have been developing 'cell' software to link together machines from various of its members. This grouping has certainly been encouraged by European initiative and indeed Fatronik Services has been created to participate in BRITE and EUREKA. However, these two programmes are not part of 1992 but of the wider process of Community integration (as, indeed, is ESPRIT in which the machine tool industry is also involved).

The link between customer and supplier has long been recognised, but has only more recently become enshrined again in the management literature, with the seven precepts of Peters and Waterman and the subsequent burgeoning literature, and, indeed, even in public purchasing guidelines. In Spain these links have been forged with the rapidly developing motor car industry, the new high-speed train contracts and Airbus Industrie. This relationship with purchaser industries is common – the siting of the Swiss industry being substantially determined by the location of the watch industry, the German industry in Baden-Württemberg by its strong engineering and car manufacturing heritage, and so on.

Looking outwards towards a developing market power by EC companies in third-country markets, CECIMO is very pessimistic:

> Unfortunately the EC machine tool industry as a whole is not sufficiently present in foreign markets. Foreign competitors, especially the Japanese, usually outdistance the Europeans in this area. Also the Taiwanese and other Far Eastern countries will probably follow the Japanese lead in the future. This evolution is all the more disturbing as the increasing complexity of machine tools makes them less and less likely to be sold on the basis of a catalogue only. Also as in the past most EC companies will be dependent upon their overseas agents or representatives in the future. However, it will grow more and more

indispensable that their activities overseas are extensively supported by resident sales engineers. Though some progress has been achieved in the field of offshore manufacturing, most EC machine tool manufacturers simply do not have the personnel and the financial means to set up factories and/or sales and service centres abroad. This will prove to be a serious disadvantage not only because foreign competitors are often better positioned but also because of hindrances from protectionism which may make it indispensable to establish a presence in one or more foreign markets. (CECIMO, 1989, p. 14)

Links in other parts of the supply chain, between producer and component supplier and between producer and research institutions, are also important in cutting production costs and developing new products. These links have two consequences, with techniques such as just-in-time production, but also with getting the supplier involved in trying to meet the purchaser's requirements and, indeed, helping to develop the product for him. Both of these tend to increase the importance of having the supplier close to the producer and hence are an incentive to 'European-ise' inputs to the European machine tool industry. Given that Europe has an export surplus in machine tools, it is inevitable that in order to increase the closeness of relation between producer and purchaser some activity will have to be transferred outside the Community into customer countries. So we see the Group 1000 in Spain, which is comprised of CME, Ibarmia, Metosa, and Sabi having outlets in Canada and the United States. Links between producers and component suppliers, however, tend to concentrate the supply chain within the Community. For example, continuing the focus on Spain, Arrasate, one of Spain's larger machine-tool-producing co-operatives, is tending to shift its emphasis towards systems work and is building up its network of local subcontractors.

These links can also run across country borders. The Danobat co-operative, which, like Arrasate, is one of the nine machine tool co-operatives under the Mondragon co-operative group, is now producing upstream machining operations for West German firms. Where the requirements are reasonably straightforward, Spanish companies using modern machines but lower-paid labour can provide inputs for the more sophisticated tools produced elsewhere in Europe.

The link-ups in the Spanish industry are complex. There are four groupings which involve co-operative R & D either because of region Fatronik (Guipuzcon Province), Etorlan (Vizcaya Province) or type of ownership Ikerlan, Ideko (both co-operatives). In the first two cases there is state participation in the scheme. Etorlan, which started in March 1987, involves the research establishment, Robotiker, DYE and the Vizcaya Department of Economic Development. Fatronik has set up a £3 million manufacturing cell which is 50 per cent financed by local and state government. Three-quarters of Spanish production occurs in Basque country, whose government has provided extensive support for the industry during the years 1985–7 (see Table 12.11).

The other major link-ups, Mondragon, Debako, Group 1000, Mayer-holding and Atera, have been mainly for exporting but some of them have also provided a degree of co-operative support for other common overheads. Although total production may appear large at £393 million the average size of the thirty-two major firms listed in Figure 12.6 is small. Hence, the need for co-operation is considerable as is the support of the industry association, AFM. (See Table 12.12.)

Similar arguments have been put forward in other countries, such as Italy with its *Sistemi per Produrre*, but the Spanish arrangements are assisted because of the size of government help, the very rapid rise in domestic demand, the great need for investment and innovation because of their lower level of sophistication and their low costs. This perhaps is quite a good indicator of the sorts of change that can be achieved by the more sophisticated industries in the lower-income parts of the Community. As an industry which does not sell to consumers but to other

Table 12.11 Government support for the machine tool industry in the Basque region

	R & D (£ m.)	Prototypes (£ m.)
1985	2.3	5.3
1986	2.7	5.7
1987	3.5	4.8

Source: *Machinery* (1988)

Table 12.12 Size of major Spanish firms

Firm	Employees	Turnover (£ m.)
Arrasate	350	20
Danobat	535	22
DYE	150	14
Ibarmia	52	4
J-2000 Juaristi	150	7½
Lealde	58	3½
Mupem	130	17
ONA	200	15
Sacem	204	8½
Soraluce	200	10½
Sprint	45	2½
Zayer	300	22½

Source: *Machinery* (1988)

producers, the machine tool industry tends to develop hand in hand with its purchasers. The concentration of these purchasers in parts of Spain, particularly in the Basque country, is an important stimulus. We thus see in the industry in each of the European countries a concentration near domestic purchasers, despite the fact that, for the more advanced machine tool builders in West Germany, Italy, the United Kingdom and France, the majority of output goes to export. The domestic market forms the initial *raison d'être* and then continues to provide a framework of support through infrastructure, research links, component supplies and close interaction with customers which helps develop products.

This helps explain the continued strength of the UK industry despite serious problems encounter and substantial closures in the 1970s and early 1980s. Despite the contraction in manufacturing industry the United Kingdom still has a strong engineering sector with substantial aeronautical and other vehicle engineering sectors, which are major consumers of machine tools.

Links between companies

It is the experience of the United Kingdom and also of France in the 1970s which gives a clear pointer to why the amalgamation route is not being followed strongly in the European Community in the machine tool industry. Although the size of machine tool companies in the United Kingdom was on average smaller than in West Germany (median 360–380 employees compared with 440 and upper quartile 740–780 compared with 820), for an industry with roughly two-thirds of the employees (Prais, 1981) the United Kingdom had some very large companies. Alfred Herbert is the best example. With government encouragement it absorbed a number of other companies, increasing its size from 6,000 employees to 15,000 (around a fifth of the industry) which made it the largest machine tool company in the world. Yet profitability declined markedly and the firm was approaching liquidation by 1974 and, indeed, went into receivership in 1980.

The reasons for this decline are various, not least the concentration on the less sophisticated volume end of the market, where the firm had no particular cost advantages. However, as Prais concludes, there is no evidence that large *plants* are required for success in the machine tool industry. Secondly, there is no evidence that the gains from centralised marketing and finance in a *firm* of that size are clear, although this assessment is hampered by poor general British marketing performance. Lastly, 'it is far from obvious that very large firms have any advantage in good engineering design [which] is most important in achieving success for a machine tool company' (Prais, 1981).

'Highly skilled manpower is an essential requirement for the design and production of technically advanced machinery.' Since the United Kingdom fell down in this regard the lack of gain from having large firms may not be sustained on this evidence alone, particularly since the Alfred Herbert case is so extreme. Nevertheless, it does not appear that horizontal merger within the industry is a particularly effective route to competitive strength.

A number of cross-border links seem to be in the process of formation in France of the major companies shown in Table 12.13, three already have strong cross-border linkages, two within the Community Huron-Graffenstaden, 85 per cent owned by Comau (Italy), Nodler-Emag, 80 per cent owned by Emag (West Germany) – and one, ETA, 58 per cent owned by Toyoda (Japan). FLD-Manurhin are forming a link with Somab which will be the second largest producer after Brisard. Sonim is to be taken over by Traub (Germany), René Clement is also forming a Franco-German link and JTC systems a Franco-British one. Of the remaining main companies, most are members of larger groups: Renault, SCEMM (Citroën), Amada, Matra. This is thus a rather different picture from Germany and particularly from the United Kingdom where, if anything, in the 1980s the strategy has been for demerger and management buyout, rather than concentration into mergers of machine tool companies or into incorporation in larger engineering or related groupings.

It is very noticeable that of the ten largest machine tool companies in the world (see Table 12.14) only the smallest is European and seven out of ten are Japanese. Clearly, these larger companies gain market power

Table 12.13 Leading French machine tool companies, 1988

	Sales (FF m.)	Employment
Brisard	967	1,100
Renault Automation	755/(400)	(460)
SCEMM (Citroën)	410/(400)	720
Ernault Toyoda Automation	(345)/270	530
Amada	260	–
Huron–Graffenstaden	(270)/220	420
Gravograph	(190)/160	250
Alcera-Gambin	(150)/140	250
Matra Manurhin	150	–
FLD	140	145
Nodler–Emag	140	160
Cazeneuve	140	230

Source: *L'Usine Nouvelle*, *Les Echos* (Figures in brackets are those from *L'Usine Nouvelle* where they differ from *Les Echos*. This does not imply that one source is to be preferred to the other)

Table 12.14   The ten largest machine tool manufacturers, 1988

Rank	Company	Sales (ECU m.)	Rank in 1987
1	Fanuc (Japan)	856	2
2	Amada (Japan)	822	4
3	Yamazaki (Japan)	735	1
4	Litton (US)	554	3
5	Okuma (Japan)	509	7
6	Nori Seiki (Japan)	451	9
7	Cross & Trecker (US)	396	5
8	Toyoda (Japan)	395	10
9	Komaisu (Japan)	368	12
10	Comau (Italy)	351	6

Source: BIPE (from *L'Usine Nouvelle*)

from their size, especially when it comes to marketing and distribution. It is, however, success which tends to lead to large size. The creation of large firms is not by itself a guarantee of success. If there are to be successful amalgamations within European industry, they need to have a logic to them which is more than size alone but which involves clear synergies from the parts of the merger. The fact that the size of Japanese firms is continuing to increase must obviously be a worry to existing European producers, especially since the trend towards setting up plants in Europe tends to increase their ability to penetrate the European market. The Single Market will tend to increase the incentive for this competition, not diminish it. While this will help drive costs down and keep them lower to the benefit of consumers, naturally we cannot expect European producers to view this so calmly.

Regional linkages

These links extend beyond those between companies to links between companies and universities and other research institutions. The links between universities and companies in Germany, particularly in Baden-Württemberg, are well known, but similar links exist between German universities and Swiss companies. These, again, are mainly with Baden-Württemberg but also with Bavarian universities. The concentration of the German industry is very noticeable (see Table 12.15). A third of the firms are in Baden-Württemberg and another third in Nordrhein-Westphalen. However, the Baden-Württemberg firms are on average over twice as large as those in Nordrhein-Westphalen and hence contribute half the German output. Thus, it is a rather easier task to develop the linkages.

Table 12.15   Regional distribution of West German machine tool industry

Region	No. of firms (%)	No. of employees (%)	Output (%)
Schleswig-Holstein			
West Berlin			
Rheinland-Pfalz	2.3	1.8	1.7
Hamburg	2.3	1.3	1.7
Niedersachsen	4.7	2.1	2.1
Nordrhein-Westfalen	35.1	22.3	21.6
Hessen	8.2	5.9	4.9
Baden-Württemberg	34.5	46.3	48.3
Bayern	12.9	20.3	19.7
Total	100.0	100.0	100.0
Total numbers	171	54,446	8,247.3[1]

Note: [1]DM m.

Source: *VDMA* (as at end December 1988)

The same sort of regional concentration occurs in Italy with 60 per cent of the plants being found in Lombardy (see Table 12.16). However, they only produce 40 per cent of the total output. A further 35 per cent comes from the Piedmont region which only has 10 per cent of the plants and hence an average plant size 4 ½ times as large. UCIMU (1988) stresses the importance of links between companies, particularly subcontracting, which they feel aids cost competitiveness. (It is also noticeable from the UCIMU figures that despite the low average firm size, thirteen firms produce 40 per cent of the country's output, and their individual behaviour will have a significant impact on the overall total.) Concentration in Germany is harder to assess but the turnover figures shown in Table 12.17 for the ten largest companies appear to account for getting on for half the output shown in Table 12.15.

In the German case the links and the development of new products through R & D have also been assisted by government intervention. This intervention was almost totally directed to the increase of the demand for advanced products by the user firms, particularly involving CAD–CAM and robotics, although there are plans and programmes of indirect promotion aimed at developing research in the technical universities, in the public institutes of research and in the industrial firms.

Intervention in R & D is a part of a broader programme which has two parts:

1. the *Fertigungstechnik* programme of 1980–3; and
2. the *Productik* programme of 1984–7.

The *Sonderprogram Fertigungstechnik* (Special Programme for the

Table 12.16 Italian machine tool manufacturers: main corporate variables (% of total) by geographical areas, 1986

Regions	Plants	Employees M.T.	Employees total	Production M.T.	Export M.T.	Total production	Total export	Invest. 1986	Invest.[1] 1987
Piemonte	11.6	28.9	29.1	28.7	31.2	35.7	32.4	24.0	23.9
Lombardia	59.1	42.4	43.9	42.4	35.4	41.4	38.2	40.7	40.2
Veneto	13.5	14.7	10.7	11.8	12.5	8.3	9.2	8.9	13.5
Emilia Romagna	12.3	10.3	11.8	12.8	14.9	11.5	15.8	18.1	14.9
Centre-Sud	3.6	3.7	4.5	4.3	6.0	3.1	4.4	8.3	7.5
Total	100.0	100.0	100.0	100.0	100.0	100.0	100.0	100.0	100.0

Note: [1]Forecast. M.T. indicates machine tools

Source: Economic studies department: UCIMU (*Sistemi per Produrre*)

Table 12.17   The ten most important West German machine tool manufacturers, 1987–88

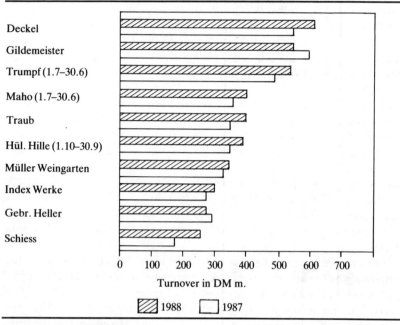

Source: *Fertigung*, July 1989

Manufacturing Technology) started in 1980 following the *Humanisierung der Arbeitsleben* (humanisation of work) programme. It was concerned with R & D in the automated factory field (robotics, FMS, CAD–CAM) and gave grants both to private businesses and to Universities and research institutes. The businesses could get up to 50 per cent of the investment whereas the universities can get up to 75 per cent. Out of over 3,000 applications received by 1986, three-quarters came from firms with less than 500 employees. The 1984–8 *Productik* programme allocated DM530 million to high-technology industries, most going to CAD–CAM and robotics, the two programmes between them funding about 1,000 projects.

Other linkages in the value-added chain

While these links relate to the earlier steps in the value-added chain, a further area of complex linkage which may be affected by the 1992 programme is distribution. A common pattern for European companies is to sell directly within their domestic market and to employ agents in the other countries. These agents may be other machine tool manufacturers which supply complementary products, often on a mutual co-operation basis so that each company sells the other's products in its own market. There are also specialist distributors who will sell a number of products from various countries. In some cases, as the relationship with these agents develops the manufacturer may actually buy out the distributor, as has happened with Hitachi-Seiki and its UK distributor recently, for example.

However, distribution of the original equipment only forms a small part of the link between customer and producer. Most machine tools have a long life expectancy and therefore require regular servicing and replacement of parts. They are also frequently absolutely central to the production process and, with the modern trends to minimise working capital by keeping work in progress between operations to a minimum, any failure rapidly brings the rest of the production process to a halt. It is thus essential that the customer has very rapid access to repair and maintenance and that the repairer has immediate access to the necessary parts.

This linkage is dealt with in a number of ways. In major customers the employees of the firm themselves will be trained by the producer in repair and maintenance and will keep a stock of many of the necessary spare parts. The smaller the customer and the more complex the machine, the more likely it is that specialist help will be required from outside the firm. If the supplier is to service the market properly these links will have to be strong and effective. The Single Market may help extend the range of any single service centre particularly in continental Europe and may extend the area which can be covered direct from the supplier.

It is not immediately apparent how this will affect the producer–agent relationship. Increasing quality of product and service tends to encourage a direct relation where the supplier can control what is provided either by doing it himself or by owning the agent. However, in so far as the arrangement is reciprocal this implies an incentive for merger or even takeover among the producers and their service partners. The trend such as it is at present is for closer linkage with independent agents. There is also an emphasis through CECIMO on improving the interchangeability of crucial parts which are liable to replacement so that a more efficient service can be provided to customers.

This element of co-operative behaviour is encouraged by the activity of CECIMO's members. It has been practised for a long time in Italy with the *Sistemi per Produrre* (UCIMU, 1989) and is rapidly being implemented in Spain. The formation of two co-operative groups, Fatronik and Debako, have spent £11½ million and £5½ million respectively on joint R & D to help the member companies support each other in export markets. This is assisted by joint exporting such as Maherholding, Atera and Group 1000. There is thus a strong national flavour to the response as we also saw in the German case. Hence, although European industry may be advantaged by the Single Market, the approach to reaping the benefits among producers tends to be national rather than transnational. However, this is not necessarily to the disadvantage of consumers, nor to the welfare gain for the economy as a whole. Provided that competition becomes more intense and unnecessary costs from frontier controls and technical barriers are reduced, then the consumer will gain even if producers co-operate on a national basis. This is more debatable when this co-operation is achieved through the use of local or central government funds as the cost of the intervention on the rest of the economy must be subtracted.

The question of strategic change was investigated by CECIMO in January 1989. They concluded:

> Although a certain trend towards concentration at production and distribution levels is discernible no decisive changes have yet taken place in these areas. Contrary to expectations the so-called 'integration' business has not widely come into being yet. As a result machine tool manufacturers have not generally had the opportunity to act as suppliers of components for flexible manufacturing systems. Although the need for it undoubtedly exists intra-EC operations such as the establishment of subsidiaries or subcontracting in other EC countries are still the exception. Although there are still many hindrances to overcome, the possibilities of the excellent European infrastructure could be better used. Also intra-EC mergers, joint ventures or cooperations are still quite uncommon. This is because the difficulties involved are hard to come to terms with, especially for small and medium companies and difficult regulations on takeovers and joint venture companies still pose many problems at present. The last few years have seen a limited movement towards horizontal integration between machine tool manufacturers on the one hand and software houses, electronic firms or automation companies on the other. More recently machine tool makers have shown a tendency towards creating similar departments for themselves. Although the present situation is not satisfactory with regard to the shifting of activities there are now at least some indications that the advent of the unified market in 1992 will provide stronger incentives towards more intra-EC activities. (CECIMO, 1989)

This paints a picture of limited change. Our discussion suggests that while the aggregate view of limited change may be correct there has been considerable change in some countries and some sectors. We have noted the co-operative efforts within the domestic economy among Spanish and Italian tool makers. Similar relationships between tool makers, the state and research institutions exist in the German *Länder*, particularly Baden-Württemberg. France seems to run rather against this line as there have been several mergers and in general few of the larger tool makers are now independent companies.

The strategies of companies differ according to whether they are in specialised or volume sectors. The market in the latter case is harsh and fewer companies offer products in it. There is some evidence of a slowing of Japanese inroads into this market, and Yamazaki's plant at Worcester, which has now been operative for a number of years, has helped shift some of the establishment pattern of operation from Japan to Europe although its main influence has been to increase market share. Partly as a result, the United Kingdom's share of the volume market has increased. In general, demand has been expanding rapidly, easing problems.

One clear need is improved marketing. While the yen has been rising rapidly the Japanese share of the European market has fallen – from 8.6 per cent in 1986 to 6.7 per cent in 1987. However, within this total Italian imports from Japan rose by nearly two-thirds and Spanish imports by one-third. European companies are thus doing well which may help explain why they have not changed markedly in response to 1992. When this demand boom is over we can expect firms to look more closely at their strategic response. Looking to maintain position, Japanese companies will be increasingly attracted to invest in the Community to avoid harsher cost competition. The strategic response to the Single Market is probably still to come.

References

Baden-Fuller, C. W. F. (1989), 'Exit from declining industries and the case of steel castings', *Economic Journal*, vol. 99.

Boston Consulting Group (BCG), (1985), *Strategic Study of the Machine Tool Industry*, Commission of the European Communities, February.

Buigues, P. and Ilzkovitz, F. (1988), The Sectoral Impact of the Internal Market, EC Brussels, II/335/88-EN.

CECIMO (1989), Second follow-up of the EC/BCG Study on the Machine Tool Industry in the European Community, Brussels, January.

GEWIPLAN (1988), The 'Cost of Non-Europe' Some Case Studies on Technical Barriers, in vol. 6, *Research on the 'Cost of Non-Europe'*, EC Brussels, Luxembourg.

Grinyer, P. H., Mayes, D. G. and McKiernan, P. (1988), *Sharpbenders: The Secrets of Unleashing Corporate Potential*, Basil Blackwell.

National Economic Development Office (1987), report from the Advanced Manufacturing Systems Task Force, London.

NMTBA (1988), *1988–9 Economic Handbook of the Machine Tool Industry*, Virginia, US.

Prais, S. J. (1981), *Productivity and Industrial Structure*, Cambridge University Press for NIESR.

Slatter, S. (1984), *Corporate Recovery: Successful Turnaround Strategies and Their Implementation*, Penguin.

UCIMU (1988), Rapporto di Settore, Milano.

13

Financial strategies

Joëlle Laudy

Introduction

Implementing company strategies, whether for internal or external growth, requires raising capital. The chosen method of finance, such as own funds, borrowing or rights issues, constitutes the firm's financial strategy. This financial strategy depends on a whole series of factors which are summarised in Figure 13.1. The three most important elements determining that strategy are as follows:

1. The characteristics of the particular national market.
2. The specific circumstances of the firm itself.
3. The preferences and requirements of the firm.

The factors determining the preferences of firms are largely the subject of the foregoing chapters on the individual sectors. The expansion strategy and the financial strategy are interrelated; the ability to raise finance by various methods affects the possible ways forward; existing gearing has a major impact on the ability to borrow further, and so on. This chapter concentrates on the first two determinants: the national characteristics and the firm characteristics.

In the first instance, the concern is whether the difference between the institutional structures of the financial markets in the various member states and the regulations governing their operation actually constitute obstacles to firms' strategies – in particular, obstacles that will continue even after the liberalisation of capital markets on 1 July 1990. The intention is that with open capital markets in Europe all firms should have the same opportunities for obtaining finance. However, such opportunities also depend on the characteristics of the individual firm, its

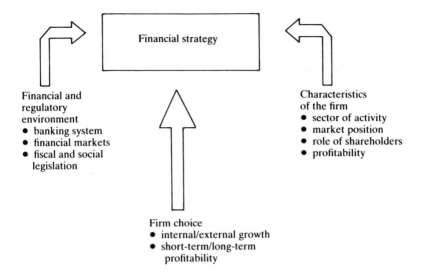

Figure 13.1 Financial strategy

profitability, indebtedness, sectoral prospects, etc., and this forms the substance of the second section of this chapter.

The effective operation of financial markets is an important ingredient in permitting the successful restructuring that firms wish to undertake in adjusting to the Single European Market. Indeed, the fragmentation of financial markets is itself a barrier to the achievements of the various possible efficiency gains. It might therefore not be desirable in this respect for the opening of financial markets to be an early step in the 1992 process rather than occurring simultaneously. As it is the two will proceed side by side, and to understand the implications for companies the European Commission has amassed a major database on the financial position of companies throughout the Community and in our main competitor markets in North America and Japan by way of comparison.

The range of structures of resources of industrial firms

Data sources

One means of measuring the diversity of financial strategies occurring in the member states is to compare their financial structures, and, in particular, their resources structures. The analysis which follows draws on the BACH database compiled by the Economic and Financial Affairs Directorate-General at the Commission (DGII).[1] This databank is comprised of information drawn from annual company accounts (balance sheets and profit-and-loss accounts) of firms in eight countries of the EC (Greece, Denmark, Luxembourg and Ireland are missing) and the US and Japan. The figures shown are sector totals, taken from the aggregated accounts produced by the relevant central banks and national statistical offices. DGII has harmonised these figures in two dimensions, first, by bringing them into line with the accounting conventions in the fourth Directive and a common sectoral classification for all the countries.

Concepts used in the analysis

The concept of resources corresponds to the notion of capital. It is defined as total debts from long- and short-term bank lending, other direct financial debts either from the market or inter-group lending, and, finally, own capital, widely defined including reserves and provisions for various risks.

Differences in recourse to debt among the countries

The contrasts for borrowing are striking as shown in Figure 13.2, ranging from nearly 60 per cent of capital employed in Portugal to less than 36 per cent in the United Kingdom. Clearly, in some countries the banking system plays a much more important role in the development of the economy, Japan, Portugal and France being the outstanding examples. In many respects this is just a matter of tradition. Self-financing is much more normal in Germany and Belgium, so in these countries lending only amounts to about 45 per cent of capital employed.

These differences are so large that they have a major impact on financial strategies of companies in the countries concerned. To some extent the discrepancies may be accentuated by the role of inflation, as accounts in Germany, France, Italy, Belgium, Portugal and Spain are provided on a historic cost basis. Although official revaluations may help overcome this, the effect is unlikely to be complete, especially when inflation rates differ substantially between countries. Nevertheless, when revalued to 'market prices' the strong diversity still exists and is quite large enough to dominate any measurement problems.

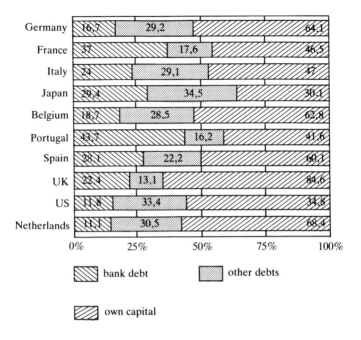

Germany 16,7 | 29,2 | 64,1
France 37 | 17,6 | 46,5
Italy 24 | 29,1 | 47
Japan 29,4 | 34,5 | 30,1
Belgium 18,7 | 28,5 | 62,8
Portugal 43,7 | 16,2 | 41,6
Spain 28,1 | 22,2 | 60,1
UK 22,4 | 13,1 | 84,6
US 11,8 | 33,4 | 34,8
Netherlands 11,1 | 30,5 | 68,4

0%   25%   50%   75%   100%

bank debt   other debts

own capital

Figure 13.2   Structure of resources: industry, 1987 (Source: BACH (Commission europ., DG II))

The influence of the national financial environment

The role of the banking system

The essential role played by the banking system is clear for the heavily indebted countries shown in Figure 13.3. Bank debts represent about three-quarters of external resources in Portuguese firms and 68 per cent in French ones. This primacy is equally important in Japan but not quite so clear from company accounts. Since the 1970s the bond market has grown strongly and firms have issued more debentures, classified under the heading of 'other debts' which have in fact been subscribed by the banking system. At the other extreme, recourse to bank borrowing is lowest in countries like Germany and Belgium, which at 40 per cent of capital employed are the least indebted.

The relative movements of bank borrowing make it possible to measure the amplitude of disintermediation from the banks that has occurred in recent years. Between 1982 and 1987 net disintermediation

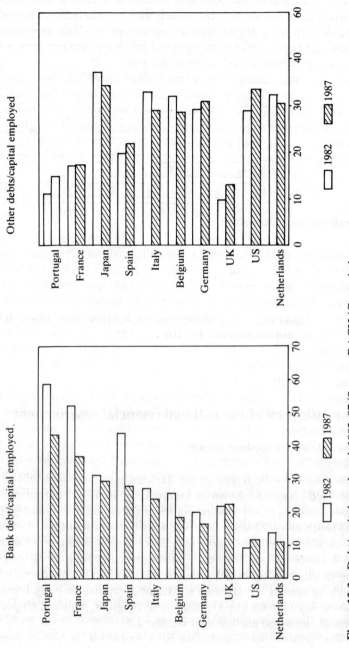

Figure 13.3 Debt/capital employed, 1982–87 (Source: BACH (Commission europ., DG II))

has occurred just as much in countries like France and Portugal where the banks are particularly important as in Spain and Germany. The change in the structure of bonds was translated into a simultaneous growth in non-bank borrowing. By contrast in four countries – Italy, Netherlands, Belgium and Japan – there was a general fall in the share of debt in total resources, irrelevant of the source of the debt.

Lastly, the United Kingdom and the United States followed a course of their own characterised by simultaneous growth in both bank and non-bank borrowing. This particular result was aided by borrowing to finance the mergers-and-acquisitions boom, illustrated clearly in the United States by the explosion of issues of junk bonds (whose popularity has diminished very rapidly more recently in the face of scandals and financial difficulties by important borrowers).

The role of stock markets

We can now see what has been the corollary of the fall in indebtedness that has taken place in most countries; in particular, what has been the role of stock markets in providing own funds to firms. The growth of own funds can develop following several patterns, including calls to shareholders and use of reserves. Unfortunately, it is not possible to obtain figures for the volumes of capital raised on stock markets for European countries in total and we therefore have to deduce it from variations in the totals of subscribed capital (which represents the value of shareholdings set out in the balance sheet).

Figure 13.4 relates the development of subscribed capital to intensity of stock market activity. Again, it is not possible to isolate stock market capitalisation relating to industrial activity alone – that is to say, value at market prices – for all countries, from the securities of industrial firms quoted on the stock exchange. Examination of the countries where this distinction can be made does not enable us to draw a conclusion about a positive role for stock markets in the development of industries' own capital. Indeed, it has been negative in Italy even though industrial market capitalisation there has been greater than in France or Spain.

We cannot, therefore, conclude that the presence of a large stock market favours an appeal by industrial firms to shareholders. On the contrary, the importance of stock market capitalisation appears to be directly linked to the frequency of mergers and acquisitions. Table 13.1 compares the ranking of six countries according to two criteria. The first measures the amount of restructuring by reference to the number of 'target' companies in mergers and acquisitions while the second measures stock market activity by the volume of transactions compared with market capitalisation. The similarity of these two rankings is obvious, the

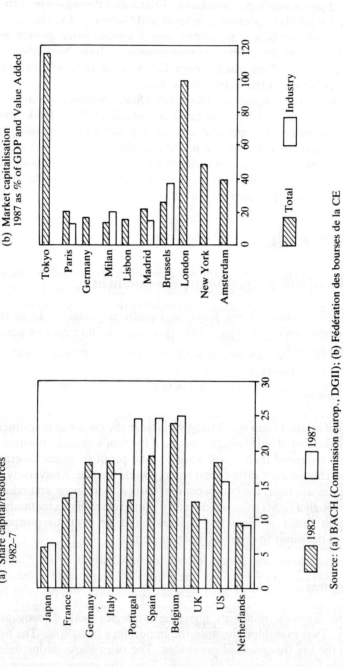

(b) Market capitalisation
1987 as % of GDP and Value Added

(a) Share capital/resources
1982–7

Source: (a) BACH (Commission europ., DGII); (b) Fédération des bourses de la CE

Figure 13.4 (a) Share capital/resources, 1982–87 (Source: BACH (Commission europ., DG II)); (b) market capitalisation as percentage of GDP and value added, 1987 (Source: Fédération des bourses de la CE)

Table 13.1   Acquisitions and stock market activity

Country	UK	GR	FR	SP	IT	NL	B	DK	P
No. of target firms	137	116	115	82	63	57	31	19	15
Ranking	1	2	3	4	5	6	7	8	9
Vol. of transactions	57.7	87.2	43.2	35.1	26.6	36.8	16.7	13.9	13.3
Market ranking	2	1	3	5	6	4	7	8	9

Source: M & A

two cases which are out of step being Germany and the Netherlands. This can be explained by the fact that stock market capitalisation is a poor measure of these countries' economic activity, being too low in the case of Germany and too high for the Netherlands.

The influence of the regulatory environment

The regulatory environment plays an equally important role in the formation of financial strategies. Take, for example, interest rate policy and the tax system.

Rates of interest

The level of interest rates is a driving variable in the choice of investment finance: if the cost of borrowing is low and if the firm's financial position is reasonably balanced then it will want to take profit from the leverage effect and choose debt rather than resort to self-finance. Conversely, if interest rates are high, the comparison of costs of borrowing and raising capital through a rights issue would lead a firm to diversify its methods of financing in order to limit the charges on it or even to postpone investment decisions in order to repay its debits.

The tax system

Corporate taxation influences financing strategies both directly and indirectly. Two examples illustrate the importance of its role. The first concerns the tax treatment of provisions. The rules about deductibility vary widely from one country to another. Thus, the annual provision for depreciation varies from 4 per cent of turnover in Germany to 6.5 per cent in Portugal. In the same way, the option of making provision for pension funds represents a very considerable source of self-finance for firms in some European countries, particularly Germany and Italy.

The second example relates to the taxation of profits where there are reduced tax rates for profits which are reinvested in order to increase the proportion put to reserves.

Characteristics of the firm itself

We have picked just four characteristics to examine from among the many which determine the choice of financial strategy – the level of profits, the sector of activity, size, and the balance of power between management and shareholders – that can be affected by the pre-1992 strategies.

The level of profits

A firm's profitability affects its ability to use self-finance. Figure 13.5 shows the relation which exists between profits and the level of own funds. The strengthening of these funds comes essentially from the improvement in profitability which can then be put to reserves. This often results from the rationalisation of production or 'niche' products.

Sector of activity

Traditionally, firms operating in the most capital-intensive sectors of the economy finance a much larger part of their global needs from own resources and hence are financially more autonomous. This feature seems to be confirmed by the gap which exists in the majority of countries between the rates of financial independence (own capital plus reserves/total resources) of the textile and the chemical industries. (Figure 13.6.)

Membership of a particular sector also conditions the competitive environment for a firm. In highly concentrated sectors, market power helps firms to be price setters and obtain high rates of profitability and hence enhanced ability to finance themselves, while for loss-making sectors, the banks tend to have the whip hand (as in the case of iron and steel).

Firm size

Firm size also affects the range of possibilities for financing. We can observe that in the course of recent years bank disintermediation has

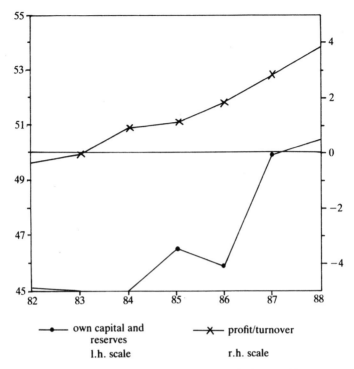

Figure 13.5 Profitability and financial independence: industry – European average (Source: Fédération des bourses de la CE)

principally involved the large companies. Small and medium-sized firms rarely have the capital – particularly in terms of human resources – necessary to have direct recourse to financial markets (especially bond and equity markets). Small firms which are part of groups can benefit from disintermediation through their parent companies (which raises non-bank lending) while independents remain firmly tied to the banking system. It is at the same time worth noting that between 1982 and 1987 the financial structure of large firms has moved nearer to that of the smaller firms and, irrespective of size, indebtedness has fallen.

The role of shareholders

The ownership structure can also influence industrial firms' financial strategies, in so far as it determines the policy for distributing dividends and hence the policy for profits and additions to reserves. A firm which is essentially family-owned can restrict the distribution of dividends fairly

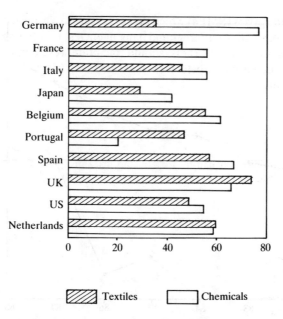

Figure 13.6   Capital and reserves (as percentage of resources), 1987
(Source: Fédération des bourses de la CE)

easily compared with a publicly quoted company. This characteristic
appears to be one explanation for the great financial independence of
Belgian industrial companies. In contrast, the link between banks and
industrial firms can explain the high level of debts in Japanese industries.

Conclusion

Like all industrial strategies, financial strategy depends largely on the
characteristics of the firm itself. The general improvement in firms'
performance across Europe has been eased by the decrease in interest
rates. It has helped relax the financial constraints in all member states.
However, we have to set against this the heterogeneity of national
environments, stemming largely from the general economic policies
followed by each country, which also limit the choice of financial strategy.
The most significant differences relate to the importance of the role of the
banking system and the intensity of stock market activity.

The great dependence of firms in France, Portugal and Spain on the
banks should make those countries more affected by the freeing of capital
markets. However, the impact will probably be less for small and

medium-sized enterprises (SMEs) which do not belong to a group, due to their propensity for dealing with regional bank agencies. Paralleling this, the development of stock markets should facilitate restructuring in countries where regulations up to now have been restrictive, such as Spain and Germany.

Note

1. After spending months speculating upon the musical allusion intended by this acronym I am disappointed to find none was intended (ed.).

Index

acquisitions, 13, 15–17, 23, 128, 427
  iron and steel, 382–3
  semiconductor industry, 239, 253
aerospace industry, 21–3, 184
  company strategies, 203–6
  industry structure, 185–99
  institutional changes, 199–203
agrochemicals, 353–6
airlines, 13, 21, 22, 162
  company strategies, 171–80
  deregulation, 170–1
  structure, 163–9, 180–2
artificial fibres (companies), 341–7
ASICs, 221, 225–6, 232, 234, 237–8, 249, 253
audio equipment, 212–13, 215, 256–7
automation, 400–1, 407, 418
automobile industry, 21–2, 28–9, 90–1
  current structures, 30–56
  Single Market, 56–73
  strategies at work, 73–89

banking system, 425–7, 431, 432–3
barriers, 11–12, 14, 18
  in automobile industry, 56–62
  fiscal, 56–7, 233, 404
  physical, 57
  tariff, 153, 162, 380, 404, 408
  technical, 58, 200–3, 404, 405–6, 420
  trade, 198–9, 203, 383
bio-technology, 357, 359
bipolar technology, 224–5, 241
Boston Consulting Group, 396–403
bottlenecks, airline, 176–9
'bow waves', 187, 188
BRITE project, 248
British Rail, 130, 143–4, 147, 150–1

Bull Group, 317

cabotage system, 110, 171
CAD, 223, 226, 229, 233, 246, 248, 253
CAD-CAM, 195, 283–4, 315, 416, 418
capital, 404, 422–3
  debt policies, 424–8, 426–7
  stock market role, 427–432
cash flow, cumulative, 194, 195
Cecchini Report, ix, 1–3, 23, 56, 58, 131, 145, 146, 148
challenger strategy, 82
Channel Tunnel, 98, 130, 134–5, 142–3, 147–9, 153–4, 156, 160
chemical industries, 24–5, 369–70
  general approach to 1992, 337–41
  impact of 1992, 347–9
  main companies, 341–7, 355
  specific markets, 349–68
chip production, 225, 227, 229–30, 232–4, 237, 249, 251–2, 254
civil aircraft, 184–5, 189, 192–4, 196, 200, 203–4, 206
CMOS technology, 225
CNC machines, 391, 398, 408
commercial strategies (IT), 302–3
commodities, 221, 347–9, 368, 369
communications, 79–80, 212, 213
compact disks, 262–3, 264, 265
  players, 212, 214–15, 256–7, 258
company strategies, *see individual industries*
Comparex, 320
competition
  aerospace, 193–5, 201
  airlines, 170, 172–3, 176–7
  automobiles, 55–6, 81–2, 89–90

435